COMMUNITY OF THE CROSS

COMMUNITY OF THE CROSS

Moravian Piety in Colonial Bethlehem

CRAIG D. ATWOOD

THE PENNSYLVANIA STATE UNIVERSITY PRESS
UNIVERSITY PARK, PENNSYLVANIA

Community of the Cross is published as part of the Max Kade German-American Research Institute Series. This series provides an outlet for books that reflect the mission of the Penn State Kade Institute: to integrate the history and culture of German-speakers in the Americas with the major themes of early modern scholarship from the sixteenth to the early nineteenth century.

Library of Congress Cataloging-in-Publication Data

Atwood, Craig D.
Community of the cross : Moravian piety in colonial Bethlehem /
Craig D. Atwood.
p.   cm.
Includes bibliographical references and index.
ISBN 978-0-271-05855-9 (pbk : alk. paper)
1. Moravian Church—History.
2. Pietism—Germany—History.
I. Title.

BX8565 .A84   2004
284′.674822—dc22
2003022440

CONTENTS

PREFACE

SOME OF THE material in this book is disturbing to modern sensibilities, and I need to assure readers that this is not a description of Moravians today, although they, too, can learn from this history. This is not an exposé but a serious attempt to make sense of an important religious community whose attitudes and theology may still have relevance. We best show respect to those whom we study when we take seriously what was most important to them, while examining it critically. That is what I try to do in this book.

There is a long history of the writing of this work that may help clarify what I try to accomplish here and at the same time acknowledge my debt of gratitude to dozens of people who participated in this project, sometimes unwittingly. Having grown up in a family with a two-hundred-year Moravian heritage, I was familiar with the Moravian story, but even as a child I sensed that something was being omitted in the telling of the history. In the hymns and liturgy of the church I caught glimpses of a poetic imagination and provocative theology that I later learned was the distant echo of one of the most fascinating figures in Protestant history, Nikolaus Ludwig von Zinzendorf.[1] I knew his name, but no one could tell me about his theology, beyond generalities. As a child, I also wondered why those old Moravians had sacrificed so much to live together in strictly regulated communities. Could there be a connection between the orderly communal buildings and the poetic theology of Zinzendorf?

Bethlehem was a natural subject of research because it was the center of Moravian activity in North America in the colonial period. All other Moravian communities in America stemmed from the work in Bethlehem. I also studied at the Moravian Theological Seminary in Bethlehem, where I had the pleasure of studying Moravian history with David Schattschneider, now the retired dean. In class we discussed the so-called Sifting Time (1743–50). It is practically a rite of initiation for future Moravian ministers to learn about the *Litany of the Wounds*, the "blue cabinet" that newly married couples supposedly used,

---

1. A similar echo profoundly influenced Hilda Doolittle, the poet H. D. See Barbara Ellen Burke, "Parallels Between Moravianism and Selected Works by H. D. (M.A. thesis, University of Louisville, 1991); Jane Augustine, "The Mystery: H. D.'s Unpublished Moravian Novel, Edited and Annotated Towards a Study in the Sources in a Poet's Religious Thinking" (Ph.D. diss., City University of New York, 1988).

hymns about bees flying around the side wound of Christ, and the Society of Little Fools. There was embarrassed laughter, and in the process what was once vital to living people was dismissed and hidden away.

I began reading the litanies of the time and found them remarkable in their vision of both the earthly and the heavenly community, as well as rich in theology and poetic imagery. I read studies of Bethlehem by scholars outside the Moravian Church, who broke the Moravian story out of pious narrative and hagiography; but I was still convinced that something was missing. Moravian mission activity and social structure seemed somehow lifeless and strangely divorced from Zinzendorf.

Arthur Freeman, now retired from the seminary (and godfather of one of my daughters), led me deeper into the study of Zinzendorf and his theology, with a view toward how that theology could be useful today. Although my work focuses on how Zinzendorf's theology was manifested in the lived experience of the Moravians rather than as a resource for modern theology, I am indebted to Arthur in many ways. He introduced me to the vast field of Zinzendorfian studies in German and helped me see that, despite claims to the contrary, Zinzendorf does make sense. Again, though, it was hard to connect Zinzendorf to the life of the Moravian communities in America. There also remained that troubling question of the *Litany of the Wounds*.

Despite my efforts to focus on other areas of research as a graduate student at Princeton Theological Seminary in the early 1990s, I was continually drawn (or driven) back to this enigma. Anthony Grafton's early modern seminar at Princeton University showed me that social and cultural historical methods could be usefully applied to the study of religious communities. I also learned how to read historiography with the same hermeneutic of suspicion that I had long applied to the study of Scripture. Every text needs exegesis because texts reveal more than they intend and obscure much that we would like to know. Moravian historiography is no exception.

Intrigued by the questions that the eminent sociologist of religion Richard Fenn asked in history department colloquia, I tackled the problem of the *Litany of the Wounds* head on with his guidance. Many of our conversations were held over breakfast as a small diner in Princeton, and I apologize to other patrons who found their eggs seasoned with snatches of conversation about bleeding wounds. Dick introduced me to classical sociological literature as I sought for a theory to explain the phenomena I was examining. Unfortunately, the Moravians seemed to run counter to the standard theories of Max Weber, Brian Wilson, David Martin, and even Émile Durkheim. What does one make of a community that creates exceedingly rational plans for building towns and efficient economic system but leaves the decision of whether and where to build to the lot? What do you do with a sect that welcomes the elaborate symbolic drama of aristocratic society and high culture, yet forbids even the simplest revels?

More helpful was the work of Mary Douglas, although the Moravians seemed to defy the categories she has developed. They were a closed community that welcomed visitors and sought converts. They had a strict structure of authority and control yet encouraged reflection and intimate conversation. Eventually I abandoned the effort to impose a theoretical construct on the Moravians in Bethlehem, preferring to develop my own description. However, Douglas's core insight that the social body and the individual body are intricately connected was the key to the Bethlehem mystery. Statements about Christ's body are also statements about the community and the individuals in it. The body of Christ that the Moravians worshipped, the body of Christ that they understood themselves to be as a community, and their individual bodies, in which Christ dwelled, were distinguishable yet inseparable.

René Girard's analysis of violence in religion also helped make sense of the violence evident in Moravian liturgy. Girard's thesis that the Christian identification with the sacrificial victim diminishes actual social violence put the *Litany of the Wounds* in a new light. In short, the methods of ritual studies illuminate my historical analysis. In addition to the work of earlier scholars, most notably Wilhelm Bettermann and Erich Beyreuther, the studies of Leo Steinberg and Caroline Walker Bynum on late medieval and Renaissance art and spirituality provided helpful background for understanding the violent and erotic imagery in eighteenth-century Moravian piety. The articles of Katherine Faull of Bucknell University and conversation with her were instrumental in refining my thesis. Recent works by Aaron Fogleman and Paul Peucker also provided key insights.

Many people assisted me in my research and writing. I am extremely grateful to Vernon Nelson and Lothar Madeheim of the Moravian Archives in Bethlehem. They taught me to read eighteenth-century German script and frequently pointed me to productive avenues of exploration. I have also benefited greatly from the assistance and encouragement of Paul Peucker, archivist of the Unity Archive in Herrnhut. Tom Minor, retired librarian of Reeves Library at Moravian College, was invaluable in providing books for me even from a distance of five hundred miles. The staff of Speer Library at Princeton Seminary, Gramley Library of Salem College, and the Moravian archives in Winston-Salem were also very accommodating.

Ricarda Fröhlich, *eine schöne Seele,* assisted me in translating the *Litany of the Wounds,* and her husband Karlfried Fröhlich helped me to be more rigorous in my historical research. Though Jean Loup Seban never understood why

I would be interested in the Moravians, he was very helpful in helping me understand the world of the Enlightenment. James Moorhead helped me become more of an Americanist and gave me the freedom to examine Bethlehem from new perspectives.

There is a growing community of scholars studying the Moravians who have played different roles in the writing and publishing of this book. Colin Podmore, whose work on the Moravians in England convinced me that I was on the right track, strongly encouraged me to publish my own research. I am grateful to Peter Vogt, Daniel Crews, Nola Reed Knouse, Elisabeth Sommer, Rachel Wheeler, Katherine Carté Engel, Otto Dreydoppel Jr., and Jon Sensbach, not only for their published work but for good conversations at key moments in my research. Peter Kaufman of my alma mater at Chapel Hill has been extremely helpful in getting my work out and involving me in a larger scholarly community. Ulrike Wiethaus of Wake Forest, who wanted to "talk about sex," helped me refine my discussion of that topic. Gregg Roeber's suggestions for improving this text were pragmatic and wise.

Some of the material in this book has appeared in different form, as "Sleeping in the Arms of Christ: Sanctifying Sexuality in the Eighteenth-Century Moravian Church," in *Journal of the History of Sexuality* 8 (1997); "The Joyfulness of Death in Eighteenth-Century Moravian Communities," in *Communal Societies: Journal of the Communal Societies Association* 17 (1997); "Zinzendorf's 1749 Reprimand to the Brüdergemeine," in *Transactions of the Moravian Historical Society* 29 (1996); "Zinzendorf's *Litany of the Wounds of the Husband*," in *Lutheran Quarterly* 11 (1997); "Theology in Song: Daily Litanies in the Eighteenth-Century Moravian Church," in *The Distinctiveness of Moravian Culture;* "The Mother of God's People: The Adoration of the Holy Spirit as Mother in the Eighteenth-Century Brüdergemeine," in *Church History* 68 (Dec. 1999); "Understanding Zinzendorf's Blood and Wounds Theology," in *Transactions of the Moravian Historical Society* 33 (2003), and is reproduced here with permission.

The faculty of Salem College were good colleagues who listened to my theories, and I wish them well. Dean Eileen Wilson-Oyelaran's wisdom and commitment to education deserve the highest praise. I also thank my many students at Salem College and Moravian Seminary who were challenged by these materials and asked challenging questions in return. Melissa Hall, Gil Frank, and the late Marian Noecker provided valuable assistance in proofreading. Christina Hawkins graciously checked the German translations.

I am very grateful to the Moravian Church, which has been vital in my development as a person, and in which I have had the privilege of serving. Tom Brady of Berkeley rightly identified my work as revisionist and warned me about how churches often respond to such scholarship. I sincerely hope that this analysis will lead to further inquiry by the Moravians as well as those interested in them. My gratitude goes to Pastor Gerald Harris, who twice found concrete means of support that allowed me the time to pursue my graduate studies and research. Home Moravian Church has given me the opportunity to teach and time to think, gifts that I cherish. I hope this book justifies their confidence and that of the United Brethren's Congregation of Staten Island. I am also grateful to the Max Kade Institute for providing support for the publication of this book.

My wife, Julie, who studied psychology at Moravian College, knows the principle of primacy and recency, so I save my deepest expressions of gratitude for last. They go to Julie and my children (Allyson, Emily, Sarah, and Madeleine) for their patience, interest, understanding, love, and tolerance through years of reading, writing, and absent-mindedness. Julie has saved me from many things, including infelicities in writing, and has been a very valuable conversation partner through the years as I've been immersed in "blood, sex, and death." Our dinnertime conversations have not been those of a typical American family, I'm afraid. She and the children remain an ever-present reminder of the Moravian conviction that Christ is most present in loving relationships. Martin Luther is reputed to have said that no one should write about the Incarnation until he has helped with the raising of babies. Even if he didn't say it, it is true.

INTRODUCTION

Dearest wounds of Jesus, *Whoever does not love you, and does not give his whole heart to you, holds nothing dear.*

Wondrous wounds of Jesus, *Holy fissures, you make sinners holy, and thieves from saints. How amazing!*

Powerful wounds of Jesus, *So moist, so gory, bleed on my heart so that I may remain brave and like the wounds.*

Mysterious wounds of Jesus, *I thank the pastors, who made the bruises and gashes of my Lamb known to me.*

Cavernous wounds of Jesus, *In your treasure hoard, roomily sit many thousands kinds of sinners.*

Purple wounds of Jesus, *You are so succulent, whatever comes near becomes like wounds and flows with blood.*

Juicy wounds of Jesus, *Whoever sharpens the pen and with it pierces you just a little, licks and tastes it.*

Warm wounds of Jesus, *In no pillow can a little child feel itself so secure before cold air.*

Soft wounds of Jesus, *I like lying calm, gentle, and quiet and warm. What should I do? I crawl to you.*[1]

These petitions are from the *Litany of the Wounds of the Husband,* a German litany that arrived in Bethlehem, Pennsylvania, on November 7, 1744. When it was read to the residents, "Everything was very bloody and heart warming," according to the community's diarist.[2] Six weeks later, August Gottlieb Spangenberg, who had recently been sent from Europe

---

1. The complete litany is found in Appendix 3. For more on the litany, see Craig D. Atwood, "Zinzendorf's Litany of the Wounds of the Husband," *Lutheran Quarterly* 11 (1997): 189–214. The German original may be found in Nicholas Ludwig von Zinzendorf, *Reden während der Sichtungszeit in der Wetterau und in Holland,* vol. 3 of *Hauptschriften in sechs Bänden,* ed. Erich Beyreuther and Gerhard Meyer (Hildesheim: Georg Olms, 1963), pages not numbered. A truncated version is found in Hans-Christoph Hahn und Hellmut Reichel, *Zinzendorf und die Herrnhuter Brüder: Quellen zur Geschichte der Brüder-Unität von 1722 bis 1760* (Hamburg: F. Wittig, 1977), 164–67. Katherine M. Faull published an English version based on eighteenth-century English texts in her article "Faith and Imagination: Nikolaus Ludwig von Zinzendorf's Anti-Enlightenment Philosophy of Self," in *Anthropology and the German Enlightenment: Perspectives on Humanity,* ed. Katherine M. Faull (Lewisburg: Bucknell University Press, 1995), 23–56.

2. Kenneth G. Hamilton and Lothar Madeheim, trans., *The Bethlehem Diary,* vol. 2, 1744–45, ed. Vernon Nelson, Otto Dreydoppel Jr., and Doris Rohland Yob (Bethlehem, Pa.: Archives of the Moravian Church, 2001), 154 and 168.

to be the leader of the new community, taught the worshippers how to sing
the *Litany*. For the next two decades this would be sung regularly in worship,
in private devotions, and at funerals. Though the eighteenth-century Moravian
community of Bethlehem continues to be admired, aspects of their religious
life often baffle those who study them. To understand Bethlehem and the Moravians, though, we need to make sense of their unusual piety.

This book is a study of colonial Bethlehem, but it is also a book about the
body: human bodies in Bethlehem, the social body of Bethlehem, and the symbolic body of Christ. It will examine the theology and piety of the Moravians
in Bethlehem in order to make sense of their religious symbolism and see how
it was intricately related to their unique social life. In doing so, this study will
shed light on the complex relationship between religion and culture as well as
give new insight into the complex world of colonial Pennsylvania.

SIGNIFICANCE OF COLONIAL BETHLEHEM

Much of the writing on American colonial history and culture, and especially
on religion, tells a story of immigration from the British Isles and the influence
of English-speaking Protestant churches on America.[3] This is certainly understandable and valuable, for the dominant story is important; but there are other
stories, voices, and influences that should be considered. The approximately
100,000 German speakers who came to the American colonies, especially to
Pennsylvania, brought with them a different approach to Christianity and culture.[4] Because of William Penn's "Holy Experiment" and the response of German dissenter groups, the Pennsylvania colony was the most religiously diverse
and tolerant in America.[5]

Within the story of German immigration and religious experimentation in

---

3. This is evident in most of the popular textbooks. On the issue of the Anglo-Saxon dominance of
American religious and cultural historiography and competing narratives, see Thomas Tweed, ed., *Retelling
U.S. Religious History* (Berkeley and Los Angeles: University of California Press, 1997), especially the editor's
introduction. The essays in *Church History: Studies in Christianity and Culture* 71 (June 2002) by Amanda
Porterfield, Stephen J. Stein, William Vance Trollinger, and Peter W. Williams cover the crucial issues and
much of the bibliography on this topic. Books that help redress the problem are Jon Butler and Harry Stout,
Religion in American History: A Reader (New York: Oxford University Press, 1998), and Julia Mitchell Corbett, *Religion in America*, 3rd ed. (Upper Saddle River, N.J.: Prentice-Hall, 1997), but even here the Germans
are largely overlooked.

4. Aaron S. Fogleman, *Hopeful Journeys: German Immigration, Settlement, and Political Culture in Colonial America, 1717–1775* (Philadelphia: University of Pennsylvania Press, 1996), gives a figure of 85,000, and
Marianne Wokeck, *Trade in Strangers: The Beginnings of Mass Migration in North America* (University Park:
Pennsylvania State University Press, 1999), estimates that it was closer to 110,000. Precise figures are impossible to determine, of course, but Wokeck's incredibly detailed graph of immigrant shipping is impressive.

5. Steve Longenecker, *Piety and Tolerance: Pennsylvania German Religion, 1700–1850* (Metuchen, N.J.:
Scarecrow Press, 1994); Patricia Bonomi, *Under the Cope of Heaven: Religion, Society, and Politics in Colonial
America* (New York: Oxford University Press, 1986); Robert Crist, ed., *Penn's Example to the Nations: 300
Years of the Holy Experiment* (Harrisburg: Pennsylvania Council of Churches, 1987); F. Ernest Stoeffler, ed.,
Continental Pietism and Early American Christianity (Grand Rapids: Wm. B. Eerdmans, 1976).

Pennsylvania, the Moravians play a prominent but little examined role. The Moravians represent a distinct voice in the history of the Great Awakening and religion in America, for they combined early evangelical sensitivities, communal living, and gender equity with Lutheran doctrine and liturgy. The Moravian community of Bethlehem, Pennsylvania, was one of the most significant, successful, and unusual religious communities in colonial North America.[6]

During the first twenty years of its existence, Bethlehem was a complete commune where labor and other resources were shared for the common mission of bringing the gospel to American natives and European colonists. Missionaries went out from Bethlehem to live and preach among the Delaware and other native tribes, Bethlehem's preachers ministered to German-speaking immigrants and other colonists, and Bethlehem established schools for girls as well as boys. The communal economy facilitated this Moravian mission, but it was also an expression of Moravian religious ideals. Residents of Bethlehem attempted to live together in a foretaste of paradise while laboring for Christ. All of life was to be a form of worship, as they experienced a daily awareness of the presence of Christ and the heavenly community. Unlike many of the sectarian German groups in Pennsylvania, Bethlehem combined a Lutheran sense of liturgy and devotion with radical Pietist spirituality and communal living.

Bethlehem is also important because it was part of an international, interdenominational religious fellowship called the *Brüdergemeine* (Community of the Brethren). The residents of Bethlehem stayed in regular contact with their religious brothers and sisters in Germany, England, the Baltic, and the Caribbean through letters, reports, and personal visits.[7] The Moravian story is transatlantic in many senses of the word, and this book will show how the ideas of a theologian in Europe profoundly shaped the lived existence of people in Pennsylvania.

For anyone wishing to study the Moravians, the use of names can be quite

---

6. Of twenty-one communal societies begun before the American Revolution listed in *The Encyclopedia of American Communes, 1663–1963*, ed. Foster Stockwell (Jefferson, N.C.: McFarland, 1998), seven are Moravian communities (the separate Wachovia villages are listed together). Apart from what would become the Amana Church Society, the Moravians had the only colonial communes to survive more than two generations. However, the Moravian settlements receive scant attention in histories of American communal societies, such as Donald E. Pitzer, ed., *America's Communal Utopias* (Chapel Hill: University of North Carolina Press, 1997), 27–31.

7. W. R. Ward notes that August Hermann Francke's regular correspondence with some four hundred people was typical of Pietists, and that there was a lively exchange between Europe and America. Ward, *The Protestant Evangelical Awakening* (Cambridge: Cambridge University Press, 1992), 1–12; see also Carola Wessel, "Connecting Congregations: The Net of Communication Among the Moravians as Exemplified by the Interaction Between Pennsylvania, the Upper Ohio Valley, and Germany (1772–1774)," in *The Distinctiveness of Moravian Culture: Essays and Documents in Honor of Vernon Nelson on his 70th Birthday*, ed. Craig Atwood and Peter Vogt (Nazareth, Pa.: Moravian Historical Society, 2003).

confusing. The *Brüdergemeine* is now known in the United States as the Moravian Church. The name "Moravian" implies a strong Czech ethnicity, but in the eighteenth century most members of the "Moravian Church" were German. Even those who came from Moravia (and Bohemia) spoke German. To complicate things further, in the eighteenth century the Brüdergemeine included Lutheran, Reformed, and Moravian groups, known as Tropoi (or Tropuses).[8] The term "Moravian" was applied only to those members of the Brüdergemeine (from Moravia and Bohemia) who claimed membership in the Unitas Fratrum, a pre-Reformation Protestant church.[9] It is common today in English, however, to refer to the Brüdergemeine as a whole as "Moravian." In this book, "Moravian" will be used primarily for ethnic Moravians in the Brüdergemeine and for the residents of Bethlehem.

One reason for the strong international and interracial character of the Moravian Church was its missionary zeal. The success of the Moravians in the eighteenth century was indeed remarkable. In a thirty-year span missionaries went to North America, St. Thomas, Surinam, South Africa, the Gold Coast, Greenland, Algeria, Russia, Ceylon, Persia, Egypt, Labrador, and Jamaica.[10] In addition to missions to non-Christian peoples, the Brüdergemeine set up less formal groups of believers within the official churches in the Baltic region, Poland, England, the Netherlands, Switzerland, Germany, France, and Scandinavia. Tens of thousands were influenced through this "diaspora" ministry.[11]

More important for my purposes, the Moravians also established several carefully regulated Christian communities (called *Ortsgemeinen*) in Europe and America. In these communities European nobles joined their voices with Moravian peasants, German students, English artisans, African slaves, and American natives in singing about the glories and blessings of Christ. During an era when the world was being torn apart by colonialism and absolutism, the Moravians created an international and interracial community, despite racial and class tensions within the community.[12] Bethlehem was probably the closest

8. A. J. Lewis, *Zinzendorf: The Ecumenical Pioneer; A Study in the Moravian Contribution to Christian Mission and Unity* (Philadelphia: Westminster Press, 1962).

9. See pp. 21–25.

10. J. Taylor Hamilton and Kenneth G. Hamilton, *History of the Moravian Church: The Renewed Unitas Fratrum 1722–1957* (Bethlehem, Pa.: Interprovincial Board of Christian Education of the Moravian Church in America, 1967); J. E. Hutton, *A History of Moravian Missions* (London: Moravian Publication Office, 1922); Hartmut Beck, *Brüder in vielen Völkern: 250 Jahre Mission der Brüdergemeine* (Erlangen, 1981).

11. Ward, *Protestant Evangelical Awakening*, 144–54; Hermann Plitt, *Die Brüdergemeine und die Lutherische Kirche in Livland* (Gotha, 1861); Valdis Mezezers, *The Herrnhuterian Pietism in the Baltic* (North Quincy: Christopher Publishing, 1975).

12. James David Nelson, "Herrnhut: Friedrich Schleiermacher's Spiritual Homeland," (Ph.D. diss., University of Chicago, 1963); Otto Uttendörfer, *Alt Herrnhut* (Herrnhut, 1925), reproduced in *Zinzendorf Materialien und Dokumente* (ZM 2:22); Hans-Walter Erbe, *Herrnhaag: Eine religiöse Kommunität im 18. Jahrhundert* (Hamburg: F. Wittig, 1988); Helmut Erbe, *Bethlehem, Pa.: Eine Herrnhuter-Kolonie des 18. Jahrhunderts* (Herrnhut: Gustav Winter, 1929); Beverly Smaby, *The Transformation of Moravian Bethlehem from Communal Mission to Family Economy* (Philadelphia: University of Pennsylvania Press, 1988); Gillian Lindt Gollin,

approximation to an egalitarian ideal in the Moravian Church, perhaps in the eighteenth-century Atlantic world.

Visitors to Bethlehem, such as Benjamin Franklin, remarked on the orderly and peaceful nature of life in the community as well as on its impressive architecture and "high" culture. Bethlehem's missionaries and converts appear in James Fennimore Cooper's *Leatherstocking Tales,* but for the most part, after the American Revolution, the Moravians receded from the larger American scene. The residents of the communities gradually adopted American values and attitudes, and by 1850 the church had given up the remnants of communal life. The Moravians who had once inspired passionate controversy in Europe and America became just another Protestant denomination.

Although Moravian archivists and historians published some material before 1960 on the history of the Moravians in America, it is really only in recent decades that Bethlehem has begun to receive the attention it deserves from critical scholars, particularly those working in the areas of colonial history, sociology, and American religious history. Many researchers have been attracted to Bethlehem because of its rich archival resources, which include thousands of short biographies of the residents and offer first- and secondhand accounts of contact with Native Americans.[13]

Missing from this research on the early Moravians has been sustained attention to theology and piety in their social context. Like visitors to colonial Bethlehem, researchers have generally been impressed with the social and economic life of the community, but the worship and spiritual life of Bethlehem during its communal period has generally offended or embarrassed Moravian and non-Moravian researchers alike.

Bethlehem was founded as a "congregation of the cross." The adoration of the crucified Jesus, especially his wounds, was the focus of intense devotion for both adults and children. The adoration of the blood and wounds of Christ, devotion to the Holy Spirit as mother, and other unusual aspects of eighteenth-century Moravian devotion were an integral part of their communal life, inter-

Moravians in Two Worlds: A Study of Changing Communities (New York: Columbia University Press, 1967). For comparative study, see Elisabeth Sommer, *Serving Two Masters: Moravian Brethren in Germany and North Carolina, 1727–1801* (Lexington: University Press of Kentucky, 2000); Jon F. Sensbach, *A Separate Canaan: The Making of an Afro-Moravian World in North Carolina, 1763–1840* (Chapel Hill: University of North Carolina Press, 1998); Jerry Lee Surratt, *Gottlieb Schober of Salem: Discipleship and Ecumenical Vision in an Early Moravian Town* (Macon: Mercer University Press, 1983); Daniel B. Thorp, *The Moravian Community in Colonial North Carolina: Pluralism on the Southern Frontier* (Knoxville: University of Tennessee Press, 1989).

13. Rachel Wheeler, "Living upon Hope: Mahicans and Missionaries, 1730–1760" (Ph.D. diss., Yale University, 1998); Maia Turner Conrad, "'Struck in their Hearts': David Zeisberger's Moravian Mission to the Delaware Indians in Ohio" (Ph.D. diss., College of William and Mary, 1998); Amy Schutt, "Forging Identities: Native Americans and Moravian Missionaries in Pennsylvania and Ohio, 1765–1782" (Ph.D. diss., Indiana University, 1995).

racial mission, economic activity, and sexual practices. It was the Moravians' liturgy and devotion that united the community and inspired both its unique social structure and its mission effort.

THEOLOGY, PIETY, AND SOCIETY IN BETHLEHEM

The major figure behind Bethlehem's piety, mission, and communal life was a Lutheran nobleman named Nikolaus Ludwig, Count von Zinzendorf. In the United States, Zinzendorf is known mainly for his role in the religious development of John Wesley and in the establishment of Protestant missions. In his own day, however, Zinzendorf was one of the most famous (and controversial) figures in Germany. He was a noted preacher, hymn writer, patron of Christian missions, advocate of religious toleration, and social critic. His hymns, litanies, sermons, and discourses presented a vision of Christian community that attracted thousands of adherents from all social classes and many different races.[14] The literature on Zinzendorf is enormous because his activities touched so many aspects of early modern German culture. In direct and indirect ways, his work influenced such luminaries as Goethe, Schleiermacher, Herder, and Novalis. He remains, arguably, the most discussed German religious figure of the eighteenth century, in part because of his controversial piety.[15]

Zinzendorf's "theology of the heart" was a creative, antirationalist approach to Christianity that offered a vigorous alternative to contemporary Protestantism, which had grown rigid in its quest for doctrinal precision and moral purity. Zinzendorf focused intently on the atoning death of Jesus and made the blood and wounds of Christ the primary object of devotion for his followers. This blood mysticism was joined to the idea of the soul's mystical marriage to Christ. All believers, men and women, were to be brides of Christ. Furthermore, Zinzendorf and his followers also worshipped the Holy Spirit as "mother." This language of motherhood and the soul's marriage to the crucified Jesus offended many of Zinzendorf's contemporaries, including John Wesley, George Whitefield, and Gilbert Tennent.[16] Despite the controversy

14. Most of Zinzendorf's published works are reproduced in two series: *Hauptschriften in sechs Bänden* (abbreviated ZH), and *Ergänzungsbände zu den Hauptschriften* (abbreviated ZE), ed. Erich Beyreuther and Gerhard Meyer (Hildesheim: Georg Olms, 1964–85). Although many of his sermons were published in English in the eighteenth century, only two modern English translations of his works have appeared: *Nine Public Lectures on Important Subjects in Religion Preached in Fetter Lane Chapel in London in the Year 1746*, trans. and ed. George W. Forell (Iowa City: University of Iowa Press, 1973), and *A Collection of Sermons from Zinzendorf's Pennsylvania Journey*, trans. Julie Weber and ed. Craig D. Atwood (Bethlehem, Pa.: Moravian Publication Office, 2002), hereafter *Pennsylvania Sermons*. The latter volume includes a bibliography of all of Zinzendorf's works ever translated into English.

15. Dietrich Meyer's *Bibliographisches Handbuch zur Zinzendorf-Forschung* (Düsseldorf: C. Blech, 1987) gives all of the literature published on Zinzendorf prior to 1987 as well as all of the editions of his writings.

16. The anti-Zinzendorfiana runs to tens of thousands of pages and deserves careful study. Aaron Fogleman has shown the connection of anti-Zinzendorf literature to early modern anxieties about race, class, and gender. In many cases this led to violence against the Moravians. Aaron S. Fogleman, "'Jesus ist weiblich': Die hernhutische Herausforderung in den deutschen Gemeinden Nordamerikas im 18. Jahrhundert," *Histor-*

generated by such polemics, Zinzendorf's heart theology attracted thousands of converts during the 1730s and 1740s, the period when this piety was being developed.

Had his ideas remained in the realm of private devotion or even been simply literary expressions, the count's writings would merit a prominent place in the history of poetry and mysticism. Unlike most poets and mystics, however, Zinzendorf gave his ideas practical expression in the life of Moravian communities such as Bethlehem. In order to make sense of transatlantic Pietism, religion in early Pennsylvania, Moravian missions to native peoples, and even the early history of Methodism, it is necessary to understand Moravian communal life and the theology of Zinzendorf together.

Although Bethlehem and the Moravians in colonial America have attracted the interest of scholars in many disciplines, Zinzendorf's vital role in Bethlehem's life has often been de-emphasized or even distorted. Zinzendorf and his theology have generally been seen as a negative influence on Bethlehem and the Moravian work in America.[17] But Bethlehem was the embodiment of Zinzendorf's vision.

As a Moravian settlement, Bethlehem was a closed society for about one hundred years. No one was allowed to live there without being accepted as part of the Moravian Church and agreeing to live according to the church's rules.[18] From the earliest days of Bethlehem, the leadership insisted that the community must be vigilant when admitting residents. "Our rule must remain that of keeping the door open for everyone to leave us, yet of being more cautious in admitting them."[19] Simply being Christian was not sufficient for living in Bethlehem. Even Moravians had to be examined before being admitted into the Bethlehem community, and the final decision on who lived and worked in Bethlehem lay with the Lord through the drawing of the lot.[20]

---

ische Anthropologie: Kultur, Gesellschaft, Alltag 9 (2001): 167–94; Aaron S. Fogleman, "Jesus Is Female: The Moravian Challenge in the German Communities of British North America," William and Mary Quarterly 60, 3rd ser. (2003): 295–332. Probably the most damning polemic was that of the Pennsylvanian Andreas Frey, who journeyed to Herrnhaag and was shocked by the liturgical and social life there. One of the most influential polemics in English was that of Henry Rimius, A Candid Narrative of the Rise and Progress of the Herrnhuters, Commonly call'd Moravians or Unitas Fratrum, With a short Account of their Doctrines, drawn from their own Writings (London, 1753). See also Milton J. Coalter Jr., "The Radical Pietism of Count Nicholas Zinzendorf as a Conservative Influence on the Awakener, Gilbert Tennent," Church History 49 (1980): 35–46.

17. Jacob John Sessler, Communal Pietism Among Early American Moravians (New York: Henry Holt, 1933), 157.

18. The discussions held prior to the writing and signing of the Bethlehem Brotherly Agreement are discussed by Katherine Carté Engel, "Br. Joseph's Sermon on the Oeconomie, February 11, 1758," in Atwood and Vogt, Distinctiveness of Moravian Culture. An English translation of the Herrnhut brotherly agreement may be found in Peter Erb, Pietists: Selected Writings (Mahwah, N.J.: Paulist Press, 1983), 325–30.

19. Kenneth G. Hamilton, trans. and ed., The Bethlehem Diary, vol. 1, 1742–1744 (Bethlehem, Pa.: Archives of the Moravian Church, 1971), 106.

20. The practice of the lot has been much discussed in the scholarly literature. The reader is directed to Sommer, Serving Two Masters, and Gollin, Moravians in Two Worlds.

The practice of drawing the lot was intended to bring the individual and the community into line with the wishes of Christ and to avoid all self-will. When there were important decisions to make, the elders would pray for guidance and then draw a slip of paper from the lot box. The paper indicated "yes," "no," or "wait," and this was accepted as the will of Christ. Thus it was Christ who had the final say on who could live and lead in Bethlehem. For this reason the Moravians often referred to their system as a "theocracy."[21]

The most unique feature of the Moravian communities was the "choir system." This will be discussed in detail in a separate chapter, but a few words may be helpful here. "Choir" referred not to a singing group but to social groups within a community. The entire Moravian community was divided into close-knit groups according to age, sex, and marital status.[22] The precise structure of the choirs varied from settlement to settlement, but all of the Moravian communities implemented some variation of this system. As we shall see, Bethlehem's choir system was the most developed in the Moravian world. Its choirs covered every stage of life, from conception to burial.

In order to gain a picture of the choir system, let us briefly trace the choirs that a typical Moravian female would progress through during her life.[23] She would begin life in the Infants' Choir, and at about age five or six she would be received into the Little Girls' Choir. At the onset of puberty she would be transferred into the Older Girls' Choir, and when she turned seventeen (usually) she would be received into the Single Sisters' Choir, which was sometimes called the Maidens' Choir. This meant that she was at an age appropriate for marriage. If she chose to marry, then she immediately became part of the Married Choir. If her husband died, she joined the Widows' Choir. There were corresponding male choirs, and men served their apprenticeship in the Single Brothers' Choir. This scheme was altered from time to time and from place to place. Sometimes the older and the younger girls, or the older girls and the single women, would be combined into one choir.[24]

Sociologists and social historians have been attracted to Bethlehem because of its unique social structure and economic system, and they have uncovered much about how Bethlehem functioned.[25] But the heart and soul of the com-

21. Dietrich Meyer, "The Moravian Church as a Theocracy: The Resolution of the Synod of 1764," in Atwood and Vogt, *Distinctiveness of Moravian Culture.*

22. The choir system has naturally attracted the attention of sociologists. Gollin, *Moravians in Two Worlds,* 67–89, gives a fairly comprehensive account of the development and usefulness of the choir system in both Herrnhut and Bethlehem; however, she implies that a choir is only a choir when it has its own separate living quarters and economy. This was not always the case.

23. See Smaby, *Transformation of Moravian Bethlehem,* 145–46, and Erbe, *Bethlehem, Pa.,* 44, for a detailed discussion of these stages.

24. *Bethlehem Diary* (Moravian Archives), Oct. 15, 1749 (¶ 2).

25. One exception is Edwin Albert Sawyer, "The Religious Experience of the Colonial American Moravians," in *Transactions of the Moravian Historical Society* (hereafter TMHS) 18:1–227.

munity was its religious life. This book will attempt to adjust our understanding of Bethlehem by examining the deep connection between life in Bethlehem and the religious symbolism of Zinzendorf. This will be an exercise in both historical theology and cultural history because it will examine the nexus between theology, religious experience, and social praxis. In doing so, it will focus attention on those aspects of Bethlehem's life that have most confused or offended outsiders (including modern scholars) but that were central to the residents of Bethlehem, namely, their liturgy and ritual.

It is in their adoration of the wounds of Jesus and their longing for mystical marriage with the Savior that the colonial Moravians appear most alien to us, and yet it was this piety that most clearly defined them and their mission. By examining this exotic and even disturbing devotion, we can come closer to unraveling the mystery of the Moravians and their mission. In many ways, this will be a study of ritual and how it shapes life. Clifford Geertz's comment that "in a ritual, the world as lived and the world as imagined, fused under the agency of a single set of symbolic forms, turn out to be the same world" describes life in colonial Bethlehem.[26]

After placing Bethlehem in the context of the eighteenth century, especially the complex and fluid Pietist movement that affected Germany, England, and America, I explore the heart religion of Zinzendorf and show how such controversial themes as the motherhood of the Holy Spirit, the mystical marriage of the soul with Christ, the full humanity of Christ, and the blood-and-wounds theology form an organic theology. Then I will show how this theology was communicated to the residents of Bethlehem through sermons, hymns, litanies, and rituals. Bethlehem tried to be a town where "the life, sufferings, and death" of the Savior were a present reality that gave meaning to the most mundane aspects of life. Employment, education, family life, and even marriage and sexuality were all understood in the light of the incarnation of the Creator in the form of the Savior. The social system, rituals, and theology of Bethlehem were so intricately joined that it would be hard to conceive of them as existing separately.

This study concentrates on the theology that Zinzendorf communicated, not his private reflections. It examines Zinzendorf's printed works produced in the period 1738–56, the time of the greatest expansion of the Brüdergemeine, the establishment and development of the community of Bethlehem, and the period when Zinzendorf was forced to defend his thoughts. Interestingly enough, it does not matter to this study whether his sermons were preached in America

---

26. Clifford Geertz, *The Interpretation of Cultures* (New York: Basic Books, 1973), 112. Cf. Catherine Bell, *Ritual: Perspectives and Dimensions* (New York: Oxford University Press, 1997).

or Europe. There were very few Moravians in America when Zinzendorf made his famous visit to Pennsylvania (late 1741–early 1743); therefore his Pennsylvania sermons had little direct impact on the community of Bethlehem.[27] It was the sermons preached in the European communities that would have been heard by the early emigrants to Bethlehem, since the majority of them had lived in one of the Moravian communities in Europe. Moreover, his printed sermons and discourses were widely distributed to all of the Moravian communities and were frequently read in Bethlehem.

Bethlehem is one of the most carefully documented communities in colonial North America. In fact, the sheer wealth of manuscript materials makes historical study more, rather than less, difficult, as it is impossible for any one person to read all, or even a significant portion, of the boxes of handwritten German papers. Past studies have focused on such official documents as the economic ledgers, synod results, membership reports, and minutes of the administrative committees. In recent years, scholars such as Katherine Faull and Beverly Smaby have made good use of the funeral biographies *(Lebensläufe)* as windows into the community's norms and individuals' experience.[28]

This book examines a neglected body of material, especially the community's litanies and hymns. Because of a bias toward the preached word and systematic theology in Protestantism, scholars of American religion tend to study formal theological discourse even when discussing popular religion; but it was the liturgical practice that was formative for many communities in America. Zinzendorf and his followers placed heavy emphasis on hymns as *theological* expressions, and the hymnbooks used in Bethlehem during the communal period are valuable sources for determining the use of Zinzendorfian themes and motifs.

Even more important than the hymns are the church's litanies, for they were explicitly intended to express the communal faith and theology. Special attention will be given to the *Litany of the Wounds of the Husband* as a powerful statement of the core of Zinzendorf's theology. Rather than simply condemning the *Litany of the Wounds,* as many previous writers have done, I attempt to understand why such devotional materials were so important in Bethlehem. Moreover, the rituals themselves, their scheduling, and descriptions of their effect on the community will be analyzed.

One of the most important sources for this study is the Bethlehem Diary, which records the events of communal life along with personal interpretation

27. Craig D. Atwood, "Introduction," in *A Collection of Sermons from Zinzendorf's Pennsylvania Journey.*
28. Katherine M. Faull, trans. and ed., *Moravian Women: Their Related Lives* (Lewisburg: Bucknell University Press, 1998). Several *Lebensläufe* have recently been translated in Atwood and Vogt, *Distinctiveness of Moravian Culture.*

and description.[29] It was kept by a variety of diarists over the years, and its character changes according to the diarist. It also includes excerpts from the diaries of the various subgroups within Bethlehem, such as the Single Sisters' Choir. The subjective aspect of the Diary, which has steered sociologists and historians away from it as an unreliable source, makes it particularly useful for our purposes. Within the Diary are notices of weddings, baptisms, and funerals, including the funeral biographies that Smaby examined. Such sources help demonstrate whether Zinzendorf's theology went to the heart of the individuals in the community at moments of existential crisis.[30]

THE QUESTION OF THE SIFTING TIME

Much of this study involves material and themes commonly associated with an obscure period of Moravian history known as the *Sichtungszeit,* or Sifting Time, and thus it is necessary to address this issue before proceeding. The term itself comes from Luke 22:31 ("Simon, Simon, behold, Satan demanded to have you, that he might sift you like wheat"), which refers to being tested. In Moravian historiography, the Sifting Time was a period of fanatical excess originating in the Herrnhaag community in Germany in the 1740s. At that time, the Brüdergemeine faced the real possibility that it would become a fanatical sect or what some today might call a "cult." In 1749 Zinzendorf was made aware of the situation in Herrnhaag and issued a long letter of reprimand.[31] He also removed his son Christian Renatus from his office as head of the Single Men's choir. A special synod was called to deal with the problems in Herrnhaag and the resulting negative publicity. Hymnals, litany books, and many collections of Zinzendorf's sermons were edited and reissued.[32]

These facts are well established, but the Sifting Time has been granted an almost mythic status in Moravian history as a time of great danger that the Moravians survived and emerged from stronger. Nearly every history of the Moravians (even those covering earlier and later periods) has used the Sifting Time as a way to make sense of Zinzendorf and his movement, but I believe that we need to reconsider the idea of the Sifting Time itself. For two centuries

29. A very helpful musicological index of the *Bethlehem Diary* is available in the Moravian Archives. Two volumes of the diary have been translated and published by the Archives: Kenneth G. Hamilton, trans. and ed., *The Bethlehem Diary,* vol. 1., 1742–1744 (Bethlehem, Pa.: Archives of the Moravian Church, 1971); and Kenneth G. Hamilton and Lothar Madheim, trans. *The Bethlehem Diary,* vol. 2, 1744–45, ed. Vernon Nelson, Otto Dreydoppel Jr., and Doris Rohland Yob (Bethlehem, Pa.: Archives of the Moravian Church, 2001).

30. Wendy Pfeifer-Quaile, in her dissertation "The Self-Expression of Moravians in North Carolina" (Ph.D. diss., Rutgers University, 2001), confirmed this thesis.

31. Craig D. Atwood, "Zinzendorf's 1749 Reprimand to the *Brüdergemeine,*" *Transactions of the Moravian Historical Society* 29 (1996): 59–84.

32. Hamilton and Hamilton, *History,* 105. Zinzendorf recorded in the *Jüngerhaus Diarium* in 1757, "I myself probably gave the occasion for our short but terrible hour of Sifting" (see ibid., 657, n. 35).

it has been used, consciously and unconsciously, to marginalize central features of Zinzendorf's theology and Moravian piety in the eighteenth century rather than to make sense of them.[33]

The traditional interpretation of the 1740s is that Zinzendorf let his theological imagination roam too far. Like Icarus, he flew too close to the sun, with catastrophic results. His provocative (and to most interpreters, erroneous) ideas led to fanaticism, but the count quickly returned to more or less traditional theology and the community repudiated his theological experiments. Through frequent repetition, this interpretation is often accepted as a fact, and the Sifting Time is seen as the watershed in Moravian history.

It is also assumed that key figures in the history of Bethlehem, such as August Gottlieb Spangenberg and Peter Böhler, who opposed the troubling activities in Herrnhaag, must have been opposed to Zinzendorf and his evocative theological style as well. The American historian Jacob John Sessler is a notable exemplar of this tendency to separate the count from his close associates; as Sessler puts it, "in these years under discussion, men like Spangenberg and Peter Böhler took exception to Zinzendorfianism."[34]

There are many flaws in this traditional view of the 1740s, but we need to address the question of why the standard interpretation has taken such firm hold on Moravian historiography. The simple answer is that the idea of the Sifting Time has served a convenient apologetical purpose. Whatever historians, sociologists, church leaders, or theologians have considered bizarre or unorthodox about the eighteenth-century Moravians has been identified as part of the Sifting Time and thus dismissed. We see this most clearly in English-language scholarship, but this apologetic approach has also affected German scholars, who have used the Sifting Time to separate the "real" Zinzendorf from his writings of the 1740s, which provided so much fuel for polemical attacks.

The desire to distance Zinzendorf from his own writings was strengthened when Oskar Pfister, a Freudian psychologist, argued that the period described as the Sifting Time was Zinzendorf's "eruption period."[35] For Pfister, the works of the 1740s were indeed the "real" Zinzendorf, a really unbalanced Zinzendorf. It was natural that pro-Zinzendorf scholars would want to distance the count from writings that may support the charge of deep-seated sadomasochistic tendencies in Zinzendorf. Gerhard Reichel answered Pfister's charge that Zin-

---

33. For more on the problem of the Sifting Time, see Craig D. Atwood, "The Persistence of Zinzendorfian Piety in Colonial America," in *German Moravians in the Transatlantic World*, ed. Michele Gillespie and Robert Benchy (forthcoming). Katherine Faull makes a similar point in "Faith and Imagination," 25–26.

34. Sessler, *Communal Pietism*, 153.

35. Oskar Pfister, *Die Frömmigkeit des Grafen Ludwig von Zinzendorf: Ein psychoanalytischer Beitrag zur Kenntnis der religiösen Sublimierungsprozesse und zur Erklärung des Pietismus* (Leipzig: F. Deuticke, 1910).

zendorf was psychologically unbalanced by demonstrating the close affinity between the expressions of the 1740s and seventeenth-century Lutheran hymnody.[36]

Reichel's approach has much to commend it, but Reichel himself was so influenced by the traditional model of the Sifting Time that he actually argued at cross-purposes. On the one hand, he rightly showed that in the 1740s Zinzendorf was drawing upon a long tradition of German piety, but on the other hand he asserted that this period was a brief aberration from which Zinzendorf quickly recovered. So, for Reichel, while the piety of the 1740s was not pathological, it was mercifully transitory. Reichel asserts that the count quickly turned away from "blood-and-wounds theology" and returned to more acceptable modes of expression.

Likewise, although Wilhelm Bettermann argued that the expressions of the 1740s are part of Zinzendorf's wider theological understanding, he still maintained that this was a brief phase in Zinzendorf's thought rather than a significant development.[37] This view is changing somewhat in modern Zinzendorf scholarship. While Peter Zimmerling uses the traditional language of a Sifting Time, he is careful to point out that Zinzendorf continued to use some of his most creative and controversial motifs, such as the family idea of the Trinity, long after the end of the Sifting.[38]

In England and America, the Sifting Time has been used to separate the Moravian Church from Zinzendorf's theology itself.[39] Zinzendorf is generally blamed for the Sifting Time, while the Moravian immigrants are given credit for restoring the church to its original discipline and order. The Sifting, we are told in the church's official history, ended when the Moravians reasserted themselves, abandoned Zinzendorfian excess, and restored proper biblical theology. "The Brethren soon found their way back to sober language and scriptural forms of thought. Few churches have passed through experiences so searching without suffering permanent harm. . . . The discipline so characteristic of the refugees of 1722 to 1727 was revived. The unhappy features of the time of Sifting disappeared; the hymnals and liturgies which had been instrumental in promoting them were suppressed."[40]

The use of the term "Sifting Time" to demonstrate that the Moravian

36. Gerhard Reichel, *Zinzendorfs Frömmigkeit im Licht der Psychoanalyse* (Tübingen: J.C.B. Mohr, 1911).

37. Wilhelm Bettermann, *Theologie und Sprache bei Zinzendorf* (Gotha: Leopold Klotz, 1935), 1–2.

38. Peter Zimmerling, *Gott in Gemeinschaft: Zinzendorfs Trinitätslehre* (Giessen/Basel: Brunnen Verlag, 1991), 169–72.

39. J. E. Hutton, *A History of the Moravian Church,* 2d ed. (London: Moravian Publication Office, 1909); Sawyer, "Religious Experience of the Colonial American Moravians"; Thorp, *Moravian Community in Colonial North Carolina,* 14–21, 28–29; Hamilton and Hamilton, *History,* 94–106; Smaby, *Transformation of Moravian Bethlehem,* 28–30; Gollin, *Moravians in Two Worlds,* 11–16.

40. Hamilton and Hamilton, *History,* 105–6.

Church was not really the fanatical sect portrayed in mid-century polemics appears already in Moravian apologetical literature in the 1760s and 1770s.[41] Everything controversial about the church supposedly ended around 1750. Thus August Gottlieb Spangenberg dismissed completely the provocative Twelfth Appendix *(Anhang XII)* of the Herrnhut songbook as unworthy of mention since it was recalled by the church after 1749.[42] What Spangenberg does not say is that *all* of the litanies and most of the hymns of *Anhang XII* continued to be republished with only minor revisions and were used for decades after 1750.[43]

This misunderstanding of the Sifting Time has of course been increased by the intentional destruction of documents by church officials in the eighteenth century and later.[44] Scholars have been too quick to assume that references to the "juicy and tasty" wounds in the surviving sources represent the Sifting Time. On the contrary, it is what was removed that represented the Sifting Time, not what was left in the records. Historians, however, have used the silence in the sources to create a Sifting Time that may or may not be accurate. It is easy to be misled by Zinzendorf's instruction that "the teaching of the little side-hole is already too old and belongs back in the sacristy until another time, so that no nonsense will be made of it" as an effective prohibition of blood-and-wounds theology.[45] Even within his letter of reprimand, though, Zinzendorf affirmed the importance of wounds theology for the community.

Hermann Plitt in many ways set the tone for the modern understanding of Zinzendorf. His dating of the Sifting Time to 1743–50 has been the norm in

41. David Cranz, *Alte und Neue Brüder-Historie oder kurz gefaßte Geschichte der Evangelischen Brüder-Unität* (Barby, 1772, reproduced in ZM 2:11); David Cranz, *Ancient and Modern History of the Brethren*, trans. Benjamin LaTrobe (London, 1780); August Gottlieb Spangenberg, *Leben des Herrn Nikolaus Ludwig, Grafen von Zinzendorf und Pottendorf* (Barby, 1773–75, reproduced in ZM 2:1–8) *(The Life of Nicholas Lewis, Count Zinzendorf, Bishop and Ordinary of the Church of the United [or Moravian] Brethren*, trans. and abr. Samuel Jackson [London: S. Holdsworth, 1838]).

42. Vernon Nelson, "The *Geistliche Gedicht* of Zinzendorf and the Brüder-Unität 1745–1748," in *"Alles ist euer, ihr aber seid Christi": Festschrift für Dietrich Meyer*, ed. Rudolf Mohr (Cologne: Rheinland-Verlag, 2000), 827–38.

43. For example, the worship of the Holy Spirit as mother has been treated as a brief experiment during the Sifting Time. Gary Kinkel's groundbreaking monograph on this topic, *Our Dear Mother the Spirit: An Investigation of Count Zinzendorf's Theology and Praxis* (Lanham, Md.: University Press of America, 1990) (see 31–33), was unfortunately limited by the traditional understanding of the Sifting Time and thus missed the further development of this devotion after 1750. See Craig D. Atwood, "The Mother of God's People: The Adoration of the Holy Spirit in the Eighteenth-Century Brüdergemeine," *Church History* 68 (Dec. 1999): 886–909.

44. Paul Peucker, "'In Staub und Asche': Bewertung und Kassation im Unitätsarchiv 1760–1810," in Mohr, *Festschrift für Dietrich Meyer*, 127–58. An example of this may be in the *Bethlehem Diary* for 1748. In more than one place, the pages of the original diary appear to have been cut to remove offending passages. For instance, one entry from 1748 states: "Moreover our congregation events today were very juicy and tasty to us, especially, however, the litany of the wounds, with which we . . ." *Bethlehem Diary* (Moravian Archives), Aug. 26 (Sept. 6, n.s.), 1748. This may have been just an error, though, since the copy sent to Herrnhut ends with "began our Sabbath blessedly." (Reference supplied by Paul Peucker.) The reason for the two dates is that England and its colonies did not adopt the Gregorian calendar reforms until later in the century. The first date is old style and the second is new style (n.s.), or Gregorian.

45. Atwood, "Zinzendorf's 1749 Reprimand," 71.

Moravian scholarship.[46] Peter Zimmerling, for instance, in his recent presentation of Zinzendorf's Trinitarian theology, follows Plitt's outline of Zinzendorf's career.[47] Recently, though, some have argued that the so-called Sifting Time really lasted from 1738 to 1753 or later, as expressions commonly associated with the Sifting Time occur both before and after 1743–50. Gary Kinkel, for instance, chose 1738 as the beginning of the Sifting Time because by that date "certain ideas and manners of expression characteristic of the *Sichtungszeit* had begun to appear."[48] As we shall see, it is more accurate to say that the expressions of 1738 and even 1744 are *not* uniquely characteristic of the Sifting Time but were part of a persistent and comprehensive Zinzendorfian piety.

The wide disparity in dates demonstrates that the concept of a Sifting Time is problematic. If the broader date is accurate, then the Sifting Time spanned a quarter of Zinzendorf's life and half of his literary career. Moravians who experienced the Sifting in Herrnhaag, in contrast, describe it as a painful episode in the history of Herrnhaag during 1748–49.[49] The idea of "a brief, terrible time" of temptation and trial loses all meaning if it extends through more than one-third of Zinzendorf's career and almost all of his published works. Paul Peucker, while serving as archivist in Herrnhut, argued convincingly that the Sifting Time originally referred only to 1748–49 in Herrnhaag.[50]

One problem with the broader dating of the Sifting Time is that the 1740s was the period of Zinzendorf's greatest literary output, in terms of both sermons and liturgical materials. The majority of Zinzendorf's important works were published during the supposed Sifting Time. Thus there has been a tendency to dismiss works such as *Vier und Dreißig homilien über die Wunden-Litaney* (Thirty-four Homilies on the Litany of the Wounds) as nothing more than Sifting Time nonsense rather than expressions of Zinzendorf's mature theology. We must keep in mind, though, that these were the works that Zinzendorf and the community chose to publish for the public arena. The hymns, litanies, and sermons of Zinzendorf from the 1740s continued to be used throughout the Brüdergemeine until the 1780s and 1790s. If the standard interpretation of the Sifting Time is accurate, then what do we do with Zinzendorf's major works? Are they expressions of the "real" Zinzendorf or not?

---

46. Hermann Plitt, *Zinzendorfs Theologie,* 3 vols. (Gotha: F. A. Perthes, 1869–74).

47. Zimmerling, *Gott in Gemeinschaft.*

48. Kinkel, *Our Dear Mother the Spirit,* 31.

49. For instance, one of the leaders of Bethlehem, Anna Seidel, said of the Sifting, "In April 1747, I traveled back to Herrnhaag. . . . I shall never forget these very months in Herrnhaag all my days for it was a quite specially blessed time. . . . In autumn 1748, I traveled to Holland, and after a two month stay in Zeist I traveled with the late Mama via Barby back to Herrnhaag, where I spent the whole winter and had a very heavy time during the Sifting Period." Faull, *Moravian Women,* 124.

50. Paul Peucker, "'Blut' auf unsre grünen Bändchen: Die Sichtungzeit in der Herrnhuter Brüdergemeine," *Unitas Fratrum* 49–50 (2002): 41–94, at 77–80.

The use of the Sifting Time in Anglo-American scholarship is more prob-
lematic than it is in German scholarship. The most influential figure in interpreting eighteenth-century Moravian history is J. E. Hutton, a Victorian-era
Moravian historian whose 1909 *History of the Moravian Church* helped define
Moravian historiography.[51] For Hutton the Sifting Time was the direct result
of Zinzendorf's antirational theology and his devotion to the wounds of Christ.
"As long as Zinzendorf used his own mental powers, he was able to make his
'Blood and Wounds Theology' a power for good; but as soon as he bade good-
bye to his intellect he made his doctrine a laughing-stock and a scandal. Instead
of concentrating his attention on the moral and spiritual value of the cross, he
now began to lay all the stress on the mere physical details. He composed a
'Litany of the Wounds'; and the Brethren could now talk and sing of nothing
else."[52] For Hutton, the *Litany of the Wounds* was itself evidence that Zinzendorf and his weaker followers quite literally lost their minds. It might be more
accurate to say that it is evidence that Zinzendorf was not the Victorian moral-
ist that Hutton thought all good Christians should be.[53]

This view of the Sifting as a time of general and unrestrained childishness
has asserted great influence and continues to serve political and ecclesiastical
purposes. However, as we shall see in more detail, the evidence contradicts this
widely accepted theory. In their efforts to invent a Moravian Church and a
Bethlehem unaffected by Zinzendorf's more creative ideas, or to invent a Zinzendorf similarly unaffected by his own ideas, scholars have in fact distorted
rather than illuminated our understanding of the entire Zinzendorfian era and
the evolution of Moravian theology and piety. This situation is changing in
contemporary scholarship on the Moravians. Thanks to the work of Paul
Peucker, Peter Vogt, Katherine Faull, Hans-Walter Erbe, and Aaron Fogleman,
a more precise understanding of the Sifting Time is emerging.[54]

One advantage of the traditional interpretation of the Sifting Time is that it
provides a neat explanation for the dissolution of Herrnhaag, the center of the
Sifting.[55] Herrnhaag was the most beautiful and the most important Moravian
community in the 1740s. Most of the men and women who led the Brüdergemeine for nearly half a century spent some time living at Herrnhaag. It was the
gem of the Moravian world, but in 1749 the secular authority, Count Casimir

---

51. Hutton, *History of the Moravian Church;* http://www. everydaycounselor.com/hutton.

52. Hutton, *History of the Moravian Church,* 276.

53. Hutton's perspective on the Sifting Time was used by Sessler and others to understand the early
history of Bethlehem as well. "Zinzendorf suffered from a pathological condition which broke out in demonstrations of emotionalism, phantasies, and morbidity" that adversely affected the community. Sessler, *Communal Pietism,* 162.

54. Hans-Walter Erbe, "Herrnhaag—Tiefpunkt oder Höhepunkt der Brüdergeschichte?" *Unitas Fratrum*
26 (1989): 37–51; Faull, "Faith and Imagination," 23–56; Fogleman, "'Jesus ist weiblich,'" 167–95.

55. For the full story of Herrnhaag, see Erbe, *Herrnhaag: Eine religiöse Kommunität.*

of Ysenburg-Büdingen, forced the residents to leave.[56] There were indeed problems in Herrnhaag among the Single Brothers, as the Moravian leadership noted, but it is not clear that this was the direct cause of the dissolution of Herrnhaag.[57]

The reason for the expulsion, in brief, was that the old count (famous for his policy of religious toleration) died in 1749. He had been a supporter of Zinzendorf, but his son and successor, Casimir, was not. Casimir himself was closely connected to the Danish court. The fiasco of the awarding and rescinding of the Danebrog in the early 1730s had embittered many in the Danish court against Zinzendorf.[58] Moreover, the hostility of Halle toward Zinzendorf was well established by 1741. In other words, the seeds of the destruction of Herrnhaag were sown in the early 1730s, long before the Sifting Time.

When Casimir came into his own as feudal lord, he ordered the residents on his estate to swear allegiance to him alone. In addition, the residents of Herrnhaag had to verbally repudiate Count Zinzendorf or face banishment.[59] Casimir was shocked when the Herrnhaagers elected to vacate their buildings rather than show disloyalty to Zinzendorf. More than a thousand residents of Herrnhaag were forced to leave. Some two hundred migrated to Bethlehem at a crippling financial cost. The Herrnhaag disaster was a major reason for the financial crisis of the 1750s in Bethlehem and the wider Brüdergemeine. While stories about the activities of the Single Brothers in Herrnhaag may have contributed to the expulsion decree, dynastic, political, and aristocratic rivalry played a great role.

In Moravian historiography, though, the dissolution of Herrnhaag served as a morality tale. Beware of embracing Zinzendorf's radical ideas or you will end up like Herrnhaag. In short, Herrnhaag has been treated like a Moravian Sodom that was destroyed because of its heresy, but the Sifting in Herrnhaag had little to do with the main themes of Zinzendorf's theology and the life of the Moravians in Bethlehem: the blood and wounds of Christ. This book will demonstrate the persistence of evocative blood-and-wounds theology long after the Sifting Time and the dissolution of Herrnhaag.

It is recorded in the Bethlehem Diary, for instance, that at a communion service the "corpse bees enjoyed the sacrament."[60] At another service, "After

---

56. Hellmut Reichel, "Das Ende des Brüdergemeine Herrnhaag 1750," *Unitas Fratrum* 26 (1989): 52–72.

57. Erbe, *Herrnhaag: Eine religiöse Kommunität,* demonstrates this convincingly. Based on his portrayal of the Sifting, we might compare it to the "Summer of Love" in San Francisco in 1968. It was a time when a youth culture frightened the authorities.

58. Reichel, "Das Ende des Brüdergemeine," 54–57. On the Danebrog controversy and its relationship to the split between Halle and Zinzendorf, see Ward, *Protestant Evangelical Awakening,* 132–40.

59. Reichel, "Das Ende des Brüdergemeine," 58.

60. Jan. 19, 1760, *Bethlehem Diary* (Moravian Archives).

those who are sick had also received their portion of the body, Br. Nathanael [Seidel] sang the corpse-bees completely to sleep with the late Christel's corpse liturgies for a blessed rest in His grave!"[61] Based on the standard periodization of Moravian history, we would date these entries to the Sifting Time, but in fact they come from the late 1750s, when the Sifting Time was over and Spangenberg was fully in control in Bethlehem.

How do we explain the persistence of such language years after the so-called Sifting Time? The simplest explanation is that these references to the "corpse bees" were connected to a deeply felt Zinzendorfian piety that was shared by Spangenberg and the Bethlehem community, rather than an aberrant form of Moravian piety. It is certainly true that Spangenberg did not use such expressions in his later apologetical works, but they appear when he was the "Vicar General of the Ordinary in America" in the decade following the Sifting Time. The examples can be multiplied.

Moreover, there is little evidence that there was a general time of Sifting that affected the entire church. To the contrary, this was the period when the Moravians were examined by governmental officials in Saxony, Prussia, and England and consistently found praiseworthy, despite the diligent work of their enemies. In 1749, when the Sifting Time was supposedly raging out of Zinzendorf's control, the English Parliament carefully studied the history and theology of the Moravians and concluded that the Moravian Church was an "antient [sic] and episcopal Protestant Church."[62] It is hard to reconcile these high-water marks of legitimation with a period of raging fanaticism.

The actual history of the *Litany of the Wounds* also challenges the traditional interpretation that this litany was part of the Sifting. Historians have allowed the theory to determine the evidence. Once it has been accepted that the *Litany of the Wounds* is a piece of Sifting Time nonsense, one tends not to notice its continued use long after 1750. The confusion over the *Litany of the Wounds* is understandable, as the name of the litany was changed to something that appears on the surface to be more traditional. In 1752 the old *Litany of the Wounds* was divided into *The Litany of the Life, Sufferings, and Death of the Jesus* and *Hymns of the Wounds*. In this form, most of the old *Litany of the Wounds,* including the infamous petitions to the wounds of Christ ("so moist, so gory") remained in publication in German and English Moravian hymnals to the end of the eighteenthth century, half a century after the Sifting Time.[63]

61. Ibid., Nov. 27, 1756.

62. Colin Podmore, *The Moravian Church in England, 1728–1760* (Oxford: Clarendon Press, 1998).

63. *A Collection of Hymns chiefly extracted from the Larger Hymn-Book of the Brethren's Congregations* (London: Brethren's Chapel, 1769); *A Collection of Hymns, for the Use of the Protestant Church of the United Brethren* (London: Brethren's Chapel, 1789); *Liturgic Hymns of United Brethren: Revised and Enlarged* (London, 1793), 55. Cf. Atwood, "Zinzendorf's Litany of the Wounds."

Colin Podmore, in his study of the Moravians in England, recognized that it was precisely those aspects of Moravian devotion that historians have often dismissed as pathological or nonsensical that attracted many English evangelicals, such as John Cennick and Jacob Rogers, to the Moravian fold.[64] The church never recovered the dynamism it had possessed during the 1740s, when Zinzendorf was most creative and the church most controversial. Part of the reason for the stagnation after 1750 was the debt crisis and Halle's persistent opposition to the Moravians, but another factor is that the Moravians became more conventional after mid-century. This was true of the church in general, but particularly of Bethlehem. As long as the Moravians in Bethlehem embraced the theology and liturgy of Zinzendorf, their community thrived.

Bethlehem needed the paradoxical imagery of the wounded Savior-God in order to deal with the contradictions of living in heaven on earth. This is where the real strength of Zinzendorf's theology manifested itself. Blood-and-wounds theology, with all of its graphic descriptions of the torture and abuse of Jesus and its eroticizing of his wounds, served to help the residents of Bethlehem sublimate community-destroying impulses. Christ became their scapegoat, not just theologically but sociologically and psychologically as well. Through evocative and provocative imagery, Zinzendorf painted the Savior before their eyes as they worshipped, worked, and slept. He offered the Moravians a God who shared their struggles and bore on his own body the strains and contradictions of their communal life, so that they could live in harmony.

64. Podmore, *Moravian Church in England*, 132–36.

FIGURE 1. Nicholas von Zinzendorf (1700–1760) receiving wampum from Native American leaders. Unity Archives, Herrnhut.

CHAPTER 1

THE MORAVIANS AND
TRANSATLANTIC GERMAN PIETISM

THE UNITAS FRATRUM

Some of the residents of colonial Bethlehem were descended from members of one of the first European churches to break away from Rome. The Unity of the Brethren (Unitas Fratrum) was established in 1457 after the end of the Hussite Wars, half a century before the Protestant Reformation. The church endured periods of persecution until it was virtually destroyed during the Thirty Years' War. Remnants survived into the eighteenth century, and in 1722 refugees from Moravia sought protection from Count Nikolaus von Zinzendorf in the hope they could revive the church of their ancestors. The period between the decree of expulsion from Bohemia and Moravia in 1627 and the arrival of the refugees on Zinzendorf's estate is called the time of the Hidden Seed in Moravian historiography.[1]

Whether this "Hidden Seed" existed, and whether any of the approximately two thousand German-speaking Czechs who eventually united with the Brüdergemeine were indeed members of the old Unitas Fratrum, remain difficult problems in Moravian historiography. It was a burning issue in the eighteenth century, as toleration of the Moravians often depended on how much credence the authorities gave to the connection with the old Unitas Fratrum.

Although Moravian Church historians continue to stress the connection between the old Hussite Unity and Zinzendorf's movement, there are reasons to doubt that the refugees had preserved their old church.[2] First, there is little concrete evidence for the continued existence of the Unity in Bohemia or Moravia. Second, it is interesting that so few members of the Unity who lived outside Bohemia (especially Poland and East Prussia) joined with the Zinzend-

---

1. Theodor Gill, "Zinzendorf und die Mähren," in *Graf Ohne Grenzen: Leben und Werk von Nikolaus Ludwig Graf von Zinzendorf,* ed. Dietrich Meyer and Paul Peucker (Herrnhut: Unitätsarchiv-Comeniusbuchhandlung, 2000), 37–42; Hamilton and Hamilton, *History,* 13–14; J. T. Müller, *Zinzendorf als Erneuerer der alten Brüderkirche* (Leipzig: Friedrich Jansa, 1900).

2. W. R. Ward, "The Renewed Unity of the Brethren: Ancient Church, New Sect, or Transconfessional Movement," *Bulletin of the John Rylands Library* 70 (1988): lxvii–xcii. Edita Sterik, "Mährische Brüder, böhmische Brüder, und die Brüdergemeine," *Unitas Fratrum* 48 (2001): 106–14, discusses the differences, for Zinzendorf, between the Moravian Brethren and the Bohemian Brethren. Enrico Molnár, in "The Pious Fraud of Count Zinzendorf," *Iliff Review* 11 (1954): 29–38, accuses Zinzendorf of intentionally and systematically deceiving the Moravian emigrants into believing that he was renewing the church of their ancestors.

orf community. Third, in the peculiarities of the Zinzendorf community, the "Moravian" tropus remained a minority within the Brüdergemeine and did not have an independent existence.

There is some evidence of ongoing Protestant life in Bohemia and Moravia after the Thirty Years' War. Pockets of Protestants met in homes, barns, and caves to worship and exchange forbidden books.[3] During the years of persecution there were no clergy, sacraments, or a church order, but the hymns they memorized and some books they hid helped keep the memory alive. Particularly important were the works of Jan Amos Comenius, who published a German version of the Moravian hymnbook, a history of the Unity of the Brethren and their church order, and a German catechism in 1661. According to the preface of his history, Comenius hoped to preserve the heritage of his church before it died. He also indicated that his publications were intended for members of the Unity living in eight cities in Bohemia and Moravia.[4]

Some of the most important Moravian settlers in Herrnhut, including the Neissers, Zeisbergers, Schneiders, and Nitschmanns, came from Zauchental (Suchdol), one of the eight villages. While we cannot say with confidence that the community led by Zinzendorf was a renewal of the pre-Reformation Unitas Fratrum, it seems clear that the refugees had an awareness of and commitment to that old church. It may be helpful to relate briefly the history of the Unitas Fratrum in order to make sense of the Moravians in Bethlehem.[5]

The Unity of the Brethren arose during the mid-fifteenth century as part of the religious turmoil that gripped Bohemia following the execution of Jan Hus in 1415.[6] By 1419 the Hussite movement had split into more radical (Taborite) and more conciliatory (Utraquist) factions that eventually went to war with each other. One unique voice at the time was that of Petr Chelčický, a lay theologian, who was initially attracted to the radicalism of Tabor; however, he rejected Taborite violence as contrary to Jesus' teaching.[7]

3. Adolf Vacovsky, "History of the 'Hidden Seed,'" in *Unitas Fratrum,* ed. Mari P. van Buijtenen, Cornelius Dekker, and Huib Leeuwenberg (Utrecht: Rijksarchief, 1975), 35–54.

4. For more on Comenius, see Mathew Spinka, *John Amos Comenius: That Incomparable Moravian* (New York: Russell & Russell: 1943).

5. For the history of the Unitas Fratrum, see Peter Brock, *The Political and Social Doctrines of the Unity of the Czech Brethren in the Fifteenth and Early Sixteenth Centuries,* vol. 11 of *Slavistic Printings and Reprintings,* ed. Cornelis H. van Schooneveld (The Hague: Mouton & Co., 1957); Rudolf Říčan, *The History of the Unity of Brethren: A Protestant Hussite Church in Bohemia and Moravia,* trans. C. Daniel Crews (Bethlehem: Moravian Church in America, 1992). Albrecht Ritschl gives a brief history of the Brethren in vol. 3 of his *Geschichte des Pietismus in der lutherischen Kirche des 17. und 18. Jahrhunderts* (Bonn: Adolph Marcus, 1886), 221–40, which stresses the Unitas Fratrum's "monkish" and Anabaptist heritage. For a brief and traditional reading of the Unitas Fratrum's history, see Cranz, *Ancient and Modern History of the Brethren.*

6. For the history of the Hussite movement, see Thomas A. Fudge, *The Magnificent Ride: The First Reformation in Hussite Bohemia* (Aldershot, Eng.: Ashgate, 1998); Howard Kaminsky, *A History of the Hussite Revolution* (Berkeley and Los Angeles: University of California Press, 1967); F. M. Bartos, *The Hussite Revolution, 1424–1437,* trans. J. Weir and ed. John Klassen (New York: Columbia University Press, 1986), and Josef Macek, *The Hussite Movement in Bohemia* (London: Lawrence & Wishart, 1965).

7. Brock, *Political and Social Doctrines,* 25–69; Murray L. Wagner, *Petr Chelčický: A Radical Separatist in Hussite Bohemia* (Scottsdale, Pa.: Herald Press, 1983).

Chelčický advocated the Waldensian theory that the Roman Catholic Church fell into error at the time of Constantine because it became an instrument of the state. He argued that the true church should not participate in the feudal system because Christians are obligated to follow *only* the law of love given by Christ. In a similar vein, he also called for the abolition of hierarchies within the Christian community.[8] Central to Chelčický's writing is that Christ calls his followers to absolute nonviolence including a willingness to suffer persecution rather than to resist evil.

Chelčický did not begin a church, but his writings had a profound impact on the origin of the Unity of the Brethren. A university student named Gregor was frustrated by the Utraquists' compromises with Rome after the Council of Basel and the fact that it was hard to tell the difference between the followers of Hus and Catholics in daily life. On the advice of his uncle, Utraquist archbishop Jan Rokycana, Gregor read Chelčický's works, and in 1457 he organized a group of like-minded believers into a religious community in Kunwald that called themselves the Unity of the Brethren. In 1467, at the Synod of Lhotka, they established a priesthood and episcopacy separate from Rome.[9]

The Brethren centered their doctrine and practice on a strict observance of the Sermon on the Mount. For the first generation, this meant absolute nonviolence and separation from government and the nobility. Apostolic poverty was strongly encouraged for those who would be perfect, and was virtually required for priests.[10] Like the later Hutterites in Moravia, the Unity was primarily made up of peasants who considered the agricultural life more holy than urban life. Members of the church were forbidden to make money from trade, usury, scholarship, or rents.[11]

The second generation of Brethren, under the leadership of Lukas of Prague, in the 1480s and 1490s moderated many of the traditional doctrines and prohibitions.[12] Although still predominantly poor and rural, the church began to

8. Chelčický's main works are "On Spiritual Warfare" (1421), "On the Triple Division of Society" (1425), and "On the Holy Church" (also called "The Net") (c. 1440). Kaminsky has provided translations and/or summaries of these in "Treatises on Christianity and the Social Order" in *Studies in Medieval and Renaissance History,* ed. William M. Bowsky (Lincoln: University of Nebraska Press, 1964), 1:105–79. It is uncertain to what degree the Moravian reluctance to swear the oath and bear arms in the eighteenth century is related to the theology of the Unity.

9. On the reputed origins of the Waldensians, see Walter Adeney, "Waldenses" in *Encyclopaedia of Religion and Ethics,* ed. James Hastings (Edinburgh: T. & T. Clark, 1980). The claim of apostolic succession through the Waldensians did help the Moravian Church to be recognized by the Parliament of England in 1749. *Acta Fratrum Unitatis in Anglia* (London, 1749); J. T. Hamilton, *The Recognition of the Unitas Fratrum as an Old Protestant Episcopal Church by the Parliament of Great Britain in 1749* (Nazareth, Pa.: Moravian Historical Society, 1925).

10. Brock, *Political and Social Doctrines,* 80–92.

11. Ibid., 98–99.

12. Brock views this change as a rejection of the principles and spirit of the original Unity and an unfortunate acceptance of traditional social norms. Molnár, by contrast, evaluates this transformation under Lukas quite differently. "By a decree in 1495 the Brethren consciously brought to an end this first stage of their journey as a period of moralistic excess and immoderation which would have dampened the prodigality of the grace of God." Říčan, *History of the Unity,* 392.

accept artisans, merchants, and eventually nobles into its membership. The oath was criticized but not forbidden, as was participation in trials and government.[13] Despite this weakening of opposition to the secular world, the Brethren still considered themselves "Brethren of the Law" and sought to live insofar as possible according to a literal reading of the Sermon on the Mount.[14]

Since they continued to hold the state suspect, the Unity attempted to settle their disputes without resort to courts of law. To assist in obedience to the law of Christ, the Brethren instituted a strict system of pastoral discipline exercised by the priest, who in turn was held accountable by Seniors (bishops) and lay "Judges" in the congregation. The priest was required "to instruct, scrutinize, criticize, advise, admonish or encourage every candidate for membership, as well as every member, regarding the life of piety and righteousness, not just regarding doctrine."[15] This discipline was one of the most cherished aspects of Unity church life, which its leaders repeatedly defended against its critics within the Unity and among other Protestant churches.[16]

The Unity was virtually destroyed during the Thirty Years' War. The war began when the Protestant nobility of Bohemia crowned the elector of the Palatinate, Frederick V, king of Bohemia in defiance of the emperor Maximilian in 1618. Bohemia and Moravia quickly fell to the imperial armies and in 1627 all Protestant subjects were forced to convert to Catholicism or go into exile. Some of the Brethren, led by Comenius, made their way to Poland, where they established a community in exile.

One of their centers in Poland, the city of Leszno (Lissa), was destroyed during war between Sweden and Poland. The other center, Thorn, was the home of the last bishop of the old Unitas Fratrum to serve a congregation of the Unity before the time of Zinzendorf. The willingness of Bishop Sitvonus of Thorn to agree to Zinzendorf's request to pass on the episcopacy of the Unitas Fratrum to the Herrnhut community in 1735 may have been motivated by the renewed persecution of Protestants in Thorn. Following a riot during a procession of the Virgin in 1724, the Catholic authorities beheaded twelve leading Protestant citizens. They also gave the last remaining Protestant church to the Catholics and closed the Protestant academy.[17]

---

13. Brock, *Political and Social Doctrines,* 113–18, 214–17. This occasioned a split within the Unitas Fratrum between the Major Party in support of moderation and the rigorist Minor Party. Ibid., chap. 5.

14. Milos Strupl, "Confessional Theology of the Unitas Fratrum," *Church History* 33 (1964): 283; Brock, *Political and Social Doctrines,* 86.

15. Marianka Sasha Fousek, "Spiritual Direction and Discipline: A Key to the Flowering and Decay of the Sixteenth-Century Unitas Fratrum," *Archive for Reformation History* 62 (1971): 211. The memory of this discipline may have had a direct impact on the development of the practice of "speaking" in the Brüdergemeine.

16. Ibid., 211–13.

17. Ward, *Protestant Evangelical Awakening,* 22.

One of the major issues in the early years of Herrnhut and the development of Zinzendorf's Brüdergemeine was to what extent the old Unity of the Brethren should be resurrected. Because it was noticeably absent from the Peace of Westphalia (and thus in the same category as Anabaptist groups), the resurrection of the church would be an act of rebellion against the Peace of Westphalia. However, the Moravian refugees resisted being absorbed into the Lutheran parish on Zinzendorf's estate, just as their ancestors had resisted absorption during the Reformation.

However one interprets this complex and confusing history, it is clear that the Moravians under Zinzendorf did not re-create the old Unitas Fratrum. Even so, there are similarities between that body and the community led by Zinzendorf. Both the old Unity and Zinzendorf's Brüdergemeine understood Christianity in terms of a close-knit community in which discipline was a way of life. Both bodies allowed peasants and artisans to hold office in the church and guide their communal life. The memory of the old church gave the new community confidence to establish its unique social life in the midst of opposition. The Moravians within the Brüdergemeine continued to sing their ancestors' hymn "Blessed be the time when I must roam, / Far from my country and my home." For some of the Moravians, this meant crossing the Atlantic.

RELIGION AND POLITICS IN THE EIGHTEENTH CENTURY

Bethlehem was an American village, but we have already seen that its history was intricately connected to the broader world of European politics. Some background into the complexities of religion and state policies in the Holy Roman Empire and neighboring lands in the years following the Reformation will help place the Moravians in proper context and explain why they came to Pennsylvania.[18]

The famous Peace of Westphalia had not truly settled the religious situation in the Holy Roman Empire in the seventeenth century. When Protestant principalities came under the rule of Catholic lords, the state generally promoted the Catholic Church vigorously. This was the case in the Palatinate when the elector Karl died in 1685 and the rule of the Palatinate reverted to the Roman Catholic house of Pfalz-Neuburg. Under the reign of Philipp Wilhelm and his son Johann Wilhelm, Protestant privileges were systematically removed. As a result of renewed religious persecution and changing economic conditions, tens of thousands of Protestants left the Palatinate.[19] So many of them arrived

18. See R.J.W. Evans, *The Making of the Habsburg Monarchy* (New York: Oxford University Press, 1979).

19. Gregg Roeber, *Palatines, Liberty, and Property: German Lutherans in Colonial America* (Baltimore: Johns Hopkins University Press, 1993); Fogleman, *Hopeful Journeys,* gives detailed immigration statistics and provides a good description of the economic pressures in the Rhineland. On the role of religious persecution

in America that it was common in colonial America to call all Germans "Palatines." French invasions in the Rhine area also contributed to the religious
unrest, particularly since France had recently revoked the Edict of Nantes
(1689) and was expelling Protestants from its territories.

A similar story of mass migration because of religious conflict is that of the
famous Salzburgers in the winter of 1731–32. W. R. Ward called this "the most
dramatic episode in the story of religious revival, an event which had its reper-
cussions throughout Protestant Europe and America, and taught lessons to the
Habsburgs."[20] The crisis began with a revival of Lutheranism inspired by an
exile named Josef Schaitberger, whose works emboldened the Lutheran miners
in the Salzburg archdiocese to be public in their dissent. Catholic authorities
took steps to stop the revival. When other measures failed, they expelled thousands of Protestants, who were forced to leave their children behind.

The example of the Salzburgers made a powerful impression on many, including the Moravians, who were threatened with a similar fate. Some of the
Salzburgers found refuge in the philanthropic venture of General Oglethorpe
in the Georgia colony. It was Salzburger Lutherans who, unintentionally, first
brought the Moravians and John Wesley together in Georgia.

Also important for the story of the Moravians is the great revival in Silesia,
which was an unexpected result of the invasion of Charles XII of Sweden into
Silesia in 1707.[21] The Protestants in the area were inspired by the preaching of
the chaplains in the Swedish army, and when the armies left, children and
youth began holding their own open-air prayer gatherings (similar to American
camp meetings a century later) against the wishes of the authorities.

The revival took firm hold in the town of Teschen under the leadership of
ordained Protestant clergy supplied by August Hermann Francke at the behest
of the Prussian crown. The key figure was Johann Adam Steinmetz, who led a
pastoral team that included a Czech-language preacher, a Polish-language
preacher and catechist, and assistants who preached in Slavic languages. Christian David, who felled the first tree in Herrnhut, was converted by Steinmetz
in 1717.[22] After Silesia came into Prussian hands in the 1740s, Frederick the
Great gave the Moravians control over the Protestant cause in Silesia, but
Teschen itself came under Hapsburg control.

---

on emigration from the Palatine and other Rhine territories, see Longenecker, *Piety and Tolerance,* and
Donald F. Durnbaugh, "Radical Pietist Involvement in Early German Emigration to Pennsylvania," *Yearbook
of German-American Studies* 29 (1994): 29–48.

20. Ward, *Protestant Evangelical Awakening,* 93. For the full account see 93–106.

21. Ibid., 71–83. For more on Silesia, see Herbert Patzelt, *Der Pietismus im Teschener Schlesien 1709–1730*
(Göttingen, 1969). On the role of the pious nobles in both political and religious life at the time, see Hans-
Walther Erbe, *Zinzendorf und der fromme hohe Adel siner Zeit* (Leipzig, 1928), reproduced in ZM 2:12.

22. Zinzendorf, "Christian David: Servant of the Lord, A Translation of the Memoir of Christian David
as written by Count Nicholas L. von Zinzendorf," trans. Carl John Fliegel and ed. Vernon Nelson (Bethlehem, Pa.: Moravian Archives, 1962).

Within Bohemia itself, there was a resurgence of Protestant vigor in the early 1700s, and hundreds of families illegally emigrated from the country. Some (mainly German-speaking Czechs) came to Upper Lusatia and joined Zinzendorf, but many did not. The exodus of Habsburg subjects led to political oppression in Bohemia and diplomatic complications within the empire.[23] Although Upper Lusatia had been absorbed into Saxony, the nobility continued to assert their independence, especially in the area of religion. Thus it is not surprising that a group of religious refugees from nearby Bohemia and Moravia, led by a man converted in the Teschen revival, would seek protection in Upper Lusatia. Nor is it surprising in light of the persistent volatility in the Holy Roman Empire that the Moravians, along with other radical Pietist groups, looked to America as a refuge.

PIETISM

The communities formed at Herrnhut and Bethlehem were shaped in large part by an international religious movement, Pietism, that contributed much to the vitality and volatility of early eighteenth-century religion.[24] Gregg Roeber's bold claim that "no other phenomenon so dominated eighteenth-century German Protestant life as Pietism did" is certainly justifiable.[25] However, as with many broad social and intellectual movements, it is hard to give a simple definition to Pietism.[26] The term "Pietism" includes many diverse movements and people, from church officials supported by the state to radicals who separated from all church structures. Furthermore, the term itself, like Puritan or Methodist, was first used by opponents of the movement.[27]

There are different schools of thought on how to describe or define Pietism. Some define it in terms of a few chief doctrines, such as repentance, sanctification, and new birth, or the "hope for better times."[28] There is no doubt that

23. Ward, *Protestant Evangelical Awakening*, 128.

24. Martin Brecht, ed., *Geschichte des Pietismus*, 2 vols. (Göttingen: Vanderhoeck & Ruprecht, 1993, 1995); Erich Beyreuther, *Geschichte des Pietismus* (Stuttgart: J. F. Steinkopf, 1978); Martin Schmidt, *Pietismus als theologische Erscheinug* (Göttingen, 1984); F. Ernest Stoeffler, *The Rise of Evangelical Pietism* (Leiden: E. J. Brill, 1965); F. Ernest Stoeffler, *German Pietism During the Eighteenth Century* (Leiden: E. J. Brill, 1973).

25. Roeber, *Palatines, Liberty, and Property*, 63.

26. W. R. Ward calls Pietism "one of the most strenuously and assiduously worked fields not only of modern church history, but of the history of religious belief and practice not ecclesiastically oriented." Ward, "German Pietism, 1670–1750," *Journal of Ecclesiastical History* 44 (1993): 476–505, at 476. According to Ward, some three hundred titles on Pietism appear in the various European languages each year. Some of the more important recent research on Pietism is found in Klaus Deppermann et. al., *Pietismus und Neuzeit: Ein Jahrbuch zur Geschichte des neueren Protestantismus* (Göttingen: Vandenhoeck and Ruprecht, 1974–). Jonathan Strom, "Problems and Promises of Pietism Research," *Church History* 71 (2002): 536–54, discusses contemporary Pietism research.

27. The difficulties in defining Pietism led at least one scholar to question whether there was such a thing. Michel Godfroid, "Le Piétisme allemande a-t-il existé? Histoire d'un concept fait pour la polémique," *Études Germaniques* 101 (1971): 32–45.

28. Strom's essay, "Problems and Promises of Pietism Reseach," offers a nice summary of these different

these were central themes of Pietist preaching and writing, but they also appear in Lutheran Orthodox literature. More helpful is Hartmut Lehmann's broader understanding of Pietism as a social movement that encouraged the formation of bands of the pious for prayer and study (conventicles) and a sense of separateness from the world.[29]

Despite the difficulties of definition, one does see a network of relationships and shared interests among those called Pietists in Germany that was qualitatively different from their interactions with opponents of the movement, particularly Lutheran Orthodox theologians.[30] This network was extended to include participants in the Great Awakening in America, such as Jonathan Edwards and Gilbert Tennent, as well as the early Methodists John Wesley and George Whitefield.[31]

What united Pietists, despite their differences, was the attempt to make Christianity a more vital presence in society and in individual lives. The Pietists wanted to "complete the Reformation" in terms of social behavior as well as inner spiritual life. Basically, Pietism was a bold attempt to make the Protestant doctrine of the priesthood of all believers visible and effective.

Pietism was in many ways a reaction to the perceived failure of the Lutheran Church to improve the spiritual life of individuals and the social life of Germany. Modern researchers have also noted the limited effect the Reformation had on daily life in Germany.[32] In addition, the religious conflicts of the seventeenth century left many areas of Germany depopulated and destroyed much of the social infrastructure, including schools and churches. Richard Gawthrop argues that one response to the turmoil of the age was an increase in authoritarian structures that included confessional orthodoxy to combat perceived heresies. This was in turn connected to an increased focus on duties reserved to the clergy, such as the sacraments and ceremonies, rather than on the subjective experience of the laity.[33] In opposition to Orthodoxy, Pietist clergy promoted "fruits of faith" more than adherence to a confessional system.[34]

---

perspectives. See also Martin Brecht, "Pietismus," in *Theologische Realenzyklopädie* (Berlin: Walter Gruyter, 1996), 20:606–13; cf. Johannes Wallman, "Was ist Pietismus?" *Pietismus und Neuzeit* 20 (1994): 13.

29. Hartmut Lehmann, "Zur Definition des 'Pietismus,'" in *Zur neueren Pietismusforschung*, ed. Martin Greschat (Darmstadt: Wissenschaftliche Buchgesellschaft, 1977): 82–90; Hartmut Lehmann, *Pietism und Weltliche Ordnung in Württemburg vom 17. bis zum 20. Jahrhundert* (Stuttgart: Kohlhammer, 1969), 14–18.

30. Harry Yeide, *Studies in Classical Pietism: The Flowering of the Ecclesiola* (New York: Peter Lang, 1997).

31. W. R. Ward, *Protestant Evangelical Awakening*.

32. Gerald Strauss, *Luther's House of Learning: Indoctrination of the Young in the German Reformation* (Baltimore: Johns Hopkins University Press, 1979).

33. Richard L. Gawthrop, *Pietism and the Making of Eighteenth-Century Prussia* (Cambridge: Cambridge University Press, 1993), 88–95. Carter Lindberg's description of the Orthodox program is helpful. "The doctrinal implications of the Reformation were carefully worked out in highly rationalistic Summae which depended upon the reintroduction of Aristotelian concepts and methods of argumentation frequently cast in polemical mold against Roman Catholic, Reformed, and even other Lutheran teachings." Lindberg, *The Third Reformation?* (Macon: Mercer University Press, 1983), 136–37.

34. Lindberg, *The Third Reformation?* 134, quoting Martin Schmidt, "Pietismus," in *Religion in Geschichte und Gegenwart* 5: 370–83.

Just as there is no clear definition of Pietism, there is no firm consensus on its sources or origins, but most would agree that the origin of the movement can best be dated to 1675, with the appearance of Philipp Jakob Spener's new edition of Johann Arndt's 1605 work, *True Christianity*.[35] Although written long before the rise of Pietism, this became the principal text of the movement and was published more than 120 times in almost as many years in at least ten different languages.[36]

What marked Spener's edition of Arndt's popular sermons as the beginning of a reform movement, though, was his preface, which outlined a pragmatic program of church and social reform. Later published as a separate work entitled *Pia Desideria*, this short work begins with a listing of the ills of the church of his day.[37] Among these were intellectualism, argumentativeness, and immorality. Spener did more than criticize; he offered practical suggestions on how to create a new reformation in the church. Luther, he said, had produced a doctrinal reformation; now was the time for a practical reformation of church and society.

Pia Desideria included the following suggestions: (1) more reading of the Bible individually and in small groups; (2) making the priesthood of all believers effective through small groups within the church; (3) recognition that Christianity is a matter of practice, not of knowledge; (4) avoiding destructive religious controversies; (5) reforming ministerial training in order to teach piety in addition to doctrine; and (6) preaching simple and edifying sermons for the laity. These were all characteristics of the Moravian Church under Zinzendorf.

After publishing *Pia Desideria*, Spener was called to a post in the court of August the Strong, the king of Saxony, in Dresden. There he established close contact with many members of Zinzendorf's family, especially Nikolaus's grandmother, Baroness Henrietta Catherine von Gersdorf. Spener's criticism of the flamboyant life in the court of August the Strong in Dresden led to his dismissal in 1691. He was made court preacher for the elector of Brandenburg (the future Prussian king, Frederick I). From there he exerted great influence on religion in Prussia and surrounding states. Even those who did not become part of an identifiable Pietist party valued Spener's work.

The Pietists' apparent criticism of Luther angered many of the theologians of Lutheran Orthodoxy, who were also suspicious of the Pietists' debt to Calvinism and mysticism. For much of the first half of the eighteenth century, a

---

35. Johannes Arndt, *True Christianity*, trans. and ed. Peter Erb (New York: Paulist Press, 1979). For more on Spener, see Johannes Wallmann, *Philipp Jakob Spener und die Anfänge des Pietismus* (Tübingen, 1970).

36. Ward, *Protestant Evangelical Awakening*, 48. Ward notes that more than 100,000 volumes were available in German.

37. Philipp Jakob Spener, *Pia Desideria*, trans. Theodore G. Tappert (Philadelphia: Fortress Press, 1964).

bitter war of polemic was waged between the Orthodox and the Pietists that
led to legal actions in some areas. For instance, the Swedish Conventicle Act of
1726 "forbade, under threat of heavy fines, the assembly of men and women,
old and young, and acquaintances and strangers in private homes for the purpose of cultivating piety or worship."[38]

Spener had earlier led a young biblical scholar named August Hermann
Francke to an experience of new birth. Francke's own account of his conversion
struggle *(Bußkampf)* and breakthrough *(Durchbruch)* to grace became one of
the standard texts in Pietist circles.[39] When Francke was forced out of his post
at the University of Leipzig in 1694 because of his Pietist activities, Spener
arranged for him to be called as a pastor in Halle and biblical professor at the
newly formed University of Halle.[40]

Francke was an energetic leader who created a distinctive form of Pietism
that stressed social service and universal education as key aspects of "Francke's
plan to eradicate ignorance and poverty."[41] This activism led to the formation
of more than two dozen institutions, including a pedagogium (primary
school), infirmary, apothecary, orphanage, publishing house, and foreign mission society, all supported by an extensive financial network created by
Francke.

Much of the research into Pietism has naturally been concerned with Halle,
the major center of "church Pietism" in the 1700s. The work at Halle was
actively promoted by the Prussian state, especially during the reigns of Frederick III (King Frederick I) and Frederick William I, because they recognized that
Pietism's blending of Lutheran and Reformed piety could ease religious tensions in their realm and that Pietism could promote educational, economic,
and social improvement in the underpopulated kingdom.[42] Halle's own efforts
to spread reform throughout German-speaking lands supported the crown's
international diplomacy.

The Francke institutes became the models for similar charitable institutions

38. Stoeffler, *German Pietism*, 57–71; Erich Beyreuther, *Der Junge Zinzendorf*, vol. 1 of *Die Große Zinzendorf—Trilogie* (Marburg an der Lahn: Verlag der Francke Buchhandlung, 1957; 1988), 153–57. At times the civil
authorities were involved.

39. Erich Beyreuther, *August Hermann Francke: Zeuge des lebendigen Gottes* (Marburg, 1961).

40. Beyreuther, *Geschichte Pietismus*, 61–122.

41. Roeber, *Palatines, Liberty, and Property*, 69–75. Roeber argues that Francke, unlike most Lutherans,
promoted an active view of stewardship that encouraged a form of worldly asceticism in which profits from
business are to be given for the common good through well-organized social ministries operating with the
authority of the state

42. Ward, *Protestant Evangelical Awakening*, 58–63 (and elsewhere). Gawthrop, *Pietism and the Making of
Eighteenth-Century Prussia*, uses Weber's theory of secularization to argue that Pietism was a key component
of the rise of the modern state. The classic work on Pietism and the state is Klaus Deppermann, *Der hallesche
Pietismus und der preussiche Staat unter Friedrich III* (Göttingen, 1961). For the extensive bibliography on this
aspect of Pietism, see Ward, "German Pietism," 484–88.

all over Europe, and Hallensian pedagogy served as the foundation for the Prussian state educational system.[43] The University of Halle trained numerous Lutheran pastors who spread the Halle form of Pietism throughout German-speaking Protestant areas. Halle also sent out the first Lutheran missionaries to native people in colonial lands. Through the Lutheran chaplains in the English court, Anton Wilhelm Böhme and his successor Friedrich Michael Ziegenhagen, Halle had a strong voice in English church politics and affected the Moravians in British North America.[44]

Halle produced a distinctive pastoral theology that promoted a standard path to salvation that led people through a difficult conversion process. This pastoral theology laid great stress on a conversion *(Bekehrung)* that took place through a repentance struggle *(Bußkampf)*, leading to a breakthrough *(Durchbruch)* to faith, peace, and morality. According to Erich Beyreuther, the usual sequence of events was (1) an awareness of sins, (2) anxiety over one's sins, (3) doubts, (4) desire for salvation, (5) struggling in prayer, and (6) sudden enlightenment and certainty concentrated in a violent conversion struggle.[45]

Moreover, Halle stressed personal morality, including a strict rejection of things that were not sinful in themselves *(adiaphora)* but could lead to sin. Such things as dancing, card playing, theater, and laughter distracted one from Christian duty and were a dangerous waste of time. Duty, sobriety, obedience, and self-control were cardinal concepts of Hallensian Christianity.

Carter Lindberg describes Francke's attitude toward sin as a deviation from Luther's understanding, in that those who have experienced new birth must refrain from worldly pleasures, especially the pleasures of the body.[46] The moralistic aspect of Halle Pietism increased under his son, August Gottlieb Francke, who became the leader of Halle after his father's death in 1727. This became another point of argument with the Moravians. Zinzendorf's love of music and ceremony (what Fogleman calls a "cosmopolitan *Weltanschauung*"), and his positive view of sexuality were a frequent source of complaint from Pietists of all types.[47]

Among the Lutherans in southwestern Germany, especially in Württemberg, a different form of Pietism took hold.[48] After some initial conflict with the authorities, by mid-century the Pietists there were allowed to form conventicles

43. Stoeffler, *German Pietism*, 39–87; Beyreuther, *Geschichte Pietismus*, 170–71.

44. Ward, *Protestant Evangelical Awakening*, 256–59, 304–10; Arno Sames, *Anton Wilhelm Böhme (1673–1722): Studien zum ökumenische Denken und Handeln eines Halleschen Pietisten* (Göttingen, 1989).

45. Beyreuther, *Geschichte Pietismus*, 135–38.

46. Lindberg, *The Third Reformation?* 177.

47. Fogleman, *Hopeful Journeys*, 108.

48. Roeber, *Palatines, Liberty, and Property*, 75–94; see also Lehmann, *Pietismus und Weltliche Ordnung in Württemberg*.

so long as the members did not separate from the official church or become disruptive. As a result, Pietism in Württemberg tended to be less activist and more sentimental than that of Halle. It focused on retreating from the temptations and vexations of the world into the quiet of one's own heart. Many German immigrants to colonial Pennsylvania came out of this Pietist setting and shared a distrust of overbearing authority that threatened the family and hearth.[49] This affected the reception of the Moravians in Pennsylvania.

MYSTICISM AND RADICAL PIETISM

The popular response to Spener's program indicates that there was "a crisis of piety" and a longing for religious experience throughout Germany. The works of late medieval mystics, especially Johannes Tauler, and more recent Catholic mystics, such as Madame Guyon, played a key role in the development and spread of Pietism. Moreover, the continuing influence of Anabaptism and Puritanism in the Netherlands and Rhineland also contributed to the rise and spread of Pietism.[50] In general, the more individual Pietists adopted mystical conceptions of the church, the more likely they were to separate from the state church. This struggle over whether to remain in the official church or to create a separate religious fellowship is evident in the Moravian Church during Zinzendorf's time.

The French mystic Madame Guyon popularized a type of mysticism that stressed the inability of humans to achieve salvation, approach God, or do anything good on their own. The essence of faith is to wait quietly in meditation for God to draw the soul into himself. All human efforts to come to God, even the sacraments and prayer, actually hinder the process of union, according to Guyon. This extreme form of religious passivity is called Quietism, and it was rejected by Catholic officials because of its low view of the sacraments. Quietist ideas were also popularized through the works of Miguel de Molinos and Pierre Poiret.[51] Quietism found an audience in Germany, in part because of the similarity between Guyon's teaching and the Lutheran doctrine of justification by faith through grace. Zinzendorf and the Moravians in Herrnhut read Mme. Guyon in the 1720s, and Quietism or "Stillness" became a major subject of controversy in the Fetter Lane Society during Wesley's day.[52]

---

49. Roeber, *Palatines, Liberty, and Property,* "Introduction."

50. According to Ward, there were 444 editions of Thomas à Kempis published in the eighteenth century, along with 100 editions of Molinos and Francis de Sales, and 59 editions of Bayly's *Practice of Piety.* Ward, *Protestant Evangelical Awakening,* 48.

51. Stoeffler, *Rise of Evangelical Pietism,* 172–74; cf. Ted Campbell, *Religion of the Heart: A Study of European Religious Life in the Seventeenth and Eighteenth Centuries* (Columbia: University of South Carolina Press, 1991), 29–35.

52. Spangenberg claimed that the Moravians read Guyon only in order to find what was worthwhile in her works and refute what was erroneous; *Leben des Herrn Ludwig,* 660. On the Quiestist controversy, see Podmore, *Moravian Church in England,* 59–62.

Jakob Böhme, a cobbler from Görlitz in the early seventeenth century, wrote several mystical treatises that became very popular among radical Pietists in the eighteenth century. Böhme's mysticism was based on a "feeling for life" *(Lebensgefühl)* that motivates all things. The divine essence in nature effects its purpose through will, not reason, and is characterized by action, not static perfection. As persons are taken up through the divine fire of God's love in Christ they attain true knowledge (theosophy). In Böhme's theology, the institutional church is unimportant and may actually hinder the soul's union with God and the ultimate manifestation of God's Spirit in the world.

Böhme's writings inspired some Pietists to make a sharp distinction between the true church of the Spirit and the corrupt church: the church of Cain and the church of Abel. Many Separatists in Germany tried to establish purified communities, often in defiance of the law.[53] The relative freedom in colonial America made it much easier for "awakened" persons during and after the Great Awakening to establish separate churches.[54]

One of the most important figures to develop and apply the ideas of Böhme was the Englishwoman Jane Leade, who enjoyed the toleration that prevailed in the Netherlands. Leade and her followers separated from the confessional churches, which were intertwined with political affairs in order to create a new type of Christian community that was supposed to transcend church divisions. Leade called this new form of church Philadelphian (Rev. 3:7–13) and saw it as part of the in-breaking of a millennial age of mutual love, intense religious experience, and social harmony.

The idea of a millennial Philadelphian Church spread throughout Germany and the Netherlands. Zinzendorf's effort to unite the German-speaking Protestants, including the radical Separatists, into a transconfessional "Church of God in the Spirit" was strongly influenced by Philadelphian ideas.[55] It is important to note that mystical and Philadelphian literature, including the hymns of Gerhard Tersteegen, helped formed the discourse of religiously minded Germans in Europe and America.

The influence of mysticism on the theology of Zinzendorf and the piety of

53. The most thorough works on radical Pietism are by Hans Schneider, "Der radikale Pietismus im 17. Jahrhundert," and "Der radikale Pietismus im 18. Jahrhundert," in *Geschichte des Pietismus,* ed. Martin Brecht (Göttingen: Vandenhoeck & Ruprecht, 1993; 1995), 1:391–437, 2:107–97. Compare Stoeffler, *German Pietism,* 170–71.

54. C. C. Goen, *Revivalism and Separatism in New England, 1740–1800* (New Haven: Yale University Press, 1962). Bonomi, in *Under the Cope of Heaven,* 152–57, makes the claim that the widespread practice of separating from "unconverted" pastors made it much easier for Americans to eventually effect political separation from England.

55. Peter Vogt, "Introduction," in *An Authentic Relation of the Occasion, Continuance, and Conclusion of the First Assembly of some Labourers out of most of the Christian Religions and other private religious People in Pensilvania kept in German Town 1st and 2nd January 1741–2,* in ZM 2:30.

the Brüdergemeine remains a controversial subject in Zinzendorf research. Most scholars follow Otto Uttendörfer's theory that Zinzendorf turned away from mysticism in the 1730s when he embraced the theology of Luther.[56] While the turn to Luther was real, it is important to note the strong influence of mysticism on Zinzendorf's theological development early on. For example, the traveling preacher Hochmann von Hochenau, who inspired many with his mystical understanding of the new birth, had a direct influence on the Moravians, and spent much of his time at the Ebersdorf estate of Zinzendorf's first wife, Erdmuth Dorothea. She admired him greatly, and according to Zinzendorf it was from von Hochenau that Erdmuth first learned the worth of Jesus' wounds. This "blood-and-wounds mysticism" was the hallmark of Zinzendorfian piety.

Radical pietists not only valued medieval mysticism, they tended to take a positive view of the various heretical movements in the history of Christianity, much to the disgust of Orthodox theologians. Gottfried Arnold, the leader of a small separatist group, published a history of Christianity, *Unparteiische Kirchen- und Ketzerhistorie* (1699), that portrayed heretics in a much better light than church officials and theologians. One Orthodox writer suggested an epithet for him in 1718. "Here lies Gottfried Arnold, not so much a theologian, as the bitterest enemy of orthodox theologians; the persistent defender of heretics, the stupid repristinator of mystical theology,—perhaps the first of all distorters of church history.—He had a mixed religion, or, none at all. Henceforth he is commended to God's judgement.—Wanderer, go hence!"[57]

Arnold eventually made his way back into the state church, serving as a pastor, but his work had a long and influential history. It was much admired by Zinzendorf's grandmother, von Gersdorf, and was a major source of Zinzendorf's knowledge of Christian history. In general, the radical Pietists drew most heavily on Arnold's work.

Radical Pietists became more bold when Count Ernst Casimir of Ysenburg-Büdingen in Wetterau issued a decree of toleration in 1712 inviting dissidents to immigrate if they were willing to live as productive subjects and pay a special fee.[58] Many of the aristocrats in the Reformed principalities of the Wetterau were already involved with Pietism, and the local people had a strong interest in Böhme. Ernst Casimir's decree encouraged various forms of radical Pietists

---

56. Arthur J. Freeman, *An Ecumenical Theology of the Heart: The Theology of Count Nicholas Ludwig von Zinzendorf* (Bethlehem: Moravian Publication Office, 1998), esp. 55–60. The most complete study of this subject is by Otto Uttendörfer, *Zinzendorf und die Mystik* (Berlin: Christlichen Zeitschriften-Verlag, 1952).

57. Quoted in Stoeffler, *German Pietism*, 176.

58. Longenecker, *Piety and Tolerance*, 14–16, 22; Ward, *Protestant Evangelical Awakening*, 162–69; see also Matthias Benad, *Toleranz als Gebot christlicher Obrigkeit: Das Büdinger Patent von 1712* (Hildesheim, 1983).

to seek refuge in the Wetterau. Many of them eventually made their way to Pennsylvania.

The Wetterau also sheltered a group of prophets known as the Inspired, who originated in the Cérvennes in France during the persecution of Protestants by Louis XIV in the 1680s. As persecution worsened, apocalyptic expectations rose among French Protestants and some began exhibiting the kinds of physical behavior associated with modern Pentecostalism.[59] When they were filled with the Spirit they made strange contortions, spoke in strange voices, and predicted future events.

After they fled France, they made quite a sensation throughout Western Europe before seeking peace and refuge in the Wetterau in 1714. They formed prayer groups, held love feasts, and tried to build a nonsectarian community, but the movement splintered when the Inspired disagreed among themselves over whose prophecies were true and whose were false. The most enduring artifact of their work was the *Berleburg Bible*, which included annotations on the true unity of the spiritual church and pointed to the expected millennium.[60]

The Inspired played a major role in the Moravian story.[61] In the early days of Herrnhut, Zinzendorf made a concerted effort to bring the leader of the Inspired, Johann Rock, into the Brüdergemeine. Not only did the count preach to the Inspired in the Wetterau, he invited Rock to visit Herrnhut. The visit did not go well, in part because of Zinzendorf's patronizing attitude and in part because of Rock's public denouncement of Herrnhut ceremonies. Having failed to convert Rock, Zinzendorf repudiated him and the Inspired. He did, however, win over hundreds of Rock's followers.[62] The Moravians also encountered the Inspired in Pennsylvania, but in an altered form.

PENNSYLVANIA

It was natural that Zinzendorf would be attracted to Pennsylvania as a colony for the Moravians. Other than Roger Williams's Rhode Island, Pennsylvania was the only American colony to establish freedom of religion in its constitution as a matter of conscience, not convenience. William Penn's efforts to recruit persecuted Protestants in the Holy Roman Empire made Pennsylvania

59. See Ward, *Protestant Evangelical Awakening*, 163–73 for a brief history of the Inspired. For more history and analysis, see Hillel Schwartz, *The French Prophets* (Berkeley and Los Angeles: University of California Press, 1980).

60. J. Steven O'Malley, *Early German-American Evangelicalism: Pietist Sources on Discipleship and Sanctification* (Metuchen, N.J.: Scarecrow Press, 1995), 271–99, includes excerpts from the Berleburg Bible.

61. Hans Schneider, "Geheimer Brief-Wechsel des Herrn Grafens von Zinzendorf mit denen Inspirten," *Unitas Fratrum* 49–50 (2002): 213–18.

62. Spangenberg, *Leben des Herrn Nikolaus Ludwig*, 630–38; cf. Ward, *Protestant Evangelical Awakening*, 172–73.

one of the most religiously diverse colonies in British North America. Of the roughly 100,000 Germans who immigrated to Pennsylvania, about 3,200, including the Moravians, were members of persecuted bodies.[63] Most of the sectarians migrated between 1727 and 1756, the period of the Moravians' greatest activity, because of complex economic and social reasons, but freedom of religious expression was also a key factor.

Not only did Penn's toleration jibe with Zinzendorf's own views, it also meant that the Moravians could work in *relative* freedom and have easy access for their mission to the native peoples for the purpose of evangelization.[64] Furthermore, they saw the eclectic and vibrant religious sectarianism in Pennsylvania as fertile ground for their type of Pietism, which combined Lutheran liturgy and doctrine with radical Pietist spirituality and communalism. In the eighteenth century, 830 Moravians came to the colonies, most from German-speaking lands.[65] The Moravians were able to establish rather stable and secure communities in the New World, but they were unable to attract many of the sectarians to their movement.

The Moravians were not the first Pietists to build a religious community in the wilderness. Among the earliest immigrants to Penn's wood were followers of Johannes Kelpius. Influenced by the Inspired, Kelpius and his companions were convinced that the end of the world was foretold by the comet of 1680. They decided to await the Second Coming in the New World. After spending time with Philadelphians in the Netherlands, they sailed for the city of Philadelphia. Heading for what was then wilderness along the Wissahickon Creek near Germantown, they established an ascetic community in preparation for the millennial kingdom. Kelpius described his community as the woman in the wilderness (Rev. 12:6) that fled the dragon of the flesh, especially marriage.[66] Life in an ascetic commune was harder than expected, though, and following the founder's death in 1708 the community gradually disintegrated, leaving a legacy primarily of poems and hymns.

The prophet Johann Adam Gruber had been a leader in the Community of the True Inspired in the Wetterau before coming to Pennsylvania in the 1720s. Gruber was one of the original members of the Skippack Brethren that provided the first entrée for the Moravians in Pennsylvania and was the basis of

63. Fogleman, *Hopeful Journeys,* 104–5.

64. For a brief account of the Moravian work in the colonies, including Zinzendorf's visit in the early 1740s, see John R. Weinlick, "Moravianism in the American Colonies," in Stoeffler, *Continental Pietism,* 123–63; Atwood, "Introduction," ix–xxiii.

65. Fogleman, *Hopeful Journeys,* 168–69.

66. Donald Durnbaugh, "Communitarian Societies in Colonial America," in Pitzer, *America's Communal Utopias,* 19–22. Longenecker, *Piety and Tolerance,* 27–32; cf. Ward, *Protestant Evangelical Awakening,* 51–52; Klaus Deppermann, "Pennylvanien als Asyl des frühen deutschen Pietismus," *Pietismus und Neuzeit* 10 (1984): 190–212.

Zinzendorf's famous Pennsylvania synods.[67] The synods themselves were a joint undertaking of Zinzendorf and the Skippack Brethren, especially Henrich Antes, a member of the Reformed Church who was on good terms with Spangenberg. Shortly after his arrival in Pennsylvania, in December 1741, Zinzendorf and Antes agreed on a plan to gather the various Pennsylvania sects and churches into a single synod of German-speaking Christians. Antes printed a circular that invited representatives of the sects to a meeting.[68]

The synods met January 12–13 in Germantown; January 21–23 at Falkner's Swamp; February 21–23 at Oley; March 21–23 in Germantown; April 18–20 at the Germantown Reformed Church; May 16–18 in Germantown; and June 13–15 in Philadelphia.[69] However, they did not accomplish Zinzendorf's goal, which he later said was "to enthrone the Lamb of God as real Creator, Preserver, Redeemer and Sanctifier of the whole world; and to introduce the catholicity of the doctrine of His passion as a universal theology for the Germans of Pennsylvania, in theory and practice."[70]

His theology proved to be too controversial for the Lutherans and Reformed, while his sacramentalism and love of ritual alienated the radical Pietists. Moreover, the count's imperial demeanor convinced Gruber and fellow Separatist Christopher Sauer that the synods were really an effort to create a new church, with Zinzendorf as the pope. Gruber became a bitter opponent of the Moravians and Sauer readily published warnings against the Moravians.[71]

Another vigorous rival of the Moravians in Pennsylvania, the Ephrata Cloister, also had roots among the Inspired in the Wetterau.[72] Conrad Beisel had associated with the Church of the Brethren led by Alexander Mack in Schwarzenau as well as the Inspired in Wittgenstein before he left for the New World in 1720. He hoped to join Kelpius's community on the Wisshickon, but when he arrived he found that they were no more.

He first associated with the Church of the Brethren in Pennsylvania, but after a few years he led a group into the wilderness in order to live according to Old Testament laws (including the Sabbath and dietary rules) and celibacy, despite the hostility of their neighbors. Beisel would also be a stern opponent of

---

67. The first trip was to the mission field of St. Thomas in 1739, where he helped secure the release of some Brethren from prison. Weinlick, "Moravianism in the American Colonies," 145.

68. Joseph Mortimer Levering, *A History of Bethlehem, Pennsylvania, 1741–1892, with Some Accounts of its Founders and the Early Activity in America* (Bethlehem, Pa.: Times Publishing Co., 1903), 75–76.

69. Vogt, "Introduction." For a long and unsympathetic presentation of Zinzendorf's ecumenical activities in Pennsylvania, see Sessler, *Communal Pietism,* chap. 2.

70. Quoted in Levering, *A History of Bethlehem,* 81.

71. Longenecker, *Piety and Tolerance,* 41–44; Vogt, "Introduction"; Donald F. Durnbaugh, "The Brethren in Early American Church Life, in Stoeffler, *Continental Pietism,* 222–65, at 245–51.

72. Durnbaugh, "Communitarian Societies," 22–26; Longenecker, *Piety and Tolerance,* 32–40; E. G. Alderfer, *The Ephrata Commune: An Early American Counterculture* (Pittsburgh: University of Pittsburgh Press, 1985).

Zinzendorf and the Moravians, particularly because of the Moravians' positive attitude toward sex within marriage.[73]

The German sects in southeastern Pennsylvania, such as the Ephrata Cloister, naturally attract a lot of attention from scholars because of their distinctiveness, but most Germans in that colony were Lutheran or Reformed and were able to provide evidence of church attendance for legal purposes.[74] Although Pennsylvania in the early eighteenth century had attracted thousands of German immigrants, there were few pastors. Most of the ones serving were poorly qualified according to church standards. By 1776 there were still only about eighty Reformed and eighty-six Lutheran ministers (most of them not ordained) serving more than 80,000 German immigrants and their growing families.[75]

This lack of ordained clergy, however, did not mean that the Pennsylvania Germans were any less religious than other settlers. In fact, Pennsylvania had more congregations proportionally than the other colonies around 1750.[76] In so far as possible, the German immigrants organized congregations, followed the normal liturgy, and read a published sermon by a popular preacher, such as von Hochenau. Despite repeated requests from congregations, the authorities in Europe were reluctant to send ordained clergy to the wilderness, where even their salaries were uncertain. It was only when news reached Halle that Zinzendorf was on his way to America that funds were allocated to send someone to organize a Lutheran church and "save Pennsylvania from Zinzendorf."[77]

For many, such diversity of churches seemed a sign of impiety rather than of great religious interest. Church officials of all denominations proclaimed that Pennsylvania was the most irreligious colony in America: "All shades of sectarians exist here down to open infidelity. Besides the English, Swedish and German Lutherans, and the Scotch, Dutch and German Reformed, there were Arminians, Baptists, 'vereinigte Vlaaminger en Waterlander,' Mennonites from Danzig, Arians, Socinians, Schwenckfelders, German Old Tunkers, New Tunkers, New Lights, Inspired, Sabbatarians or Seventh-Day Baptists, Hermits, Independents, and Free Thinkers."[78] In fact, the phrase "Pennsylvania religion" was

---

73. Peter Vogt, "*Ehereligion:* The Moravian Theory and Practice of Marriage as a Point of Contention in the Conflict Between Ephrata and Bethlehem," *Communal Societies* 21 (2001): 37–48.

74. Fogleman, *Hopeful Journeys*, 146.

75. Ibid., 111.

76. Bonomi, *Under the Cope of Heaven*, 81. While the number of congregations is not an infallible guide to actual church adherence, it does give some indication of religious vitality, particularly in a region where congregations must be established by the worshippers themselves, not by ecclesiastical or governmental authorities.

77. Walter H. Wagner, *The Zinzendorf-Muhlenberg Encounter: A Controversy in Search of Understanding* (Bethlehem, Pa.: Moravian Publication Office, 2002); Roeber, *Palatines, Liberty, and Property*, 243ff.

78. Julius Friedrich Sachse, *The German Sectarians in Pennsylvania, 1708–1742* (Philadelphia, 1899–1900), quoted in Sessler, *Communal Pietism*, 20.

a synonym for atheism. The disorganized nature of life in colonial Pennsylvania was quite different from the life of a German parish, with its clear lines of authority, intimacy, and order.[79]

Marianne Wokeck's work on mass migration to British North America demonstrates the great difficulties faced by those who chose to leave the relative stability of the German village for the New World.[80] In addition to being exploited and abused during the journey, there was the difficulty of adjusting to a strange land. The church played a role in helping Germans settle, but in America the church had to be organized in a different way than in Europe.[81]

Pietism offered a more pragmatic and flexible approach than Lutheran Orthodoxy to ecclesiastical structure. Because of their focus on individual conversion, Pietist pastors were also better prepared to persuade people to make a commitment to the church in a setting where the established church had difficulty paying salaries. Pietism also provided an extensive network of interested benefactors who provided the resources to send personnel, Bibles, and other devotional literature to America.[82]

Henry Melchior Muhlenberg, the man sent to counter the Moravians in Pennsylvania, shared Francke's commitment to pragmatic organization, ecclesiastical loyalty, zealous encouragement of new birth, and opposition to worldly amusements. He was able to bring scattered, poorly served congregations into a new church structure that negotiated American freedom and clerical authority. He also stamped the new American Lutheran church with Pietism, complete with displays of tears in worship and the singing of Tersteegen's hymns.[83]

The Moravians arrived in Pennsylvania during the Great Awakening. Although Jon Butler has raised important objections to treating the series of revivals that affected many areas of the colonies as a single phenomenon, he does indicate that the revivals of the 1740s played a role in the spread of popular Christianity in America.[84] There is no need here to give the history of the Great Awakening, except to note the religious fervor that gripped many communities, including eastern Pennsylvania, in the wake of George Whitefield's grand revivalistic tours.[85]

79. Fogleman, *Hopeful Journeys*, 36–67.
80. Wokeck, *Trade in Strangers*.
81. Fogleman, *Hopeful Journeys*, 86–92.
82. Ward, *Protestant Evangelical Awakening*, 255–65.
83. Theodore G. Tappert, "The Influence of Pietism in Colonial American Lutheranism," in Stoeffer, *Continental Pietism and Early American Christianity*, 13–33.
84. Jon Butler, *Awash in a Sea of Faith: Christianizing the American People* (Cambridge: Harvard University Press, 1990), 98–128.
85. The literature on the Great Awakening and its participants is vast. Much of it deals with the role of the Awakening in awakening revolutionary forces in the colonies. Among the classic studies are Edwin Scott Gaustad, *The Great Awakening in New England* (New York: Harper and Bros., 1957); Goen, *Revivalism and*

Pietism was an important, if frequently overlooked, element in the Great Awakening. The Awakening was not an expression of Pietism in the form familiar in Germany, but the leading figures of the Awakening, George Whitefield and Gilbert Tennent, drew on Pietist writings and methods. Tennent was tutored in the Dutch style of Pietism by Theodorus Jacobus Frelinghuysen in New Jersey.[86] The animosity toward the Moravians expressed by Whitefield and Tennent should not be interpreted as a rejection of Pietism but as another expression of Halle's rejection of Zinzendorf.

In short, the renewal of the Moravian Church and its establishment in Pennsylvania was part of a major religious revival fueled by Pietism in Europe and America. It was a tumultuous time, and the Moravians were one of the most controversial movements. Zinzendorf united Lutheran liturgy, radical Pietist mysticism, and Moravian communalism in a creative and provocative mix.

Separatism in New England; Alan Heimert, *Religion and the American Mind: From the Great Awakening to the Revolution* (Cambridge: Harvard University Press, 1966); William McLoughlin, *Revivals, Awakenings, and Reform: An Essay on Religion and Social Change in America, 1607–1977* (Chicago: University of Chicago, 1977); and Bonomi, *Under the Cope of Heaven.*

86. Milton J. Coalter Jr. attempts such a study in *Gilbert Tennent, Son of Thunder: A Case Study of Continental Pietism's Impact on the First Great Awakening in the Middle Colonies* (New York: Greenwood Press, 1986); however, he appears to be less interested in Pietism than in the career of Tennent.

FIGURE 2. Anna Nitschmann (1715–1760), founder of the Single Sisters Choir. ÖL auf
Leinwand von J. V. Haidt. Unitätsarchiv (Moravian Archives) Herrnhut.

CHAPTER 2

ZINZENDORF AND THE
THEOLOGY OF THE HEART

I n order to make sense of life in Moravian Bethlehem, it is necessary to
understand Zinzendorf's theology, including its most provocative features, such as the motherhood of the Holy Spirit and the adoration of the
wounds of Christ. Zinzendorf's theology is connected to his life and development; however, since the story of his life has been told many times, we will
look only at those parts of his biography that bear particular relevance for
understanding his theology.[1] First of all, though, we need to understand what
"heart theology" meant to Zinzendorf.[2]

HEART

Zinzendorf is such a singular figure that it is sometimes forgotten that he drew
on a long tradition of affective theology and devotional literature, including
the works of Jan Amos Comenius, Andreas Weigel, Johannes Arndt, and Paul
Gerhard in formulating his theology of the heart. In fact, it was Pierre Poiret
who coined the phrase "theology of the heart" in a 1690 work, *La théologie du
coeur,* that enjoyed a wide circulation among the German Pietists.[3]

In the intellectual struggles of the day, Zinzendorf, like Poiret and the Ro-

---

1. John R. Weinlick, *Count Zinzendorf* (New York: Abingdon Press, 1956; rept., Bethlehem, Pa.: Moravian
Church in America, 1989); Mary B. Havens, "Zinzendorf and the Augsburg Confession: An Ecumenical
Vision?" (Ph.D. diss., Princeton Theological Seminary, 1990), is essentially an intellectual biography. Dietrich
Meyer, *Zinzendorf und die Herrnhuter Brüdergemeine, 1700–2000* (Göttingen: Vandenhoeck & Ruprecht,
2000), reflects a lifetime of work on Zinzendorf materials. Erich Beyreuther's three-volume biography, *Der
junge Zinzendorf, Zinzendorf und die sich allhier beisammen finden,* and *Zinzendorf und die Christenheit* (Marburg an der Lahn: Francke Buchhandlung, 1957, 1959, and 1961, republished in one volume as *Die große
Zinzendorf Trilogie,* 1988) remains the best account in any language. Two eighteenth-century biographies are
still worth reading: Spangenberg, *Leben des Herrn Nikolaus Ludwig,* which appeared in an abridged English
translation by Samuel Jackson fifty years later as *The life of Nicholas Lewis, Count Zinzendorf, Bishop and
Ordinary of the Church of the United (or Moravian) Brethren* (London: S. Holdsworth, 1838), and Ludwig
Carl von Schrautenbach, *Der Graf von Zinzendorf und der Brüdergemeine seiner Zeit,* ed. Frioedrich Wilhelm
Kölbing (Gnadau and Leipzig, 1851).

2. Freeman, *An Ecumenical Theology of the Heart.* The bibliography on the theology of Zinzendorf in
general is daunting, but the following works were helpful in formulating my reading of Zinzendorf's sermons
and his concept of religion of the heart: Zimmerling, *Gott in Gemeinschaft;* Bernhard Becker, *Zinzendorf und
sein Christentum im Verhaltnis zum kirchlichen und religiosen Leben seiner Zeit,* 2d ed. (Leipzig: F. Jansa,
1900); Uttendörfer, *Zinzendorf und die Mystik;* Leiv Aalen, *Die Theologie des jungen Zinzendorf* (Berlin and
Hamburg: Lutherisches Verlagshaus, 1966); Gösta Hök, *Zinzendorfs Begriff der Religion* (Uppsala: Lundequistska Bokhandeln, 1948).

3. Campbell, *Religion of the Heart.*

mantics later, perceived that the real threat was not to doctrines or beliefs; it was to human heart. Heart *(Herz)* for Zinzendorf is not simply the seat of emotion, it is really the center of a person.[4] Like the physical heart, the metaphorical heart is the foundation of life, the moving force. *Herz* includes emotion but, more important, it is the location of the will and desires. If the heart is dead, then the person is dead and unfeeling, even though the body may be alive.[5]

One can see close similarities between Zinzendorf's understanding of the heart as the center of personality and the Hebrew understanding that the heart is the location of both emotion and intellect. In the Old Testament, the heart is the point of contact with God. "Heart" is more visceral and affective than the Greek word for the personality, ψυχή(psyche).[6] Zinzendorf also uses the words *Seele* (soul) and *Geist* (spirit), employing a body-soul dualism common in Western thinking; but such a dualism is less central to his theology than the concept of the *Herz* that unifies all aspects of the person. In this Zinzendorf follows the lead of St. Paul.[7]

Zinzendorf is notoriously imprecise in his use of words, and he uses several related but different words to describe religious experience. The most important of these are *Gefühl* (feeling or an intuitive grasp), *Empfindung* (sensation), *Gemüt* (disposition, cast of mind), and *Erfahrung* (experience). Feeling *(Gefühl)*, for Zinzendorf, is much more than a passing emotional state, although it may and does include the emotions.[8] More precisely, it is the heart's way of knowing. Just as persons sense physical objects through bodily feelings or sensations, so too they sense spiritual objects (i.e., God) through inner feelings.

According to Zinzendorf, we do not have to see God to sense him, just as we do not have to see our souls to know that we have souls. We know that there is a God because we feel God in our hearts.[9] Religious experience is different from physical experience, but it is truly an experience nonetheless. It is a subjective experience of an objective reality that existentially affects one's

---

4. Bettermann, *Theologie und Sprache,* 12.

5. Zinzendorf, *Nine Public Lectures on Important Subjects in Religion Preached in Fetter Lane Chapel in London in the Year 1746,* trans. and ed. George W. Forell (Iowa City: University of Iowa Press, 1973), 88.

6. R. C. Dentan, "Heart," in *The Interpreter's Dictionary of the Bible,* ed. George Buttrick (Nashville: Abingdon Press, 1962), 2:549–50; N. W. Porteous, "Soul," ibid., 4:428–29.

7. Rudolf Bultmann, *Theology of the New Testament,* trans. Kendrick Grobel (New York: Charles Scribner's Sons, 1954), 1:220–21.

8. Bettermann, *Theologie und Sprache,* 22–24, emphasizes that "feeling" for Zinzendorf was different from sentimentalism or emotionalism.

9. "From the first we maintain that faith is nothing less than the object of evidence; for it deals with things that are not visible. Secondly we maintain that faith is nothing less than a thought that says, I believe, a thought set in concrete, I will believe. And therefore we believe that it is such a reality that is as certain as our lives and our souls are certain, which we also do not see." *Gemeinreden,* ZH 4:37:148–49; cf. ibid., 4:4:85; cf. Zimmerling, *Gott in Gemeinschaft,* 147–55; Bettermann, *Theologie und Sprache,* 23.

entire life. This understanding of religious feeling would later be developed by Schleiermacher in a more rigorous philosophical manner, but the roots are in Zinzendorf's Pietist upbringing, his exposure to the philosophy of the early Enlightenment, and his personal experience.

ZINZENDORF'S EARLY DEVELOPMENT

Zinzendorf was born on May 26, 1700, the only child of two pious members of the Saxon nobility, George Ludwig von Zinzendorf and Charlotte Justine von Gersdorf, a baroness in Upper Lusatia. After his father died, Zinzendorf's mother moved with the six-week-old Nikolaus to her familial estates to live with her mother, Baroness Henrietta Catherine von Gersdorf, a most remarkable person. The baroness read the Bible in its original languages, corresponded with the great philosopher Leibniz in Latin, and even studied Syrian and Chaldean.[10] Gersdorf was a major patron of the Pietist leader Philipp Jakob Spener, and later of August Herman Francke, his protégé. Spener was one of Zinzendorf's godfathers at his baptism.[11]

Zinzendorf's father's brother, Otto Christian, was the boy's guardian. In 1704, when his mother married a Prussian field marshal, Gneomar Ernst von Natzmer, Zinzendorf was left in the care of the Baroness von Gersdorf in her castle, Gross-Hennersdorf. Zinzendorf's entire life would be profoundly shaped by his upbringing as an aristocrat of very high lineage (if not great wealth) and the competing claims of Pietism.

Since Zinzendorf was raised in such a pious home, it is not surprising that from a very early age he demonstrated a predilection for the religious life. Later in life he could recount several religious experiences he had had before he reached his tenth year. Young Zinzendorf treated Jesus like a friend and companion. "For many years I associated with him [Jesus] in a childlike manner [and] conversed with him as friends for hours."[12] This experience of intimacy with Jesus as an invisible playmate played a major role in the development of his heart theology and his attitudes toward the spiritual life of children.

When Zinzendorf was ten, his mother and stepfather insisted that he be sent to Halle to be educated at the recently established pedagogium. Because of his high status, Zinzendorf ate regularly at the table of the elder Francke

---

10. Beyreuther, *Geschichte des Pietismus,* 178.

11. Beyreuther, *Junge Zinzendorf,* 51–58.

12. Spangenberg, *Leben des Herrn Nikolaus Ludwig,* 27. Spangenberg also reports that Zinzendorf even wrote notes to the Savior and threw them out the window so he could read them (30). Pfister, *Die Frömmigkeit des Grafen Ludwig von Zinzendorf,* 4–6, makes much of Zinzendorf's supposedly unnatural childhood and the pathology of his religious precocity, but Beyreuther shows in great detail that the Zinzendorf's upbringing was not radically different from that of any German noble, except for the increased attention to religion. Beyreuther, *Junge Zinzendorf,* 66–77.

and learned directly from the great Pietist leader. Although Zinzendorf later repudiated Halle's style of Pietism and was rejected by the younger Francke in return, it is undeniable that Pietism was the dominant influence in his formative years.

When he was approved to take communion at Halle, he dedicated himself to a Pietist lifestyle. This included forming small religious communities *(ecclesiolae)* dedicated to world evangelism. Zinzendorf led regular prayer and spiritual direction meetings in his room despite being "much envied and persecuted" by his classmates.[13] Included in these meetings were several individuals who would figure prominently in his life, among them his closest companion, Frederick von Watteville.[14]

For his sixteenth birthday, his grandmother minted a medallion for one of Zinzendorf's student societies. On one side of the gold medal appeared Jesus wearing the crown of thorns, with the inscription *Vulnera Christi* (the wounds of Christ). The other side depicted a man carrying a cross under the words *Nostra Medela* (our healing). We see here the early linking of wounds devotion and Christian community for Zinzendorf.

Although Zinzendorf turned against Halle in later years, he continued, in his own way, to pursue the reform efforts of Spener. Wherever he traveled, he established meetings modeled on Spener's conventicles.[15] At least part of his later separation from the mainstream of Pietism was his turn toward Luther's theology beginning with his studies at the University of Wittenberg, a center of orthodoxy.[16] The reason the count left Halle for Wittenberg was that his guardian was uncomfortable with his close attachment to Pietism. Because Zinzendorf was one day supposed to assume the duties of his rank, he was under strict orders to improve his dancing, riding, and the other skills needed in society. He was also supposed to study law at Wittenberg, not theology.

Without directly disobeying his family's orders, Zinzendorf attended theology classes and spent much of his spare time at school reading the Bible, theology, and church history. It was at Wittenberg that he began to appreciate the theology of the Orthodox theologians, with their insistence on justification by faith, although he rejected their intellectualism.[17]

As a former student of Francke, Zinzendorf was caught in the midst of the major conflict over the Pietist program to "complete the Reformation" of Lu-

---

13. Spangenberg, *Leben des Herrn Nikolaus Ludwig,* 43–44.

14. Beyreuther, *Junge Zinzendorf,* 121–25.

15. Becker, *Zinzendorf und sein Christentum,* 178–221, 426–29, 465–67; cf. Spangenberg, *Leben des Herrn Nikolaus Ludwig,* 42–43, 50 n. 10; cf. Beyreuther, *Junge Zinzendorf,* 85–90, 116–18.

16. Spangenberg, *Leben des Herrn Nikolaus Ludwig,* 57–58; Beyreuther, *Junge Zinzendorf,* 130–35.

17. Spangenberg, *Leben des Herrn Nikolaus Ludwig,* 72–76; Becker, *Zinzendorf und sein Christentum,* 218–19. Spangenberg emphasizes that Zinzendorf was self-taught in theology.

ther. Zinzendorf's first ecumenical effort was an attempt to reconcile his teachers at Wittenberg with his former teachers at Halle. The failure of this effort increased Zinzendorf's distrust of polemics and theological debate.[18] It also worried Zinzendorf's family that the young count was involving himself in such controversies.

Zinzendorf's guardian hoped that his *Wanderjahr* (similar to the grand tour) in France and the Low Countries after his formal education would open Zinzendorf more to the pleasures of the world and break him out of his exclusive focus on religious matters. Things turned out a bit differently than expected, though, as Zinzendorf sought out the company of religious people, including Mennonites and members of Philadelphian societies. Among his contacts was the reform-minded bishop of Paris, Cardinal Noailles. His close friendship with a Roman Catholic cardinal convinced Zinzendorf that no one denomination was the true church. This was just one manifestation of Zinzendorf's active and life-long ecumenism, based on the conviction that religion of the heart is prior to all church structures.[19]

Soon after his *Wanderjahr* he met and married Erdmuth Dorothea von Reuss, the sister of his close friend Heinrich von Reuss XXIX. Erdmuth's home of Ebersdorf, not far from Zinzendorf's own estate, was a center of mystical Pietism and hosted a thriving Pietist community for years.[20] Erdmuth shared the count's religious convictions and married him under terms of what the Pietists called a *Streiter Ehe* (militant marriage) contracted for the service of Christ rather than romantic love. This understanding of marriage would be institutionalized in the Moravian Church during Zinzendorf's lifetime, as we shall see.

Having finished his education, Zinzendorf entered state service in Dresden as an aulic and judicial counselor. The legal profession held little interest for him, however, and he devoted much of his time to Pietist conventicles in town. Once he came of age and received his inheritance, he purchased the estate of Berthelsdorf from his grandmother. He and his new wife moved there in 1723, and he increasingly devoted his attention to being a proper feudal lord. The Zinzendorfs' piety was revealed in the words inscribed over the door of their new home, which indicated that they were merely guests passing through on their way to heaven.[21]

---

18. Spangenberg, *Leben des Herrn Nikolaus Ludwig*, 84–86.

19. Ibid., 118–28. Zinzendorf's ecumenism was much criticized in his time but was highly praised in the twentieth century. A. J. Lewis, *Zinzendorf, the Ecumenical Pioneer*, is the only major work on this topic published in English.

20. Uttendörfer, *Zinzendorf und die Mystik*, 39–40.

21. *"Hier übernachten wir, als Gäste: Drum ist dies Haus nicht schön, noch feste. So recht: wir haben noch ein Haus Im Himmel: das sieht anders aus."* Quoted in Weinlick, *Count Zinzendorf,* 59.

By the time he assumed his place in society, Zinzendorf was well schooled in the major aspects of Pietism, had contact with several Separatist groups, including Anabaptists, was on good terms with a Catholic cardinal, and had come to appreciate Luther's theology. Soon he would mold these influences into a provocative and exciting mix. First, though, came his theological break with Halle.

CONVERSION, SIN, AND ETHICS

In 1727 a Halle-trained pastor named Mischke questioned Zinzendorf's conversion because Zinzendorf had not lived through a conversion struggle *(Buß-kampf)*. Zinzendorf spent nearly two years struggling over this issue and finally rejected Halle's view of salvation. He concluded that humans have no need for a conversion struggle since Christ did penance for all in Gethsemane.[22] He decided that the Pietist approach to salvation was Pelagian; that is, it was an effort to earn salvation through human effort. Moreover, Pietism offered an incomplete cure because it was mired in self-righteousness. True salvation, Zinzendorf was convinced, came only through grace effected on the cross once and for all. This and all the "truths of Scripture, [are] things which we experience as true as soon as we become sinners, as soon as we throw ourselves at the pierced feet of our Creator and beg for grace."[23]

Although Zinzendorf describes conversion in different ways, there does not seem to be much progression in his understanding of conversion from the late 1720s to his mature theology, as Bernard Becker has shown in detail.[24] Early in his career Zinzendorf decisively rejected the Pietist teaching of a *Bußkampf* as being a type of this-worldly purgatory in which present suffering obviates the need for future punishment. Instead, Zinzendorf saw conversion as a renouncing of human value before God and an acceptance of the penance of Christ for all people.

Zinzendorf believed in original sin and the fall from grace of the first humans, but he also asserted that this original sin had been atoned for, once and for all, on the cross.[25] There was no longer any power or punishment connected with original sin. All humans had been freed from that ancient curse because Christ "died for the sins of the whole world," even those who had died before the time of Jesus.[26] The blood of Christ "flowed out of his body and cascaded

---

22. Becker, *Zinzendorf und sein Christentum,* 183–95.

23. Zinzendorf, *Nine Public Lectures,* 8.

24. Becker, *Zinzendorf und sein Christentum* 193–97, 205–9.

25. Zinzendorf, *Einundzwanzig Diskurse,* ZH 6:5:124. For this reason, all infants die already saved. See *Nine Public Lectures,* 68. Freeman, *An Ecumenical Theology of the Heart,* 168–73, discusses Zinzendorf's understanding of the effect of the Fall. Freeman connects this to the human inability to know God.

26. *Einundzwanzig Diskurse,* ZH 6:5:124. This includes the souls of those who died before the coming of Christ. Zinzendorf affirmed the doctrine of Christ's harrowing of hell. Ibid., 127–28.

like a dammed stream which flooded over and blessed the entire world in an instant."[27] This meant that all people had already been redeemed and could not achieve redemption on their own. All souls had been purchased from the devil, even those of wicked people; but most people remained ignorant of this truth. They did not even know they were lost, much less redeemed; thus they did not enjoy the benefit of this redemption.[28]

Zinzendorf came very close to a doctrine of universal salvation in his early discourses, but he drew back from this implication by asserting that those who do not believe are surely damned. He handled the question of election that divided Lutherans and Calvinists by proposing a doctrine of "first fruits." The first fruits are those who have been set aside for salvation from the foundation of the world. All other people must be saved by their own acceptance of their redemption.[29] This idea of first fruits was foundational for Moravian missions to non-Christian peoples, including the native tribes of America. It was also the subject of several Valentine Haidt paintings depicting converts from many peoples.[30]

Although Zinzendorf rejected the Pietist emphasis on a conversion struggle, he held on to the idea of conversion, or a new birth. The new birth for him was both an emotional process and one of achieving enlightenment. It produces *Glückseligkeit,* an experience of "happy blessedness." Since the converted person is filled with love for Christ, he "lives already in heaven, and his happiness is eternal, for he need no longer be anxious, he need not think of death any longer for he can die no more."[31]

This "blessed happiness" is the result of conversion, but the process itself is not always pleasant and joyful. In fact, it is a highly individualized experience that varies greatly and may be painful. The experience itself will be different for each person: "Whether this experience afterwards turns first into a joy of your heart, into a surprising joy such as you have never felt before in your whole life, or into a dreadful shame or profound sorrow, it is all the same, for this depends on the circumstances."[32] The pain comes because a person must recognize his or her own misery in order to long for salvation. The heart must

27. Zinzendorf, *Wundenlitanei Homilien,* ZH 3:1:10.

28. Zinzendorf, *Berliner Reden* (Men), ZE 14:7:82–89.

29. Zinzendorf, *Nine Public Lectures,* 15–16.

30. For more on the First Fruits concept and how this was overshadowed in Moravian missions after Zinzendorf, see David A. Schattschneider, "Souls for the Lamb: A Theology for the Christian Mission According to Count Nikolaus Ludwig von Zinzendorf and Bishop August Gottlieb Spangenberg" (Ph.D. diss., University of Chicago, 1975). On Valentine Haidt's painting and "First Fruits," see Vernon Nelson, "John Valentine Haidt's Life and Work" (Bethlehem, Pa.: Moravian Archives, 1996).

31. Zinzendorf, *Nine Public Lectures,* 6. Peter Zimmerling explores this in more detail in *Nachfolge zu lernen: Zinzendorf und das Leben der Brüdergemeine* (Moers: Brendow-Verlag, 1990).

32. Zinzendorf, *Nine Public Lectures,* 66.

feel itself so "broken, shattered, and timid" that it knows it cannot save itself; only then can it be saved by the Lamb of God.[33]

Thus conversion may be a painful, ego-shattering experience, but Zinzendorf denies that it *must* be traumatic. He compares it to cutting teeth. It is better that a child go through the pain of cutting teeth than not cut teeth at all; but no doctor would forbid a child to cut teeth without pain.[34] Zinzendorf summed up the difference between the Pietist method of conversion and his own with this analogy: "as if a person were to fall into the hands of a miserable quack who had caught only a small piece of the cure, and hurts, torments, cuts, rips, and burns his patient and still accomplishes hardly anything in some months; and between a skilled person who in half a hour is finished with his operation."[35]

Zinzendorf not only broke with Halle over the nature of conversion, he also developed a different view of the nature of sin and ethics.[36] Zinzendorf claimed that converted Christians "are led by the Holy Spirit, every day in all their knowledge, in all their affairs, in all their actions."[37] They are the most moral of all people, but not through their own efforts. Morality is the consequence of faith, not of law. "And to such people, says the apostle, no law is given: these people steal less than other people, they whore less than other people, they give false witness less than others, they covet things that are not theirs less than others, and less than all other people."[38] This conviction changed the whole approach to preaching and building a Christian community because the written law was deprived of its force. Zinzendorf has the Spirit say, "I will write a summary of the law in their heart."[39]

Zinzendorf built his ethics on St. Paul's notion that Christians develop the mind *(Sinn)* of Christ (1 Cor. 2:16), combined with Jesus' statement that a good tree cannot produce bad fruit (Matt. 13:33). The result of faith is that the heart and mind of a Christian are transformed by Christ through the Spirit so that the believer wants to do nothing but the will of Christ.[40] However, when a

---

33. Zinzendorf, *Gemeinreden*, ZH 4:13:219.

34. Zinzendorf, *Naturelle Reflexionem*, ZE 4:67; cf. Becker, *Zinzendorf und sein Christentum*, 195. Ward, *Protestant Evangelical Awakening*, 136–38, notes that Zinzendorf's "quick" approach to conversion was a major point of contention with other evangelicals.

35. Zinzendorf, *Gemeinreden*, ZH 4:31:66.

36. For more on Zinzendorf's Christocentric approach to ethics, see Helmut Bintz, "Die Begründung der christliche Ethik in der Inkarnationslehre bei Zinzendorf," in *Pietismus-Herrnhutertum-Erweckungsbewegung: Festschrift für Erich Beyreuther*, ed. Dietrich Meyer (Cologne: Rheinland-Verlag, 1982), 177–302; cf. Zimmerling, *Gott in Gemeinschaft*, 202–36.

37. Zinzendorf, *Gemeinreden*, ZH 4, Anhang, 9.

38. Ibid., 4:16:253–54.

39. Ibid., Anhang, 7–8.

40. "We have the mind of Christ, we think like Jesus Christ. Each one has a mind like Jesus Christ also had; that is a real thing." *Gemeinreden*, ZH 4:18:275; cf. ibid., 4:10:172–73. On the trinitarian grounding of Zinzendorf's ethics, see Zimmerling, *Gott in Gemeinschaft*, 209–36.

specific individual, especially someone with the charisma of Zinzendorf, says, "I live no more; he lives in me. I speak no more; he speaks in me. When you speak with me, you speak with him,"[41] it can sound delusional and messianic. This was not the intention of his theology, however. He held that every believer was being molded in the image of Christ and could speak thus.

Every attempt to develop a code of behavior or even rules for determining ethical decisions was fundamentally unchristian because Christian ethics flow simply from Christian hearts, according to Zinzendorf. Law *(Gesetz)* and heart are contraries.[42] Ethics, traditionally understood, lead people into hypocrisy and idolatrous system building, but when the heart has been purified by the Spirit and directed toward the Savior, there will be no distinction between one's thoughts, words, actions, and feelings. The believer is thus an integrated person. "I believe it, therefore I speak it; I feel it, therefore I confess it."[43]

Life in Bethlehem was structured around this idea that life flows easily and naturally from the disposition of the heart. One's words and confession should flow from the heart and say no more than the heart knows. Moreover, closing one's heart to others and especially to God was a grave error that stood in the way of a happy relationship with God.[44]

Drawing on Luther's idea of being a justified sinner, Zinzendorf expressed the paradox of salvation in the phrase "No one is more holy than a sinner who has grace."[45] Such provocative statements make it easy to depict Zinzendorf as either an antinomian or a perfectionist. He certainly revealed antinomian tendencies in his rejection of the law; however, in sum, he attempted to express a creative paradox between the complete redemption of sin purchased by Jesus and the reality of continuing human sinfulness since the Atonement. Salvation is entirely in the hands of the Savior. Zinzendorf asserted that the hardest thing for a believer to do is to accept that salvation comes only by grace, not by any merit or effort, or, for that matter, by any theology.

FAITH AND REASON

At the same time that Zinzendorf was turning away from Halle Pietism, he was also struggling with the issues of reason, faith, and belief.[46] He began his writing

---

41. *Gemeinreden,* ZH 4:12:207.

42. Ibid., 18:270.

43. Ibid., 21:311.

44. Zinzendorf points to the biblical story of Adam, who hid from God after sinning: "Take note; this gives a clear insight into the modesty, the self-righteousness, the equity, the humility present when a person, out of great discretion and with ever so many compliments and an exaggeration of his misery, wants to evade the Saviour; an insight into these things as seen through the eyes of God. . . . No! For once one must approach just as one is." Zinzendorf, *Nine Public Lectures,* 92.

45. Zinzendorf, *Gemeinreden,* ZH 4:43:221. Likewise, he informed the children that they must become sinners in order to be saved. *Kinder Reden,* ZE 6:2:8.

46. As Bettermann shows, Zinzendorf was not alone in struggling with these issues. Pietism in general was a response to the radical doubt of the early Enlightenment. *Theologie und Sprache,* 170–76.

career in Dresden in 1725 with an anonymous series of tracts called *Der Dresdenische Socrates* (republished later as *Der Teutsche Socrates*).[47] These tracts were
in the spirit of much anonymous or pseudonymous writing of the early eighteenth century critical of contemporary society.[48] In these pamphlets Zinzendorf attempted to be another Pierre Bayle. In fact, he claimed that the only
book, other than the Bible, that he carried on his travels was Bayle's *Historical
and Critical Dictionary*. It may be surprising at first to hear that Zinzendorf
had such a high regard for Bayle, whom many considered an enemy of Christianity, but as Beyreuther aptly argues, Bayle is a two-edged sword who cuts
against secular philosophy as much as for it.[49]

Paul Hazard credits Bayle as one of the principal causes of the revolution in
European thinking at the turn of the eighteenth century. Along with such factors as increased contact with foreign cultures and Newtonian science, Hazard
sees Bayle's works as changing Western attitudes toward tradition, authority,
and God.[50] Every area of human thought and life was assaulted by Bayle's
rigorous intellectual critique and biting wit. For the average reader as for the
philosophes, Bayle's *Dictionnaire* proved an inexhaustible gold mine of information on the foolishness of humans in general and religious leaders in particular.

Relying heavily on the earlier thought of the French philosopher Montaigne,
Bayle's attacks on theology were in fact attacks on reason itself.[51] Far from
inaugurating an Age of Reason, Bayle raised serious doubts about the very
concept of reason. This helped fuel Zinzendorf's own rejection of rationalism,
and supported his effort to base spiritual truth on religious experience rather
than philosophy.

Zinzendorf had been struggling with the issue of faith and reason long before he encountered Bayle, first in childhood in Hernersdorf and then in school
at Halle, where he learned the new scientific theories and empiricism of English
thinkers Isaac Newton, Francis Bacon, and John Locke. He was also familiar
with Leibniz's *Theodicy* and Descartes's methods of philosophical doubt.[52]

Whereas many of his contemporaries were comforted by the predictability

---

47. *Socrates* is reproduced in ZH 1. For an examination of the theology of *Socrates*, see Aalen, *Theologie
des jungen Zinzendorf*.

48. See Paul Hazard, *The European Mind: 1680–1715*, trans. J. Lewis May (Cleveland: Meridian Books,
1963), 3–28, for a discussion of several of the more interesting and important of such critical works around
1700.

49. Erich Beyreuther, *Studien zur Theologie Zinzendorfs* (Neukirchen-Vluyn: Kreis Moers, 1962), 202,
223–26.

50. Hazard, *European Mind*, chap. 5.

51. Beyreuther, *Studien zur Theologie*, 207–18.

52. Hazard, *European Mind*, and Paul Hazard, *European Thought in the Eighteenth Century: From Montesquieu to Lessing*, trans. J. Lewis May (London: Hollis & Carter, 1954); Peter Gay, *The Enlightenment: An
Interpretation*, 2 vols. (New York: Norton, 1966, 1969).

and order of the Newtonian universe, Zinzendorf grasped as early as his eighth year the frightening implications of an infinite, mechanistic universe in which the human person is an irrelevant piece of matter.[53] The only source of security for Zinzendorf lay in his personal experience of Christ within his own heart. This childhood experience of doubt followed by faith was the foundation of his heart religion. When the heart grasps the truth of salvation, all of the mind's doubts are put to rest.[54]

First during his *Wanderjahr* and then throughout his life, Zinzendorf confronted urbane Deists, and he offered them his own religion of the heart as an alternative to "religion within the limits of reason alone." It might appear at first that the best way to reach out to Deists and intellectual despisers of Christianity whom Zinzendorf met in Paris would be to present the gospel in terms they could understand, that is, according to the discourse of contemporary philosophy. But Zinzendorf rejected this approach as dangerous to the faith that he wanted to promote. "As soon as they want to demonstrate to atheists and common deists and people like that that our religion is a wisdom rooted in their heads . . . then they are obviously threshing empty straw."[55] Instead, Zinzendorf tried to ground religion in experience rather than in rational certainty.

In the 1720s Zinzendorf refined his understanding of faith and reason through his failed effort to bring Conrad Dippel, the philosopher and alchemist who rejected "Word, Sacrament, and Orthodoxy," back into the Lutheran fold.[56] He failed to convert the radical Pietist, but he learned to distinguish between two types of reason: *Verstand* and *Vernunft*. Both words can be, and are, translated as "reason," but there is a subtle distinction. It is perhaps best to render them as "understanding" and "speculation," respectively.[57]

When Zinzendorf railed against reason, it was generally *Vernunft* he had in mind, although he did on occasion refer to a "corrupted *Verstand*." *Vernunft*

53. Zinzendorf's account of this experience can be found in *Büdingische Sammlung*, ZE 4, Vorrede. Beyreuther, *Junge Zinzendorf*, 78–80, speculates that the hymn that caused Zinzendorf such angst was "O Ewigkeit, du Donnerwort, O Angang ohn Ende" (O eternity, you word of thunder, O beginning without end) which praises the infinity of God within an infinite universe. Freeman, *An Ecumenical Theology of the Heart*, 78–83, associates Zinzendorf's early poem *Allegegenwart* with this awareness of the comfortless reality of modern cosmology and understands the poem as one of the crucial moments in Zinzendorf's development. On the comfort many found in the Newtonian universe, see Hazard, *European Thought in the Eighteenth Century*, 309ff.

54. Zinzendorf, *Gemeinreden*, ZH 4:17:264.

55. Zinzendorf, *Nine Public Lectures*, 78; Bettermann, *Theologie und Sprache*, 185–86.

56. Stoeffler, *German Pietism*, 182–91.

57. Zinzendorf, *Büdingische Sammlung* I, Vorrede, ZE 7. Freeman quotes Zinzendorf's definition of these terms in *An Ecumenical Theology of the Heart*, 76. It may have been confusion over the distinction between *Verstand* and *Vernunft* that caused Wesley to warn the English world of Zinzendorf's efforts to take away their reason. Many later interpreters have also failed to observe this distinction. Hutton, for example, says "They were not to use their own brains" (*History of the Moravian Church*, 274).

is the type of reason that seeks to create God after its image and speculates about unknowable things. It is usually a characteristic of philosophy, but Zinzendorf claimed it is also found in abundance among "fanatics" and "dreamers."[58]

Anticipating some of the ideas of Kant, Zinzendorf attacked metaphysics as fruitless speculation into the inner reality of the incomprehensible God. Such speculation is not only impious; it is also foolish because it seeks to know the unknowable.[59] "To reason over the deity, to draw conclusions from it, to mold it into concepts, is already a criminal act similar either to six blasphemies or to absolute, certifiable lunacy. For God is neither time nor eternity, nor nature, nor anything else that the head can think about nor the mouth express."[60]

In contrast, true geniuses "who actually raised themselves above the level of what is ordinarily human" understand that they cannot think the thoughts of God. They are bashful of divine things, unlike "petty geniuses" who try to penetrate the mystery of God through philosophy.[61] The problem with philosophers and mystics, according to Zinzendorf, is that they seek to go beyond reason, searching out what cannot be known. A would-be philosopher should restrict himself to the things that the *Verstand* can grasp, such as "his mathematics, his geometry, his calculations, his logarithms . . . or stay with his physics experiments, with research into longitudes or perpetual motion. Those are materials for an acute understanding."[62]

Zinzendorf praised *Verstand* or practical philosophy, however, as useful. It helps people to avoid falling into intellectual errors; thus Christians should use their practical reason to understand what God has given them to understand.[63] Here is a key to understanding how the Moravians could reject "reason" and yet be so rational in their organization and economy. Philosophy and science can increase knowledge of the natural world, but it is dangerous to mix philosophy, particularly metaphysics, with religion.

The unsystematic character of true faith means that Christianity cannot really be called a religion, for it is nothing more and nothing less than the experience of salvation, when the heart understands and accepts that the Creator has died for all people.[64] This was a conscious repudiation of the rational-

---

58. Zinzendorf distinguishes between philosophers and fanatics in his sermon *Von der Wage-rechten Auseinandersetzung der Philosophie und des Fanaticismi* (1746), *Gemeinreden,* ZH 4, Anhang, 37–52.

59. Zinzendorf, *Einundzwanzig Diskurse* ZH 6:8:155. We clearly see the stamp of Bayle here and the early stages of modern theology's rejection of metaphysics. Zimmerling, *Gott in Gemeinschaft,* 147–61, distinguishes Zinzendorf's theological method from the Enlightenment and Pietist spiritualism.

60. Zinzendorf, *Litaneirede* 2 (3.11.1756), quoted in Beyreuther, *Studien zur Theologie,* 245.

61. Zinzendorf, *Einundzwanzig Diskurse* ZH 6:6:134ff.

62. Ibid., 142.

63. Zinzendorf, *Gemeinreden,* ZH 4, Anhang, 38.

64. "Thus there should not be a Christian religion in the sense that one only adopts a certain system, that [expresses] different opinions and thoughts about Christ, his teachings and his life; rather, his death and

ism exhibited in Protestant Orthodoxy. No matter how much effort someone puts into making Christianity a rational and consistent system, there will always be elements left unexplained *(viele Dubia vexata übrig bleiben)*. After all that effort, the task of systematizing has to be abandoned.[65]

Zinzendorf may have had in mind philosophers such as Leibniz and his disciple Christian Wolff, or he may have been thinking of the scholastic *Summa* or even a Reformation-era *Institutio*. In any case, a systematic theology could not allow for contradictions or paradoxes that violated the laws of human logic but might be necessary within the divine logic. Theology as well as piety had to be carried out under the form of the cross. The cross form is always paradoxical, and thus not subject to rational laws.[66]

Rationalist apologetics fail because no one can be convinced of the gospel through reason alone. Arguments and demonstrations only raise more doubts. Certainty in religion lies in the heart and only in the heart. Thus religion is not a matter of convincing intellectual arguments but of conviction, will, and faith. Zinzendorf, drawing on Augustine, distinguished different types of belief *(Glaube):* (1) dead knowledge, or *scientia Satanae;* (2) the attachment and love of a human heart to the Savior; (3) a living spiritual knowledge and experience of divine things.[67] Even Satan has the faith of a philosophical Christian, since he knows that there is a Creator, but he is not thereby saved.

Although the unbelief of scoffers and philosophes threatened people's immortal souls, the blind acceptance of doctrinal statements demanded by the church was just as damning, in Zinzendorf's view. Reasoned acceptance of a theological or creedal system may be belief, but it is not faith. At best, orthodox theologians and preachers "who think that if they have them memorize the catechism or get a book of sermons into their heads or, at the most, present all sorts of well-reasoned demonstrations concerning the divine being and attributes"[68] can lead someone to mere belief but not to saving faith.

Faith is not a matter for rational debate; it is nothing more or less than the transformation of the human heart through an inner union with the Savior.[69]

What is faith *[Gläuben]* then? Faith is a connection, stemming from the supposition of the truth of the thing, of the soul *[Gemüth]* with the Creator who is the Savior, from which

---

suffering must be buried in our hearts. Therefore, we must be blessed because he died for us." *Gemeinreden,* ZH 4:42:215.

65. *Gemeinreden,* ZH 4:37:147–48. See Zimmerling, *Gott in Gemeinschaft,* 147–60.

66. Zinzendorf, *Wundenlitanei Homilien* 5, ZH 3:61. On Zinzendorf's understanding of the distinction between the deep God of the mystics or God as he can be known through revelation and experience, see Zimmerling, *Gott in Gemeinschaft,* 110–56, esp. 114–17.

67. *Gemeinreden,* ZH 4:5:96–100. See Hök, *Zinzendorfs Begriff der Religion,* 11ff., for a discussion of these different types of belief. Hök relates these to Augustine's *credere de Deo; credere Deo; credere in Deum* (56).

68. Zinzendorf, *Nine Public Lectures,* 35; cf. *Gemeinreden,* ZH 4:17:260–61. Likewise, religious language must be able to be understood even by children. Bettermann, *Theologie und Sprache,* 18.

69. *Gemeinreden,* ZH 4:17:263–64; *Kinder Reden,* ZE 6:1:3.

ultimately follows also, the resolution, through the nature of the thing itself, to endure everything with the Creator, who is the Savior, as long as one lives, to suffer for his sake, to risk oneself for him in his affairs, to not be ashamed of him and his words, to be satisfied having him day and night in his thoughts, to comfort, to rejoice, to correct, and to get everything, which one needs, from him.[70]

This understanding of religion as nonrational (rather than irrational) allowed Zinzendorf in *Socrates* to address a significant failure of rational religion, whether of the Deist or orthodox variety. If salvation is in some way based on concepts or knowledge or rational understanding, what is the fate of those whose capacities are impaired? "Religion can be grasped without rational means, otherwise no one could have a religion except for those with an enlightened head, and the most rational would be the best students of divine matters, but that is not believable and is also contradicted by experience. Religion must be a matter that one can grasp through mere feeling, without any concepts, otherwise, no deaf person, yet alone a person blind from birth, or especially a child, could have the religion necessary for blessedness."[71]

Zinzendorf frequently used the biblical story of Mary's visit to her cousin Elizabeth (Luke 1:39–45) to demonstrate that faith is not based on reason. Both women were pregnant, Mary with Jesus and Elizabeth with John the Baptist. When Mary approached Elizabeth, the unborn John leaped in his mother's womb in recognition of Jesus.[72] John knew Christ without the need of systematic theologies, creeds, or even the Bible. No rational discourse could equal the direct encounter he had with the Christ.[73]

It was this nonrational approach to Christianity that made Moravians such effective missionaries to premodern peoples, but it also helped European nobles to overcome the doubts of their age.[74] Zinzendorf accepted the Deist assumption that all peoples everywhere have an intuitive sense that there is a Creator and, more important, a longing for the Creator. This is not only universal, it is indubitable. "To believe that there is a God, or not, is not within

70. *Gemeinreden,* ZH 4:37:154–55.

71. *Socrates,* ZH 1, *Anhang,* unnumbered. Cf. Bettermann, *Theologie und Sprache,* 12; Freeman, *An Ecumenical Theology of the Heart,* 98–99.

72. For instance, *Einundzwanzig Diskurse,* ZH 6:3:83–84, *Kinder Reden,* ZE 6:50:255; cf. *Kinder Reden,* ZE 6:81:400.

73. "There were two children, Jesus and John, who knew nothing of each other and naturally could not see each other, but who, through the mediation of the Holy Spirit, had a strong impression of one another. When Mary greeted Elizabeth, her child rejoiced with such a great joy that the text cannot exactly describe it. And it happened so quietly that no one would have known about it if Elizabeth had not told it." *Kinder Reden,* ZE 6:50:254–55. Zinzendorf also instructed pregnant women to care for the spiritual development of their embryos. Bettermann, *Theologie und Sprache,* 19.

74. Zinzendorf, *Gemeinreden,* ZH 4:17:264. Zinzendorf maintained this perspective throughout his life; see *Kinder Reden,* ZE 6:81:398.

us. We naturally believe. . . . The foundation lies too deep in our nature and feelings [Gemüth] [to deny it]."[75]

An innate feeling for the numinous is not sufficient for salvation, however. One must also understand in one's heart that the Creator whom all peoples know is also the Savior who died for everyone.[76] All Christian theology must proceed from this sensible reality, the heart's true knowledge of and love for the Savior, otherwise theology is just empty metaphysical speculation.[77] In fact, the entire Augsburg Confession, which was the basis of true theology for Zinzendorf, is really an expression of heart religion; "it is a hearty, careful, cross-theological confession that agrees with the doctrine of the suffering [of Christ] and the ideas of the heart that flow from that."[78]

Zinzendorf's rejection of rational religion raises the question of whether he should be called a theologian at all. Certainly if one defines theology as a system of rational propositions about God, then Zinzendorf is not a theologian. But he may be seen as a theologian in a larger sense, much as antirationalist writers such as Pascal, Kierkegaard, and Nietzsche can be considered philosophers. Zinzendorf plumbed the depths of the mystery of divinity and language, and found that rationality is inadequate for the primary task of theology, namely, to speak about God. As Arthur Freeman says in interpreting Zinzendorf, "We are born into a world that is mystery to us, and as we mature, observe, and reflect, we push back the walls of this mystery. We may take advantage of the great religious and philosophical traditions which in themselves are the results of attempts to understand. But whatever wisdom we gain, the mystery remains and we know that we know in very limited ways."[79] Zinzendorf himself acknowledged that his approach to Christianity would destroy theology as it had been practiced. "Hundreds of questions will be eliminated, a hundred affairs would answer themselves, and in the end there will be a system that someone can generally write down on two pages."[80]

Among the people who followed Zinzendorf in this new approach to doctrine and practice were the Moravians who were establishing the community of Herrnhut at the same time that Zinzendorf was publishing Der Dresdenische

---

75. Zinzendorf, Berliner Reden, ZE 14 (Men), 3.

76. According to his Berlin sermons, this was how Satan had deceived the Deists and others of his day. Ibid.

77. That now is our confession, that is the heart religion that all the creeds, which they accept for true, make an overt heart confession. "One, indeed only One," it says, "and none other is loved by me, Jesus the faithful in whom I rejoice. If I do not notice his arm around my shoulders, if I do not feel his warmth in my heart, then I am left out, thus everything remains to me of love for nothing else holds me." Gemeinreden, ZH 4:1:6.

78. Zinzendorf, Einundzwanzig Diskurse, ZH 6:10:203.

79. Freeman, An Ecumenical Theology of the Heart, 70.

80. Zinzendorf, Gemeinreden, ZH 4:35:108.

Socrates. The combination of Moravian discipline and Zinzendorf's religion of the heart produced a new type of Pietist community at Herrnhut. From that Herrnhut community, the Moravians spread Zinzendorf's vision to much of Europe, the Caribbean, and Pennsylvania.

HERRNHUT AS A RELIGIOUS *GEMEINE*

In 1722 an event occurred that would change the course of Zinzendorf's career, but at first he was unaware of it. His estate manager, Heitz, gave permission for a group of Protestant refugees to settle on the count's estate. The Moravians who came to Zinzendorf's estate knew little about their ancestors' church, but they knew they wanted to resurrect it. They began a small town in an undeveloped portion of the estate about a mile from Berthlesdorf, where both the parish church and Zinzendorf's home were located. Christian David cut the first tree and christened the new town Herrnhut, which can be translated "on watch for the Lord" or "under the Lord's watch."[81]

More Protestants fled Moravia and Bohemia and found refuge at Herrnhut, and soon the toleration granted at Herrnhut attracted radical Pietists of all stripes. Separatists, mystics, and seekers came to Herrnhut in search of a more genuine form of Christianity. Some stayed, but others, like the philosopher Christoph Oetinger, continued seeking.

Eventually Zinzendorf noticed the presence of the new settlers and was impressed by their fortitude and steadfast faith in the midst of adversity; however, relationships between the Pietist count and the Herrnhuters were not always cordial. The Moravians resented the fact that they were forced to worship in the Lutheran parish of Berthlesdorf.[82] The pastor, Rothe, insisted on such things as private confession and the wearing of vestments, which the Moravians and Separatists saw as "popish." Zinzendorf was worried about the separatist tendencies of the Moravians and the legal difficulties they could cause by resurrecting the old Unitas Fratrum, a church that had no legal standing in the Holy Roman Empire.

The new community almost collapsed just five years after it was founded. Things came to a crisis in 1726, and the Moravians considered this a time of trial, or "sifting," when Herrnhut was in danger of becoming a "nest of heretics." A wandering apocalyptic preacher named Krüger encouraged a group of the Herrnhuters to separate themselves from the impious before Christ returned in judgment. He soon gathered a large faction that considered Zinzend-

---

81. Hamilton and Hamilton, *History*, 23–33; Otto Uttendörfer, *Alt Herrnhut: wirtschaftsgeschichte und Religionssoziologie Herrnhuts während seiner ersten zwanzig Jahre (1722–1742)* (Herrnhut: Missionsbuchhandlung, 1925).

82. Beyreuther, *Der Junge Zinzendorf,* 164–204.

orf and Rothe the agents of the Antichrist. Krüger moved on to preach in other places, but Herrnhut was left fragmented.

Zinzendorf, in his capacity as feudal lord, intervened directly in the conflict of opinions in Herrnhut. In 1727 he moved his residence to Herrnhut and, as Spangenberg put it, "gave himself completely to the service of the poor exiles. From then on, his effort was to further their temporal and spiritual welfare."[83] On May 12, 1727, Zinzendorf issued the *Herrschaftliche Gebote und Verbote* (Manorial Injunctions and Prohibitions) to order the civil life of Herrnhut. Joined to these civil rules was the *Brüderlicher Verein und Willkür* (the Brotherly Agreement), which addressed the spiritual life of Herrnhut.[84]

Zinzendorf convinced the residents that the new Brotherly Agreement expressed the same ideals as the *Ratio Disciplinae* of the old Unitas Fratrum. Zinzendorf's statutes established Herrnhut as a religious *Gemeine* (fellowship or community) within the Lutheran parish of Berthelsdorf. The rules attempted to balance Herrnhut's status as a separate religious community with its full participation in the established church.

This desire to maintain the uniqueness of the Unitas Fratrum within the structure of the Lutheran Church motivated many of Zinzendorf's actions that appear contradictory. For instance, in 1728, when the Berthelsdorf pastor convinced many of the Moravians simply to become Lutheran and let the Unitas Fratrum die, Zinzendorf opposed the proposal vigorously. Spangenberg, along with a hundred fellow students at Jena, where Zinzendorf was visiting at the time, urged the Brethren to hold on to their ancient faith.[85]

However, in 1731 it was Zinzendorf who urged the Moravians to become Lutheran. When the lot spoke against his plan for assimilation, Zinzendorf bowed to the lot's decision. According to Becker, Zinzendorf's basic plan was for the Brüdergemeine to remain Lutheran in Germany, although the Moravians could still live by their discipline and order of worship. Outside Germany, the Unitas Fratrum could be established as an independent ecclesial body with a self-ordained ministry under the authority of its own synods and bishops.[86]

The process of ordering the life of Herrnhut and overcoming dissension led to a Pietist-style revival experience in Herrnhut. August 13, 1727, is still celebrated in the Moravian Church as a type of Pentecost when the Moravian Church was reborn. From 1727 on, the life of Zinzendorf and the Moravians

83. Spangenberg, *Leben des Herrn Nikolaus Ludwig*, 348–57, 406. Cf. Weinlick, *Count Zinzendorf*, 70–74.

84. These documents are reprinted in Müller, *Zinzendorf als Erneuerer*, 106–15; cf. Sommer, *Serving Two Masters*, 10–28.

85. Hamilton and Hamilton, *History*, 40; Spangenberg, *Leben des Herrn Nikolaus Ludwig*, 492; and Ritschl, *Geschichte des Pietismus*, 3:245–46. See also *Büdingische Sammlung*, ZE 9:631; cf. Hamilton and Hamilton, *History*, 94–98.

86. Becker spells out the details of this arrangement in *Zinzendorf und sein Christentum*, 449–63.

became permanently joined. David Nitschmann, the first Moravian bishop in the renewed church, is quoted as saying, "From that time on, Herrnhut became a living congregation of Jesus Christ."[87]

Zinzendorf used his status and education to defend Herrnhut and the Moravians before the Saxon government on several occasions. He also served as the regular catechist and helped structure Herrnhut according to his plan of a religious community, or Gemeine, within the confessional church. Over the next decade, Herrnhut developed a distinctive organization and devotional life, which will be discussed in detail in another chapter.[88]

In 1735 Zinzendorf negotiated with the court chaplain of Prussia, Daniel Ernst Jablonski, to continue the succession of Moravian bishops. Jablonski, the grandson of the great Moravian bishop Jan Amos Comenius, had been consecrated a bishop of the Unitas Fratrum even though he served in the Reformed Church.[89] A murky situation became even more confusing when Zinzendorf, already a Lutheran minister, accepted consecration as a Moravian bishop in 1737. The continuation of the episcopacy remains one of the strongest ties between the old Unitas Fratrum and the Moravian Church reorganized under Zinzendorf, but this also increased opposition to Zinzendorf from Halle and the Saxon authorities.

Opposition to Zinzendorf's activities increased in his native Saxony in the 1730s. He had angered many of the aristocracy, including members of his family, by mingling with peasants, and there were many sore feelings from the Socrates. He was accused of encouraging religious separatism and urging people to leave their feudal lord, the Habsburg emperor. One Moravian leader, David Nitschmann the Martyr, was imprisoned in Austria, where he died in 1729, despite Zinzendorf's efforts to have him released.

Saxon officials examined Herrnhut on two occasions in the 1730s. After the second visitation, in 1736, it was decided that the residents of Herrnhut could remain and observe their own form of worship, but the count was exiled. Having had the foresight to sign over his estates to his wife, the banishment did not affect Zinzendorf's property, but from 1736 on he considered himself a pilgrim with no fixed abode. He traveled with a large retinue called the Jüngerhaus (household of the Disciple) that included most of the leadership of the growing church.[90]

The Moravian settlers were allowed to stay in Herrnhut, but the threat of

87. Weinlick, Count Zinzendorf, 79.

88. Nelson, "Herrnhut: Friedrich Schleiermacher's Spiritual Homeland."

89. Weinlick, Count Zinzendorf, 114–18, 136–37. Hermann Dalton, Daniel Ernst Jablonski (Berlin: Warneck, 1903); Norman Sykes, Daniel Ernst Jablonski and the Church of England (London: SPCK, 1950).

90. Hamilton and Hamilton, History, 63.

exile had an effect on them as well. In fact, Zinzendorf's exile contributed directly to the spread of the Brüdergemeine, particularly to the formation of religious towns modeled after Herrnhut. Zinzendorf wanted to have places of refuge for the residents of Herrnhut, particularly the Moravians, should the Saxon court banish them as well. These towns were more than just safe havens, though; they were vital centers of Zinzendorf's religious vision, an expression of his understanding of the Gemeine. This was one of Zinzendorf's most creative notions, which he developed from the Pietist conventicle and the idea of the Philadelphian church.

THE *GEMEINE* IDEAL

It is difficult to translate the word *Gemeine* because it means congregation, church, and community all at once. The Gemeine was an extension of Spener's notion of the *ecclesiola in ecclesia,* where a group of like-minded individuals motivated by the love of Christ establish a community for study and mutual edification within the established church.[91] Zinzendorf, however, expanded the notion to encompass entire villages and towns founded for Christian mission and mutual edification. In fact, there are several levels of Gemeinen: the local congregation/religious community, the worldwide Brüdergemeine, and the invisible Gemeine, or the true church through the ages. The word *Kirche* refers to the institutional church, but Gemeine refers to the intimate community bound by mutual love of the Savior.

There was no one type of Gemeine, but each was an expression of local needs. Two types of Gemeinem were related to the diaspora work within established churches and two others were types of closed settlements. Diaspora congregations were called *Stadtgemeinen* or *Landgemeinen,* depending on whether they were located in town or countryside. They followed Moravian liturgy but had a less rigorous discipline.

Settlement congregations were either *Ortsgemeinen* or *Pilgergemeinen.*[92] Both were regulated communities operated directly by the church. Only members of the Brüdergemeine could live in one of these towns. Even members had to

---

91. There has been some controversy over the use of terms for these small groups devoted to piety. Some avoid the word "conventicle" because of its factional connotation. For an introduction to the topic, see Markus Matthias, "Collegium pietatis und ecclesiola" in *Pietismus und Neuzeit* 19 (1993) 47–59; Erich Beyreuther, "Einleitung" to Spener's *Sendschreiben* in Philipp Jacob Spener, *Schriften,* vol. 1, ed. Erich Beyreuther and Dietrich Blaufluß (Olms: Hildesheim, 1979) 79; Johannes Wallmann, "Die Anfänge des Pietismus," *Pietismus und Neuzeit* 4 (1977–78), 50–51; Hartmut Lehmann, "'Absonderung' und 'Gemeinschaft' im frühen Pietismus. Allgemeinhistorishe und sozialpsychologische Überlegungen zur Entstehung und Entwicklung des Pietismus," *Pietismus und Neuzeit* 4 (1977–78): 54–82. Jonathan Strom's article "Early Conventicles in Lübeck," in *Pietismus und Neuzeit* 27 (2003), examines this discussion in detail.

92. See Smaby, *Transformation of Moravian Bethlehem,* 25, for a taxonomy of the types of Gemeinen. There is a typographical error in n. 42, on page 48, however. The date should read 1848. Cf. Hamilton and Hamilton, *History,* 184–85.

receive special permission (often through the lot) to reside in a Gemeine, and every resident had to agree to the covenant for that community. Since the congregational towns were very intimate, the Moravians exercised a level of discipline that would have been unthinkable in the state church. In Zinzendorf's view, normal church discipline, particularly if backed by civil laws, only leads to hypocrisy, but mutual discipline in a Gemeine was to be based on honesty and brotherly love.[93]

Through such discipline, the Gemeine was to be a foretaste of heaven on earth and serve as a living witness to the saving grace of Christ. The 1764 Synod described Ortsgemeinen thus:

The Ortsgemeinen are places that the Saviour himself has chosen, on which a peculiar grace certainly rests. . . . They should give off a witness to the world that [is] more effective than so many sermons. . . . They are establishments which are brought together to the end that the Holy Spirit has a free hand [so] that each inhabitant becomes a child of God, and . . . the opportunity for temptation is cut off and prevented, and where the youth obtain an impression of the Saviour from their first years on.[94]

Members of a Gemeine were to display an intense interest in each other's hearts and souls. Not only should their hearts be united in their love for Jesus, their thoughts and desires should be similar, flowing as they did from the same love for God.[95] Every relationship must be viewed from the perspective of the Savior, who forms the center of all relationships. Because of this emphasis, the Moravians sought also to love the world for the sake of Christ and accept as brothers and sisters all those who live in Jesus. For Zinzendorf, this was the proper motive for evangelism and the source of a true Gemeine: each believer is connected to all human souls and is concerned about their eternal happiness, just as Christ was.[96]

According to Zinzendorf, the earthly Gemeine is modeled on the Holy Trinity, which was the original Gemeine and the original church. The earthly Gemeine reflects the nature of the Triune God that was tarnished by the fall of Adam and Eve. Jesus Christ restores this original Gemeine.[97] Children who grow up in this Gemeine of God should no more be able to doubt the reality of their membership in the household of God than children who grow up in an earthly household can doubt that they were born into their own family.

93. Becker, *Zinzendorf und sein Christentum*, 121–54. See Sommer, *Serving Two Masters*, chap. 5, for details on the development of communal discipline. For Zinzendorf's views on hypocrisy, see Bettermann, *Theologie und Sprache*, 189.

94. Synod Report of 1764, sec. 43, p. 49, quoted in Sommer, *Serving Two Masters*, 19.

95. Atwood, "Zinzendorf's 1749 Reprimand," ¶ 10.

96. Zinzendorf, *Gemeinreden*, ZH 4:23:317, 325–26.

97. Ibid., 4:77–95.

Children born and baptized in the community will have a natural desire for God.[98]

However, this Gemeine includes more than just the visible members of the Brüdergemeine. It includes souls around the world and even those in heaven. "Because of that we are certainly gaining a heaven on earth; this makes the Gemeine into the Kingdom of God on earth, when we are in such a familiarity with the Savior, with his Father, the dear Mother the Holy Spirit, with the servants, the liturgists (Heb. 1), with the saints in heaven, with the Lady [Virgin Mary], with the brothers and sisters among us, and with the invisible Gemeine of God in the world."[99] This is one of Zinzendorf's strongest statements of a realized eschatology. Until Jesus returns, there will be a mystical, invisible communion between the saints in heaven and on earth. Though he never denies a future return of Christ, more important to Zinzendorf is that Christians are already living in a heaven on earth through the ministry of the Holy Spirit.

To love and follow Christ means that one makes Christ the center of existence and in turn becomes a sign of Christ in the world, living as Christ lived. All activities of daily existence in a Gemeine, from work to sex, should be done only in the context of love for and worship of Christ. All of life's daily activities thus become a part of the divine liturgy: "When you spin, knit, sew, and anything else, do it as love for the Prince, and, as I have told you before, as a Liturgy. Walk and stand for him, eat and drink for him, and when you lie down, you lie in his arms. In short, if everything you do, you do for him, if you liturgize to him from early in the morning until night, you will enter into his joy and do blessed labor."[100]

Thus we see that, ideally, there should be no difference between the sacred and the secular within a Moravian community like Bethlehem. I disagree with Dieter Gembicki's statement, "The 'law' stated by sociologists of religion [i.e., Durkheim], on the absolute dichotomy of things sacred and profane, applies to Bethlehem, PA, too."[101] This may apply to Bethlehem after 1762, but not to Bethlehem in the 1740s. The process of moving from *Kairos* to *Chronos* that Gembicki so eloquently describes can be interpreted as a movement from a totally sacralized society to one in which the sacred and secular are clearly distinguished. In other words, it was part of the movement away from Zinzendorf's understanding of the Christian life.

98. Zinzendorf, *Einundzwanzig Diskurse,* ZH 6:2:67; Bettermann, *Theologie und Sprache,* 159.

99. Zinzendorf, *Einundzwanzig Diskurse,* ZH 6:1:51. Bettermann, *Theologie und Sprache,* chap. 10.

100. Zinzendorf, *Kinder Reden,* ZE 6:67:324. Related to this is Zinzendorf's notion that every day should be a Sabbath to the Lord. The Christian life is an "ever continuing Sabbath." Ibid., 77:377.

101. Dieter Gembicki, "From *Kairos* to *Chronos:* Time Perception in Colonial Bethlehem," *Transactions of the Moravian Historical Society* 28 (1994): 48.

THE MOTHER OFFICE OF THE HOLY SPIRIT

August 13, 1727, was understood to be a day of outpouring of the Holy Spirit that formed Herrnhut into a true community of those who had been reborn. Such a revival made sense to both church and radical Pietists in Europe and America. It was an awakening, but Zinzendorf's way of understanding the Holy Spirit that was poured out created great controversy, for he came to the conclusion that the Holy Spirit was the mother of the Gemeine.

This is one of Zinzendorf's most original contributions to the history of Christian thought, but it has not received much notice until recently.[102] This concept has frequently been ridiculed and dismissed as part of the Sifting Time. Again we can quote Hutton: "He gave free rein to his fancy, and came out with an exposition of the Trinity which offended the rules of good taste. He compared the Holy Trinity to a family. The father, said he, was God; the mother was the Holy Ghost; their son was Jesus; and the Church of Christ, the Son's fair bride, was born in the Saviour's Side-wound, was betrothed to Christ on the Cross, was married to Christ in the Holy Communion, and was thus the daughter-in-law of the Father and the Holy Ghost."[103] Bishop Hamilton, in his official history of the Moravian Church, could only bring himself to deal with this matter in a footnote that states, "The designation of the Holy Spirit as our 'Mother' . . . is an illustration of the danger of substituting vivid figures of speech for logical ideas."[104]

Whether or not it is dangerous to call the Spirit "Mother," we see here how the theory of the Sifting Time has caused researchers to overlook key aspects of Moravian life in the Zinzendorf era. Since it has been assumed that this was a brief Zinzendorfian fancy, quickly suppressed, virtually no one has looked for evidence of its use after 1750.[105] It has been treated as tangential to Zinzendorf's theology, but the count insisted that the mother office of the Holy Spirit is "an extremely important and essential point. . . . All our Gemeine and praxis hangs on this point."[106]

Gary Kinkel and Peter Zimmerling have examined the development of Zin-

---

102. For more on the mother office of the Holy Spirit, see Zimmerling, *Gott in Gemeinschaft;* Kinkel, *Our Dear Mother the Spirit.* For a review of the literature on this topic, see Kinkel, 15–30.

103. Hutton, *History of the Moravian Church,* 275.

104. Hamilton and Hamilton, *History,* 657, n. 33. Kinkel, on the contrary, argues "that to the extent one recognizes Luther's teaching about the Holy Spirit to represent or reflect classical Christian trinitarian teaching, one must also recognize Zinzendorf's idea of the motherly office of the Holy Spirit to be an authentic doctrine of classical Christianity." *Our Dear Mother the Spirit.*

105. Thus Kinkel states, "Beginning in about 1750, during Zinzendorf's own lifetime, his communities backed away from this language, apparently concerned about 'excesses,' of which they considered the motherly office of the Spirit one." *Our Dear Mother the Spirit,* 10. Actually, the use of the mother metaphor by the Moravians increased significantly after 1750. It was nearly a decade after the death of Zinzendorf that the community drew back from this practice. Atwood, "Mother of God's People."

106. *Gemeinreden,* ZH 4, Anhang, 2.

zendorf's concept of the "mother office" of the Spirit in the 1730s and 1740s. Both show that Zinzendorf was not discussing the divine essence as somehow gendered, but was attempting to describe God's relationship to humans.[107] Motherhood was connected with the "economic" Trinity. Zinzendorf continued to use male pronouns for the Spirit, but it is awkward in English to refer to a mother as "he"; therefore I will use female pronouns for mother.

Kinkel argues that the mother metaphor was an outgrowth of Zinzendorf's reading of Luther's theology of the Spirit, although Luther himself did not use the word mother.[108] I think Luther was less important for this development than the inner logic of Zinzendorf's own thought. Zimmerling shows that Zinzendorf's understanding of the mother office of the Holy Spirit was closely connected to the rest of Zinzendorf's theology and helped shape the distinctive worship and ecclesiology of the *Brüdergemine*.[109]

The development of this doctrine illustrates how Zinzendorf's commitment to heart religion fueled his theological reflection as he sought ways to make the doctrine of the Holy Spirit "good for the heart." The motherhood of the Spirit was not intended to be creative image building and wordplay, but was the best expression of the reality of God revealed in Scripture and experience.[110] Zinzendorf was confident that those who have not experienced the Spirit as mother cannot understand such language, but those who have the Spirit understand the rightness of the "mother" name intuitively as soon as they hear it because they experience the Spirit as a mother.[111]

Zinzendorf acknowledged that although he knew the words about the Spirit in the various creeds and confessions, he did not understand what the creeds and the theologians were trying to communicate about the Holy Spirit; thus he could not speak or write about it until he developed better metaphors:

I did not understand the deity of the Holy Spirit, and whoever knew me knows that I never spoke of it. There are people who are offended at this and remind me of it, but I could not speak about it, since I did not know how I should define it. I simply believed that he is the third person of the Godhead, but I could not say how this was properly so. Instead I thought of him abstractly. . . . The Holy Spirit had known me well, but I did not know him before the year 1738. That is why I carefully avoided entering in the matter until the Mother Office of the Holy Spirit had been so clearly opened up for me.[112]

Because Zinzendorf held that abstract thought is contrary to religious faith, he could not properly worship or preach about the Spirit until he learned

---

107. Kinkel, *Our Dear Mother the Spirit*, 85–90; Zimmerling, *Gott in Gemeinschaft*, 59–73.
108. Kinkel, *Our Dear Mother the Spirit*, 193–220.
109. Zimmerling, *Gott in Gemeinschaft*, 216–36, 254–58.
110. Ibid., 161–63; cf. Atwood, "Mother of God's People."
111. Zinzendorf, *Gemeinreden*, ZH 4:36:135–36.
112. August Gottlieb Spangenberg, *Apologetische Schluß-Schrifft*, ZE 3:576.

experientially and scripturally what the Spirit meant for the heart. He confessed that he had some difficulty in coming to an adequate understanding of the Spirit, but he defended this slow development, stating, "the theologians have the problem, or the advantage, that they understand everything all at once. Therefore they have no new blessings, but they are perfect as soon as they complete their course of study."[113]

Zinzendorf maintained that he was not the only one who had difficulty in grasping the concept of the Holy Spirit. People have ascribed all kinds of properties to the Holy Spirit without being able to say exactly who she is because of the lack of clear and vivid language. For years, Zinzendorf wrote, "songs have called the Holy Spirit advocate, comforter, intercessor, and . . . titles that contain much nonsense."

For before they regarded her as a finger, a dove, a mirror, and they published, preached, and sang a hundred other foolish fancies about her in which there was no sense and understanding. So now they may rather attain a childlike, simple heart concept of her, since one is better than the others: for the hearty, childlike concept can still bring them to a true, living knowledge and to a feeling of the office of the Holy Spirit in their hearts. But all hieroglyphical, allegorical and transcendental titles . . . only confuse humans and are without the least effect on their heart.[114]

In contrast, those who experience the Trinity in their hearts know that "God is also our dear husband, his Father is our dear Father, and the Holy Spirit is our dear Mother, with that we are complete, with that the family idea is established, the oldest, the simplest, the most respectable, the most endearing idea among all human ideas, the true biblical idea, in the application of the holy Trinity for us, for no one is nearer to one than *Father, Mother, and Husband.*"[115] This was the breakthrough that Zinzendorf experienced in 1738.[116] Even when preaching to non-Moravian audiences in America in 1742, he used maternal language for the Spirit. In his first sermon in Pennsylvania, he boldly stated "that his Father must become our Father and his Mother our Mother," without giving an explanation for such terminology.[117]

113. Ibid.

114. Zinzendorf, *Gemeinreden*, ZH 4, Anhang, 3. He complains of "der dunkeln, unexplicirten, unausgewikkelten art davon zu reden." Ibid., 4:3:52. See also Kinkel, *Our Dear Mother the Spirit,* 95–103.

115. Zinzendorf, *Gemeinreden* ZH 4, Anhang, 3; Kinkel, *Our Dear Mother the Spirit,* 95–96.

116. Becker, *Zinzendorf und sein Christentum,* 400–401, discusses the details on the dating of the origin of Zinzendorf's concept of the Mother Office. Zinzendorf himself gives two separate dates, 1738 and 1741; Spangenberg, *Apologetische Schluß-Schrifft,* ZE 3:576–77. Becker points out that there is a further difficulty in dating, since the first recorded instance of this usage was in a hymn of the Brüdergemeine written in 1736.

117. Zinzendorf, *Pennsylvania Sermons,* 21–22. This raises doubts about Kinkel's assertion that this language was used only within the Moravian community, particularly in light of the fact that the Gemeinreden and the Gesangbücher were published for the public (*Our Dear Mother the Spirit,* 74). Spangenberg first promoted the view that the motherhood of the Spirit was connected to the so-called Sifting Time. *Leben des Herrn Nikolaus Ludwig,* 1573–76.

Having found a name for the Spirit, Zinzendorf was glad to find support for it in the Church Fathers and the tradition.[118] Ultimately, though, tradition was far less important than conformity to the sense of Scripture and the experience of the heart. On both of these counts, he found the metaphor of the mother office to be the best language available.[119]

Zinzendorf argued for the biblical basis of the mother office by linking a verse from the Old Testament (Isa. 66:13) with one from the New Testament (John 14:26).

> By that time the Savior, who was a very great Bible student, had doubtlessly read the verse in the Bible "I will comfort you as a mother comforts one." Then the dear Savior thought, "If I should say to my disciples that I am going away, then I must give them some comfort. I must say to them that they will receive someone who will comfort them over my departure. It will not be strange to them, for they have already read it in the Bible. . . . There it reads, they shall have a Mother: "I will leave you my Spirit."[120]

Many theologians rejected the linking of these two verses and the subsequent naming of the Holy Spirit "mother" based on her motherly activity, but Zinzendorf countered that this should not be a problem for theologians, as it is stated in the Bible.[121]

Although Zinzendorf maintained that his language of motherhood for the Holy Spirit had nothing to do with a feminizing of the Trinity, it is suggestive that he used the example of Anna Nitschmann as a way to describe the work of the Holy Spirit.[122] Nitschmann had been elected an eldress in 1730, when she was only fifteen, and remained the leader of the single women of the Brüdergem-

---

118. E.g., "the church father Victorinus who said, *Non falletur, si quis subintellexerit, Spiritum Sanctum Matrem esse Jesu.*" Spangenberg, *Apologetische Schluß-Schrifft,* ZE 3:577, cf. 3:283. Zinzendorf credits Luther and Francke with helping him come to the understanding of the Holy Spirit as mother; *Gemeinreden* ZH 4:46:251; cf. Becker, *Zinzendorf und sein Christentum,* 400. On patristic and medieval support for maternal images of the deity, see Ritamary Bradley, "Patristic Background of the Motherhood Similitude in Julian of Norwich," *Christian Scholar's Review* 8 (1978): 101–13; Elaine Pagels, "Whatever Happened to God the Mother? Conflicting Images of God in Early Christianity," *Signs: Journal of Women in Culture and Society* 2 (1976): 193–303; and Bynum, *Jesus as Mother,* 110–65.

119. See Zimmerling, *Gott in Gemeinschaft,* 39–67, for a thorough discussion of Zinzendorf's use of Scripture and experience in formulating his understanding of the Trinity; cf. Kinkel, *Our Dear Mother the Spirit,* 134–40.

120. Zinzendorf, *Gemeinreden,* ZH 4:3:64 and 65. He also uses the Song of Solomon as support, but Spangenberg records vigorous disagreement over the exegesis of this passage. Spangenberg, *Apologetische Schluß-Schrift,* ZE 3:79–80.

121. "Now no theologian is irritated if the word 'comfort' is taken out of the passage and applied to the Holy Spirit, for they call him the Comforter. But if we take out the word Mother and signify it to the Holy Spirit, then people are opposed to it. I can find no cause for such disputes and arbitrariness, and therefore I pay no attention to it. For if one passage of the paragraph is devoted to the Holy Spirit, then the title is also devoted to the Holy Spirit." *Gemeinreden,* ZH 4, Anhang, 2. One of the most persuasive critics of this practice of Zinzendorf's was the biblical scholar Albrecht Bengel. See Kinkel, *Our Dear Mother the Spirit,* 110–18, for a summary of Bengel's objections.

122. Dietrich Meyer, *Der Christozentrismus des späten Zinzendorf* (Bern: Herbert Lang, 1973), 61. See Kinkel, *Our Dear Mother the Spirit,* 117–28, for a discussion of mother language and gender.

eine until her marriage to Zinzendorf in 1756. It is intriguing that Mutter Nit-schmann participated in ordination services for women and wore purple, typically a symbol of episcopal office.[123] She was one of the most important female leaders of the international community and was routinely referred to as *Mutter* (mother), as was the Holy Spirit.[124]

Albrecht Bengel in the eighteenth century used this as evidence that Zin-zendorf's use of the word "mother" to describe the Holy Spirit did indeed feminize the Trinity, despite claims to the contrary.[125] Kinkel tries to answer Bengel's objection, using Zinzendorf's insistence that he was not making meta-physical claims about the gender of God, but I have to agree with Aaron Fogle-man that the use of mother language is a feminization of the Trinity.[126] Fogleman is justified in his claim that this contributed to the public, and occa-sionally violent, opposition to the Moravians, but it is important to note that this was just one of many points of bitter controversy.[127] It is also important to recognize that this language also attracted people who found it deeply mean-ingful. Mother language was more than a feminization of the Trinity, it was a way to deepen spirituality.

In Zinzendorf's view, believers may call the Spirit "mother" because of her many types of motherly activity. She was the true mother of Jesus, since she "prepared him in the womb, hovered over him, and finally brought him into the light. She gave him certainly into the arms of his mother, but with invisible hands carried him more than his mother did."[128] However, the Spirit can also be called the mother of all living things, since she has a special role in the ongoing creation of the world.[129] Thus the Holy Spirit is truly the mother of all living beings in a general way.

Therefore the pagans were not wrong in thinking that there was a great

---

123. Vernon Nelson, "The Ordination of Women in the Moravian Church in America in the Eighteeenth Century," *TMDK: Transatlantic Moravian Dialogue Correspondence* 17 (1999): 14–23.

124. There is little scholarly literature on Anna Nitschmann, and the original documents related to her work appear to have been suppressed by church officials after the death of Zinzendorf. See Peter Vogt, "Herrnhuter Schwestern der Zinzendorfzeit als Predigerinnen," *Unitas Fratrum* 45–46 (1999): 28–60, esp. 51; Peter Vogt, "A Voice for Themselves: Women as Participants in Congregational Discourse in the Eighteenth-Century Moravian Movement," in *Women Preachers and Prophets Through Two Millennia of Christianity*, ed. Beverly M. Kienzle and Pamela J. Walker (Berkeley and Los Angeles: University of California Press, 1998), 227–47. Cf. Peter Zimmerling, "Zinzendorfs Bild der Frau," *Unitas Fratrum* 45–46 (1999): 9–27; Otto Utten-dörfer, *Zinzendorf und die Frauen: Kirchliche Frauenrechte vor 200 Jahren* (Herrnhut, 1919). On the repression of women's leadership after the death of Zinzendorf, see Paul Peucker, "Gegen ein Regiment von Schwestern: Die Stellung der Frau in der Brüdergemeine nach Zinzendorfs Tod," *Unitas Fratrum* 45–46 (1999): 61–72.

125. Kinkel, *Our Dear Mother the Spirit*, 117ff.

126. Fogleman, "'Jesus ist weiblich,'" 171–74.

127. Ibid., 189–94; Wagner, *Zinzendorf-Muhlenberg Encounter*, 66–68.

128. Zinzendorf, *Gemeinreden*, ZH 4:27:371.

129. "It is known that the Holy Spirit brings everything to life, and when a human was made from a clump of earth (and from that one blood the entire human race on the globe was derived by and by), the Holy Spirit was very near by the breathing of the breath of God into the man." Zinzendorf, *Wünden Reden* 7:75. She is thus the mother of "all living beings, in the vegitative sense." *Gemeinreden*, ZH 4:36:135.

goddess and earth mother, Zinzendorf claimed. This was simply a "dark idea" of the truth, a mere inkling of the divine reality. "People had a vague idea in ancient times, before the incarnation of the Savior, that the Holy Spirit is such a special nurse-mother to humans . . . that she was the proper Mother of all souls, the *Chava* [Eve] of souls, the Mother of all the living. It was, however, vague and equivocable."[130]

The Holy Spirit is the mother in a third and more important sense: she is the Mother of the church and all those who have been reborn. Zinzendorf based this understanding of the Spirit giving birth to converted souls in large part on Jesus' conversation with Nicodemus in John 3. Jesus told Nicodemus that he must be born again, not from his mother's womb, but from God. According to Zinzendorf, Jesus told Nicodemus that we are spiritually born from a mother, not a father.[131]

The Holy Spirit, then, is the mother in the sense that she is the active agent in conversion. The Spirit works to prepare souls for the reception of the gospel and is the true preacher of Christ.[132] Conversion and the formation of the Christian community are both activities of the Holy Spirit, not of human beings.[133]

The Spirit also gathers the children of God into a single, universal community that is under her special care. This house of God will remain until eternity because the "Church Mother" *(Kirche-Mutter)* protects "the Savior's household here on the earth" just as an earthly mother protects her own home. When Jesus left the earth, he placed the mother in charge of his church, just as a man on a trip leaves his wife in charge of the estate.[134]

The Holy Spirit also creates a community, dispensing her gifts as she sees best. At Pentecost, she came upon 120 people and anointed them to the apostolic office. Through that action, "an equality in the teaching office between the sisters and brothers" was made that has not stopped.[135] The Spirit works through human agents in the community, such as the elders and eldresses, who

---

130. Zinzendorf, *Gemeinreden,* ZH 4:27:369.

131. Ibid., 46:254.

132. Kinkel, *Our Dear Mother the Spirit,* 141–74.

133. "[The Holy Spirit] makes the soul acknowledge that she would not have received the wounds, and would not have gotten to know her redeemer, that she would never have understood the article regarding redemption and reconciliation, if the Holy Spirit had not preached to her through unknown means." *Gemeinreden,* ZH 4:35:113.

134. Zinzendorf, *Gemeinreden,* ZH 4:40:197–98 and 4:3:66; *Einundzwanzig Diskurse,* ZH 6:8:155. No doubt when saying this Zinzendorf had in mind his wife, Erdmuth, who was manager of his own estates. Zimmerling, "Zinzendorfs Bild der Frau," 29–21. For the life of Erdmuth, see Erika Geiger, *Erdmuth Dorothea Gräfin von Zinzendorf: Die 'Hausmutter' der Herrnhuter Brüdergemeine* (Holzgerling: Hännsler, 2000), which appears in an abridged English version as *Countess Erdmuth Dorothea von Zinzendorf: 300th Anniversary of Her Birth,* trans. Irene Geiger (Niesky: Gudrun Schiewe, 2000).

135. Zinzendorf, *Gemeinreden,* ZH 4:32:69 and 4:34:91.

are attentive to all and examine them for signs of spiritual disease.[136] This is particularly true when it comes to the sacraments. "I consider our dear Mother to be the proper consecrator and transformer in this sacrament."[137]

In short, for Zinzendorf, the mother Spirit cares for her spiritual children as a human mother cares for her physical children. This includes protecting, guiding, admonishing, and comforting the children of God throughout the changing years of their earthly lives. Just as a human mother teaches her child proper ways of behaving by saying, "My child, you must do it this way, [and] you must not do that," so too does the Holy Spirit teach believers.[138] "The Mother who is over all mothers [says], 'I will comfort you. I will remind you. I will lift you up. I will advise you. I will wean you from all rudeness and uncivil things. I will make a well-bred child out of you, better than any mother does in all the world.'"[139]

This school of the Holy Spirit is not like any human educational institution because it is "a family school, that is a school on the lap, in the arms of the eternal Mother" who tenderly loves her children.[140] When a child believes in the Savior, "Then it sits on the Mother's lap, is received into the school, and is led through all classes; then it is under the special dispensation, under the motherly regimen of the Holy Spirit, who comforts, punishes, and kisses the heart, as a mother comforts, punishes, and kisses her own child."[141]

The idea of the Spirit as mother demonstrates clearly Zinzendorf's application of religion of the heart and his understanding of the Christian community. The image of the mother is clear and evocative. It was also useful in developing an inclusive, intimate community that was intended to be an earthly reflection of the heavenly community.[142] Zinzendorf's heart religion, with its emphasis on spiritual formation and experience, depended on personal intimacy with other Christians and daily devotion to God. Herrnhut, and later Bethlehem, were important manifestations of this "lap school" of the Spirit.

THE LANGUAGE OF THE HEART

In order to appreciate eighteenth-century Moravian religion, it is necessary to understand Zinzendorf's view of religious language. In contrast to philosophi-

---

136. Zinzendorf, *Kinder Reden*, ZE 6:41:201.

137. Zinzendorf, *Einundzwanzig Diskurse*, ZH 6:8:166–67.

138. Zinzendorf, *Gemeinreden*, ZH 4, Anhang, 4. See also Kinkel, *Our Dear Mother the Spirit*, 174–82.

139. Zinzendorf, *Gemeinreden*, ZH 4, Anhang, 12–13. Notice the emphasis on noble decorum here. The child of God is not only raised to be moral but also "well-bred."

140. Zinzendorf, *Gemeinreden*, ZH 4:27:375.

141. Ibid., 3:71.

142. I am in agreement with Kinkel that Zinzendorf's metaphor of the mother spirit was connected to spiritual formation in the communities, as will be shown in the specific case of Bethlehem (*Our Dear Mother the Spirit*, 74–78).

cal and mystical language, the language of the heart is simple and affective. According to Zinzendorf, the Brüdergemeine does not waste time on "double-meaning written words or dark prophecies and allegorical speeches," but instead has "the privilege of simplicity."[143] The more the heart rules the head, the more clear and understandable concepts become.

Zinzendorf had great contempt for those who made overly subtle distinctions and dealt in abstractions that even they did not understand. "The stupidest people can learn to repeat things which they do not understand, and the learned, sharp-witted people trouble themselves to learn to understand the most subtle things and to speak of them, but the more simplicity there is, the more the matter is grasped by simplicity."[144]

Heart language has a holistic and unmediated quality, while rational language is always analytical and mediated. In putting a heart experience into speech, one can lose the experience itself, especially if inappropriate language is used.[145] Zinzendorf said he was loath to explain liturgies and hymns to those who do not understand them, because liturgical language is a heart language that communicates the most profound truths directly to the heart and the understanding. If one has to explain it, then something is lacking either in the hymns or in the heart of the hearer.[146]

Litanies and hymns are the most appropriate way, therefore, to express faith. Zinzendorf reminded children that singing has been a natural expression of heart religion since the days of Moses, Miriam, Deborah, and David.[147] With such singing "come beautiful thoughts and blessed expressions into the heart; nourishment that comes indeed from the Savior himself."[148] Music is the natural response to salvation, since singing comes from the heart. But it is better to be quiet than to sing about something you do not believe or have not experienced. "Light-minded singing," Zinzendorf warned, is a grave sin.[149]

For Zinzendorf, the Bible is also an expression of heart religion rather than dogma, and it is a great mistake to get caught up in the mere words of the Bible.[150] It does not speak objectively as a uniform and authoritative expression

---

143. Zinzendorf, *Gemeinreden*, ZH 4:3:53–54.

144. Ibid., Part 2, Intro., 2 (unnumbered).

145. In Zinzendorf's terms, an explanation of religious language runs the danger of "cooking out the juice and strength," as such expressions are intended for the heart, not the understanding. *Wundenlitanei Homilien*, ZH 3:1:2. It appears to me that Zinzendorf is attempting to ground religious discourse as separate from all other discourse, such as Kierkegaard would later attempt to do.

146. Ibid., 1:1. Zinzendorf goes on to say, however, that there are times when such explanations are necessary, since some members of the community have misconceptions.

147. Zinzendorf, *Kinder Reden*, ZE 6, *Vorerinnerung*.

148. Ibid., 9:42.

149. Ibid., 72:354–56. For more on the use of music in Moravian worship, see C. Daniel Crews, "Die Stellung der Musik im gottesdienstlichen Leben der Brüdergemeine," *Unitas Fratrum* 47 (2000): 12–28, and C. Daniel Crews, *Zinzendorf: The Theology of Song* (Winston-Salem, N.C.: Moravian Archives, 1999).

150. Bettermann, *Theologie und Sprache*, 14–17.

of a single viewpoint. Like everything else this side of the eschaton, the Bible is *catoprisches* (in a mirror) and partial.[151] For instance, the prophets received dark and confusing revelations, and "even they had no clear concept of it in the understanding, but only a heart concept *[Herz-Begriff].*"[152]

Furthermore, the Bible includes a number of individual voices speaking out of their own experience; therefore the personal histories and personalities of the biblical authors shape their expression of revelation.[153] Zinzendorf openly acknowledged that the Bible is flawed in its historical details and lacks the artificial beauty of the classics, but this only proves that it is true to God's purpose and to human life.[154] Zinzendorf argued that it was a terrible error, perhaps even a sin, to try to force the Bible to speak with a single voice, or to "improve" it. "The fact that the Bible has so many errors (scarcely a book today would be published with as many), is, for me at least, an unassailable proof for its divinity. Why? It was so much the desire of the Lord that not a syllable in the divine teaching of the Holy Scriptures be altered."[155]

Zinzendorf brought together the many strands of heart religion into a single biblical image: the child (Matt. 18:31).[156] He thought that children were the living embodiment of his ideal of simplicity of heart, because they do not have to overcome the opposition of their reason and education in order to embrace the Savior in genuine love.[157] They also do right without any concept of wrong.

It is true that they must learn and grow, but Zinzendorf saw it as unfortunate that as they grow they lose their simple, innocent, and graceful immediacy. In fact, one could describe the goal of the Christian life as reclaiming lost innocence, the innocence of both Eden and childhood. "Oh! If only I had remained a child! If I could have always proceeded from grace! If I knew nothing other than what a child knows."[158] Christians should remember what they learned in the cradle.[159]

---

151. Zinzendorf, *Gemeinreden*, ZH 4:1:3. Zinzendorf's rejection of an analytical approach to the Bible in favor of a narrative and affective approach may indicate that he is simply pre-critical; however, he was very much aware of contemporary criticism and was accused of undermining confidence in the Bible by pointing out its many flaws. *Wündenlitanei Homilien*, ZH 3:33:336. For more on hermeneutics, see Freeman, *An Ecumenical Theology of the Heart*, 124–52.

152. Zinzendorf, *Gemeinreden*, ZH 4, Anhang 2, 18.

153. Zinzendorf, *Wundenlitanei Homilien*, ZH 3:15:145. Even errors in astronomy were tolerated by the Holy Spirit; Spangenberg, *Apologetische Schluß Schrift*, ZE 3:146.

154. "Therefore it is a great thing that the Holy Scripture was brought together with a great heavenly wisdom out of a hundred pieces, and their proper purpose is not at all to run together a series of thoughts in a flowing connection, like a system. Instead it [concerns] faith matters which concern the ground point of our blessedness and way of life." *Gemeinreden*, ZH 4, part 2, Intro., 2–3 (unnumbered). In Bettermann's judgment, "The many historical mistakes of the scriptures are to him [Zinzendorf] a sign of their divine truth, because here human ambition which always must improve and correct until no one can find any more fault with the book fails" (*Theologie und Sprache*, 17).

155. Zinzendorf, *Wünden Reden* 15, ZH 3:144.

156. E.g., *Gemeinreden*, ZH 4:5:105.

157. Zinzendorf, *Kinder Reden* ZE 6:5:21–22.

158. Ibid., 11:57.

159. Ibid., 5:23.

Zinzendorf also stressed the dependent nature of childhood. All of children's emotional and physical needs are taken care of by others, and they can live joyfully in the love of Christ. This is the proper condition for the Christian who lives in and by grace. All of life must be a liturgy and a daily intercourse with the Savior *(tägliche Umgehen mit dem Heiland)*.[160] God is to be the center and sum of a believer's life, just as a mother is the center of an infant's life. The Moravians were to live and move and have their being in God alone (Acts 17:28).[161] The residents of Bethlehem used their minds and bodies to create a vibrant community in the wilderness while attempting to maintain a childlike faith in their Savior.

THE EXPANSION AND DECLINE OF ZINZENDORF'S PROGRAM

One of the important events in the expansion of the Moravian Church was the curious affair of Jesus being selected as Chief Elder of the church on September 16, 1741, an event still celebrated in the Moravian Church.[162] The story is often repeated, and the details remain somewhat obscure, but a few words may be helpful here. The event took place in London during a meeting of the leadership of the Church, including such figures as Anna Nitschmann. Leonard Dober, the first missionary to St. Thomas, had been serving in the office of Chief Elder and was feeling overwhelmed by the burdens of office. Previously he had asked to be relieved of his duties and the lot had refused his request.

On September 16, the lot agreed. Unfortunately, none of the names selected as a replacement was approved by the lot. Finally, on Zinzendorf's suggestion, they asked if Jesus was reserving this office for himself. The lot answered that he was, and so he was officially proclaimed Chief Elder on November 13, 1741 (giving time for the news to reach all of the communities). Interestingly, this did not apply to America until 1748.

It is hard to know how one should interpret this event, but the Moravians in Zinzendorf's time took it as divine sanction for their work and evidence of a special relationship with Christ. It encouraged the growing understanding that the Gemeine was to be a theocracy ruled by Christ through his chosen agents and the lot. It also gave the Moravians courage for the rapid expansion of the church during the 1740s.

The 1740s and 1750s were the high-water mark for Zinzendorf and his Brüdergemeine. Missions were established on five continents and diaspora work spread over much of central and northern Europe. Early in the 1740s he made an eighteen-month visit to Pennsylvania and New York, where he attempted to establish an ecumenical synod for German-speaking Christians.

160. Ibid., 4:17; 10:53.
161. Hamilton and Hamilton, *History*, 68–75; Beyreuther, *Zinzendorf und die Christenheit*, 207–9.
162. Hamilton and Hamilton, *History*, 77ff.

Furthermore, in 1746 and 1747 the Saxon court reconsidered the count's banishment from Saxony. The king of Saxony even visited Herrnhut and was impressed by the industry and order of the community. In October 1747 the order of banishment was removed, and Zinzendorf was able to return home.[163] In 1748 the community of Barby was established on the Elbe and the theological seminary was soon moved there. Zinzendorf established a permanent base of operations in England, and in 1749, with the help of James Hutton and General Oglethorp, was able to secure full recognition for the Unitas Fratrum as "an antient and episcopal church" within British lands.[164]

By 1749 the Brüdergemeine was a vigorous international movement and Zinzendorf was a European-wide celebrity. This was also the period of Zinzendorf's greatest literary activity. He produced a prodigious number of hymns, litanies, and sermons between 1745 and 1755. The Moravians published much of Zinzendorf's work, often with little editing by Zinzendorf. The works from this period show the full development of Zinzendorf's theology of the heart, and its contrast to the rational and moralistic language common in his day.

But 1749 was a year of crisis as well as victory. At about the same time that the Unitas Fratrum was recognized by Parliament, it came to Zinzendorf's attention that there were problems in the life and devotion of the Single Brothers in Herrnhaag, the flagship community of the Brüdergemeine.[165] The dissolution of Herrnhaag and the resulting debt crisis of the early 1750s nearly destroyed the movement. The church managed to separate its finances from Zinzendorf's, but it took decades to recover from the debt incurred in the 1740s.[166] The financial crisis forced the church to scale back its global vision. Interestingly, though, despite the real threat of bankruptcy, the church made its boldest venture by purchasing 100,000 acres of land in North Carolina to start a new colony.

In 1756 Erdmuth Dorothea, Zinzendorf's wife of more than forty years and chief financial administrator of his estates, died. Zinzendorf went through a period of depression, but, at the urging of his closest advisors, in 1757 he married his longtime co-worker and companion, Anna Nitschmann.[167] They eventually settled in Herrnhut, where both died in 1760. Losing both "Papa" and "Mutter" within a few weeks was a severe blow to the movement.

The next two decades were spent in trying to institutionalize Zinzendorf's

---

163. Weinlick, *Count Zinzendorf*, 194–95. It is worth noting that this was during the so-called Sifting Time.
164. Podmore, *Moravian Church in England*, 226–65.
165. See Introduction; Atwood, "Zinzendorf's 1749 Reprimand."
166. Hamilton and Hamilton, *History*, 107–12, 165, 178. See Podmore, *Moravian Church in England*, 266–83.
167. Weinlick, *Count Zinzendorf*, 224–28; Spangenberg, *Leben des Herrn Nikolaus Ludwig*, 2058–59, 2103–4.

charisma while moving the church to more traditional Lutheran theological expressions, in part to calm the fears of creditors. One of the key figures in this transition was August Gottlieb Spangenberg, the head of the Bethlehem Gemeine. Before discussing Bethlehem, however, it is necessary to examine the most important and controversial aspect of Zinzendorf's theology: his understanding of Christ and the Crucifixion.

FIGURE 3. August Gottlieb Spangenberg (1704–1792). Leader of the Bethlehem community. Ölgemälde im Unitätsarchiv. Unity Archives, Herrnhut.

CHAPTER 3

THE BODY OF CHRIST

Having seen how Zinzendorf developed his religion of the heart in the context of his own experience, it is easier to understand his approach to Jesus Christ. The person of Jesus was the object of heart religion, but Zinzendorf's devotion to Jesus was quite different from that of his Protestant contemporaries and of present-day Moravians. It was far more intense and central to his whole religious program.

The basic feature of Zinzendorf's theology, his Christocentrism, was evident in his childhood, but the period 1727–44, from the signing of the Brotherly Agreement and subsequent revival on August 13 to his return from America, was crucial for the full development of his doctrine of Christ.[1] During this period the Moravian Church also began its phenomenal mission enterprise, developed the Ortsgemeine concept, and attracted thousands of converts and supporters.[2] Zinzendorf's Christology and the mission of the Moravian Church went hand in hand.

CHRIST JEHOVAH

Zinzendorf rejected devotion to the invisible, unknowable God of the abyss promoted by Meister Eckhart. Mystical and philosophical language for God, such as the Cause of Causes or the One or the Nothing, held little attraction for Zinzendorf.[3] The source of being was shrouded in such a thick "cloud of unknowing" that no one could relate to this God. The God of the philosophers was also too awesome and frightening for mortals to love. Jesus Christ was a different matter, however.

From all these three things: [1] from not knowing God; [2] from the dangerous familiarity with the bottomless abyss over which one would have plunged into the darkness, into places horrid and ghastly, into the horrifying eternity, before which mortal philosophers

---

1. Zimmerling, *Gott in Gemeinschaft,* 27–38.
2. Hamilton and Hamilton, *History,* 34–127.
3. Zinzendorf, *Wundenlitanei Homilien,* ZH 3:1:7. For a comprehensive treatment of Zinzendorf and medieval mysticism, see Uttendörfer, *Zinzendorf und die Mystik.* Beyreuter perceptively deals with Zinzendorf's use of mystical language in developing his version of Luther's theology of the cross. Beyreuther, *Studien zur Theologie,* 21–22.

have also trembled; and finally [3] from the same childish worship which intelligent people (who do not think widely enough and do not understand the reality of it) untimely mock. From all these we have been freed by the blessedly happy thought that our Creator became a human and that the divine essence has finally, after a long wait, assembled an image. Therefore we can rejoice forever.[4]

For Zinzendorf, the most important idea in Christianity was that Christ became human. People saw him, touched him, and recorded his words. Unlike the Father, Christ remains concrete and accessible to the human heart and mind, even the mind of a child. "My child, you will see him, and when you see him, he will look like you. About seventeen hundred and twenty years ago, he was born a human just as you are."[5] Jesus was not an abstraction but a concrete entity with whom one could be in relation. Jesus is God in relationship to humankind; God made manifest on earth.

This childhood conviction became the foundation for Zinzendorf's understanding of the Trinity. Zinzendorf has sometimes been accused of being a "Unitarian of Christ" or a "Christomonist" rather than a Trinitarian, but Zimmerling demonstrates convincingly that Zinzendorf developed a consistent Trinitarian theology based on the Incarnation.[6] Unlike many theologians, such as Aquinas or Anselm, who begin with a concept of the impassability and perfection of God taken from Greek philosophy, Zinzendorf began his thinking about God with Jesus Christ.[7] He accepted as truthful the early church's proclamation that Jesus was both fully human and fully divine. Zinzendorf used the Apostles' Creed, the Nicene Creed, the so-called Athanasian Creed (the *Quincumque vult*), and the Augsburg Confession, but he went beyond the traditional understanding of the creeds in promoting the full humanity and full divinity of Christ.[8]

The Incarnation was so essential to Zinzendorf's theology that he tolerated no diminution of this reality. The Son is the *only* mediator between the deity and humankind. Christ is "God your Creator, God your Redeemer and Sancti-

4. Zinzendorf, *Wundenlitanei Homilien*, ZH 3:2:19–20. We can hear echoes of Pascal's *Pensees* and the rejection of the "God of the philosophers" here. Freeman connects Zinzendorf's understanding that the Son is the one who reveals the Trinity to Zinzendorf's struggle against rationalism (*An Ecumenical Theology of the Heart*, 79–84). For Zimmerling, this was Zinzendorf's way of defending the idea of biblical revelation and the doctrine of the Atonement from Deism. *Gott in Gemeinschaft*, 32–33.

5. Zinzendorf, *Kinder Reden*, ZE 6:69:363. For Zinzendorf's anthropomorphism, see Beyreuther, *Studien zur Theologie*, 22–23.

6. Zimmerling, *Gott in Gemeinschaft*, esp. 137–46. On the charge of "Christomonism," see H. Schmidt, H. Bintz, and W. Günther, eds., "Protokoll des Gespächs zwischen Professor Karl Barth und Vertretern der Brüdergemeine am 12. Oktober 1960 in Basel," *Civitas Prasens*, no. 13, special issue (1961): 3.

7. Zinzendorf claims that the devil wants people to think "Platonisch," "Pythagorisch," or "Socratisch" about God and wonder at subtle metaphysical distinctions. *Gemeinreden*, ZH 4:3:59. Zimmerling's assertion that Zinzendorf overturns traditional dogamtics is sound. *Gott in Gemeinschaft*, 35ff.

8. He is particularly critical of the Apostles' Creed, which he recognized was not written by the Apostles themselves. *Einundzwanzig Diskurse*, ZH 6:2:61.

fier, indeed your God and, at the same time, your mediator between the deity and humankind."[9] The Son of God is not an emanation of God, a part of God, or a demigod, but is God in all of God's reality. Echoing the theology of the Greek Fathers, especially Athanasius, Zinzendorf preached, "Since we could not become like God, he became as we are."[10] This idea of deification is unusual in Western Christianity, but it is fundamental in Eastern Orthodoxy.[11]

The Son is the *Archon,* and the Incarnation involved no loss of divinity. According to Zinzendorf, when Christ "emptied himself and took on the form of a servant" (Phil. 2), "he did not empty himself of divinity but only of his majesty and his divine office, his government of the world, for the moment."[12] The Son offered up to the Father his authority over the cosmos and became a person like any other, but he still remained God. He forgot his divinity while on earth, as if he were asleep and dreaming.

He made himself at home in his human clothing so that he does not appear to be longing for the immeasurable greatness, according to the majesty of the holy God which is his own and is still inseparable from him and which he must now rightly feel and accept. For here in time he had loosed himself from it. He had laid it away and forgotten it. He had put it to sleep, as one sleeps and at the same time forgets in sleep, that he is the God of the earth . . . so he had actually spent some 30 years as in a dream.[13]

True to his rejection of theological speculation, Zinzendorf did not enter into ancient Christological debates about *how* Jesus was God and human but simply affirmed the Chalcedonian declaration that it is true.[14] He blamed confusion over the Trinity and Incarnation on the arrogance of humans who attempt to delve into secrets of God.

Zinzendorf's approach to the Trinity had practical application in ecumenical efforts. For instance, in 1740 the patriarch of Constantinople, Neophytus, sent a letter that affirmed the orthodoxy of the Moravian Church to all of the metropolitans of the Eastern Orthodox Church. In his view, the Moravian Church held to the ancient faith.[15] In light of this affirmation from the Greek Orthodox patriarch, it is very interesting that a non-Chalcedonian church, the

9. Ibid., 66. For more on Zinzendorf's understanding that Christ is the Creator, see Beyreuther, *Studien zur Theologie,* 11–15.

10. "Wir konnten nicht werden wie GOtt, so ist Er worden wie wir." *Gemeinreden,* ZH 4:39:189.

11. Jaroslav Pelikan, *The Spirit of Eastern Christendom,* vol. 2 of *The Christian Tradition* (Chicago: University of Chicago Press, 1989).

12. Zinzendorf, *Einundzwanzig Diskurse,* ZH 6:5:121–22; *Gemeinreden,* ZH 4:4:89–90.

13. Zinzendorf, *Gemeinreden,* ZH 4:4:90–91.

14. Zinzendorf, *Einundzwanzig Diskurse,* ZH 6:2:68–69; cf. ibid., 5:117–18.

15. *Acta Fratrum Unitatis in Anglia,* 35–36, 48–49; cf. ZE 8, *Büdingishe Sämmlung,* 1–2. Arvid Gradin, the emissary from Herrnhut, felt obliged to return the letter since it implied full acceptance of Orthodox doctrine.

Coptic Church, also affirmed the orthodoxy of Zinzendorf's teaching. Mark, the patriarch of the Coptic Church, commended the Moravian Church for adhering to "the simple doctrine of the Apostles, without mingling in the controversies which afterwards arose."[16]

According to Zinzendorf, the Incarnation is a great mystery, but it is nonetheless true that when Jesus suffered and died on the cross, God died on the cross. "The Savior . . . who is God and human in one person and indeed in such a hypostatical union that one can say, 'God has suffered.' In preference to this truth one can and may excuse the hard expression that has even been used in the church, 'God himself is dead, He has died on the cross.' "[17]

Zinzendorf defended himself from charges of promoting the *Patripassism* heresy (that the Father suffered on the cross) by affirming that it was not the Father who suffered and died but the Son; however, the Son is also fully and completely God. Zinzendorf states that the eternal Father certainly did not die, but in a mysterious way God experienced death through Jesus, who did die. Thus it is a misunderstanding of the unity of the Trinity and the reality of the Incarnation to deny that God suffered on the cross.[18]

Zinzendorf asserted that the Son is not merely divine, he is actually Jehovah, the God of the Old Testament. "And then he [Christ] says to them: it is true, there is only one maker of all creatures, who is and remains I. The entire Old Testament is about me."[19] Christ is not simply found allegorically or typologically in the Old Testament, as (for example) the rock in the wilderness (1 Cor. 10:4; Heb. 5:6): Christ is God in the Old Testament.

Zinzendorf had reached this conclusion at least by 1742. The first of his published Pennsylvania sermons treats this subject extensively. "In the Old Testament people knew about no other God at all except our Lord Jesus, who at that time was called Jehovah."[20] Every mention of God, every theophany, every prophecy in the Old Testament is of Christ. Christ is the Creator of the universe. Christ is the one who made the covenants with the patriarchs, gave Moses the law, and spoke through the prophets.[21] The Creator was incarnate in Jesus. This may be Zinzendorf's most radical rethinking of traditional Christian doctrine, and it is absolutely central to his theology and interpretation of scripture.

16. Cranz, *Ancient and Modern History of the Brethren*, 491. For Zinzendorf's view of Athanasius, see Beyreuther, *Studien zur Theologie*, 27.

17. Zinzendorf, *Einundzwanzig Diskurse*, ZH 6:2:65. Zinzendorf maintained this perspective throughout his career. As late as 1756 he could preach that the God who made heaven and earth died on the cross for us. *Kinder Reden*, ZE 6:70:349.

18. Zinzendorf, *Einundzwanzig Diskurse*, ZH 6:2:64.

19. Zinzendorf, *Gemeinreden*, ZH 4:3:59. See Beyreuther, *Studien zur Theologie*, 22–24; Zimmerling, *Gott in Gemeinschaft*, 74–85.

20. Zinzendorf, *Pennsylvania Sermons*, First Sermon, 19.

21. Zinzendorf, *Gemeinreden*, ZH 4:35:109.

Indeed, when they [the theologians] ask us for a single axiom from which we derive with our doctrine all other principles; when they ask us for the two chief lines of the Bible without which the Bible is and remains a chaos of nonsense; when they ask I say, the two chief propositions upon which scriptural doctrine stands and falls: the first is that there is a Savior, and the second is that the Savior is the Creator. . . . The Creator had entered into our sinful nature, truly poor and despised, for thirty years and finally was slaughtered in order to be the ransom for us and for the whole world.[22]

The doctrine of salvation is simply this: "Your Creator is your Savior" *(dein Schöpfer ist dein Heiland).*[23]

Zinzendorf reported that he arrived at this conviction at an early age. It was the center not only of his theology but also of his piety, and he defended it on biblical grounds.[24] The first chapter of the Gospel of John clearly paints Jesus as the preexistent *logos* who is the creative force in the universe. Christ was not simply present with God at creation; Christ was the active agent in creation. In addition, Zinzendorf accepted the tradition that Isaiah 9:6 is a messianic prophecy, but he focused on the idea that the messiah would be called "almighty God, the everlasting Father, the Prince of Peace." Therefore the messiah is none other than the everlasting Father.

Zinzendorf points to other passages of the New Testament that explicitly or implicitly identify Christ as the Creator (e.g., Heb. 1:8–9, and especially Col. 1:16) in order to show that those who deny that Christ is the Creator are denying the plain truth of Scripture.[25]

When challenged on this idea, Zinzendorf offered an interesting biblical argument. He agreed with modern biblical scholars that the Gospel of John was indeed the last to be written, but he argued that this makes it superior to the others because the Holy Spirit had more time to reveal the truth about Jesus as God.[26] Furthermore, he continually asserted that no creed, not even the Apostles' Creed, could contradict the plain evidence of Scripture.[27]

Zinzendorf's study of church history at Halle and Wittenberg confirmed his belief in Christ as the Creator. Those who challenge this idea "are not aware

22. Ibid., 37:153–54.

23. This frequently repeated phrase of Zinzendorf's is seen, for example, in *Gemeinreden,* ZH 4:33:88 (1747), and *Kinder Reden,* ZE 6:58:287 (1756).

24. Zinzendorf, *Kinder Reden,* ZE 6:84:411–12; Beyreuther, *Studien zur Theologie,* 11–12.

25. Zinzendorf, *Pennsylvania Sermons,* Sermon 1.

26. Beyreuther, *Studien zur Theologie,* 38; Zinzendorf, *Einundzwanzig Diskurse,* ZH 6:4:101.

27. "The article for today is taken for the most part from the so-called Apostles' Creed, concerning which there is no real doubt in our day that the Apostles did not write it, but it is an ancient and for the most part beautiful creed, and it has preserved a great wisdom and truth about God, (but unfortunately it had one or more than one author who were schoolmen, and who on the one hand had the fancy of dividing the Trinity into the Creator and the Redeemer and the Sanctifier, and who in particular knew nothing much about the Holy Spirit, as one can see from the short, truncated line which concerns him." *Einundzwanzig Diskurse,* ZH 6:4:92–93; cf. August Gottlieb Spangenberg, *Antworten,* ZE 5:50–56.

that it has been sung now for two, three, four, and five hundred years in Greek, Latin, and German in all Christian churches."[28] The doctrine of Christ as Creator was so important to Zinzendorf that he dared publicly to disagree with the Apostle Paul, who in 1 Cor. 15:24 subordinates the Son to the Father.[29]

Since the Savior is the Creator, there is no separation between creation and redemption. The same God who made human creatures also came to redeem them. It was part of the divine plan from eternity. "He thought about us when we still could not think; he promised us himself into eternity . . . that he as the Creator Jesus Christ would enflesh himself as a man."[30] This is the source of all blessedness, that the creature has been redeemed by the Creator. "Whoever can say 'Jehovah Elohim, who has created mankind and all things, whose handiwork we are, who is exalted above all heavens, is my Saviour, is my infant Jesus in the womb, in the cradle and in the temple.' Such a person is an angelic, heavenly and divine man."[31]

The Creator did not send his son to be a child sacrifice for the world; the Creator of the heavens and earth became a creature and died for the creation. This idea radicalizes the concept of God, making it impossible to view God from any perspective other than that of the cross. Moreover, it means that all souls belong to Christ who has redeemed them, even the hospital prostitutes in London.[32]

Christ as the Creator thus formed the basis for Zinzendorf's world mission that was put into effect in 1732. No race, no people, no nation is automatically excluded from the offer of salvation. Humans still have to choose to accept Christ, though. "*Whoever hears it; in whoever's heart, 'Why do you want to die?' rings,* 'No, I do not want to die. I want to live. I want to be with the Savior. I do not want to let his precious blood be shed in vain for me. I want to experience it in my heart.' To that one, the answer is given immediately, 'Yes, Amen!'"[33]

Not only is Christ the God of the Old Testament, he is the only God experienced by the world. His office *(Amt)* is to be the unique bridge between the

---

28. *Gemeinreden,* ZH 4:36:134. He even offers as evidence the fact that around the year 800 official documents were dated in number of years after the "birth of God" *(im Jahr na GOttes Geborte). Einundzwanzig Diskurse,* ZH 6:19:309. Incidentally, Discourse 19 reveals a fairly sophisticated historical sense.

29. Zinzendorf, *Einundzwanzig Diskurse,* ZH 6:4:96.

30. Zinzendorf, *Gemeinreden* ZH 4, Anhang, 34.

31. Zinzendorf, *Nine Public Lectures,* 49.

32. Ibid., 4. He did, however, reject universal salvation on the grounds that it undermines evangelism. See *Einundzwanzig Diskurse,* ZH 6:10:194–98, esp. 197: "I have also observed that most ministers who believe in the eternal gospel (and more believe it than it seems) are false people who do not perform their office, for when they see that they produce nothing with their preaching in this time, they comfort themselves with the future redemption."

33. Zinzendorf, *Pennsylvania Sermons,* Supplement, 116. The question here comes from God. When the soul gives the response "I want to live," God gives his "Amen."

Triune God and the world. He is the mediator and "the actor between God and people." People may think that this Creator is God the Father or a monotheistic God, but in truth it is the Son of God who made them.[34]

According to Zinzendorf, the devil has tried to pervert this knowledge of Christ. Before the Incarnation, Satan used idolatry, polytheism, and paganism to resist the true knowledge of God, but these methods have failed since the Incarnation. Since then, the devil has used a different tactic to keep people from the knowledge of God. He tries now to make them all strict monotheists, like the Deists. "The devil focuses on the Unity and no more on multiplicity. . . . Now he delights in making all people Deists. He no longer brings them a cat or an ox to pray to; now even a wild person in the American wilderness is so shrewd that he knows they are nothing."[35] Preaching must overcome this natural Deism because people may think they are saved when they are not.

Without experiencing the Savior as the Creator, a person is really an atheist, regardless of whether he or she claims a belief in the Creator. "One must pray to the right God, otherwise one is not God-fearing." Thus the Christian dispute with the Socinians is not really over the Trinity; it is over "who is the only God. The only God . . . is Jesus Christ whom we preach. The only God of the world is he who made the world and who is also the one who hung on the cross."[36] Instead of trying to convince people that there is a God who made them, one has to show them that this God is also their Savior, Jesus Christ.[37]

THE TRINITY

It might appear that Zinzendorf is proclaiming a form of Unitarianism or Christomonism.[38] He leaves himself open to this charge when he claims that his only debate with the Socinians is over "who is the only God."[39] However, that statement relates to God's actions in the world, not the divine essence. Zinzendorf insists that the Trinity can be understood only through Christ. The Trinity is not a doctrine for the world at large.

---

34. Zinzendorf, *Berliner Reden* (Men), 3–4.

35. Zinzendorf, *Gemeinreden*, ZH 4:3:58. For more on Zinzendorf's opposition to Deism, see Beyreuther, *Studien zur Theologie*, 24–25.

36. Zinzendorf, *Gemeinreden*, ZH 4:3:67; cf. ibid., 52:325. "Wer der einige GOtt ist? Der einige GOtt, den wir predigen, ist JEsus Christus, der einige GOtt der Welt ist der, der die Welt geschaffen hat, und das ist auch der, der am Creutz gehangen hat." *Gemeinreden*, ZH 4:35:114.

37. "Fr. Wer hat den Menschen gemacht? A. GOtt der HErr. Fr. Wie heißt man Ihn? A. JEsus Christus. Fr. Bedeuten die Worte etwas? A. Ja. Fr. Was denn? A. JEsus heißt ein Erlöser und Christus ein König." *Büdingische Sammlung* III, ZE 9:404 (the pages are out of order). See also Freeman, *An Ecumenical Theology of the Heart*, 118.

38. There is much literature on Zinzendorf's view of the Trinity. Peter Zimmerling's *Gott in Gemeineschaft* is a very comprehensive account. See also Freeman, *An Ecumenical Theology of the Heart*, 83–90.

39. See Beyreuther, *Studien zur Theologie*, 9–36, and for a defense of Zinzendorf from the charge of Christomonism.

Nothing is more certain than that the entire matter of the mystery of the Trinity does not at all belong to a catholic system for the entire world and which has been put into writing. If someone wants to write a catechism that should be scriptural and for the whole world, for all people, it must deal with Jesus Christ alone, who is the God of the world, the object of the universal liturgy.[40]

There is a Father and a Spirit, but they are known only through the revelation of Jesus. According to John's Gospel, the world did not know the Father until the Son appeared, and no one had the Spirit until the Son had sent her (John 13). The world has no other God than "the Universal God, namely, their Creator Jesus Christ," but those who have come to Christ will learn of the Trinity.[41] Part of Christ's mission was to reveal his Father to his followers and to lead people to him; however, this revelation is reserved for those who are united with Jesus.

It is a great privilege that we can consider Jesus Christ's Father as our God. Not all people can and may do this. In their minds, natural people have nothing to do with Jesus Christ's Father. "No one comes to the Father except through Jesus" (John 14:6, altered). Whoever has not experienced forgiveness for all his sins, whoever has not been born anew, "whomever Jesus Christ has not shown to the Father and shown that he has done enough for him," has no other God but the common God of all creatures whom he must have, whom he and everyone *must* accept as their God whether they know how to name him or not, because this lies within them. It is their inborn idea (Romans 1:19).[42]

Zinzendorf never denied the reality of God the Father, but the Father clearly does not play a significant role in either the theology or the piety of Zinzendorf.[43] Most of the properties generally associated with the Father are assumed by the Son while the Father is seen primarily as a substitute for Christ after the Incarnation. "Because he [Christ] has since established himself newly in the quality of our Brother and Bridegroom, he no longer calls himself Father, but he has given us another Father; therefore we always speak of the heavenly Father, Mother, and Bridegroom."[44]

Zinzendorf was even known to refer to the Father as actually being more of a Grandfather, since Christ is the true Father.[45] It is easy to speculate that

40. Zinzendorf, *Einundzwanzig Diskurse*, ZH 6:2:64. On Zinzendorf's understanding of the Trinity as a doctrine only for the church, see Zimmerling, *Gott in Gemeinschaft*, 39–43.

41. Zinzendorf, *Gemeinreden*, ZH 4:3:67; ibid., 35:116–17; ibid., 33:80. The Trinity is only known through Christ "because although we have glimpsed a little of our Father and Mother, we have not seen their form, but only their office and activity, their connection with the wife of the Savior, with his bride, of that we have received what is necessary." Ibid., 51:315.

42. Zinzendorf, *Pennsylvania Sermons* 1:42.

43. Zimmerling, *Gott in Gemeinschaft*, 100–105; Freeman, *An Ecumenical Theology of the Heart*, 118–22.

44. Zinzendorf, *Kinder Reden*, ZE 6:9:38.

45. Spangenberg, *Antworten*, 72; cf. Sessler, *Communal Pietism*, 145.

growing up without a father may have contributed to his view of God the Father as inaccessible, but Zinzendorf is clearly struggling with the Gospel of John and German mystical literature.

THE INCARNATION

Zinzendorf fully appreciated the tension within the Chalcedonian formula that Christ was fully human and fully divine, but he saw this as a matter for the heart, not for the head. He stressed the absolute divinity of Christ and his complete identification with humanity as a "real, practical truth" and "a matter for the heart" which must be believed, even though it might offend others who only mouth the creedal formulas. Such people look at the Moravian Church and say:

These people speak of the mystery of the holy Trinity as if there really was one. These people act as if there really were three persons in the Deity. . . . These people speak of the Savior as if he really had been in the world, like another human. They speak of his childhood, of his diapers, of his sweat, of his sleeping, of his efforts and diligence, of his learning in school, of his faithfulness in his craft, of his peasant language, of his skill in explaining himself, of his way of encountering his opponents; and all that with such simplicity, credulity, and application as if they were talking about a man who had thus come among us and left us a lasting tradition.[46]

When the universal God of creation became a particular man in the midst of historical contingency, the entire world changed. No longer were humans dependent on the dark and confusing revelations of God evident in nature, in prophecies, and in the law; now there was a person to whom everyone could look for the definitive revelation of God. Humans cannot understand the thoughts of the Creator; therefore the Creator condescended not only to speak human thoughts but even to become human.[47]

Those who had longed to see God could now see him in flesh and bone. If people want to know who God is, they only have to look at Jesus as portrayed in the Gospels and painted in their hearts. He spoke words that every ear could hear. He had a body that his followers continue to taste, see, smell, and touch through the Eucharist.

Once God became incarnate in Mary's womb and was born as a child, the second commandment was no longer in force, according to Zinzendorf. God forbade images of himself before the Incarnation, but since he clothed himself in visible form, believers can see "the picture of his holy humanness, of the Son of Man who is no longer an immeasurable something but a circumscribed

---

46. Zinzendorf, *Gemeinreden,* ZH 4:35:107–8.
47. Ibid., 14:215.

one, no longer incomprehensible but understandable, and no longer presents a mere spirit to the imagination but flesh and bone."[48]

The prevalence of plain white interiors and clear glass windows in the places of worship for the Moravian Church has been misinterpreted by many as evidence that Zinzendorf and his followers were iconoclasts, or at least stressed simplicity over ornamentation. More research is needed on the perspective of the community, but as far as Zinzendorf was concerned, there is no barrier to iconographic depictions of Christ and the saints. He was a student of Luther in this regard and may even have been drawing upon the iconophile tradition of Eastern Orthodoxy.

The community of Herrnhaag was famous for the vividness of its religious art. Paintings and transparencies were used frequently in worship, as were elaborate ritual processions that had a dance-like quality in their complexity. The worship at Herrnhaag was a feast for the ear and the eye.[49] Pennsylvania shared in this rich iconographic tradition and made frequent use of Valentine Haidt's paintings.[50] I believe that the white walls of a Moravian Saal (worship room) served the same function as the white walls of an art museum.

Not only did the Moravians use visual arts; they employed imaginative language. Preachers, with the aid of the Holy Spirit, were encouraged to use graphic and affective language to paint Christ before the eyes of their listeners.[51] There is a natural connection between preaching Christ and the concrete and affective language of heart religion. The worshippers should become aware of the presence of Christ with them and be able to feel and see his suffering for their sakes.

Katherine Faull has demonstrated the effectiveness of this type of preaching in Moravian spirituality. She argues convincingly that it was connected to Zinzendorf's understanding of the self, which was distinct from the rationalism of the Enlightenment.[52] Zinzendorf embraced the complete human being, body as well as soul, emotion as well as reason. For Zinzendorf, the full divinity of Christ was seen in his full suffering humanity, and through Christ human nature is redeemed. Persons were to be defined by their sharing in the Incarnation of Christ rather than by gender, race, or class.

The proclamation of the historical reality of the suffering God separates

48. Ibid., Anhang, 49–50; Bettermann, *Theologie und Sprache*, chap. 11.

49. Erbe, *Herrnhaag: Eine religiöse Kommunität*, 105–23.

50. For an introduction to Haidt and his work, see Vernon Nelson, "Johann Valentin Haidt und Zinzendorf," in Meyer and Peucker, *Graf Ohne Grenzen*, 152–58. Many of Haidt's paintings and other examples of Moravian art appear in this book. Moravian iconography included more than Haidt's works. For a Moravian painter other than Haidt, see Paul Peucker, "A Painter of Christ's Wounds: Johann Langguth's Birthday Poem for Johann Jakob Müller, 1744," in Atwood and Vogt, *Distinctiveness of Moravian Culture*.

51. Zinzendorf, *Gemeinreden*, ZH 4:8:141; *Nine Public Lectures*, 28.

52. Faull, "Faith and Imagination," 31–32.

Christianity from all forms of natural or philosophical religion, for Zinzendorf. True Christianity stands in marked contrast to the refinement and rationalism of Western culture. "That, therefore, certainly separates the two great religions of Christ and Belial because that is the *Ikker*, the ground point: Did your God, your Creator, your husband, who has made you become like you? Did he go about in your bodily person, in the form of your sinful flesh, truly poor and despised for thirty years, and finally was slaughtered as the ransom for you and all the world? Is this a novel or a history?"[53]

HUMAN LIFE AND THE INCARNATION

In Zinzendorf's theology, the humanity of Christ is itself salvific. Although he did not try to define it philosophically in terms of essences, he frequently discussed the way in which God's assumption of human body affected human nature. In a beautiful and marvelous way, human life, in all of its physical finitude, has been especially blessed by the Creator since he assumed human form.[54]

We ought to consider the Savior in all things as a mere man and to take all comfort for us from his humanness, from his equality with us, from his weakness which is not merely the same as our weakness but a yet greater weakness than we have, a compounding of all weaknesses in his suffering person, and all helplessness, and all uneasiness, and all humility, which scarcely a hundred men together could endure, so that a miserable creature can say that one cannot imagine a poorer, weaker, and more oppressed Jesus.[55]

God could have come into the world as a mature man and accomplished the work of the Atonement, but it is significant that he chose to be born an infant and grow into maturity. This blesses every stage of human life. "A person just grows up with the Savior; he is everything to each person that that person is at that time: one is a child, so he is a child to him; one is a boy, so he is a boy to him; one is a youth, so he is a youth to him; one is a man, so he is a man to him. For the sisters, it is the same; he is a maidenly heart for them, with a particular tenderness and a special knowledge. And so one grows up with him into human maturity and he is always just so to each."[56]

That Christ was once an infant sucking the breasts of Mary proves that infancy is a blessed stage of human life. A nursing mother should meditate upon Christ as a baby and see Christ in her own sucking child.[57] From the time

---

53. Zinzendorf, *Wundenlitanei Homilien,* ZH 3:5:53.

54. Faull, "Faith and Imagination," 32.

55. Zinzendorf, *Einundzwanzig Diskurse,* ZH 6:5:118–19.

56. Zinzendorf, *Gemeinreden,* ZH 4:43:225.

57. Zinzendorf even goes so far as to claim that birth is good only because of Jesus' birth; however, since Christ was born from a woman, it is now a "liturgical idea" that the entire community takes part in. *Wundenlitanei Homilien,* ZH 3:7:81; cf. *Gemeinreden,* ZH 4:1:31 and, Anhang, 35–36.

they rise in the morning until they say evening prayers, little children should remember that their Lord had been a child such as they. The thoughts that Jesus thought and spoke as a child can help the children avoid falling into numerous sins; therefore they should pray to be Jesus-like children all day.[58] This understanding of the Incarnation was the theoretical foundation of the choir system.

Christ was a faithful child of Mary and Joseph who labored and sweated in his father's shop even though he could have been born a prince and lived in leisure. He chose to be a laborer so that humans may all know that labor is a blessing from God. Whenever a Christian is fatigued and oppressed by labor, he or she should meditate upon the diligence and faithfulness of Christ in his own manual labor.[59]

Even suffering, illness, and death are blessed by the Incarnation. When Christians suffer from any pain or illness, they can comfort themselves by meditating upon the sufferings of Christ. "I have a headache or a toothache, and I also see that other children become sick and their bodies are even laid in the ground. I thus see well enough that I have a mortal body. But my beloved also had such a body, 'Our dear Lord God was also a sick person.'"[60]

Sickness, therefore, is one sign of our similarity to Christ; another is that the Son of God died, just as all humans do. According to Zinzendorf, it is better to lie in death than to go directly up to heaven, as Mary did, because Christians want to be like Jesus, not Mary. His rest in the grave sanctified the grave and made it a blessed bed for all who die in Christ. The grave is now a "sleep chapel" where all of Christ's comrades lie in peace.[61] In short, Christians should "rejoice that a person can experience nothing which the Savior did not also experience."[62]

The sanctification of normal human existence through the Incarnation took many forms, including the blessing of human sexuality. Zinzendorf rejected the long Christian tradition of contempt for the body, particularly the sexual organs.[63] He shocked many of his readers, then and now, with his discussions

58. Zinzendorf, *Kinder Reden,* ZE 6:66:320–21; *Gemeinreden,* ZH 4:1:31–32.

59. Zinzendorf, *Kinder Reden,* ZE 6:77:377.

60. Ibid., 11, 56; cf. ibid., 39:189, where Zinzendorf tells the children to thank God when they are sick because Jesus was also a sick person. Cf. ibid., 15:76.

61. Zinzendorf, *Gemeinreden,* ZH 4:20:295. The allusion to the bodily assumption of Mary is particularly intriguing when one considers the catholic nature of Zinzendorf's theology and Ritschl's charge that Zinzendorf had rejected Protestant theology.

62. Zinzendorf, *Kinder Reden,* ZE 6:15:77.

63. The literature on the Christian attitude toward the body is too extensive to cite. Suffice it to say that the main source of debate is not whether Christianity has denegrated bodily existence but to what extent it has done so. All types of asceticism, whether monastic or "worldly," share a desire to escape in some way the realities of physical existence, particularly sexuality. Peter Brown, in *Body and Society: Men, Women, and Sexual Renunciation in Early Christianity* (New York: Columbia University Press, 1988), demonstrates that asceticism varies greatly according to a culture's view of God and society; however, a constant theme is that

of the human anatomy, but this frankness is a natural result of his intense interest in proclaiming the full humanity of Christ. Zinzendorf gives special attention to Jesus' genitals. Since Christ was circumcised at the appropriate time, it is clear that he did indeed have sexual organs; thus "a man must either deny his own manliness or he must accept that the manliness of Jesus was as natural, complete, and simple as his own which he carries on himself."[64]

For Zinzendorf, it was nothing short of blasphemy to deny that Jesus had genitalia or to be embarrassed by this fact.[65] He stood in a long tradition in Renaissance religious art that draws attention to the genitals of the infant Jesus as a way of asserting the full humanity of the Christ child, to which Leo Steinberg has called attention.[66] Renaissance artists used various means to draw the viewer's attention to the genitals of Jesus precisely in order to emphasize the doctrine of the Incarnation. As with the writings of Zinzendorf, the vitality of this theological perspective in Renaissance art was obscured in the nineteenth and twentieth centuries.

The circumcision of Jesus was very important in Zinzendorf's theology because it was proof of Christ's full humanity. There is strong medieval precedence for linking the circumcision of Jesus to the Incarnation and salvation. John O'Malley writes, "There was no better occasion for Renaissance preachers to capitalize on the wonderful paradox of true-God/true-man than in sermons on the Circumcision. . . . The sermons generally dealt with two things: the physical act of circumcision (and its possible mystic meaning as well), and the giving of the Name, JESUS—that is savior, MAN-GOD, if you will. There is an earthiness and concreteness in some of these sermons on the Circumcision that would surely offend our contemporary tastes."[67] The same is true of Zinzendorf's sermons and Moravian hymns for the Fest of the Circumcision.

The "covenant member" of Jesus does more than establish the true humanity of the Son of God, however; it also establishes the holiness of the penis itself. It is no longer a pudendum (a thing of shame), as the medieval preachers styled it, but a holy member of the body.[68] Boys and men especially should remember this, for they bear a special affinity to Christ. They "can say, Jesus

---

of escaping from the limitations of human needs and desires, whether sexual or dietary. Elaine Pagels, *Adam, Eve, and the Serpent* (New York: Random House, 1988), offers an intriguing theory on how the Christian rejection of the goodness of sexuality arose.

64. Zinzendorf, *Einundzwanzig Diskurse,* ZH 6:7:147.

65. Ibid., 7:148. Zinzendorf also claimed that the enemies of the Moravian Church were trying to "spiritually castrate" them. Ibid., 149.

66. Leo Steinberg, *The Sexuality of Christ in Renaissance Art and in Modern Oblivion,* 2d ed. (Chicago: University of Chicago Press, 1996).

67. Quoted ibid., Excursis 39, *The Sexuality of Christ,* 215.

68. Pfister completely misrepresents this aspect of Zinzendorf's view of sexuality, e.g., *Die Frömmigkeit des Grafen Ludwig von Zinzendorf,* 40.

carried you, my members. Of that there is no doubt. . . . 'May the painful [ritual of] the first birth make our manhood dear.' "[69]

Zinzendorf was not advocating a form of phallus worship. If anything, this was an inversion of the pagan fascination with priapism.[70] Rather than focusing on the sexual potency of Christ, Zinzendorf argued that the Incarnation removed the shame long associated with the sexual organs, including those of women, as, through the Incarnation, both genders have a covenant sign.[71] Christ was conceived in a woman's uterus and born through her vagina.

Since the female sexual organs have also been blessed through the Incarnation, women's bodies ought to be honored by men. "And from that same hour the womanly member, the womanly mother, was no more a shame but the most honorable of all members."[72]

For the sake of this holy boy, whom Mary carried in her sisterly womb, the sisters are venerated by the brothers, and the brother [sic] by the sisters. The former because he became one with our physical being in the womb of a maiden but the latter because we [i.e., the brothers] actually carry on ourselves an external resemblance to him. The sign of that by which we resemble Christ, we also venerate with a deeply inward humility.[73]

The blessing of women's nature, however, is in part vicarious since they have to become like Mary and look to their children or husbands to find blessing in their procreative and nurturing natures.[74] Christ's maleness gives a certain superiority to the male gender, so that even the nurses for the infants in the community give a special respect to the baby boys. The circumcision of Jesus was the sign that each man was to be king and priest in his own home.[75]

Another weakness in this theology is that Jesus did not grow old; therefore there is no direct parallel between the life of the aged Christian and Christ. Zinzendorf actually has little to say about old age, and in some passages he indicates that it is somehow improper for a Christian to live too long.[76] In the 1740s and 1750s, the Moravian Church was primarily a youth movement. One

69. Zinzendorf, *Kinder Reden*, ZE 6:46:231.

70. Again we can see connections between what Zinzendorf was doing with language and what Renaissance artists were doing with paint. Steinberg sees this as an inversion of pagan phallicism, similar to other inversions of pagan symbolism. The phallus of Christ is powerful precisely because of his abstinence. In speaking of the popularity of the circumcision of Christ in art, Steinberg notes: "The erstwhile symbol of the life force yields not seed, but redeeming blood" (*The Sexuality of Christ*, 47).

71. Zinzendorf, *Gemeinreden*, ZH 4:1:32.

72. Ibid., 1:29.

73. Zinzendorf, *Einundzwanzig Diskurse*, ZH 6:7:149–50.

74. Zinzendorf, *Gemeinreden*, ZH 4, Anhang, 36.

75. Zinzendorf, *Einundzwanzig Diskurse*, ZH 6:7:150. One day all ranks and division of gender will be abolished, says Zinzendorf, but that is when Christ returns, not now. *Gemeinreden*, ZH 4:1:25; *Wundenlitanei Homilien*, ZH 3:7:82–83.

76. E.g., *Kinder Reden*, ZE 6:4:18. This may be a key to understanding why the Moravian Church modified its choir devotions in the 1780s as the first generation of leaders were becoming elderly.

of the factors that contributed to the conservatism of the Moravians after the death of Zinzendorf was that the once-youthful leadership remained in power as they aged.

Moreover, since Jesus never married, the blessing of the married state must be based upon a different foundation, namely, the mystical marriage to Christ.[77] Zinzendorf was obviously influenced by the marriage mysticism of late medieval Europe, but he connects this marriage imagery with the Atonement in a unique fashion. I agree with Wilhelm Bettermann that Zinzendorf connects his marriage mysticism closely to a Lutheran cross theology.[78]

MARRIAGE MYSTICISM

Beginning in the late 1730s, Zinzendorf expressed the human longing for connection with the divine in the very physical terms of human marriage and sexuality. "The complete religion, the chief religion, the one that most properly merits the name religion, is marriage, the marriage of the soul, the *mega myste-rium* which the Vulgate calls '*magnum sacramentum*' and Dr. Luther '*das grosse geheimniß*'" (1 Tim. 3:16).[79] One of Zinzendorf's favorite descriptions of Christian doctrine is "Your Creator is your husband" *(dein Schöpfer ist dein Mann)*.[80]

In Zinzendorf's theology, the Creator of all visible reality desires his human creatures to enter into a deep and blessed relationship with him, to sleep peacefully in his arms, and to be happy. This is another expression of the experience of happy blessedness *(Glückseligkeit)* in this life, which is the fruit of conversion. The greatest comfort to suffering human souls are the words, "We are created to sleep in his arms."[81] Among the principal titles that Zinzendorf used for Christ are *Bräutigam* (Bridegroom) and *Mann* (Husband), taken from biblical texts such as Matt. 9:15, 25:1–12; Luke 5:34; John 3:29; Eph. 5:23–28; and Rev. 18:23.

Zinzendorf strengthened this marriage imagery of the New Testament by

---

77. Beyreuther, "Ehe-Religion und Eschatology," in *Studien zur Theologie Zinzendorfs* (Neukirchen-Vluyn: Kreis, Moers, 1962), 35–71, gives a very perceptive theological analysis of Zinzendorf's marriage mysticism and demonstrates that it is connected to the Lutheran idea of the union with Christ.

78. Beyreuther, "Ehe-Religion und Eschatology," in *Studien zur Theologie*, 42; Atwood, "Zinzendorf's Litany of the Wounds," 194–204.

79. "Die ganze Religion, die haupt-religion, die den namen einer religion aufs eigentlichste verdienst, ist die Ehe, die Selen-Ehe, mega mysterion, die Vulgata sagt: magnum sacramentum, D. Luther, das grosse geheimniß." (1 Tim. 3:16.) *Gemeinreden*, ZH 4:5:106; *Nine Public Lectures*, 28; *Wundenlitanei Homilien*, ZH 3:5:53; cf. Otto Uttendörfer, *Zinzendorfs religiöse Grundgedanken* (Herrnhut: Missionsbuchhandlung, 1935), 161–65.

80. Zinzendorf derives this formulation from Isaiah 54:5, "The one who has made you is your husband." *Gemeinreden*, ZH 4:7:123–24; *Nine Public Lectures*, 77–78.

81. Zinzendorf, *Kinder Reden*, ZE 6:11:55. It is important to note that this was said to children in the community long after the end of the so-called Sifting Time. See also Atwood, "Sleeping in the Arms of Christ: Sanctifying Sexuality in the Eighteenth-Century Moravian Church," *Journal of the History of Sexuality* 8 (1997): 25–51; Beyreuther, *Studien zur Theologie*, 56.

connecting it with the Incarnation. Christ became one with humankind by taking on flesh and bone, just as a man and a woman become one flesh and bone (Gen. 2:23; Mark 10:7–8).[82] Like many mystics, Zinzendorf applied texts about the bride of Christ not simply to the community of believers but also to the individual Christian. The heavenly host "are liturgists and bride servants who are sent out to each one who attains eternal blessedness, who are candidates to the bridal bed."[83]

With conversion a person enters into a personal and intense marriage with Christ, the Bridegroom of the soul. Zinzendorf described conversion in terms similar to those used to describe falling in love. "And as soon as they are with him, there is an embrace, a kiss, a heart, thus he draws like a magnet, rises them all up to himself, lays them all deep in his holy side, so that a soul in that hour and at that moment when she has experienced it can say: much happiness to eternal life, if only my whole life could remain like this!"[84]

However, Zinzendorf indicated in some passages that this marriage to Christ is not fully consummated until the eschaton, when the true marriage supper of the Lamb is to be celebrated. In the between time, the converted soul is being prepared for marriage while enjoying bliss as the betrothed of Christ, not the wedded wife. She has not yet been led to the marriage bed.[85] Thus happy blessedness is an experience of the in-breaking eschaton, which was understood as complete union with the Bridegroom.

In Zinzendorf's theology, human marriage is not simply a metaphor for the mystical relationship with Christ; it is a result of that primary relationship with God.[86] The primary purpose of human marriage is not procreation; it is to express the soul's union with the divine. Childless couples are still married in the eyes of the Savior, no matter what civil or canon law may say. Children are a gift, not the goal of marriage.[87] It is not surprising, then, that wedding ceremonies in Bethlehem made little or no mention of future children to bless the marriage.

In Zinzendorf's view, it would have been good if all people only had Christ

---

82. Zinzendorf, *Gemeinreden,* ZH 4:29:25.

83. Ibid., 50, 305; cf. *Zeister Reden,* ZH 3:26:205.

84. Zinzendorf, *Gemeinreden,* ZH 4:50:310. The Father and Mother are entrusted with this task of preparing the bride for her wedding. Ibid., 303–11. For the connection of this to Zinzendorf's eschatology, see Beyreuther, "Ehe-Religion und Eschatology," in *Studien zur Theologie,* 58.

85. Zinzendorf, *Wundenlitanei Homilien,* ZH 3:7:7–77; cf. *Gemeinreden,* ZH 4:8:143.

86. In reality, according to Zinzendorf, all souls are brides of Christ, but humans have committed adultery and need to be forgiven and brought back into intimacy with their husband. *Gemeinreden,* ZH 4:7:127. Zinzendorf appears to be drawing upon Old Testament prophecy here, especially the prophet Hosea, but instead of the marriage being between Israel and God, it is between God and all humankind.

87. Zinzendorf, *Gemeinreden,* ZH 4:7:124–25. Zinzendorf blames philosophers for developing the doctrine that procreation is the purpose of marriage, and he points out that many married couples have no children and that many children are born outside of marriage. Ibid., 135.

as husband, but humankind has been divided into two genders. The purpose of this division is so that man and woman can play the roles of Christ and the Gemeine, but only the Moravians recognized this truth. For Zinzendorf's followers, sexual intercourse was a liturgy in which the woman plays the Gemeine and the man Christ. Sexual intercourse was the physical expression of the intimacy of the soul and her beloved. The man acts as a proxy for Christ until the soul is forever joined to her true husband. Men were to sacrifice themselves to meet the needs of their mates. They were liturgists and angels for the sake of the sisters.[88]

There is a problem with this view of sexuality, as Zinzendorf freely admits. The engendering of humans and physical intercourse between different genders is an expression of the mystical union of souls with their Creator; however, the souls of men must also be brides of Christ in order to be saved. Zinzendorf gets around the difficulty of human maleness by pronouncing that all souls are essentially feminine.[89] "All souls are Sisters. He knows that secret; he has made all souls; the soul is his wife. He has formed no *animos*, no manly souls among human souls, only *animas*, [feminine] souls, who are his Bride, [female] Candidates of rest in his arms and of the eternal sleeping room."[90] Therefore it is not only women who enjoy the mystical marriage. A man can also act "as a consort, as a playmate for the marriage bed of the blessed Creator and eternal Husband of the human soul."[91] Christ is the only true male, and men will be married to him, just as the sisters are.

The psychologist Oskar Pfister saw this as evidence of Zinzendorf's repressed homosexuality.[92] Gerhard Reichel argued strenuously against Pfister's charge; however, the fact that there was never any evidence of homosexual activity on Zinzendorf's part does not counter Pfister's claim that he was a *repressed* homosexual.[93] It is difficult to make a judgment on the question of homoeroticism in Zinzendorf's writings because his position is a natural consequence both of his own theological principles and of the biblical texts relating to the mystical marriage. Still, the final formulation does sound quite homoerotic. But the charge of homosexuality is a little hard to swallow when one considers that he fathered so many children and made sexual intercourse between a man and a woman central to his theology.

88. Zinzendorf, *Zeister Reden* 26:213; *Gemeinreden*, ZH 4:7:129.

89. Bynum shows that this idea of the feminine soul was common in medieval mystical literature. *Jesus as Mother*, 138.

90. Zinzendorf, *Zeister Reden* 26:208.

91. Zinzendorf, *Nine Public Lectures*, 86; cf. *Einundzwanzig Diskurse*, ZH 6:7:152. See also Beyreuther, *Studien zur Theologie*, 53–54.

92. Pfister, *Die Frömmigkeit des Grafen Ludwig von Zinzendorf*, 6off.

93. Reichel, *Zinzendorfs Frömmigkeit*, 3off.

This view of the soul's relationship to Christ has interesting implications for Zinzendorf's anthropology. Whereas earlier we saw that men are more blessed than women because their bodies resemble that of Christ, women are more blessed than men in the mystical marriage. Women can love and enjoy Christ unreservedly because their physical being and their souls are at one. They experience ever more blessed and sweeter joys through the service of their husbands, their vice-Christs, but "It is not permitted to us men to be images of the Gemeine in the perception of our sisters, but we must be priests, liturgists; we must serve at the altar; we must care for the divine worship for them. For it happens now as at all times, it is better to enjoy something than to care for it. The worker in his daily life does not have the same sensation of blessedness as the others have."[94]

Zinzendorf appears to have been striving toward an anthropology of androgyny, at least for men. He does say that in the future there will be only one gender, the female.[95] In this life, however, men remain fundamentally divided. They have to be brought out from one gender to another and experience a metamorphosis. They lead a double life as a Christ to the woman and a bride to Christ. "When one considers our manly gender, then it is the most wretched; for we are not people who throw themselves bluntly with heart and body into the Savior's arms, to depend on him, to remain lying at his side, to be able to conceive, as the sisters do."[96]

There seems to be a conflict in Zinzendorf's thought between his acceptance of traditional gender roles and his new vision of the blessing of the Incarnation and the mystical marriage. For example, women have a priestly role, just like men, but it is not clear whether they performed sacramental functions in the church.[97] "Since the Creator, who was born of a woman, has been raised up, and now the sisters belong just as well as men to the class of those whom the Savior declared to his heavenly Father to be priests, so there is in general no question at all that the entire betrothal, the entire fellowship, the entire choir of his maidens and brides are priest women, and not only priest women, but priesterly women."[98]

This should not be taken as proof that women were ordained as priests in the Moravian Church, however, since in the context of the statement Zinzend-

94. Zinzendorf, *Gemeinreden,* ZH 4:7:131.

95. Ibid., 1:25.

96. Zinzendorf, *Berliner Reden,* foreword to the sermons to the men, 6 (unnumbered), cf. *Gemeinreden,* ZH 4:7:130. The patriarchalism of this understanding is made explicit by Zinzendorf himself. "The *Gemeine* may be as beautiful as it will, but it is still only the *Gemeine,* so it is the wife, so it is the weakest part." *Gemeinreden* ZH 4:23:315. See also Beyreuther, *Studien zur Theologie,* 55–56.

97. Peter Vogt, "A Voice for Themselves." *Unitas Fratrum* 45–46 (1999) has several articles on women in the Moravian Church.

98. Zinzendorf, *Gemeinreden,* ZH 4:4:89.

orf defines a priest as someone who helps another to heaven, as in Luther's concept of the priesthood of all believers. Women deacons served communion to women in the Moravian Church, but only an ordained presbyter could consecrate the elements.

Even so, the sanctification of the body (combined with the teaching about the motherhood of the Spirit) led to a strong endorsement of women's leadership beyond the hearth and cradle.[99] This theology is one reason why the Single Sisters' choir in Bethlehem was a much stronger choir than all of the others.[100] Most of the pastoral care of women was conducted by women.

Zinzendorf's theology is commonly called Christocentric, but we need to clarify what that meant. For Zinzendorf it meant that every aspect of the Christian life, including doctrine, worship, and ethics was focused on the living reality of Christ in the community. Christ is the Creator of the universe and individual souls. Christ is the Redeemer who experienced death for the sake of those souls. Christ is the Bridegroom and lover of those who have been redeemed. Through the Incarnation, Christ is the one who has removed all shame from human bodily existence. Every aspect of human life, from birth to death, is to be understood in the light of Christ's Incarnation, sacrifice, and contemporary reality. For Zinzendorf, though, the most important aspect of the Incarnation was the death of Jesus.

BLOOD AND WOUNDS

Commenting on a recent book on the cultural significance of blood, Umberto Eco writes: "In other centuries blood was a daily reality: people knew its aroma, its viscosity. Are we really strangers to blood? Are we really so far removed from those centuries of which Camporesi tells? . . . Camporesi reconstructs feelings, terrors, and loves that have seemed ancient to us, and invites us to *look within ourselves.* To grasp the obscure rapport between rites and myths of the past and our impulses of today."[101] The study of Christianity requires that we do likewise and examine more than formal theological propositions. In order to understand Christianity, and the Moravians in particular, we must ponder the significance of blood.

Christianity is a religion in which worshippers symbolically (or, for some,

---

99. Zimmerling, "Zinzendorf's Bild der Frau," esp. 15–17.

100. Beverly Prior Smaby, "Forming the Single Sisters' Choir in Bethlehem," *Transactions of the Moravian Historical Society* 28 (1994): 1–14, examines the success of the Single Sisters' choir in Bethlehem. Katherine Faull's work on the autobiographical narratives of women in Bethlehem, *Moravian Women: Their Related Lives,* shows that the marriage mysticism of Zinzendorf played a vital role in the Single Sisters' choir, particularly in the reluctance of the single women to marry. Paul Peucker points to a reaction against this feminization of Moravian religion after Zinzendorf's death in "Gegen ein Regiment von Schwestern."

101. Eco, "Foreword," Piero Camporesi, *Juice of Life: The Symbolic and Magic Significance of Blood,* trans. Robert R. Barr (New York: Continuum, 1995), 10–11.

literally) drink the blood of their Savior on a regular basis. This focus on blood begins in the New Testament itself. The Gospel of John, Zinzendorf's preferred gospel, focuses the reader's attention on the blood pouring from the side wound of Jesus, who has earlier in the gospel urged people to drink his blood. Medieval artists depicted Joseph of Arimethea collecting the blood of Christ in the Holy Grail.

In the fifteenth century, central Europe was convulsed by the Hussite Wars, in which the forerunners of the Moravian Church carried the chalice into battle as a symbol of their struggle for access to the blood of Christ. As Caroline Walker Bynum shows, medieval devotion was focused on blood streaming out of the wounds of Christ. We see it in mystical literature and early Renaissance art.[102] Mary Magdalen dei Pazzi, for instance, in the seventeenth century "saw Jesus crucified, with his wounds dripping blood, and his open side, and beseeching him, she said, 'Make those beautiful rills to descend and bathe all hearts, all.' "[103]

In interpreting medieval and Renaissance blood visions, Piero Camporesi says, "The ambiguity of the metaphors, and the erotic symbolism of these visionary experiences, far from canceling the sensual language of the flesh, actually reinvigorate and excite it, expressing as they do the omnipresence of bodiliness and the senses, through which even religious allegories must necessarily pass. We all possess an anatomical, physiological sieve, without which it seems that discourse cannot begin, cannot be ordered with any rationality, cannot render itself intelligible. At the origin of mystical language is a sensual alphabet, which strives, by its innermost calling, to be delivered from the sense and from the body, not by canceling them, but by sublimating them, by transferring them to God, by immersing them in a laver of 'thirsting, slaking . . . concupiscence.' "[104] In other words, the desire for the blood of Christ expressed theological and mystical concerns without losing its sensuality.

Zinzendorf's focus on the blood of Christ was thus not unique, but he developed this Christian devotion in particularly striking ways. Zinzendorf even reinterpreted the Protestant theory of the history of "witnesses to the truth," those persons throughout church history who maintained pure doctrine in the midst of Catholicism, in terms of blood-and-wounds theology. Among the witnesses to the sufferings of Jesus he mentions are Elisabeth of Thuringia, Count Eger, St. Bernard, Tauler, the Bohemian Brethren, and Luther.[105]

---

102. Caroline Walker Bynum, "The Blood of Christ in the Later Middle Ages," *Church History* 71 (2002): 685–714.

103. Moreover, she connects the blood of Christ with mother's milk: "the milk of his flesh, and the blood, in the sacrament." Camporesi, *Juice of Life,* 70.

104. Ibid., 70.

105. Zinzendorf, *Einundzwanzig Diskurse,* ZH 6:19:306–7.

Zinzendorf felt that it was the unique calling of the Moravian Church to preach the Crucifixion in an age that was becoming too refined and philosophical for it. "This is the great hour of temptation when the time will come when religious people will be thoroughly ashamed to speak about the Savior, and to that things are already becoming accustomed. For almost as soon as a teacher in the Lutheran Church, in the Reformed, in England, America, etc., opens his mouth to speak about the Savior, of his blood and wounds, of his penitential struggle for our sins, then he is [considered] a Herrnhuter, that is proof enough."[106]

Zinzendorf had been fascinated by the Crucifixion as a child. He particularly loved the Christmas and Easter seasons, the former for the songs about the Incarnation of God and the latter for songs about the love of Jesus seen in his suffering.[107] Zinzendorf was not unique in connecting Christmas and Easter. As Sarah Beckwith reminds us, late medieval mysticism also concentrated attention on "Christ the incarnate God, and more specifically Christ both as an infant and as crucified, the two moments of birth and death, which insist on the claims of the body most emphatically and obviously."[108]

Hymns were the source of Zinzendorf's earliest images of the crucified Savior. Especially important to him was Bernard of Clairvaux's hymn "O Haupt voll Blut und Wunden" (O head full of blood and wounds), which was sung while his father was dying. This hymn invites the worshipper to gaze deeply and longingly at the blood streaming from the head of Christ and from his various wounds. Zinzendorf observed the anniversary of his father's death every year as a religious festival,[109] and his followers sang this hymn in its entirety every Friday evening. They would also sing it as they themselves lay dying, so that their final thoughts would be on the blood streaming down the face of the Savior.

During his *Wanderjahr* (1719) something happened that was to enter into the mythology of the Moravian Church. While at Düsseldorf, Zinzendorf encountered a painting by Domenico Feti of Jesus as the Man of Sorrows. It depicts, in a sentimental style, Jesus suffering under the crown of thorns before his Crucifixion. What gripped Zinzendorf was the caption: *Ego pro te haec passum sum; Tu vero, quid fecisti pro me?* "All this I have suffered for you, but what have you done for me?" He related that these words had a profound impact on him, and he prayed that the Savior would force him into the fellowship of his suffering if he would not do so voluntarily.

---

106. Ibid., 5:111.
107. Beyreuther, *Studien zur Theologie*, 11.
108. Sarah Beckwith, *Christ's Body: Identity, Culture, and Society in Late Medieval Writings* (London: Routledge, 1993), 17; cf. Bynum, *Jesus as Mother*, 130.
109. Beyreuther, *Junge Zinzendorf*, 42.

Later generations pointed to this experience as Zinzendorf's conversion; however, as Beyreuther perceptively indicated, this experience of the painting *Ecce homo* was not a conversion in the usual sense. Rather, it was a strengthening of a religious conviction that Zinzendorf had never lost.[110] This reproach from the suffering Savior helped strengthen Zinzendorf's tendency to connect the mission of the church with the suffering of Christ.

For several years, Zinzendorf's view of the cross remained at the level of devotion without a need to theologize over its meaning. It was sufficient to acknowledge the cross and venerate its bearer. However, this naive attachment to the cross was challenged by Conrad Dippel, who sought to make Christianity conform to reason. In his *Vera demonstratio evangelica,* Dippel set forth the proposition that God is love and that God loves his enemies. God has no wrath, because wrath would violate the nature of God.[111] The cross, for Dippel, cannot be an instrument of divine justice. God has no wrath to appease, nor would he torture anyone to appease his wrath if he could be angry. Both of those propositions violate the nature of God. Instead, the willing death of Jesus serves as an example for humankind. Jesus' passivity before the cruelty of the world is a model for humans to follow.[112]

Zinzendorf appears to have been greatly attracted to Dippel's doctrine of divine love, and throughout his life he had difficulty in speaking of God's wrath and judgment. But he believed that Dippel trivialized the cross, emptying it of its power to save souls. In his sermons to the men in Berlin in 1738, Zinzendorf rejected Dippel's subjective theology, without naming him directly, in favor of the traditional language of ransom and satisfaction.

Those who lead reason into the affair and wish to abolish the misuse of the doctrine of the cross and satisfaction speak thus: The Savior wanted only to make us his pious and divinely blessed people through his death, and through his suffering he revealed the way to holiness. But the true cause of the suffering on his body was "the ransom *(Loskauffung)* of humankind from the slavery to sin and the devil, and that he might do penance for us on the cross," as the Bohemian Brethren sing.[113]

---

110. Spangenberg, *Leben des Herrn Nikolaus Ludwig,* 99. "My blood rushed because I was not able to give much of an answer, and I prayed to my Savior to make me ride in the comradeship of his suffering with force" (quoted in Beyreuther, *Junge Zinzendorf,* 169).

111. Becker, *Zinzendorf und sein Christentum,* 268–76, gives the history of Zinzendorf's encounters with Dippel and his followers. Hans Schneider identifies Dippel as one of the four most important radical Pietists and notes that his works, especially his criticism of the state church, contributed to the German Enlightenment. Schneider, "Der radikale Pietismus in 18. Jahrhundert," 152–56. For Zinzendorf's own comments on the role of Dippel in moving him to a theology of the cross, see *Büdingische Sammlung,* Vorrede, n. 23 (unnumbered).

112. Becker, *Zinzendorf und sein Christentum,* 276.

113. Zinzendorf, *Berliner Reden* (Men) 12:146.

According to Becker, Zinzendorf answered Dippel's criticism of traditional soteriology by drawing a distinction between God's being and the human experience of God. God in his essence is love without wrath, but humans in sin perceive God as wrathful. Christ came to reconcile the world to God, not God to the world. The creature feels its utter worthlessness and its need to be punished, but the Crucifixion stands as the assurance of forgiveness.[114]

Christ did not die to appease a wrathful deity but to purchase his own creatures from "sin, death, and the power of the devil." "We are truly paid for, as a person purchases one item from another, as one can ransom a prisoner, so are we purchased from wrath, from judgment, from the curse, from the Fall and all ruin, from sin, death, the devil and hell through a true, alone in the treasury of God, legal and complete payment, namely, 'through the blood of the one who tasted death for us all through the grace of God.'"[115] Salvation is represented here as a legal payment by God to the devil that the devil was compelled to accept as binding. Once Christ died, the devil had to return all souls to God. "With a word, we are free from the devil."[116]

The whole life and ministry of Jesus must be viewed from the cross because salvation was achieved in the death, not in the Resurrection, of Jesus. "The origin of all grace is to be sought only in the merits and satisfaction of Christ alone who must become everything for us in his bloody form on the cross, and must be the only cause of our blessedness."[117] One may question whether this does not undermine Zinzendorf's insight into the soteriological function of the Incarnation itself; however, we also see this same type of incarnational spirituality in the late Middle Ages. Carolina Walker Bynum's assessment of the tenor of medieval piety applies to Zinzendorf as well:

Christ is seen as the mediator who joins our substance to divinity and as the object of a profound personal union; God is emphasized as creating and creative; the cooperation of the Trinity in the work of creation is stressed. The dominant note of piety is optimism and a sense of momentum toward a loving God. Concentration on the eucharist and on Christ's suffering in the passion, which increases in thirteenth- and fourteenth-century devotions, is not primarily a stress on the sacrifice needed to bridge the enormous gap between us in our sin and God in his glory; it is rather an identification with the fact that Christ is what we are.[118]

We see this same curious blend of violent imagery and joyful spirituality in Zinzendorf, but as one would expect from an antirationalist and unsystematic

114. Becker, *Zinzendorf und sein Christentum*, 276–80.
115. Zinzendorf, *Berliner Reden* (Men) 8:98.
116. Ibid., 99–100.
117. Ibid., 25.
118. Bynum, *Jesus as Mother*, 130.

theologian, Zinzendorf does not critically address other soteriological schemes. Nor does he attempt to make explicit all of his own assumptions about the Atonement.

The ransom of Christ for human souls lost in perdition is his stated theology; however, it is evident that the Crucifixion was more than just a purchase of souls from the devil. The subjective experience of the worshipper who contemplates the sacrifice of Christ is essential to Zinzendorf's soteriology and formed the heart of life in Bethlehem. The Atonement must be appropriated by the individual through loving and faithful contemplation of the crucified Savior.[119] Mere intellectual acceptance of the fact of the ransom is not sufficient for salvation; the heart must see and feel its connection with the dying Redeemer. Zinzendorf has the Holy Spirit say of the Crucifixion, "I can lay hold upon their hearts and say, 'What your guilt deserved, He has endured.'"[120] Such concrete images impress upon the worshipper the reality of Christ's life-giving sacrifice.

But in what form does He always come to his "Christians"? I answer, never in any other than His suffering form. All meditations upon the Deity, upon the omnipotent Being, upon the original Loving-being, yes, even upon the virtuous and wonderful life of the Saviour when He is in our thoughts and minds as the Son of God, as God of God and Light of Light, nicely orthodox, and true enough—all this is, however, nothing more than a refined, reasonable Methodism, just a little bit better than pure morality.[121]

BLOOD MYSTICISM

Christ's blood is thus symbolic of the healing of the soul and the release from sin and death. Zinzendorf makes the connection between the blood of Christ and eternal life explicit when he connects the statement in Leviticus (17:11) that "the life of the flesh is in the blood" with Christ's triumph over death. The blood of Christ has given eternal life to God's children by pouring life into their dying bodies. It is "the proper principle of life."[122] The blood of Christ gives life to Christians much as a literal blood transfusion gives life to the body.

This concept is easily connected with Zinzendorf's longing for daily union with the Savior. Christ's blood becomes the lasting connection between the heart of the Christian and the heart of the Savior. Therefore "we have indeed the great blessing that we are bathed in and swim in Jesus' blood."[123] Swimming in the blood of Christ was not a morbid image for Zinzendorf but an expres-

119. Faull, "Faith and Imagination," 32; Faull, *Moravian Women,* "Introduction."
120. Zinzendorf, *Berliner Reden* (Men) ZE 14:6:74–75; cf. ibid., 8:93–111; *Einundzwanzig Diskurse,* ZH 6:5:112.
121. Zinzendorf, *Nine Public Lectures,* 67.
122. Zinzendorf, *Gemeinreden,* ZH 4:33:86; *Wundenlitanei Homilien,* ZH 3:1:8.
123. Zinzendorf, *Gemeinreden,* ZH 4:2:40.

sion of the soul's desire for eternal life in Christ; a life purchased only by the spilling of Christ's blood.[124]

Zinzendorf went even further to say that this spilled blood was the conduit of the Holy Spirit and the means of re-creating the entire world. Its power ultimately affected all of creation. It brought new life to everything that God made and restored all things to their original purity. "When the dear Savior had died and his blood poured out, when his side was opened up, then the Holy Spirit, like a dammed stream, broke out again. She burst through and made the entire earth a streambed. As a part of its surface is covered with water, so is the entire world, at least by and by, covered with the Holy Spirit."[125] Blood is thus a symbol of immersion in the divine life; it is a fountain in which the believer swims and from which she drinks. It is a fluid symbol of vitality and strength.[126] "His blood of reconciliation is the *proprium quarti modi* of the entire holy creature, of the entire blessed universe."[127]

Because eternal life was purchased by the sacrifice of the Lamb of God, and human happiness is the fruit of redemption, it is only natural that Christians rejoice over the death of Jesus, not in ridicule but in gratitude. Zinzendorf acknowledged that others were offended by the joyful Passion hymns of the Moravian Church, but "one should see that it is biblical to be joyful while bent over the suffering of God, to play as a sinner . . . to form a playful idea of his suffering form."[128] This is not impiety or blasphemy but a true appreciation for the gift of salvation.

In a later chapter, we will examine how this joyful view of the Atonement was expressed in Bethlehem. It allowed the believer to live in childlike joy and simplicity in the midst of a difficult world. For this transformation to take place, however, the heart must be affected by the death of Jesus, and the best way for this to happen is through affective and realistic language, the language of the heart. Wilhelm Bettermann describes Zinzendorf's religious language as "biblical realism," meaning that he stressed the historical and affective reality of that which is related in the Bible.[129] This connection of affective and graphic language with the goal of joyful, childlike simplicity helps to explain some of Zinzendorf's phrases, particularly relating to the corpse of Jesus, that have offended many observers.

---

124. "From the fountain of suffering, from the fountain of blood from the heart ground of the little Lamb, there is always something supernatural, that is connected with the same Creator's Spirit and grace, that brings life into all conversation and association, in the love among one another, in all life from Jesus' blood." *Gemeinreden*, ZH 4:44:237.

125. Zinzendorf, *Einundzwanzig Diskurse*, ZH 6:8:160–61.

126. In this, Zinzendorf was following the main lines of Renaissance thought about blood. Even figures such as Marsino Ficini promoted the use of blood to increase vitality. Camporesi, *Juice of Life*, 27–52.

127. Zinzendorf, *Wundenlitanei Homilien*, ZH 3:1:8.

128. Zinzendorf, *Gemeinreden*, ZH 4, part 2, intro., 3 (unnumbered).

129. Bettermann, *Theologie und Sprache*, chap. 6.

WOUNDS THEOLOGY

Zinzendorf's view of the Crucifixion became more intense in the 1730s and 1740s. In 1734 he was burning some old papers and, as David Cranz related it,

They were all consumed, excepting one small billet, on which . . . the old Lutheran verse stood: "O let us in thy nail-prints see / Our pardon and election free." All the Brethren and Sisters who saw this billet, the only one which remained unconsumed among the cinders, were filled with a childlike joy; and it gave them an occasion to a heart-felt conversation with each other upon the wounds of Jesus, which was attended with such a blessed effect, as to make a happy alteration in their way of thinking and type of devotion.[130]

From this we see that the adoration of the wounds was not unique to the Moravian Church. Gerhard Reichel identified numerous "wounds hymns" popular in the Moravian Church that are found in Freylinghausen's 1704 hymnal.[131]

Twenty years later, Zinzendorf recalled that on that day, February 14, he and the community began to look only to Christ's wounds for their salvation and direction. "We signify the Glory to God in the highest to God on the cross, and we know that the highest thing, the *summum Bonum* for all souls, is his wounds."[132] The many strands of his heart religion came together when he discovered the power of wounds theology. The Moravians' attachment to wounds theology increased during the 1740s at the same time that they grew more vigorous in their worldwide evangelism and building of communities.

In December 1743 John Nitsche, a member of the Polish Branch of the Unitas Fratrum, died in Herrnhut. According to Cranz, Nitsche "departed this life at Herrnhut with uncommon joyfulness, incessantly addressing himself to the holy wounds of Jesus, had proved a great edification to many, encouraging them, in all circumstances, to look with particular devotion to the blood and wounds of Jesus."[133] Nitsche's devotions formed the basis of the famous *Litany of the Wounds of the Husband (Litaney zu den Wunden des Mannes)* that was first used at Gnadenfrey in 1744.

Although Cranz identified Zinzendorf as the author of the litany, early manuscripts list Johannes von Watteville, Christian Renatus von Zinzendorf,

---

130. Cranz, *Ancient and Modern History of the Brethren,* 180–81. The hymn preserved was the 1644 hymn "O Jesu Christi, meins Lebens Licht," by Martin Behm, which was contained in the 1704 Freylinghausen Songbook (#561). "Laß mich durch deine Nägel-mal Erblicken die Gnaden-Wahl. Durch deine Aufgespaltne Seit Mein arme Seele heimgeleit." Reichel, *Zinzendorfs Frömmigkeit,* 37.

131. Reichel, *Zinzendorfs Frömmigkeit,* 71.

132. Zinzendorf, *Jüngerhaus Diarium,* Feb. 14, 1754. Quoted in Beyreuther, *Zinzendorf und die Christenheit,* 63; cf. "Wir deuten das Deo Gloria in excelsis auf GOtt am Creuz, und wissen, daß die höchste Sache, das summum bonum aller Seelen, *seine Wunden* seyn." *Wundenlitanei Homilien,* ZH 3:5:55.

133. Cranz, *Ancient and Modern History of the Brethren,* 298.

Polycarp Müller, and someone named Jakob as the authors.[134] Although the *Litany of the Wounds* is often associated with the Sifting, Polycarp Müller was the one who most strongly resisted the Sifting Time. Von Watteville was the lieutenant who was given the task of bringing the Moravian Church back into order after 1749. Therefore the *Litany* it should not be dismissed as a product of Sifting Time fanaticism. The litany did offend many people outside the church, but it quickly became the most beloved litany inside the Moravian Church.

Zinzendorf himself acknowledged that his way of speaking about the suffering of Jesus aroused opposition, but that this was misguided. "If one or another reader should wonder at the newness of the expressions and at the candid utterance of such paradoxes . . . then I would not have much really to suggest in return and would only have to be sorry that I cannot send such a person my glasses, through which I see when I speak."[135] In fact, Zinzendorf claimed that the Moravian Church had always preached a theology of the wounds, even if the language was at first not as vivid as it became after 1744. In 1747 he reminded the community of Herrnhaag that before the first *Gemeinhaus* was built in Herrnhut more than twenty-four years earlier, they had "had the wounds of the Savior in their prospect."[136]

Bettermann makes the bold but justifiable claim that wounds theology represents the high point of Zinzendorf's overturning of Pietism through a Lutheran theology of the cross.[137] Wounds theology was an expression of the idea of salvation through grace alone. The wounding of Christ was seen by Zinzendorf as bringing salvation in several ways. First of all, the suffering of Jesus served as a penance for human failing. This penitential struggle for all people reached its height during the agony in Gethsemane, when Christ bore the weight of the world's sins and faced all temptations. His bloodlike sweat was the sign and seal of this penitential grace that continues to bless and heal the believing community.[138] "This is the chief goal of our entire existence in the world, since the Savior has endured the death grief on his head, by which his sweat broke out, and with such a quantity that finally instead of the usual watery moisture, blood came out of his veins and pores, and fell like water drops on the earth. With such a gruesome anxiety he won for us an eternal blessedness that can never come to an end."[139]

---

134. Reichel, *Zinzendorfs Frömmigkeit*, 52.

135. Zinzendorf, *Nine Public Lectures*, xxxii.

136. Zinzendorf, *Gemeinreden*, ZH 4:40:196.

137. Bettermann, *Theologie und Sprache*, 55. Bettermann quotes Martin Dober, one of the Moravian residents of Herrnhut, who identified the mid-1740s as the crucial period in the development of the Moravian Church and its theology (62).

138. Zinzendorf states that the sweat in the garden was not only poured out in penance for humankind but is also the medicine for human healing. *Kinder Reden*, ZE 6:41:203.

139. Ibid., 12, 60. (Incidentally, this was preached to children about three years old.) Cf. *Nine Public Lectures*, 31.

Second, the suffering of Christ keeps people from loving him for any other reason than in response to this love. Christ does not want people to love him because of "His miracles, His glory, and His benefits" but only because he first loved his creatures and suffered for them. "As He is described in Isaiah 53, no man would desire Him. Why? Because the Creator absolutely refuses to be loved for any other reason than because one does love [Him]."[140] The terrible suffering and disfigurement that Jesus endured ensures that no one can create a theology of glory around him.

The historical and graphic reality of the cruelties endured by Jesus turns the believer away from all theologies of glory and self-righteousness. The only way to happiness is through the sweat and anguish of Jesus. Zinzendorf imagines Jesus speaking thus to the individual:

Do you want me? Do you receive me? Do I suit you? Am I acceptable to you? Do I please your heart? See, here I am! This is the way I look. For your sake I was made to be sin (II Cor. 5:21), and for your sake I was made a curse (Gal. 3:13); for the sake of your sins I was torn, beaten, and put to death. I have sweated the sweat of fear and anguish, the sweat of death, the sweat of the strife of penance; I have laid down my life for your sake. I have been laid into the dust of the grave for your sake. Does this suit you? Is this important to you? Are you satisfied with me? Do I in this way please you? Do I please you better in the idea of a mangled slave who is thrown to the wild beasts in the circus, or in the form of the emperor who sits high on the throne and takes pleasure in the destruction of the poor creature? How do I please you the best?[141]

A third important reason for the suffering of Jesus was that this has a profound and lasting effect on the human heart. The natural heart is so hardened that it cannot respond to a simple decree of forgiveness; it must be melted and convinced of the extent of human ruin and the cost of human redemption. "Like wax before the fire, I / Want to melt in Jesus' suffering."[142] An easy death would have proved nothing and, more important, would have no effect on the heart. Many brave people, such as Socrates, die without fear. Christ had to suffer all that humans as a race must suffer, not just physical pain but anxiety and fear of death as well. Zinzendorf particularly stressed Jesus' cry from the cross, "*Eli, Eli, lama sabachthani*" (My God, my God, why have you forsaken me?), as evidence of Christ's complete identification with the human race and of the depth of his psychological suffering for humankind.[143]

The wounds carry further meaning, however. For Zinzendorf, the wounds

140. Zinzendorf, *Nine Public Lectures*, 90.

141. Ibid., 83. The transfigured body of Christ, on the other hand, leads one into various forms of mysticism. *Kinder Reden*, ZE 6, Intro., xxxi.

142. Zinzendorf, *Nine Public Lectures*, 41; cf. *Berliner Reden* (Men) ZE 14:6:65–67.

143. Zinzendorf, *Berliner Reden* (Men), ZE 14:12:146–47.

are an everlasting sign of Christ's Atonement. The cross has long since been destroyed, but the marks of the Crucifixion on the person of Jesus remain, since his body did not decay in the grave. Therefore "the Saviour is never in all eternity without his sign, without his wounds." When Christ returns to earth, the five cross wounds "will be the sign of the Son by which the nations, the tribe of Israel, and the entire world will recognize who the man on the clouds is."[144]

In this regard, Zinzendorf had special praise for Thomas, commonly called the Doubter. Thomas refused to believe that Jesus had been resurrected until he could see and feel the print of the nails in his hands (John 20:25). Far from criticizing Thomas for his doubting, Zinzendorf used him as an example for all Christians. Persons should not believe until in their own hearts they see the marks of the nails that prove he was truly crucified.[145] According to Zinzendorf, there are many "Thomas Christians" who have laid hands in the side of Christ.[146]

Zinzendorf was very fond of the legend that St. Martin of Tours once encountered Satan, who tried to convince the bishop that he was really Christ. Martin replied, "If you are Christ, then where are your wounds?" When Satan responded that he wanted to show Martin his glory, not his suffering, Martin answered, "You are the devil; a Saviour who is without wounds, who does not have the mark of his sufferings, I do not acknowledge."[147] The wounds of Christ are his true identifying feature, which Satan cannot imitate because Satan is a spirit.

Again, there is ample medieval precedent for such a fixation on the side wound of Jesus. In the late Middle Ages, according to Bynum, prayers to the wounds proliferated to the point that some counted as many as 6,666 wounds in Christ. But the side wound remained the most important. There was even a popular woodcut of Jesus entirely as a side wound.[148]

Many medieval devotional treatises placed the reader in the role of Thomas. It is interesting that William of St. Thierry records that, "like Thomas, that man of desires, I want to see and touch the whole of him and—what is more—to approach the most holy wound in his side, the portal of the ark that is there made, and that not only to put my finger or my whole hand into it,

---

144. Zinzendorf, *Nine Public Lectures*, 28. *Wundenlitanei Homilien*, ZH 3:1:4; cf. *Kinder Reden*, ZE 6:42:211 and 69:340.

145. Zinzendorf, *Nine Public Lectures*, 82.

146. Zinzendorf, *Gemeinreden*, ZH 4:32:72.

147. Zinzendorf, *Nine Public Lectures*, 28; cf. *Kinder Reden*, ZE 6:42:209–10. It is interesting that Zinzendorf here acknowledges the possibility that humans can experience the stigmata.

148. Caroline Walker Bynum, "Violent Imagery in Later Medieval Piety," Fifteenth Annual Lecture of the German Historical Institute, Nov. 8, 2001, published in *Bulletin of the German Historical Institute* 30 (2002): 3–36. Bynum covers some of this material in her article "The Blood of Christ in the Later Middle Ages."

but wholly enter into Jesus' very heart, into the holy of holies, the ark of the covenant, the golden urn, the soul of humanity that holds within itself the manna of the Godhead—then, alas! I am told: 'Touch me not!' and I hear that word from the Book of Revelation: 'Dogs go outside!' "[149]

The wounds of Christ, then, in late medieval and Zinzendorfian piety are a potent and multivalent symbol of salvation, and as such are a fitting object of veneration and meditation. The Christian should never lose sight of the wounded hands and feet of Jesus, because they are the proof of redemption and thus the source of health and life.

In fact, all knowledge of God is focused on the wounds of Christ. They formed the catechism and the rosary of the eighteenth-century Moravian Church. "And so that we will never forget them, we will treat them, as the Catholics do with their rosary, we never omit counting one wound after the other."[150] The meditation on the wounds formed an essential part of the daily intercourse with the Savior and became a source of comfort and healing for sin and the burdens of the world.

Therefore we need the wounds. They are not only our comfort; we speak and relate not only always how much it cost him that we are released but we also have need of them every day. If an ordinary person were to take medicine every day, so would he finally become accustomed to it. But if the Savior likewise takes us every day in his arms, let us catch blood drops from the wounds and let us pick and use our death-healing herbs, in the rose-red heart garden, so they [the wounds] are never impotent, and we become healed by them every day.[151]

The wound in the side of Jesus caused by the centurion's spear at the time of Jesus' death became the proper object of Moravian devotion. "A soul most tenderly in love with the Saviour may be ignorant of a hundred truths and only concentrate most simply on Jesus' wounds and death. Oh, how ardently this soul meditates on this part of the body, which on the day of His coming will be the sign of the Son of Man, the hole in His side, His heart, out of which flowed blood and water."[152] This particular fissure in the body of Christ became a compact symbol that Zinzendorf used to communicate many of the themes already addressed in this study. It included all of the concepts related to the

---

149. *On Contemplating God; Prayer; Meditation,* vol. 1 of *The Works of William of St. Thierry,* trans. Sister Penelope, in Cistercian Fathers Series, no. 3 (Spencer, Mass.: Cistercian Pub., 1971), 38–39.

150. Zinzendorf, *Gemeinreden,* ZH 4:39:190–91; cf. ibid., 33:87–88.

151. Zinzendorf, *Kinder Reden,* ZE 6:26:129–30.

152. Zinzendorf, *Nine Public Lectures,* 31. It would be worth exploring the history of the spear/side-wound symbolism in German thought. When Jesus predicts his death in the ninth-century Saxon gospel, *The Heliand,* he ignores the cross in favor of the piercing with the spear, presumably because the warrior audience could understand the latter form of death better. G. Ronald Murphy, trans., *The Heliand: The Saxon Gospel* (New York: Oxford University Press, 1992), 101.

Incarnation, Atonement, and the new birth in Christ. Salvation, sanctification, community life, and divine protection were all brought into a single striking symbol, that of Jesus with an opened side. "The holy side of Jesus is a central point from which one can derive everything spiritual."[153]

John's Gospel asserts that there is no way to the Father except through Jesus, but Zinzendorf presents this as a literal entering through the side hole of Jesus. "No one is directly adopted by the Father, he passes first through the Savior; no one is directly born through the Holy Spirit, he goes first through the Canal of the Savior."[154] The side wound is the narrow door, the portal to paradise, the means of entry into the body of Christ.

Zinzendorf also connects heart religion and the Atonement in the graphic image of the Savior embracing souls and pressing them against his open, bleeding side. "We could not sleep in his arms without touching the side hole, without being near, lying beside and resting in the side hole."[155] According to Zinzendorf, the spear wound was made over the heart of Jesus, and thus there is a physical as well as a metaphorical connection between the believer and the heart of Christ. The side wound is "the door to his heart." "When we thus lay ourselves in the heart of the Savior we lay ourselves at the same time in his wounded heart; the one in order to be rightly loved by him, the other in order to be made sound."[156] Furthermore, the piercing of Jesus' side is also compared to the ripping of the curtain to the Holy of Holies.[157]

Zinzendorf asserted that those who know they are redeemed have experienced being "led with body and soul into the side hole." This is the place of healing and salvation, a place where Christians are as safe as a child in its cradle, or a dove in the crevice of the rock.[158] This last image of the Christian being a bird in the side of Christ may strike the modern reader as bizarre, but it is based on two biblical images: the dove in the cleft of the rocks in Song of Songs 2:14, and Jesus as the Rock. Combining them, one sees Jesus' side wound as the cleft in the Rock in which the dove (the believer) hides.[159]

The popular Protestant hymn "Rock of Ages, Cleft for Me" uses this same imagery, although most people are not aware that they are singing about the side wound of Christ when they sing "let me hide myself in thee." Zinzendorf carried this image further, repeatedly telling his followers that whenever Chris-

153. Zinzendorf, *Gemeinreden*, ZH 4, Intro., 2 (unnumbered).
154. Zinzendorf, *Einundzwanzig Diskurse*, ZH 6:4:102.
155. Zinzendorf, *Wundenlitanei Homilien*, ZH 3:5:63–64.
156. Zinzendorf, *Kinder Reden*, ZE 6:33:163 and 26:128. There is an obvious parallel here with the devotion to the Sacred Heart of Jesus in French Catholicism; see Campbell, *Religion of the Heart*, 36ff.
157. Zinzendorf, *Wundenlitanei Homilien*, ZH 3:5:64; *Gemeinreden*, ZH 4:3:68 and 13:216.
158. Zinzendorf, *Kinder Reden*, ZE 6:11:59; *Gemeinreden*, ZH 4:12:206.
159. Bettermann, *Theologie und Sprache*, 69–75. We see this same linking in one of Zinzendorf's favorite medieval authors, Bernard of Clairvaux; see Bynum, *Jesus as Mother*, 117.

tians are in trouble or fearful, they should crawl into Jesus' wound and find peace and comfort there. It is the resting place and Sabbath bed for all who know the Savior.[160]

For Zinzendorf, the opening of the side wound of Christ was the origin of the church. Since there could be no salvation without the death of the Son of God, there could be no church until there was a cross. The church is nothing other than a "Cross Community" *(Creutz Gemeinschaft)* that depends on the wounds of Jesus. "The entire craft of the Gemein Plan is to draw it by and by through the entire Gemeine so that no heart remains which does not believe in the wounds, that no more souls would be found in the group that do not stick to the wounds and remain dependent on them. Thereafter is the Gemeinschaft complete so that no death edict can ever destroy it."[161]

Baptism is the normal means of entry into the Christian church, but for Zinzendorf the baptism that truly counts is the one in the side wound of Jesus. "I stand and cry, 'I have been baptized, I have been anointed and bloodied from the side hole, I am in the Gemeine, *Kyrieleis!'* [sic]."[162] In 1747 Zinzendorf baptized a child named Gertraut. While the child kneeled, the worshippers sang: "The water, which flowed from his side after the spear pierced, may that be your bath, and all his blood enliven your heart, mind, and spirit." After water was poured on her head, and during the blessing, the congregation sang: "O Jesus, hear me, take and hide her entirely in yourself, enclose her in your wounds and in the church covenant."[163]

The connection between the death of Jesus and baptism was expressed by Zinzendorf in even more graphic terms in his *Twenty-one Discourses on the Augsburg Confession,* in which he wrote, "For to be baptized out of the side of Jesus, to pour the entire stream of the death-water and the heart's blood of Jesus Christ over a soul, and make her so swim into the sea of the wound, and directing her entire future economy, even her homeland, and everything which will happen to her until the last day and beyond the last day under the river bed of the baptismal waters and in the sea of grace."[164] Clearly, the side wound of Christ is the entry port for the Christian to come into the fellowship of

160. Zinzendorf, *Kinder Reden,* ZE 6:11:59. Cf. "In unsere Gemeine nicht Ein Herze übrig bleibe, das nicht an die Wunden gläube, das nicht in die Wunden hineinfahre, und darinnen hier in der Zeit seinen Sitz und Ruhe-Stätte bestelle, das sanfte Bett der Sabbaths-Herzelein, davon so viel geredt, gedacht, gesungen und gespielt wird, davon aber noch vielmehr gefühlt, und alle Tage erfahren wird." *Gemeinreden,* ZH 4:49:301.

161. Zinzendorf, *Gemeinreden,* ZH 4:44:237–38. The idea of the Gemeine is discussed in the next chapter.

162. Zinzendorf, *Einundzwanzig Diskurse,* ZH 6:3:85; cf. 84.

163. Zinzendorf, *Gemeinreden,* ZH 4:4:87–88.

164. Zinzendorf, *Einundzwanzig Diskurse,* ZH 6:18:296.

believers. Zinzendorf even made the point that it is not a "little side hole" (*Seiten-Höhlgen*), as the songs of the Brüdergemeine often describe it, but is a large cave in which all Christian souls safely sit.[165]

The fact that the church was created on the cross affects the nature of the true Christian church. It is not a hierarchy of glorious servants of God, such as the angelic choir, but the bride of the Savior enthroned on the cross. It exists in "the air of the corpse, the atmosphere of the holy grave" that is "our element," and "the healthy air for our hearts, without which we could not exist." Members of the Gemeine are like "cross-air birds" that fly continually around the cross.[166]

The primary purpose of the church is to help individuals love the Savior and meditate on his merits. The whole goal of heart religion is for the heart to be so deeply impressed with the suffering and merits of Jesus that all else fades away except the view of the cross.[167] From this love of Christ, all community feeling will follow. "I do not love you [pl.] for your own sake but for his sake. I love you as my fellow little cross-air birds, as my playmates, my close playmates around his side. I love you as my fellow little swarming bees on his corpse."[168]

Zinzendorf also connected the world mission of the Moravian Church to the sufferings and death of Christ. "The meaning and entire plan of Jesus Christ's servants is to serve and thereby to neglect oneself so that others will be helped."[169] The blessing of being a pilgrim of Christ in the world was purchased by the blood of thousands of martyrs who covered the earth and blessed it and made it a certain ground for evangelism.[170]

These martyrs have prepared the way but that does not mean their followers will not also suffer.[171] Suffering is part of the Christian mission, as Zinzendorf realized when viewing the *Ecce homo*, but despite the reality of pain in suffering, the true bride of Christ can rejoice and rest happy, being protected in his wounds.

It has already been shown that the blood of Christ was an important feature of Zinzendorf's theology. Zinzendorf took very seriously the fact that most of

165. Ibid., 3:85, note. Zinzendorf excuses the effort of hymn writers to describe the side hole in a "childlike" and "tender" fashion.

166. Zinzendorf, *Gemeinreden*, ZH 4:4:79–80; *Kinder Reden*, ZE 6:71:350–51; *Gemeinreden*, ZH 4:30:35; cf. Erbe, "Herrnhaag—Tiefpunkt," for a perceptive explanation of the "cross-air bird" imagery of the Moravian Church.

167. Zinzendorf, *Nine Public Lectures*, 31; *Kinder Reden*, ZE 6:11:58, 6:24:123, 69:341.

168. Zinzendorf, *Gemeinreden*, ZH 4:23:324.

169. Ibid., 28:13.

170. Ibid., 52:333.

171. "We observe with deep respect what they suffered. We also know what we have to suffer. Each one, whom the Savior calls to begin a new plan, knows what he must endure for his part. But we must set fast that all our humiliation and trial and suffering cannot in the least hinder his purpose." Ibid., 333.

the blood that Jesus shed on the cross came from the spear wound. This wound, then, is the source of the sacrificial and healing blood that is life to the believer. This flowing stream from the heart of Jesus can never dry up and Satan cannot dam it, so it continues to flow from Christ into the heart of his bride. Zinzendorf naturally connected this symbolism to the Holy Communion, which is the most "palpable" way for the Christian to experience the embrace of Christ.[172]

Zinzendorf affirmed the Lutheran doctrine of the real presence of Christ in the communion. "We hold before our communicants the belief in the real, essential presence."[173] He presented John 6:53, "unless you eat the flesh of the Son of man and drink his blood, you have no life in you," as a eucharistic text in support of his own blood-and-wounds theology. In the Holy Communion the communicants sacramentally eat the flesh and drink the blood of Christ on the "Cross-Delicatessen."[174] Holy Communion is a form of union with God in which "We go there and present ourselves, that our minds may be made like the mind of the Lamb and our bodies like His corpse. Then we experience that through the tormented body of Christ we are united with the divine nature and come into a condition that foreshadows something of the resurrection."[175]

This union with the divine nature occurs whenever the worshipper approaches the person of Christ and sets his "mouth to his side and drinks" of the blood from the wound "ever opening itself anew."[176] In essence, the side wound of Christ becomes the breast that pours forth nourishment for the believer who rests tenderly in the arms of the Savior.[177] We see here an androgyny in Zinzendorf's Christology comparable to his view of human beings. Aaron Fogleman describes this as a "feminization of the Trinity,"[178] and that is partially correct. The feminization of Christ does not diminish the maleness of Jesus in Zinzendorf's theology. The circumcision and the side wound together paint Jesus as both the ultimate man and the nourishing mother.

This feminization of the Son of God becomes even more pronounced in a final set of images Zinzendorf offers related to the side wound. The side of Christ is the organ of spiritual birth in Zinzendorf's theology.[179] He directly

---

172. Zinzendorf, *Wundenlitanei Homilien*, ZH 3:4:43, 49.

173. Zinzendorf wards off charges of being Roman Catholic by adding that "the idea of transubstantiation is removed completely with the words, 'that the bread is no sacrament outside of the use.'" *Einundzwanzig Diskurse*, ZH 6:18:293.

174. Zinzendorf, *Kinder Reden*, ZE 6:51:259, 70:345.

175. Zinzendorf, *Nine Public Lectures*, 20.

176. Zinzendorf, *Kinder Reden*, ZE 6:56:282; *Einundzwanzig Diskurse*, ZH 6:3:89.

177. This image of Christ as a mother nourishing believers with his own blood is not original with Zinzendorf. Bynum has examined numerous examples of this motif in late medieval and renaissance art and literature. See *Jesus as Mother*, 115–24.

178. Fogleman, "'Jesus ist weiblich,'" 171–81; cf. Atwood, "Sleeping in the Arms of Christ."

179. Bettermann, *Theologie und Sprache*, 82–87. Bettermann stresses the theological meaning of this imagery. Birth through the side wound emphasizes that redemption comes only through Christ.

compared it to female reproductive organs. Zinzendorf recorded with pleasure that the sisters had the "clear image on the holy side of Jesus, which was opened on the cross, when he had birthed our souls."[180]

To help clarify his understanding of souls being born out of the side of Christ, Zinzendorf introduced a rather unusual concept. Little souls are created or "begotten" in "the matrix" (womb) of the side wound and then proceed through that orifice into the world and the bodies of the believers.[181] The Holy Spirit was given to the world along with these little souls when "the spear went into the little Lamb" (John 7:38–39) and the blood and life of Jesus poured out from the side hole. Notice that the mystical language of the divine spark has been transposed into a cross theology. There is a spark of the divine in the souls of Christians, but it proceeds through the side wound of Jesus.

The connection between the side wound and women's bodies is made explicit in the *Twenty-One Discourses* when Zinzendorf says that the Christian "wants to enter again into his womb."[182] "If one says, I believe it, now I will see whether you are a divine child. That I will see in your longing for your Mother's womb, in whether you have entered into the new world through the right door, through which the pleroma [fullness] of the new Spirit exited, namely through the side of Jesus."[183]

In another set of intriguing images, Zinzendorf compares the rebirth of the soul to the creation of Eve from the side of Adam. When Jesus fell asleep on the cross, his side was opened, and God grabbed human souls from the side, just as God opened the side of the sleeping Adam and "took out his future wife from his side."[184]

The significance of wounds piety in Bethlehem will be examined more deeply later, but for now it is important to see that Zinzendorf was able to focus an entire Christian theology by use of a single compelling symbol: the side wound of Christ. The doctrine of justification by grace through faith, which in Lutheran Orthodoxy had become a sterile academic debate, was recast in terms of the ever-present paradox of the beautiful and horrible wounds of Christ. The wounds of Christ are repulsive and gory to the world but are beautiful, glistening, and succulent to the believer.[185] It is in the light of this primal paradox that the paradox of being a justified sinner is to be understood and *experienced.* Salvation comes through the death of the incarnate Son of God.

This symbolism may appear bizarre to those outside his circle, but it had a

---

180. Erbe, *Herrnhaag: Eine religiöse Kommunität,* 102, n. 14.
181. Zinzendorf, *Einundzwanzig Diskurse,* ZH 6:4:104.
182. Ibid., 2:76 and 9:188.
183. Ibid., 2:73.
184. Zinzendorf, *Gemeinreden,* ZH 4:19:286; *Einundzwanzig Diskurse,* ZH 6:4:105.
185. Bettermann, *Theologie und Sprache,* 49–54.

powerful effect on his followers. They entered into the mental world of Zinzendorf. They visualized the sufferings of Christ and feasted on his corpse. They longed to become Christ's lovers lying in his dead arms. Their communities were truly born out of the side of Christ. Zinzendorf's theology, especially his wounds theology, was not divorced from the communal mission of the Moravian Church. It was literally the life-blood of the church.

Prosternation devant le Seigneur.

FIGURE 4. The *Anbeten* or Prostrate Prayer, circa 1757. Unity Archives, Herrnhut.

CHAPTER 4

BETHLEHEM

Bethlehem in Pennsylvania was a visible expression of Zinzendorf's imaginative theological vision even though Zinzendorf himself spent little time there. It was the headquarters of Zinzendorf's Brüdergemeine in British North America and a living embodiment of Zinzendorf's understanding that the sacred and secular dimensions of life should be joined in the daily union with Christ, the wounded Bridegroom. Before examining the piety and ritual life of Bethlehem, it will be helpful to begin with a brief account of the history of Bethlehem as a communal society (1741–62).[1]

THE FOUNDING OF BETHLEHEM

In 1735 several Moravians sailed to Georgia to work among the native tribes and African slaves. This was the famous sea voyage during which John Wesley first encountered the Moravians. The Georgia enterprise failed for many reasons. Their refusal to swear an oath of allegiance and their reluctance to bear arms in self-defense led to tensions with the other colonists, but there were also public confrontations over their Zinzendorfian piety. There was internal dissent as well, and many members of the community left.[2] When Peter Böhler came to Savannah in October 1738, he found that the community there had nearly disintegrated. Only Anton Seiffert, Martin Mack, and the Zeisbergers remained. Pennsylvania became a place of refuge for Moravians leaving the Georgia colony.

August Gottlieb Spangenberg had earlier reconnoitered Pennsylvania, and when he returned to Europe in 1739 he reported to Zinzendorf on favorable conditions in Pennsylvania. Not only could it provide a place for those leaving Georgia, it was also a fertile field for Moravian mission work among natives

---

1. This chapter relies heavily on the work of Helmut Erbe, *Bethlehem, Pa.,* Smaby, *Transformation of Moravian Bethlehem,* and Levering, *A History of Bethlehem.* Levering's history is based on an intimate familiarity with the original documents in the archives, but it lacks scholarly apparatus.

2. Aaron S. Fogleman, "The Decline and Fall of the Moravian Community in Colonial Georgia: Revising the Traditional View," *Unitas Fratrum* 48 (2001): 1–22, corrects the older view of the Georgia mission found in Hamilton and Hamilton, *History,* 82–85, and Adelaide Fries, *The Moravians in Georgia* (Raleigh, N.C.: Edwards and Broughton, 1905). Fogleman rightly concludes that the Georgia colony should be viewed as a failed experiment in community building in the New World (22). As such, it is directly related to the way Bethlehem was organized.

and colonists.[3] Spangenberg's plan was expansive. It included preaching stations in the settlements, schools for boys, Indian missions, and a town to be
the center for all of this activity and organization. At the second General Synod
(at Ebersdorf) later that year, the Brüdergemeine endorsed his plan, and the
first colonists were selected at the third General Synod (at Gotha) in 1740.[4]
There would be a central trading town surrounded by farms so that the community would not be dependent on trade with outsiders. The town was to be
named Bethlehem, as it would be the town where Christ would be born in
America.

In the meantime, the evangelist George Whitefield transported some of the
Moravians from Georgia on his personal ship to Pennsylvania. Whitefield had
grand plans of his own for a Halle-style complex in eastern Pennsylvania, and
he hired the Moravians from Georgia as carpenters and laborers on his estate,
Nazareth. What seemed at first to be a close collaboration between two types
of Pietism soon fell apart when Whitefield and Böhler disagreed over the doctrine of election. Whitefield rejected the Moravians' view of universal redemption, preferring the Calvinist idea of a limited atonement. Whitefield tried to
force the Moravians to leave his lands, but friends of Spangenberg intervened.

They were allowed to stay until winter was over, when they relocated a few
miles south of Whitefield's estate. A local miller named Irish was sympathetic
to the Moravians and agreed to sell them five hundred acres of land where the
Monocacy Creek meets the Lehigh River, and in 1741 the Moravians began
construction of Bethlehem.[5] Eventually they were able to buy Nazareth from
Whitefield and build it into a major agricultural center for the Brüdergemeine,
an irony the Moravians appreciated.[6]

Shortly after the land for Bethlehem was purchased, a group of missionaries
arrived from Herrnhut. Among them were both aristocrats and commoners
who shared communal living. Included in the number were Bishop David Nitschmann, David Nitschmann the Senior (called Father Nitschmann), Christian
Froehlich, Anna Nitschmann, and Johanna Sophia Molther. They were an experienced and diverse group.

The sixty-four-year-old Father Nitschmann was from Zauchenthal in Moravia and had been on St. Croix in 1734 when ten missionaries, including his
wife, had died. Anna Nitschmann was only twenty-three when she came to

3. Levering, A History of Bethlehem, 32–36.
4. Ibid., 55–56.
5. Ibid., 41–42, 52.
6. Peter Böhler stated, "The Brethren, who formerly were day laborers there and exiles, afterwards became the owners and inhabitants of the place." Vernon Nelson, trans. and ed., "Peter Boehler's Reminiscences of the Beginnings of Nazareth and Bethlehem," Transactions of the Moravian Historical Society 27
(1992): 15.

Pennsylvania, but she had been an eldress since she was fifteen and was the founder of the Single Sisters' Choir in Herrnhut. She returned to Europe with Zinzendorf in 1743 and became one of his most important partners. Johanna Molther was only twenty-two and was Baroness von Seidwitz. Christoph Pyrlaeus also came to assist in the mission to the native tribes.[7]

In September 1741 the cornerstone for the Gemeinhaus in Bethlehem was laid. This large building, which is still standing, served as a worship place, community center, and eating hall, and for several years was the main dormitory of Bethlehem. It was more or less finished in time for the first major immigration of Moravians to Bethlehem in 1742, when the first so-called Sea Congregation *(See-Gemeine)* arrived from Europe, led by the recently married Peter Böhler.[8] The experience of most Moravians immigrating to British North America was far different from that of other German colonists, as Fogleman has shown.[9] The Moravians arrived in organized groups that were carefully prepared for their mission in the New World.

Bethlehem was far enough along to house Zinzendorf when he arrived in December 1741. He led the celebration of Christmas Eve according to the new calendar, which the English had not yet adopted, and at that service officially named the community Bethlehem.[10] Zinzendorf helped with the organization of the fledgling community, and his daughter, Benigna, founded the Single Sisters choir as well as a school for girls.[11]

Of equal or greater interest to Zinzendorf were his visits to the native tribes. He made three visits to the wilderness to meet with representatives of the nations. His longest trip took place from September 21 to November 8, 1742, with a small party that included Anna Nitschmann, whom he called "the most courageous of our number and a heroine."[12] Conrad Weiser, his German wilderness guide, took him to Shawnee country, where no one had yet preached

---

7. Levering, *A History of Bethlehem*, 54–56, note; 69–70.

8. Ibid., 107–14. They were welcomed into the community at a meeting of one of Zinzendorf's Pennsylvania synods. On pages 119–26, Levering gives the names and biographies of all members of the Sea Congregation. For more information on the building and use of the Gemeinhaus through the years, see Vernon Nelson, *The Bethlehem Gemeinhaus: A National Historic Landmark* (Bethlehem, Pa.: Moravian Congregation of Bethlehem, 1990).

9. Fogleman, *Hopeful Journeys*, 111–16.

10. Levering, *A History of Bethlehem*, 77–78.

11. Faull, *Moravian Women*, 3. There has been very little written about Benigna von Watteville. The manuscript of her funeral biography is located in the Unity Archive in Herrnhut, and the only published biography is by Johann Friederich Wihelm Ritter, *Leben des Freiherrn Johannes von Watteville, Bishofs des Evangelischen Büderkirche und dessen Gemahlin Frau Henriette benigna Justine, Freifrau von Watteville, gebornen Grafin von Zinzendorf* (Altoona, Pa.: Jacob Schultz, 1800). Katherine Miller has published a short but helpful sketch of the countess's life, "A Short History of the Life of Benigna, Baroness von Watteville, nee Countess von Zinzendorf," *Transactions of the Moravian Historical Society* 27 (1992): 53–61.

12. Quoted in Paul Wallace, *Conrad Weisser (1696–1760): Friend of Colonist and Mohawk* (Philadelphia: University of Pennsylvania Press, 1945), 139.

the gospel. Weiser's account of this venture illuminates Zinzendorf's shortcomings. "He is pretty hot-headed and likes to give orders, the Indians on the other hand won't take orders in the least and consider a dictator non-sensical [unsinnig]."[13] Zinzendorf left Bethlehem for good on January 1, 1743, convinced of both the need for evangelical missions to the natives and the problem of theological argumentativeness among the whites.[14]

In June 1742 Bethlehem was divided into the *Hausgemeine* (home community) and the Pilgergemeine (pilgrim community) proper. This was done in some cases by request and in others by lot, but the boundaries between the two were permeable. As Levering puts it, pilgrims "were to devote themselves to evangelistic work among Indians and white people, adults and children, according to arrangements to be made from time to time. The others were to 'tarry by the stuff' (I Sam. 30:24). They were to develop the material resources, erect buildings, provide sustenance for the 'pilgrims,' care for their necessities as they went and came; and, at the same time, spiritually keep the fire burning on the home altar."[15]

This led to the development of the General Economy, by which Bethlehem was structured along strict communal lines. The church owned the land, buildings, and businesses. Residents exchanged work for food, clothing, medical care, and shelter. Children were also raised together by the community in order to free men and women for missionary and economic activities.

Helmut Erbe argues that the communalism was designed to enhance the missionary activity of the "pilgrims," not to serve as an end in itself. Thus it was not a utopian adventure but a practical way to meet the needs of an active missionary enterprise. In saying this, however, Erbe downplays the internal drive toward communalism in the life of the Brüdergemeine. A distinction needs to be made between the full economic communalism of the Pilgergemeine and the communal social structure of an Ortsgemeine. The principal difference between Bethlehem and the other settlements was the full sharing of a communal economy, but it is unlikely that this would have been accomplished had it not been for the social communalism already established in Herrnhut and Herrnhaag.

Scholars have debated whether the General Economy was intended to be a

---

13. Ibid., 141. The episode with the Shawnee was almost a complete disaster, since Zinzendorf could not stop being an imperial count and the natives did not trust his motives. Despite his frustrations over Zinzendorf, Weisser remained on good terms with the Moravians and as late as 1745 was addressing letters "To the worthy Herr Ludwig von Thürnstein Somewhere in the World on his Pilgrimage." Ibid., 123.

14. Beyond the difficulties of the Church of God in the Spirit, Zinzendorf also had a bitter controversy with Muhlenberg, the Lutheran missionary to America. See Wagner, *Zinzendorf-Muhlenberg Encounter;* Samuel R. Zeiser, "Moravians and Lutherans: Getting Beyond the Zinzendorf-Muhlenberg Impasse," *Transactions of the Moravian Historical Society* 28 (1994): 15–29.

15. Levering, *A History of Bethlehem,* 129.

permanent part of the Bethlehem plan or was merely a temporary response to the immediate exigencies of life in the wilderness. John Ettwein, one of the later leaders of Bethlehem, asserted the latter, perhaps in an attempt to justify Bethlehem's situation at the time.[16] If Ettwein is correct, then the system was never intended to endure; however, Smaby's work demonstrates the extreme personal and social tensions caused by the abolition of the old system. Such tensions indicate that the transition was neither anticipated nor desired by the residents but was in fact legislated from Europe.[17] Put simply, Bethlehem worked best when it was a communal society.

SPANGENBERG

August Gottlieb Spangenberg arrived in Bethlehem on November 30, 1744, as the *Vicarius Generalis Episcoporum et per Americam in Presbyterio Vicarius.*[18] This exalted title made him the supreme authority over all the Moravian work in North America, especially in Bethlehem. He was the vicar of the bishops and the Chief Elder in America.[19]

One of Spangenberg's goals was for Bethlehem to be as nearly self-sufficient as possible. This would not only avoid the debt cycle that he had witnessed in the European Gemeinen, it would also reduce the disruptive influence of outsiders. To this end he organized the General Economy and personally directed its diverse enterprises. Writing in 1906, Gerhard Reichel described Spangeberg's General Economy as "an unending cycle, an intricate interlocked machine!"[20] The Bethlehem complex included the trade and manufacturing center, Bethlehem, the farming community of Nazareth, and the smaller farming communities of Christianbrunn, Gnadenthal, and Friedensthal. The Moravians were thus able to manufacture most of what they needed for their own use and for trade, and they were able to grow most of their own food. There was frequent interaction between these settlements, and the children's schools and houses were at times in Nazareth and at times in Bethlehem.

The economic success of communal Bethlehem is evident in the records of the community. Although the population in the entire complex never numbered more than nine hundred adults, in twenty years the Moravians housed

---

16. Gollin, *Moravians in Two Worlds,* 138–43; Hamilton and Hamilton, *History,* 137; Erbe, *Bethlehem, Pa.,* 104–7.

17. Smaby, *Transformation of Moravian Bethlehem,* 32–36, 83.

18. Levering, *A History of Bethlehem,* 177. The only modern biography of Spangenberg is that of Gerhard Reichel, *August Gottlieb Spangenberg* (Tübingen, 1906). Sawyer, "Religious Experience of the Colonial American Moravians," 45–68, gives brief biographies of Spangenberg and his assistant, Böhler.

19. In 1741 Christ had been proclaimed the Chief Elder of the Moravian Church, but for reasons that are still obscure, that was not extended to the work in America until 1748. Hamilton and Hamilton, *History,* 72–75.

20. Reichel, *Spangenberg,* 135, "Ein unedlicher Kreislauf, eine Kunst-voll ineinander greifende Machine!"

more than fifty trades and industries. They also built more than fifty buildings in Bethlehem (and another fifty in the rest of the complex), some of which are still used by the church.[21] Most of the larger buildings, such as the Single Brothers' House, the Single Sisters' House, and the Gemeinhaus, were among the larger structures in Pennsylvania (outside of Philadelphia) in the 1740s and 1750s. Such industry is even more remarkable in light of the fact that the primary purpose of the community was not economic advancement.

All of the major histories of Bethlehem have rightly identified Spangenberg as a capable and efficient administrator. He had a difficult job that required, as Böhler later described it, "a man full of spirit and power, to direct this business in a Godly manner, and one who at the same time has understanding for the old patriarchal economy of cattle raising and agriculture, as well as in the new economy of commerce, handicrafts and building construction."[22] Spangenberg was also trained theologically (at Jena) and served as the worship leader of Bethlehem for most of his tenure, although he shared these duties with others.

Often overlooked in descriptions of Spangenberg by American and English historians are his early connections with radical Pietism. As a young man Spangenberg embraced the teachings of the Dutch mystic J. G. Gichtel, and even adopted celibacy.[23] Spangenberg's Separatist tendencies led to his ouster from his post in the orphanage at Halle in 1732.[24] Zinzendorf welcomed him to Herrnhut (which furthered the breach with Halle) and soon placed him in charge of the orphanage there in 1733. His talents were quickly recognized and before long he became one of Zinzendorf's chief aides and treasurer for the Brüdergemeine. In 1735 he led the first Moravian colonists to British North America, but the controversy he had caused in Halle followed him to the New World.[25]

Because of his practical economic gifts, theological training, and previous experience in America, Spangenberg was chosen to establish Moravian work in Pennsylvania. He left Europe in 1744 with a set of sixteen instructions for Bethlehem that established the Pennsylvania Plan and the Pilgergemeine idea.[26]

21. Smaby, *Transformation of Moravian Bethlehem*, 86–89; see 90–91 for a chart of the various buildings and industries. Sessler, *Communal Pietism*, 90–91, lists the various occupations in Bethlehem-Nazareth.

22. "Es ist wohl nicht zu leugnen . . . es gehört unstreitig ein Stephanus, ein Mann voll Geistes und Kraft dazu, diese Sache göttlich zu dirigieren, und der zugleich ökonomischen Verstand in die alte patriarchalische Haushaltung von Viehzucht und Feldbau, als in der neuen Haushaltung des Commercii, der Handwerke und des Bauwesens hat." Letter from Böhler to Zinzendorf, March 9, 1759, quoted in Erbe, *Bethlehem, Pa.*, 31.

23. Reichel, *Spangenberg*, 29. For more on Gitchel's rejection of marriage, see Gottfried Beyreuther, "Sexualtheorien im Pietismus," (Ph.D. diss., Ludwig-Maximillians-Universität, Munich, 1963), 22–28; reproduced in ZM 2:13;509–96.

24. Reichel, *Spangenberg*, 62–81.

25. Fogleman, "Decline and Fall," 1–2; Ward, *Protestant Evangelical Awakening*, 3, 139–42.

26. "General-Plan mit welchem ich anno 1744. von Europa nach America abgereißt" by Spangenberg. Folder 1, 1-a, Moravian Archives. Sessler, *Communal Pietism,* 80–84, offers a translation of this plan, essentially that of Levering, *A History of Bethlehem,* 178–79, with interpretation for each paragraph; however, I

Among the features of this plan that directly concern Bethlehem was the provision that there were to be as many smaller congregations as necessary to keep up the work of the Brüdergemeine, but that Bethlehem would be the rendezvous for the pilgrim missionaries who were to move "like a cloud of grace wherever the wind of the Lord drives them, making everything fruitful."

Nazareth was to be a plantation, and the large house in Nazareth (the Whitefield house) was to be a children's institution, a *Kinder Anstalt*.[27] There were also instructions for the mission to the native peoples and for continuing the Pennsylvania synods. It is interesting that Spangenberg was forbidden to call the Brethren "Protestant or Lutheran or Moravian." They were to be known simply as the *"evangelische Brüder—und Brüdergemeine."* Only if Nazareth were to become a full Ortsgemeine for the members of the Unitas Fratrum (distinguished from the Brüdergemeine) could the name Moravian be used there.[28]

Spangenberg and his new wife, Mary, threw themselves into their work, and slowly a thriving community arose in the wilderness. In July 1742 there were 131 persons in Bethlehem, 59 of whom were members of the Pilgrim congregation. By 1745 several boatloads of European immigrants had increased the population to 400, mostly of German origin.[29] The community continued to grow throughout the period of the General Economy, so that in 1761 there were 659 residents. Interestingly, the population declined after the communal system was abolished and did not begin to increase until 1818. In 1848 Bethlehem was only about 200 persons larger than it had been in 1761.[30]

The Spangenbergs deserve much of the credit for ordering and guiding this

find the translation and the interpretation flawed in certain places. For example, both Sessler and Levering translate item 4 as "A house for the single women and one for single men . . . are to be held in view." Actually it refers to a Single *Sisters* House, and I believe that the original document says (it is very difficult to make out) that "In Bethlehem solte nie ein lediges-Schwesters-Haus werden; wol aber ein led. br. Haus, desgleichen ein Knaben- und Mädgen-Chor," which is explained in no. 5: "die led. br. u. Schwestern könten ohne Heyrathen nicht zu rechte kommen in America, wären auch ohne das nicht so brauchbar, und es sey nicht der Sinn des Heylandes, die dortigen leute so lange ledig zu lassen." My translation reads: "4) In Bethlehem a Single Sisters House should *never* be erected, but there should be a Single Brothers House, likewise a boy and girls choir [house]: 5) the single brothers and sisters will not be able to manage that well in America without being married; they would not be as useful either. And it is not the mind of the Savior, that the people there should remain single so long."

27. The location of the boys' and girls' schools changed several times between Bethlehem and Nazareth over the first twenty years. Eventually the boys settled in Nazareth and the girls in Bethlehem. For a firsthand account of the *Kinder Anstaten*, see the *Lebenslauf* of Anna Boehler in Faull, *Moravian Women*, 68–71.

28. Incidentally, Erbe, *Bethlehem, Pa.*, 27, reports that in 1748 there were fewer than two dozen Moravians among the four hundred residents of Bethlehem. This, combined with the prohibition in the General Plan against the name Moravian, raises questions about the propriety of calling the denomination that emerged in America the "Moravian" Church.

29. Ibid., 26–28. The diverse nature of Bethlehem is evident in the nationalities of the immigrants and their international worldview. At a special festival on Aug. 21, 1745, a hymn was sung in German, English, Swedish, French, Czech, Dutch, Greek, Irish, Latin, Mohawk, Mohican, Welch, Wendish, Danish, Polish, and Hungarian. Erbe, *Bethlehem, Pa.*, 27.

30. Smaby, *Transformation of Moravian Bethlehem*, 61–62.

thriving religious and economic enterprise. As "House Father" and "House Mother" for Bethlehem, they were the absolute authorities in America. Because of his capable administration Spangenberg became known to the people of Bethlehem as Brother Joseph, in memory of the biblical Joseph who was placed in charge of Pharaoh's household.[31] Despite his very practical nature, Spangenberg always kept the missionary purpose of Bethlehem primary, sometimes to the distress of the more economically minded leaders. As Mary Spangenberg informed Zinzendorf in 1746:

But what do you think then of my little son, Henrich Antes [the general overseer], no, you should see the little fool [a term of endearment], he has come out of the rain under the eaves [out of the pan and into the fire]: if he had a lot of work at the plantation, then here in Bethlehem it really piles up, and sometimes he doesn't know where his head is. Just when he has arranged his builders, masons, tile makers, log-splitters, and drivers in the best way, then Joseph comes and sends one out as a preacher, another to be a fisher [evangelist], and the third to make a necessary visit. Then the poor heart sits and scratches behind his ears. If it comes to it, he has to do it himself.[32]

Despite such possible conflicts of interest, Spangenberg was unusually gifted and kept the operation running smoothly, and Antes proved to be one of his stoutest supporters. But the strain of leadership soon began to wear on both Spangenbergs. Mary was frequently ill and at least once broke into tears over the strain. She continually insisted that they needed more help.[33] In December 1746, when Joseph wrote to Zinzendorf pleading for more preachers and scholars, Mary added the note: "The field that we have to tend is amazingly large, and there is a true desire, hunger and thirst for the true grace; if only we had more fellow workers, which we very much need. My poor Joseph must care for too much himself. Now he goes to Nazareth, then to Gnadenhütten [the mission station for the natives], then to Philadelphia, Modecreek, etc., and because it goes on, we see no way that we could make it all as good as before if you don't send us more workers."[34]

31. Reichel, *Spangenberg*, 171, states that Spangenberg himself took the name Joseph to correspond to his wife Mary. This may be the preferred explanation as it is the more difficult. If it is true, then one can hardly miss the significance of Mary and Joseph coming to Bethlehem. Another biographer argues that Joseph was the Hebrew equivalent for the Latin name August. Jeremias Risler, *Leben August Gottlieb Spangenbergs, Bischofs der evangelischen Brüderkirche* (Barby: Brüdergemeine, 1794), 238.

32. "Aber was denken Sie denn zu meinem Kleinen Sohn, den Henrich Anthes, nein, das Närrgen sollen Sie doch sehen, er ist aus dem Regen unter die Trauffe gekommen: hat er Viele Arbeit auf der plantage gehabt, in Bethlehem kommt Sie zusammen, Er weiß manchmal nicht wo Ihm der Kopf steht. Wenn er sich seine bauleute, Kropper, Tiegel-, Splitter- und Fuhrleute aufs Schönste eingeteilt, da kommt der Joseph und schickt einen Predigen, den andern Fischen, den dritten ein nötigen Besuch zu tun. Da sitzt das arme Herz und kratzt sich hintern Ohren, wenn's um und um kommt, muß Er selber dran." Mary Spangenberg to Zinzendorf, 1746. Quoted in Erbe, *Bethlehem, Pa.*, 87.

33. Levering, *A History of Bethlehem*, 184–85.

34. Risler, *Leben Spangenbergs*, 238.

The very success of the Spangenbergs' work was making it difficult to continue, and so Zinzendorf sent them John Frederick Cammerhof and his wife Anna von Pahlen (a Livonian baroness) as assistants. They arrived in Bethlehem in January 1747.[35] Spangenberg trusted Cammerhof's leadership sufficiently to make two extended missionary trips in 1748. It was during the latter trip, which took him all the way to North Carolina, that Spangenberg came down with a serious illness that nearly took his life. In fact, the community had already begun the dying rituals for him when he suddenly recovered.[36] Clearly, though, by 1748 the Spangenbergs were exhausted by their work and needed relief.

THE TIME OF CRISIS

Soon after this, Bishop Johannes von Watteville made a visit to America to reorganize the Pennsylvania Plan, apparently against the wishes of Spangenberg. Von Watteville ordered that the ecumenical Pennsylvania synods become exclusive synods of the Brüdergemeine, a frank admission of the failure of Zinzendorf's efforts to build a Philadelphian church in America.[37] Moreover, work among the natives would be increased, while efforts with the European settlers would be de-emphasized.

This may have been an admission that the work among the settlers was generating as much controversy as conversion, or that in light of the Great Awakening there was less need for evangelism among the Euro-Americans.[38] It may also have represented a reluctance to bring new converts, raised in the freer lifestyle of the colonies, into the Brüdergemeine. In any case, this turning away from the settlers would have lasting consequences for the future of the Brüdergemeine in America, as it failed to develop into a growing American denomination for nearly a hundred years.

Von Watteville further announced a restructuring of the clerical orders by which administrative duties were to be removed from the episcopacy. In light

35. Levering, *A History of Bethlehem*, 185. Gollin, *Moravians in Two Worlds*, 42, is in error when she states, "In spite of his [Spangenberg's] obvious talents he was replaced in 1749 by John Cammerhoff at the Count's insistence." Cammerhof arrived in 1747 at the direct request of Spangenberg and never replaced him. His replacement was Bishop Johan Nitschmann.

36. Risler, *Leben Spangenbergs*, 239–40. The *Bethlehem Diary* records the Married Choir's surprise and pleasure when Spangenberg came to join them in worship despite his severe illness. *Bethlehem Diary* (Moravian Archives), Aug. 22 and 29, 1748. In light of this serious illness it is hard to understand Gollin's statement: "Having been unable to find a single letter in which Spangenberg requests a transfer, even though it is true that his wife, but not he, had been seriously ill, I tend to agree with Erbe that Cammerhoff's appointment was carried out at the insistence of Zinzendorf and had nothing to do with Spangenberg's own desires in the matter." Gollin, *Moravians in Two Worlds*, 235, n. 73. Gollin's citation of Erbe, *Bethlehem, Pa.*, 33, in support of this contention is curious, since Erbe says nothing there about Spangenberg's wishes in this matter. In fact, there is only praise of Cammerhof as one of Spangenberg's chief assistants.

37. These were not "Moravian" synods, as is sometimes indicated, but Brüdergemeine synods.

38. Fogleman, *Hopeful Journeys*, 119–20; Fogleman, "'Jesus ist weiblich,'" 189–94.

of that decision, Henrich Antes was ordained as "senior civilis" and given the charge of representing the Moravians legally.[39] During the course of his visit, von Watteville also made the announcement on November 13, 1748, that the Chief Eldership of Christ had been extended to America.[40]

This move may have come from a desire to bring America into conformity with the rest of Europe, or it may have had ulterior purposes, as Sessler asserts. "The election of Christ as Chief Elder in America served as a convenient ground for deposing Spangenberg from his office of General Elder."[41] It is interesting that whereas Sessler, Gollin, and others blame Bethlehem's problems on Zinzendorf's autocratic rule, it was actually Spangenberg who had autocratic powers in Bethlehem. The appointment of Christ as Chief Elder in Bethlehem actually resulted in more authority being delegated to the community.

Risler reports that Spangenberg took that opportunity to declare to the Gemeine that he and Mary were turning again to the gracious Lord and Savior. He and his wife "had plenty of reason to sink in the dust before the Lord, but for the sake of his wounds, through which they were healed, and for the sake of the blood which he had shed, they hoped for full forgiveness for any neglect of their duty."[42] This statement indicates that Spangenberg felt that he was being removed from office for somehow failing in his duty and for pridefulness.

According to von Watteville himself, the major reason for removing Spangenberg was that he had grown proud in his office, was openly criticizing the Brethren in Europe, and was in danger of forming an American sect under his leadership. Considering Spangenberg's early attraction to Separatism and that even the Lutherans under Muhlenberg established themselves as a separate national church, it would hardly be surprising if Spangenberg had been moving in that direction in 1748.

Von Watteville wrote to Bishop Nitschmann, who was en route to Bethlehem:

I found the Josephs [Spangenbergs] in a very bad disposition and they were full of argument *[raisonments]* against Papa [Zinzendorf] and our European Gemeinen and they were about to leave the Gemeine and to make a splinter group. They were then set aside and the Lambkin took the Elder's office for himself. . . . But since I saw that they neither got along with the brothers and sisters nor made a blessed work in Bethlehem, and especially that your wife would have a difficult time on her arrival if Mary were still in Bethlehem, because she is an austere ruler, I thus requested from the Savior that they might come to

39. Levering, *A History of Bethlehem*, 226–27, 237.
40. Hamilton and Hamilton, *History*, 77ff.
41. Sessler, *Communal Pietism*, 183.
42. Risler, *Leben Spangenbergs*, 240.

another post, and then the Lambkin ordered them through the lot, which they drew themselves, that they should remain in Philadelphia until my return from St. Thomas and form a small pilgrim household with several brothers and sisters.[43]

Spangenberg did indeed object to the reorganization that von Watteville wanted to make in the American plan, so he laid down his primary office and returned to Europe in late autumn 1749.

Spangenberg went through a long period of depression following his removal from Bethlehem. He was concerned over what he perceived to be frivolity among Zinzendorf's younger workers, and he had even began to doubt Zinzendorf himself. But he felt he could not share his concerns with anyone other than Zinzendorf. The greatest moment of crisis between the two men came when Spangenberg revealed his heart to Zinzendorf and requested a transfer to Jamaica, where he wanted "to preach the gospel to the poor blacks and with that to close out his race."[44]

Zinzendorf rejected that idea and worked to clear up any confusion between them. He sent Spangenberg on a tour of Europe and made him head of the seminary at Barby. Zinzendorf also assigned him the task of responding to the numerous critics of the Brüdergemeine, and in the process Spangenberg was able to interview Zinzendorf on many theological points he found questionable in the count's writings.[45] Whatever the precise cause of the breach with Zinzendorf, by 1751 it was completely resolved.

Things went badly in Bethlehem during Spangenberg's absence. In fact, the community almost collapsed without Spangenberg.[46] He had been the architect of the entire Bethlehem-Nazareth system, with its integration of economics and religious mission. Moreover, he was a very popular and well-loved leader with a unique blend of administration, decisiveness, and diplomacy. It would have been hard for anyone to take his place.

Spangenberg's successor was Bishop Johann Nitschmann, a relative of the Nitschmanns who had been among the first refugees from Moravia. Nitschmann was very well respected in Europe and had been one of the leaders of the theological seminary at Marienborn as well as the tutor for Zinzendorf's son, Christian Renatus. Moreover, he was an early opponent of the Sifting in Herrnhaag.[47]

43. Report of visitors to Johannes Nitschmann, April 6, 1749, quoted in Reichel, *Spangenberg,* 151–52.
44. Risler, *Leben Spangenbergs,* 245.
45. The fruit of this activity were three books: *Declaration über die Zeither gegen uns ausgegangene Beschuldigungen, Sonderlich die Person unsers ORDINARII* (Leipzig, 1751; ZE 5), *Apologetische Erklärung über einige Beschuldigungen gegen den Ordinarium Fratrum* (Barby, 1750, ZE 5); and *Apologetische Schluß-Schrift* (Barby, 1752, ZE 3).
46. Erbe, *Bethlehem, Pa.,* 87–92.
47. See Erbe, *Herrnhaag: Eine religiöse Kommunität,* for more on Nitschmann and his role in the Sifting.

Nitschmann arrived as the leader of more than a hundred new people in the so-called Third Sea Congregation in 1748; thus he had closer ties to the newer immigrants from Europe than those who had built Bethlehem.[48] The sudden influx of more than a hundred new residents severely strained the economy and the personal relationships in Bethlehem. The strain was compounded when the community had to absorb two hundred more people from Herrnhaag after its dissolution in 1750.

This was a trying time for Bethlehem, and Nitschmann was not up to the task before him. In fact, many of the problems during the crisis of 1748–52 center around his personality. Nitschmann was regarded as imperious and undiplomatic. Far from being lax in discipline, as Sessler indicates, he had to be warned by the senior civilis, Antes, that his disciplinary measures were so harsh that he was in danger of being questioned by the civil authorities in Pennsylvania.[49]

Nitschmann also failed to appreciate the differences between Europe and Pennsylvania. One of his greatest offenses was suddenly introducing the surplice (alb) in Holy Communion. The bishop's unexpected appearance in a clerical robe in May 1750 aroused great animosity. Antes in particular was angry. Clerical dress had important ecclesiastical and political implications. The English Civil War, fought just one hundred years earlier and very much a part of the American consciousness, was fought in part over the question of vestments, and Pennsylvania was the home of every form of dissenter and Quaker.[50]

Other things associated with Nitschmann illustrate his unsuitability for Bethlehem. His portrait stands in marked contrast to all other portraits of Bethlehem men of the time. He is not dressed as a laborer or even an evangelist but wears fine clothes and an episcopal hat. He also has a prominent pectoral cross on a ribbon.[51] This costuming, combined with his introduction of the surplice, could well have been interpreted as frivolous extravagance or an assertion of superiority.

Another clue is the grave of his wife, Johanna. She was not buried with her choir but in the middle of the cemetery, and her grave was marked with a large stone, giving her a place of prominence. As we shall see, this was in opposition to the normal procedure in Bethlehem and a violation of the spirit that bound the community together. It was also a rejection of simplicity of heart and the theology of the cross. It would appear that the Nitschmanns sought to be spiritual royalty in the midst of an egalitarian communal society.[52]

---

48. Levering, *A History of Bethlehem*, 233–34, 248.

49. Ibid., 249. According to Levering, Nitschmann was opposed by Cammerhof as well as by Antes.

50. Ibid., 251–52, n. 11, downplays this event and Antes's reaction, asserting that there must have been more behind it, but he failed to appreciate colonial hostility toward episcopacy.

51. Levering, *A History of Bethlehem*, 184–85. The original is in the Moravian Archives.

52. Ibid., 260, n. 17. Johanna was one of the Moravian emigrants. She had been among the original Single Sisters in Herrnhut and had been an effective and popular leader in Europe. The fact that both Nitschmanns

The crisis during Spangenberg's absence has generally been interpreted as part of the Sifting Time and blamed on Spangenberg's assistant, John Frederick Cammerhof, who delighted in the more graphic expressions of Zinzendorf's blood-and-wounds theology.[53] Opinions of Cammerhof vary greatly. Baron von Schrautenbach, Zinzendorf's friend and biographer, characterized him as a "young man of a sympathetic, friendly disposition, full of spirit, courage and energy and with a valuable education in philosophy."[54] Sessler, by contrast, stated that "he caused more trouble to Spangenberg than he gave assistance, for he introduced the Herrnhaagian fanaticism [i.e., the Sifting]." Hutton called him "a fanatic of the fanatics."[55]

In point of fact, those who accuse Cammerhof of hindering Spangenberg have brought forward no evidence other than the language he used in his letters and worship. Cammerhof was one of the most devoted missionaries to the native tribes and died in that service in 1751, having been adopted into the Oneida Nation and given the name *Gallichwio* (good words), a tribute to his eloquence in the native languages. Three decades later the missionary Zeisberger heard his name mentioned with respect among the native tribes.[56]

I think that it is misleading to blame the crisis of 1748–52 on Cammerhof or on Zinzendorf's blood–and-wounds theology. There was less difference in the religious language and symbolism used during the time of Cammerhof and the periods immediately before and after than is often asserted. An examination of the details of the crisis during Spangenberg's absence reveals that the cause lay in factors other than blood-and-wounds piety.

The dissolution of Herrnhaag did contribute to the economic crisis in Bethlehem, however. The great influx of new residents, many of whom were refugees from Herrnhaag with no strong calling to come to Pennsylvania, strained the economic system. The frontier conditions were no doubt a shock after the comparatively luxurious lifestyle at Herrnhaag. Furthermore, according to Levering, the refugees from Herrnhaag also possessed a sense of spiritual superiority, viewing themselves as persecuted martyrs who had been forced out of their homes.[57]

This sense of spiritual elitism was dangerous to communal life, and Nitsch-

---

were Moravians and early residents of Herrnhut casts doubt on the frequent assertion, e.g., Sawyer, "Religious Experience of the Colonial American Moravians," 91, that the Sifting was a conflict between the Moravians and the Pietist fanatics from Wetteravia.

53. Gollin, *Moravians in Two Worlds*; Smaby, *Transformation of Moravian Bethlehem*; Sessler, *Communal Pietism*, 179–81.

54. "Jungen Mann von teilnehmendem, freundschaftlichem Gemüt, vielem Geist, Mut und Energie und einer schätzbaren Gelehrsamkeit in Philosophie." Schrautenbach, *Der Graf von Zinzendorf und die Brüdergemeine Seiner Zeit*, ZM, series 2, 9:417.

55. Sessler, *Communal Pietism*, 183; Hutton, *History of the Moravian Church*, 279.

56. Edmund de Schweinitz, "Some of the Fathers of the American Moravian Church: John Christian Frederick Cammerhoff," *Transactions of the Moravian Historical Society* 2:175–83.

57. Levering, *A History of Bethlehem*, 248.

mann, who was close to many of the Herrnhaagers, made it worse. It is evident that he failed to understand the unique sense of communal mission in Bethlehem when, in November 1749, he founded a religious society, the One Hundred in One Soul. This society was to "constitute a body of hearts who are bound together in one body and soul and should be regarded as a special liturgical folk of the Lamb, from whom He will choose, in His time, His qualified hearts for field expeditions if they quite blessedly pass through their sabbath times."[58] There were similar societies in Europe, but such a special group was unnecessary in a Pilgergemeine where everyone was already dedicated to a common mission. Spangenberg disbanded it when he returned in 1752.

The more difficult problem was economic. The strain between Nitschmann and Antes led to the latter's voluntary removal from Bethlehem and the appointment of Br. Hermann as overseer. Antes was experienced in colonial economics, having already prospered before the arrival of the Moravians. Hermann, by contrast, attempted to apply European capitalist principles in a setting where barter was still prominent.[59] Bethlehem soon ran up high debts and found that it was difficult to collect on the debts owed to them. This led to a dangerous financial situation that Spangenberg had to address immediately upon his return to Bethlehem. Spangenberg reported to Zinzendorf that he had to remove Hermann from office for two reasons:

1. That his economic principles differed entirely from those upon which you and I agreed and which you had sent to America.
2. That the brothers and sisters in Bethlehem and Nazareth were so prejudiced against him so that I was afraid that it would never go well, if I should let him continue.[60]

The great difference in principles to which Spangenberg refers was that Hermann believed in the European Ortsgemeine model, under which the Moravians did not raise their own food. He did not appreciate Bethlehem's goal of self-sufficiency. Instead of agriculture, he concentrated on crafts, trades, and building. "For a couple of years," Spangenberg lamented upon his return to Bethlehem, "our brothers have looked too much to building and too little to the fields and animals."[61]

---

58. *Bethlehem Diary* (Moravian Archives), Nov. 23, 1749.

59. Erbe, *Bethlehem, Pa.,* 89–91.

60. Spangenberg to Zinzendorf, April 1753. Herrnhut Archives 14, No. 19, 11, quoted in Erbe, *Bethlehem, Pa.,* 99.

61. "Die eigentlich Ursache von der Not war diese, daß unser Brüder ein paar Jahre . . . aufs Bauen zuviel und auf den Acker und Vieh zu wenig gesehen." Spangenberg to Zinzendorf, April 1752. Herrnhut Archives R. 14, A 31, 78, quoted ibid., 99. Erbe's picture of Hermann differs greatly from that of Levering, who calls him "a man of uncommon executive ability and capacity for affairs" (*A History of Bethlehem,* 261).

Spangenberg's statement does not support the claim that during the Nitschmann reign the brothers and sisters were so consumed with religious devotion that they spent all their time in worship, to the detriment of labor.[62] Rather it indicates that they focused on building instead of farming. There was no lack of industry in the years 1748–52. In fact, there was a massive building up of the community that included the erection of the spacious Single Brothers House (1748), the first separate place of worship (the Old Chapel, 1751), shops for several trades, general civic improvement, and a major road to Nazareth.[63] Some of these ventures, such as the Old Chapel, took only a few months to complete, indicating great diligence and industry, but this sudden shift in economic priorities created a crisis in the General Economy that nearly destroyed Bethlehem.

Instead of raising a surplus of crops, as the community had done when Spangenberg was in charge, they had to buy food in the years Hermann was overseer. Things that they had provided by their own labor now had to be purchased with their minimal capital. Instead of supporting the Brüdergemeine worldwide, Bethlehem became a financial drain on the European community at the very time that the great economic crisis threatened the Brüdergemeine. Hermann blamed his problems on the socialism of the economy, a complaint that some in Europe acted on after Zinzendorf's death. But as Erbe describes it, "Of course he attributed the problem to the existing communist system, forgetting thereby that it was less the system than his own incompetence which had so intensified the economic crisis."[64]

SPANGENBERG'S SECOND TERM

Johanna Nitschmann died in February 1751 and Cammerhof followed on April 28, making it necessary to reorganize Bethlehem's leadership. Nathanael Seidel was already in Europe complaining to Zinzendorf about Bishop Nitschmann, and Antes was alienated from Bethlehem. It was clear that a change was needed. Eventually Zinzendorf had to agree that it had been a mistake to send Nitschmann to Bethlehem, although he did not condemn Nitschmann himself. As he wrote to Antes, "What he does, he does completely. He cannot, however, do many things so well, for he is no genius like Spangenberg but a weak little vessel, a beautiful vessel for the mantel, on the altar, etc. but not a wagon wheel, nor an axle, nor a rudder."[65]

---

62. Sessler, *Communal Pietism,* 180–81.

63. According to one visitor there were as many trades in Bethlehem in 1751 as in a major city. Levering, *A History of Bethlehem,* 254–59; cf. Smaby, *Transformation of Moravian Bethlehem,* 87–91.

64. Erbe, *Bethlehem, Pa.,* 100.

65. "Was er tut, das tut er ganz. Er kann aber so gar viel nicht tun, denn er ist kein Genie wie Sp., sondern ein schwaches Gefäßchen, ein schönes Gefäß fürs Kamin, auf den Altar etc., aber nicht ein Wagenrad, noch

Gottlieb Pezold was temporarily given charge of the administrative duties at which Nitschmann had failed so noticeably. Nitschmann concentrated on pastoral care, a task for which he was more suited, but even that proved divisive.[66] The decision was soon made in Europe that Nitschmann would have to be recalled. The formal order arrived in Bethlehem on November 14, 1751, almost exactly three years after Spangenberg laid down his office. Nitschmann left Bethlehem just three days later, having been warned to expect this decision.[67]

The situation in Bethlehem was deemed so sensitive that both von Watteville and Zinzendorf considered taking personal charge, but it was recognized that Spangenberg had the best chance for success. He had spent much of his hiatus in Germany, primarily at Barby. His first wife died on March 21, 1751, after a series of painful illnesses. Her dying delayed Spangenberg from departing on time for a planned journey to Greenland, which would have prevented him from sailing for America when the decision was made to recall Nitschmann.[68]

Spangenberg clearly felt that he and Zinzendorf were in agreement on the plan for Bethlehem and Pennsylvania. His new title was *Ordinarii Unitatis Fratrum Vicarius Generalis in America* (Vicar General of the Ordinary of the Unitas Fratrum in America), indicating that he was acting directly on behalf of Zinzendorf, the Ordinary.[69] As he was waiting to sail from England, Spangenberg sent a letter to the synod meeting at London urging them not to allow Zinzendorf to lay down his offices. He was convinced that only Zinzendorf could guide the Brüdergemeine through the current financial crisis.[70]

Spangenberg arrived in Bethlehem in December 1751 and immediately convened a synod in order to set things right.[71] He reorganized and strengthened the governing bodies of Bethlehem, which consisted of the Jünger Collegium (highest central authority), Richter Collegium (which would become the Commission, the Committee for Outward Affairs, and eventually the Aufseher Collegium, or Board of Supervisors), the Oeconomische Conferenz, Diaconat's Conferenz (financial), Kinder Conferenz, Chor Conferenzen, Diener Confer-

---

eine Achse, noch eine Ruderstange." Zinzendorf to Antes, July 1751, quoted in Erbe, *Bethlehem, Pa.,* 99, n. 506.

66. Levering, *A History of Bethlehem,* 260.

67. Ibid., 261–62. He publicly announced his imminent departure on Nov. 16, 1751 (*Bethlehem Diary,* Moravian Archives).

68. Risler, *Leben Spangenbergs,* 258–59. Bethlehem was informed of this in a letter dated Sept. 27, 1751, when Zinzendorf announced the appointment of Spangenberg, the *amerikanische Originalmann.* Erbe, *Bethlehem, Pa.,* 101.

69. "Ordinary" is an archaic word for prelate, but it can also refer to the chief liturgist. Therefore this title emphasizes Zinzendorf's spiritual authority over the entire *Brüdergemeine.*

70. Risler, *Leben Spangenbergs,* 262–63. Assuming that Risler had accurately recorded this letter of Spangenberg's, this raises doubts about the common assertion that Zinzendorf and Spangenberg were opposed to each other. Spangenberg at least, though not sparing Zinzendorf from all blame, saw no reason for him to renounce his offices.

71. Levering, *A History of Bethlehem,* 262.

enz (sacristans, etc.), Kranken-Wärter Conferenz, Handwerker Conferenz, Ackerbau Conferenz, Helfer Conferenz, Gemein Rath, and the Polizei Tag (general town meeting).[72] Spangenberg took a firm hand in restoring the communal economy and removed Hermann from office. Antes was brought back into the fold, and Spangenberg went on a personal visitation of the various mission stations, interviewing the workers.

As late as May 1752 he wrote to Zinzendorf that he was still healing the injuries from the time of Nitschmann.

Some weeks ago I came to Nazareth in order to hold the Holy Communion there. I discovered there an old scandal among the brothers and sisters who came into this land with Brother Joh. Nitschmann. At first I was frightened over it so that I went aside and wept bitterly. But the Lord soon gave me courage: then I seized the situation without hesitation. And before 24 hours had passed, the Savior had won the game. The hearts melted away in tears, and everyone was so enraptured that I could do nothing other than call them to grace. And so on the same day we had a blessed footwashing and Holy Communion.[73]

Unfortunately, Spangenberg does not inform us of the details of this "old scandal," but it is interesting that it was so shocking that he cried bitterly over it and needed divine help to confront it, yet was able to solve the problem within twenty-four hours. It is important to note that this action of Spangenberg flowed out of his Zinzendorfian theology and was made effective through community ritual. I can agree with Levering that "From this time, all that was abnormal in the tone, language and manner of the preceding few years rapidly disappeared."[74] However, as we shall see below, what was normal in language and manner in Bethlehem was the Zinzendorfian theology and piety that others have considered abnormal.

Soon after Spangenberg came back from Europe, he developed plans to turn Nazareth into a typical Ortsgemeine along the lines of Herrnhut. This would be a place for those who found the rules of the Pilgergemeine too confining. Surprisingly, this plan was abandoned because no one in Bethlehem wanted to move to the new village. They were willing to build the village but not live there. They expressed general satisfaction with life in the communal system, even if there had been some problems in recent years.

Erbe lists some of the reasons members gave for not wanting to move to Nazareth. Some were economic, others spiritual. One person preferred "to lie

72. Ibid., 263–64, n. 20.

73. Spangenberg to Zinzendorf, May 14, 1752, Herrnhut Archives R. 14, A18, 80, quoted in Erbe, *Bethlehem, Pa.*, 101, n. 522.

74. Levering, *A History of Bethlehem*, 262.

dead than to move." One brother expressed the wishes of many succinctly: "It is a grace to him to live in the communal economy."

It should be noted that despite the fact that families in the Nazareth plan were to have their own homes, they would not live as typical nuclear families. There were to be two bedrooms and two living rooms "so that the Father with his people and the Mother with her people could live apart and take care of their own."[75] It is clear that husbands and wives were not expected to share living quarters even within their own home. Since Spangenberg was the originator of this plan, we can safely assume that he had convictions on the separation of the genders that were at least as strong as Zinzendorf's.

In May 1752 the Lawatsches, formerly of Herrnhaag, arrived as helpers for Spangenberg. The restoration of Bethlehem proceeded so rapidly that in the summer of 1752 Spangenberg could leave on an extended venture to North Carolina to survey land for a possible future settlement there. He went with Antes and Timothy Horsefield on an arduous journey in August and did not return until February 1753. Almost immediately he left for Europe to report on his findings to Zinzendorf.[76]

Böhler returned to Bethlehem in 1753 to take charge in Spangenberg's absence. He also brought information on the growing financial crisis affecting the entire Brüdergemeine. We cannot go into the details of the debt, but the long and the short of it is that the bill came due on Zinzendorf's bold scheme for world evangelism. The residents of Bethlehem had to be reminded that they were part of the reason for the debt, having been transported back and forth free of charge on ships built by the Brüdergemeine.[77]

Spangenberg returned to Bethlehem on April 22, 1754, and on May 19 he married Elizabeth Miksch, whom he called Martha.[78] His remaining years in Bethlehem were among the most fruitful for the religious town. In order to finally close the wounds opened during Nitschmann's tenure, Spangenberg held open discussions with the residents of Bethlehem about the future. As Katherine Carté Engel has recently shown, there were a number of complaints about life in Bethlehem, but when pressed to decide whether to abandon the General Economy, the residents overwhelmingly chose communal living.[79]

To seal this decision, Spangenberg had all the residents of Bethlehem and Nazareth sign a Brotherly Agreement in September 1754. This was the first

75. Erbe, *Bethlehem, Pa.*, 103–5.
76. Levering, *A History of Bethlehem*, 271–72.
77. Hamilton and Hamilton, *History*, 110–11.
78. Levering, *A History of Bethlehem*, 278–79.
79. Engel, "Br. Joseph's Sermon."

formal agreement by which they agreed to live under a communal economy. Such a step had not been necessary in the 1740s, but it became necessary after the difficulties experienced under Nitschmann. The agreement reaffirms the original Zinzendorfian ideal that economic and religious matters should be united:

It should at no time be forgotten that Bethlehem-Nazareth were established for no other purpose than to be able to give a hand to the work of the Savior not only in Pennsylvania but everywhere in America, etc. The intention of the said economy is thus, if one should speak precisely, that we should by all means treat one another with respect and in a God-pleasing manner, to raise our children according to his mind; to watch over our youth (sisters as well as brothers) for him until they are adapted to be used by him; to nurse our poor and weak, old and sick, and to show to them the proper service faithfully; also to conduct our married lives so that we may give a double concern for that which belongs to the Lord.[80]

The remainder of the agreement states that the members are free to leave the commune at any time but that they give up all claims to wages or benefits from their labor when they do so. Also, members agree to use all their talent as the Gemeine sees fit, whether it be in labor or in going into the mission fields. Children of members are to be cared for in the schools so that members are free to work. In short, all members are "to present themselves agreeably as children toward the institutions which are either made or renewed for us from time to time."

Under the reorganized economy, Bethlehem was stronger than ever and began to prosper. The town was thus prepared for the strain created by the Seven Years' War (commonly called the French and Indian War) and the resulting warfare with several tribes. In late November 1755 the mission outpost, Gnadenhütten, was destroyed and most of its inhabitants were slaughtered by hostile natives.[81]

Bethlehem was caught in a struggle between the hostile tribes and those white settlers who wanted to kill all natives, including those who belonged to

---

80. "1. Es sollte zu keiner Zeit vergessen werden, daß Bethlehem-Nazareth zu keinem andern Zweck sind angefangen worden, als daß dem Werk des Heilands nicht nur in Pennsylvanien, sondern überhaupt in Amerika etc. dadurch die Hand möge geboten werden. Die Absicht besagter Ökonomie geht also, wenn man deutlich reden soll, wohl freilich darauf, daß wir uns miteinander ehrlich und gottgefällig durchbringen, unsre Kinder nach Seinem Sinn erziehen; unsre jungen Leute, sowohl Schwestern als Brüder, vor Ihn bewahren, bis sie geschickt werden, von Ihm gebraucht zu werden; unsre Armen und Schwachen, Alten und Kranken verpflegen und ihnen die gehörigen Dienste treulich erweisen; auch unseren Ehestand so führen, daß wir das, was dem Herrn angehört, doppelt besorgen mögen." The complete text of the Brotherly Agreement is found in Erbe, *Bethlehem, Pa.,* Anlage III.

81. For a firsthand account of this tragedy, see the *Lebenslauf* of Susanne Luise Partsch, in Faull, *Moravian Women,* 111–13.

the Brüdergemeine.[82] Despite this, hundreds of refugees, both settlers and natives, flocked to Bethlehem. The Moravians took them in, trying hard to maintain their normal discipline and routine despite the near doubling of the
population of Bethlehem for several months.

The Moravians also prepared for a possible attack. Spangenberg's description of the defenses shows the tension between pacifism and self-defense at this
time.

At night the watchmen shouted one to another at intervals of an hour, so that the sound
rang out loudly into the forest. We also built block houses and mounted them with guns,
and when a gun was discharged it was a signal to the vicinity that hostile Indians were
near. Thus when the savages came spying at night, they always found us in readiness. Then
I called all the Brethren together and begged them for Jesus' sake by all means to spare the
life of every hostile Indian (shooting low if they were forced to shoot), and if one was,
perchance, shot in the legs, we proposed to take him in for treatment and care for him
with all faithfulness until he recovered. I fell upon my face and besought the Saviour
to graciously prevent all bloodshed at our place, and, to Him be thanks, He heard our
prayer.[83]

The efficiency of the General Economy helped Bethlehem survive the war
years without serious harm, and things continued to improve financially until
the death of Zinzendorf.[84] According to the figures reported by the Moravians
to Governor Denny in 1756, in the Bethlehem-Nazareth complex there were:[85]

Married (157 pairs)	314
Widowers	14
Widows	17
Single Brothers	191
Single Sisters	67
Total Adults	603
children in boarding schools	
(96 outsiders)	418
Total natives	82
Grand Total of residents	**1103**

82. Levering, *A History of Bethlehem*, chap. 9, gives a great deal of detail about the massacre and the
tensions between the Brethren and the whites. It is too complex to render here.
83. Quoted in Levering, *A History of Bethlehem*, 337–38.
84. Erbe, *Bethlehem, Pa.*, 124–36.
85. Ibid., 87–88.

Of the 603 adults, 290 were at times absent or involved in the spiritual work of the community:

In mission field	48
Itinerant preachers	54
Working in schools	62
In North Carolina	
(46 Single Brothers and 8 married persons)	54
Clergy in Bethlehem	72
Total	**290**

Thus the General Economy supported a population of more than a thousand people with only about three hundred adult laborers. In 1761 the total population of Bethlehem-Nazareth had grown to 1,300, with the economic burden resting on about five hundred persons.

Erbe demonstrates quite convincingly that the dissolution of the General Economy came about from external, i.e., European, factors, not internal ones. This contradicts those who assert that the General Economy had outlived its usefulness and that people were chafing under the system. Financially the community was stronger in 1760 than it would be until the nineteenth century, despite the war crisis. Moreover, strategic land purchases and capital investments pointed toward continued economic growth. It is important to understand, though, that this incredible industry and efficiency was supported by the worship life of the Gemeine and inspired by Zinzendorf. Throughout the period of the General Economy, Bethlehem was connected to Zinzendorf and his vision.

CONNECTIONS BETWEEN ZINZENDORF AND BETHLEHEM

Although the distance of Pennsylvania from Europe meant that Bethlehem had a certain amount of practical autonomy, there appears to have been little desire in Bethlehem for independence from European control until well after the breakup of the General Economy. The Brüdergemeine stressed the preservation of its worldwide unity, and there is little indication that the residents of Bethlehem resented their relationship to the Brüdergemeine in Europe, particularly in the first twenty years. These European ties were strengthened in a number of ways, including travel, letters, and the *Gemein Nachrichten*, a manuscript circular that shared news from the various centers of the Brüdergemeine's activity.

It is not necessary for this study to examine the details of this European contact, but we should note that in its first two decades Bethlehem was populated primarily by Europeans who were specially selected to emigrate there. These were individuals who had been part of the great communities, such as Herrnhaag and Herrnhut. Moreover, all of the leaders of colonial Bethlehem were educated by the Brüdergemeine in Europe, and these leaders frequently returned to Europe to renew their personal ties to Zinzendorf.[86] Zinzendorf also sent personal emissaries, such as his eldest daughter, Benigna, and her husband, Johannes von Watteville, to examine the conditions in Bethlehem and make any necessary changes. Such direct contacts kept Bethlehem in conformity with the Brüdergemeine in Europe and continually strengthened the loyalty of the residents to Zinzendorf.

This sense of personal attachment to Zinzendorf, his family, and the leaders of the Brüdergemeine was symbolized in birthday celebrations. Birthdays of important persons were big events in Bethlehem and illuminated the power structure of the church. These celebrations strengthened the emotional ties of the community to its leaders, but they also connected earthly governance of the community to God's providence. Leaders in Europe were honored in a similar fashion even though they were not physically present in Bethlehem. The birthdays of the Zinzendorfs (Nikolaus, Erdmuth, Benigna, Christian Renatus) and Anna Nitschmann were celebrated as religious festivals every year in Bethlehem. Special music and sermons were prepared for the celebrations and sent to Europe as birthday gifts. They were often included in the *Gemein Nachrichten* for the benefit of the whole Brüdergemeine.

A typical celebration was the one by the children for the birthday of Erdmuth (Mama) in 1752. First the older boys sang *Geschöpfgen zur Geburt gebracht* (Creator brought to birth). Then the younger boys sang *Papa, Mama,* followed by the older girls with the Passion hymn *Sein Creuz, die Schmach, die Angst, der Schmerz* (His cross, the shame, the anxiety, the pain), and finally the younger girls sang the side-wound stanza *Schaut auf und seht die Felsen-Kluft* (Look up and see the crevice in the rock).[87] The words of the hymns would be altered slightly to apply to the person being honored.

The Bethlehem leaders felt that it was particularly important for the children to learn about the leaders in Europe, as they would have little or no opportunity to see them. Thus in 1751 the children gathered for the annual celebration of Anna Nitschmann's birthday. "They nicely sang some stanzas composed by the dear Mother [Nitschmann] herself, with application to herself. For example: Question—'What is so good to the dear Mother?' Answer—'The feeling of his blood flowing from the wounds.'"[88] "Mother" here refers to Nitschmann.

It is not surprising that the most important birthday celebration was that of

86. Spangenberg himself made two such trips, in 1749 and 1753.
87. *Bethlehem Diary* (Moravian Archives), Nov. 11, 1752, 1145.
88. Ibid., Nov. 28, 1751, 493.

Zinzendorf, who was known to the people of Bethlehem both as Papa and as the Disciple of the Lord *(Jünger des Herrn)*. His birthday was a time to renew the emotional attachments between the residents of Bethlehem and its absent lord, while impressing his theology upon the younger generation. It is ironic that, because of the delay in communication, the last celebration of his birthday in Bethlehem actually occurred after his death in 1760:

At the lovefeast of the children, Brother Joseph [Spangenberg] in particular related to the children how the Disciple of the Lord had an especial love for children, for whom he had composed many beautiful sermons, their *Losungen,* and beautiful odes, which they had received. And afterwards he recommended to them their beautiful *Losung* for that occasion, applying to themselves and asking the Savior, "Do I Love you, etc.", the children's Gemeine also sang their "Ave Little Lamb" for the dear Disciple.[89]

These celebrations were more than an expression of a sentimental attachment to the person who funded the Bethlehem enterprise; they were an annual ceremony renewing allegiance to Zinzendorf, his household, and his theology.

Such rituals were not the only way in which Bethlehem maintained its ties to the European Gemeine and to Zinzendorf. A more important connection was the distribution of hundreds of volumes of Zinzendorf's sermons to the Bethlehem bookstore that served the entire Moravian network in North America. In this way Zinzendorf's sermons and theological works became the major source of reading material for the Gemeine, particularly during the General Economy, when all economic transactions were centrally regulated.

The catalog of the bookstore in 1755 is thus very illuminating. There were nearly 3,500 volumes of Zinzendorf's writings and sermons available in Bethlehem.[90] Of the works not by Zinzendorf, the majority, excluding writing textbooks, are apologetical pieces, principally those of Spangenberg. The only exception is *Wilcoks honig Tropfen,* a devotional work.

This interest in Zinzendorf's works continued throughout the decade. In 1758 the Gemeine purchased an additional two hundred *2nd Theils der Londonischen Predigen* from the Brüdergemeine print shop in Barby, and in 1759 two hundred copies of *Kinder Reden,* three hundred *Berliner Reden,* and three hundred *Bethelsdorfische Reden.* In 1760 the Gemeine received:

20	revidirte Zeister Reden
200	revidirte Reden über die Wunden Litaney
100	Berlin Reden
20	Kinder Reden
100	Berthelsdorfishe Reden
50	Londonische Predigten 1st Part

89. Ibid., May 26, 1760.
90. See Appendix 2.

Some of these were sent gratis in compensation for volumes that had been lost at sea during the Seven Years' War.[91] Interest in selling Zinzendorf's works declined toward the end of the century. It is striking that none of Zinzendorf's works is listed in the catalog for 1792–93.

Not only were Zinzendorf's published sermons read in the Gemeine, his unpublished ones were as well. Zinzendorf regularly preached to the leaders of the international Brüdergemeine who traveled with him, the so-called *Jünger Haus* (Disciple House), and these discourses were distributed to all communities as part of the *Gemein Nachrichten.* Zinzendorf's sermons, even in manuscript, were often read in place of a discourse by the local pastor.[92] In this way the individual Gemeinen were kept in contact with the latest aspects of Zinzendorf's thought. For instance, his last public discourse (given in Herrnhut in 1759) was read in Bethlehem on July 13, 1760, six weeks before Bethlehem received news of Zinzendorf's death.[93]

The year following Zinzendorf's death was devoted to reading his discourses throughout the Moravian Church worldwide. Vernon Nelson's index to the *Gemein Nachrichten* indicates that there were 121 sermons by Zinzendorf in the *Gemein Nachrichten* from 1760, but none recorded for the rest of the decade. After Zinzendorf's death Johannes von Watteville, Zinzendorf's closest associate and frequent nuncio, became the main spokesman, with a total of 1,490 sermons (1760–82). He had 378 in 1761 alone. Spangenberg was the next most frequently cited preacher in the *Gemein Nachrichten,* with 586 sermons from 1760 to 1791.[94]

Thus we see that through the distribution of published and manuscript copies of the sermons of Zinzendorf and his two major lieutenants, the thought of Zinzendorf was readily available to the people of Bethlehem. It is reasonable to assume that the degree to which individuals read and heard these sermons was related to their role in the community. Preachers, teachers, and other spiritual workers would have had greater access to Zinzendorf's works than those whose occupation was more related to handiworks and commerce. Yet it should be noted that there appears to have been near-universal literacy among those who resided in Bethlehem; thus we should not dismiss the possibility of a wide audience for these sermons.[95]

---

91. Journal of the Diaconat, Dec. 1, 1757–March 30, 1761, Moravian Archives.

92. For example, throughout 1759 Zinzendorf's sermons on the *Gemein Litany,* which are unprinted, were read during normal worship periods, e.g., *Bethlehem Diary* (Moravian Archives), June 23, 1759.

93. Ibid., July 13, 1760. This merits further research, especially since the *Mutter Fest* of the Holy Spirit was reintroduced in 1774.

94. Vernon Nelson, "Index to the *Gemein Nachrichten,*" manuscript, Moravian Archives.

95. This judgment is based on the fact that all of the children were educated in the *Kinder Anstalten* and that numerous documents from both men and women of all stations of life are preserved in the Moravian Archives.

Bethlehem was founded to be the center of the Brüdergemeine's activity in America, and the European leaders maintained close connections with Bethlehem. More important, Spangenberg served as the personal representative of Zinzendorf and made sure that Zinzendorf's theology was communicated to the inhabitants of Bethlehem. The success of Bethlehem owed a great deal to the administrative and economic skills of Spangenberg, but the theology and devotion of the community were equally important, as we shall see in the following chapters. Although he was physically absent, Zinzendorf remained the dominant influence on the life and thought of the brothers and sisters in Bethlehem.

FIGURE 5. Footwashing, circa 1757. Unity Archives, Herrnhut.

CHAPTER 5

RITUAL

Ritual is one of the primary ways in which humans communicate. It is a symbolic system that helps to create, preserve, and change societies; therefore the study of rituals can be an effective way of understanding humans.[1] This is true of any society, but it is particularly true of a society that was self-conscious about its religious and ritual life. Clifford Geertz's definition of religion is particularly helpful in analyzing life in Bethlehem: "Religion is (1) a system of symbols which acts to (2) establish powerful, pervasive, and long-lasting moods and motivations in men by (3) formulating conceptions of a general order of existence and (4) clothing these conceptions with such an aura of factuality that (5) the moods and motivations seem uniquely realistic."[2] For the Moravians, the liturgy, with its focus on the Incarnation of Christ and the Motherhood of the Holy Spirit, formed the system of symbols that made sense of their existence and communal life.

MUSIC

For Zinzendorf and the Brüdergemeine in Bethlehem, the truths of the Christian religion were best communicated in poetry and song, not in systematic theology or polemics. This was expressed by one of the leaders of Bethlehem in 1748: "Whoever wants to get acquainted with us and to learn our first principles and progress of grace can acquire that knowledge better from our hymns, our *Litany of the Wounds,* and the homilies upon the same, than if we respond to such writing against us."[3] In the *Jüngerhaus Diarium,* Zinzendorf even raised the possibility that liturgists are more important than preachers and teachers.[4]

1. "We engage in rituals in order to transmit collective messages to ourselves." Edmund Leach, *Culture and Communication: The Logic by Which Symbols Are Connected* (Cambridge: Cambridge University Press, 1976), 45. The literature on ritual and society is vast. Bell, *Ritual: Perspectives and Dimensions,* provides a good introduction to the various approaches. See also Émile Durkheim, *Elementary Forms of the Religious Life,* trans. J. W. Swaim (1915; New York: Free Press, 1965); Victor Turner: *The Ritual Process: Structure and Anti-Structure* (Ithaca: Cornell University Press, 1969); Arnold Van Gennep, *The Rites of Passage,* trans. M. B. Vizedom and G. L. Caffee (1906; Chicago: University of Chicago Press, 1960); Mary Douglas, *Natural Symbols: Explorations in Cosmology* (New York: Vintage Books, 1973); Mary Douglas, *Purity and Danger: An Analysis of the Concepts of Pollution and Taboo* (1966; New York: Ark Paperbacks, 1989); Clifford Geertz, *Interpretation of Cultures.* In general, I prefer the structuralist understanding of ritual so long as it is understood that ritual is dynamic rather than static, as Geertz and Turner have shown. Ritual reinforces the social order while providing an arena for social change.
2. Geertz, *Interpretation of Cultures,* 90.
3. Nov. 8 (Nov. 19, n.s.), 1748 (¶ 6), Helpers Conference Minutes, Moravian Archives.
4. Sept. 1, 1759, *Jüngerhaus Diarium,* Moravian Archives.

In 1759 Peter Böhler, one of the pastors in Bethlehem, described the power of hymns to illuminate the doctrines of the church and bring them to life for the believer. "The thoughts and ideas of our redemption, healing, and the Divine Family are no longer just old truths but have been more clarified, illuminated and made more lively through the dear Holy Spirit, than they were even thirty years ago, especially since the song, 'You, our elected Head.'"[5] Thanks to music, what were once abstract ideas in Zinzendorf's sermons became existentially important. Music communicated doctrines directly to the heart of the believer. From 1727 to 1760 the Brüdergemeine wrote, translated, or adapted thousands of hymns, many of which were distributed to people outside the community.[6]

The *Bethlehem Diary* and the *Gemein Nachrichten* contain hundreds of hymns written for specific occasions such as birthdays, weddings, funerals, and even travel accounts.[7] Residents of Bethlehem were encouraged to learn the songs of the community "by heart" so they could join spontaneously in communal singing.[8] Many worship services were entirely in song, most notably the *Singstunde*. The liturgist selected verses from a variety of hymns organized around a particular theme. The worshippers were expected to follow the liturgist's lead. Although this could prove confusing, Zinzendorf believed that "liturgical confusion is better than an enforced order."[9]

Music was so vital to Moravians that the "organist also has an office of the Spirit and must be led by the Mother."[10] At a musicians' lovefeast in 1748, the participants discussed the distinction between the music of the Gemeine and that of the world. "The former stands under the direction, drive, and impulse of nature and the spirit of the world; however, the latter, if it is of the proper sort, is directed by the Mother in a blessed poor-sinner spirit, with a heart in love with the Lamb and his side, according to the heart of, and to the joy of, the Savior and his angels, and is justification and testimony in the hearts of the songs of God."[11]

5. "Die Gedancken und Ideen von unsrer Erlösung, Heiligung und der Gottes-Familie, nicht mehr die vorzeitigen sind, sondern mehr erleuchtet, aufgeklärt und belebt durch den H. Geist, als sie waren, auch nur vor 30 Jahren, sonderlich seit dem Liede: Du unser auserwehltes Haupt." *Bethlehem Diary* (Moravian Archives), July 10, 1759.

6. The Herrnhut *Gesangbuch* is now available on CD-Rom from the Unity Archive in Herrnhut.

7. See, for instance, *Bethlehem Diary* (Moravian Archives), Dec. 22, 1751, where Spangenberg's cantata relating his sea travel is recorded.

8. Alice May Caldwell, "Music of the Moravian 'Liturgische Gesange' (1791–1823): From Oral to Written Tradition" (Ph.D. diss., New York University, 1987), examines the transition from a spontaneous singing style in the Brüdergemeine to the creation of a written musical tradition.

9. Sept. 1, 1759, *Jüngerhaus Diarium*, Moravian Archives.

10. Gemein and Chor Committee—Bericht von dem Engern Synodo gehalten in Bethlehem in Januario 1757, Jan. 14, 1757, Moravian Archives.

11. *Jene stetet unter der Direction, und den trieben und bewegungen der Natur und des Weltgeistes; diese— wie sie rechten arte ist—aber wird in einen solchen armen-sünder-gefühl, [blotted out] mit einem im Lämmlein und sein Seitlein verliebsten Hertzen, nach dem hertzen und zur freude des Heylands und seiner heilig. Engel,*

MAIN THEMES OF BETHLEHEM'S HYMNS

It is a daunting and unnecessary task to try to determine exactly what hymns were sung when and then analyze them individually for content. Even this method would not be entirely accurate, as it would fail to account for private usage of the hymns. Instead, we can focus attention on the printed hymnals of the Brüdergemeine that were used in Bethlehem in order to determine the dominant motifs. Before examining the contents, though, it is important to determine which hymnals were actually used in Bethlehem during the period of the General Economy.

The Brüdergemeine produced a surprising number of hymn collections during the life of Zinzendorf. Twelve appendices and four supplements were appended to the original Herrnhut *Gesangbuch* of 1735. As part of the response to the Sifting in Herrnhaag, the church published a revised hymnal, the *Alt und Neuer Brüder-Gesangbuch* of 1753, that included original Moravian compositions along with a variety of hymns from different periods of Christian history.[12] The awkwardness of such a large hymnal led to the publication of shorter hymnals, such as the *Sarons-büchlein.*

The *Bethlehem Diary* records that from the earliest days of Bethlehem, there was a desire to have the latest hymnals. In 1742, when Zinzendorf was preparing *Appendix IX* for publication, he distributed copies of the hymns to the residents of Bethlehem so that they could begin learning them even before the supplement was published.[13] One hundred copies of *Appendix XII,* often associated with the Sifting Time, arrived in Bethlehem on June 17 (June 28, n.s.), 1748, and "our brothers and sisters devoured them and enjoyed them with an especially good appetite."[14]

The bookstore catalog of March 1755 reveals the extent to which Bethlehem valued the hymnals published in Europe. There were fifteen different hymnals (including revisions) with a total of more than five thousand volumes available.[15] This is an impressive number of hymnals for a community of fewer than

durch Mutterlein dirigirt und hat eine legitimation und Zeugniß in hertzen der Lieder Gottes. Bethlehem Diary (Moravian Archives), Dec. 10 (Dec 21, n.s.), 1748.

12. Verses like 1945:2 were omitted from the 1753 Gesangbuch: "Des wundten Creuz-GOtts bundes-blut, die wunden-wunden-wunden-wunden- fluth, ihr wunden! ja, ihr wunden! eur wunden-wunder-wunden-wunden-muth, und wunden, herzens-wunden. Wunden! Wunden! Wunden! Wunden! Wunden! Wunden! Wunden! Wunden! Wunden! Wunden! Wunden! O! ihr Wunden!"

13. Hamilton, *Bethlehem Diary* 1:80.

14. *Bethlehem Diary* (Moravian Archives), June 17 (June 28, n.s.), 1748 (¶ 7).

15. 56 *Großneu brr. Gesangbuch, 1st theil* Lond. 1753; 5 *Einigebunden;* 116 *Sarons-Büchlein,* Lond. 1753; 10 *Einigebunde;* 100 *Kinder Gesangbüchlein,* Lond. edit.; 32 *Einigebunde;* 19 *Collection of Hymns,* 2 Edit., Lond. 1742; 6 *Collection of Hymns,* 3 Edit. Lond. 1743, 22 Part 3, 2d ed.; 3 *Some other Hymns and Poems,* 1752; 20 incomplete; 85 *IX und Xter Anhang des alten Gesangbuch;* 280 *XIter Anhang;* 238 *XIIter Anhang;* 177 *Erste Zugabe zu altem Gesangbuch;* 200 *Zweyte, 3te, 4te;* 3000 *Kinder Gesangbüchlein,* Germany; 96 *Zweyter Theil des grossen neuen Gesangbuch;* 500 *Kinder Oden.* Bookstore Catalog 1755, Moravian Archives. Notice that *Anhang XII* was still available in 1753. It was not suppressed, as is commonly asserted.

one thousand people. We can safely conclude from the record that the residents of Bethlehem used the German hymnals of the Brüdergemeine as soon as possible after their publication and made them available to those outside the community.

Tables 1 through 3 display the distinctive Zinzendorfian vocabulary that is found in the hymnals used regularly in Bethlehem. While this is not a very subtle tool, it does reveal the extent of Zinzendorfian language in the hymnals and allows for a comparison between hymnals before and after the so-called Sifting Time. The hymnals studied were those actually used in Bethlehem. Table 1 gives the number of hymns in which certain words, phrases, or concepts appear in the three appendices/supplements that appear during the so-called Sifting Time. Table 2 charts the same terms for the hymns of the 1753 hymnal that was published after the Sifting, and table 3 breaks things down verse by verse. Since the 1753 hymnal is divided between general hymns and those for the individual choirs, these are presented in separate columns, allowing com-

TABLE 1: ANALYSIS OF HYMNS OF THE 1740S

WORD OR CONCEPT	Appendix XI 1742 108 HYMNS		Appendix XI-Supplement 70 HYMNS 288 HYMNS		Appendix XII 1747	
	HYMNS	%	HYMNS	%	HYMNS	%
Wounds	60	55.6	56	80.0	157	69.0
Blood	67	62.0	52	74.3	146	61.3
Death/Corpse	40	37.0	23	32.9	59	24.8
Cross	60	55.6	43	61.4	83	34.9
Atonement	28	25.9	12	17.1	28	11.8
Lamb	77	71.3	59	84.3	159	66.8
Christ: Creator/Jehovah	13	12.0	16	22.9	53	22.3
Heiland	39	36.1	17	24.3	23	9.7
Christ: King/Prince	30	27.8	20	28.6	25	10.5
Herrn/Lord	47	43.5	31	44.3	63	26.5
Mystical Marriage/ Christ Bridegroom	34	31.5	27	38.6	75	31.5
Heart	77	71.3	48	68.6	138	58.0
Emotions/feeling	58	53.7	38	54.3	124	52.1
Childlikeness	28	25.9	25	35.7	71	29.8
Father	29	26.9	20	28.6	59	24.8
Holy Spirit	24	22.2	12	17.1	27	9.4
Mother	6	5.6	7	10.0	51	21.4
Morality/purity	18	16.7	12	17.1	49	20.6
Incarnation	13	12.0	19	27.1	62	26.1
Sin/Righteousness	63	58.3	44	62.9	93	39.1

TABLE 2: 1753 GESANGBUCH—BY HYMN

96 total hymns in selection Hymns of the Brethren: 21 choir; 75 Gemeine

WORD OR CONCEPT	TOTAL	%	CHOIR	%	GEMEINE	%
Wounds	63	65.6	14	66.7	49	65.3
Blood	62	64.6	16	76.2	46	61.3
Death/Corpse	32	33.3	8	38.1	25	33.3
Cross	45	46.9	11	52.4	34	45.3
Atonement	19	19.8	3	14.3	16	21.3
Lamb	66	68.8	14	66.7	52	69.3
Christ: Creator/Jehovah	27	28.1	4	19.0	23	30.7
Heiland	22	22.9	4	19.0	18	24.0
Christ: King/Prince	20	20.3	6	28.6	14	18.7
Herr	44	45.8	8	38.1	36	48.0
Mystical Marriage/ Christ Bridegroom	44	45.8	15	71.4	29	38.7
Heart	79	82.3	18	85.7	61	81.3
Emotions/feeling	53	55.2	13	61.9	40	53.3
Childlikeness	31	32.3	9	42.9	22	29.3
Father	38	39.6	6	28.6	32	42.7
Mother/Spirit	36	37.5	11	52.4	25	33.3
Morality/purity	21	21.9	12	57.1	9	12.0
Incarnation	32	33.3	13	61.9	19	25.3
Sin/Righteousness	47	48.9	9	42.9	38	50.7

parison between choir and general (Gemeine) hymns. Since the 1753 hymnal was published intentionally in response to the Sifting, and since the smaller hymnals were based on it, we can safely use it as the normative hymnal for the Moravians.

One of the most important things generated by this analysis is that there are more similarities than differences in the hymnody of the 1740s (the so-called Sifting Time) and the 1750s. There is indeed less use of diminutives in the 1753 hymnal than in earlier collections, and many of the most exotic or bizarre images (bees, maggots, worms, and similar creatures sucking thirstily at the side of Christ) are virtually absent from the hymns of the 1753 *Gesangbuch*. However, wounds imagery is still prevalent, and there are frequent references to the dove resting in the crevice of Jesus' side.

One can conclude that after 1749 the Brüdergemeine moderated its liturgical and imaginative life; but this should not be seen as a retreat from Zinzendorf's blood-and-wounds theology. There are twice as many references to the wounds of Christ as to God the Father in the 1753 hymnal. Nearly half of the hymns in 1753 refer to the mystical marriage with Christ. This contradicts the commonly held notion that the hymnody of the Moravians was purged of wounds theol-

TABLE 3: 1753 GESANGBUCH—BY VERSE

1,237 total verses: 267 choir; 970 Gemeine

WORD OR CONCEPT	TOTAL	%	CHOIR	%	GEMEINE	%
Wounds	137	11.1	23	8.6	114	11.2
Blood	109	8.8	26	9.7	83	8.6
Death/Corpse	46	3.7	9	3.3	37	3.8
Cross	67	5.4	17	6.4	50	5.2
Atonement	25	2.0	5	1.9	20	2.1
Lamb	111	9.0	26	9.7	85	8.8
Christ: Creator/Jehovah	28	2.3	8	3.0	20	2.1
Heiland	24	1.9	4	1.5	20	2.1
Christ: King/Prince	24	1.9	9	3.4	15	1.5
Herr	46	3.7	11	4.1	35	3.6
Mystical Marriage/ Christ Bridegroom	59	4.8	26	9.7	33	3.4
Heart	136	11.0	30	11.2	106	10.9
Emotions/feeling	56	4.5	15	5.6	41	4.2
Childlikeness	35	2.8	10	3.7	25	2.6
Father	50	4.0	7	2.6	43	4.4
Mother/Spirit	50	4.0	14	5.2	36	3.7
Morality/purity	45	3.6	26	9.7	19	2.0
Incarnation	35	2.8	20	7.5	15	1.5
Sin/Righteousness	87	7.0	18	6.7	69	7.1

ogy and mystical marriage imagery. More than 50 percent make direct reference to the wounds of Jesus, while only three hymns mention the Resurrection of Christ. One could hardly call the Moravians in the 1740s and 1750s "the Easter People," as Moravians like to style themselves today.

The hymnals in Bethlehem reflect the main themes of Zinzendorf's theology. About a fourth of the hymns explicitly identify Christ as either the Creator or Jehovah, the God of the Old Testament. Sometimes this identification is made in passing but at other times it is a central focus. More important, nowhere is the Father designated as the Creator. Nearly a third of the hymns deal directly with the Incarnation, and those hymns are of two main types. In the general hymns, the focus is on the reality of the Creator taking on human flesh and dying on the cross.[16] It is the historicity of Christ's sacrifice that is most important.

The second type of Incarnation hymns, most prevalent in the choir section, stresses Christ's identification with the weaknesses of the flesh. Christ experienced the human condition and thus has sympathy for human weakness. He can help overcome temptation. Incarnation hymns were valued in Bethlehem

16. E.g., Hymn 2074, 1753 *Gesangbuch.*

and sung in many *Singstunden* in which "the Creator of our souls and the husband of our humanity in his merits was ardently celebrated in song."[17] In short, worship in Bethlehem stressed the paradox of the Creator dying for the creatures, which is confirmed in the *Bethlehem Diary*.[18] Such devotion to the Creator Christ was evident from the very beginning of the Bethlehem settlement.[19]

It is not surprising that there are twice as many references to the wounds of Christ as to the cross. Instead of using the cross as the primary symbol of salvation, Moravian hymns used blood-and-wounds imagery. This follows Zinzendorf's own preference for concrete, emotive symbols over symbols once removed. This focuses the worshipper's attention on the person of Christ rather than on the means of his death, thus enhancing the Christocentric message and its emotional impact. The worshipper is encouraged to identify with the disciple Thomas, who, in the understanding of the Brüdergemeine, actually placed his hand in the side of Christ (John 20:27–28).

A surprising feature of these hymns is the lack of interest in morality and purity. Few hymns make explicit reference to morality or purity and none of them is devoted to that theme. The tone is that those who love Jesus are moral and chaste but there is no need to stress moral behavior. It is not surprising that there is a greater emphasis on morality in the choir hymns than in the Gemeine hymns. The choir hymns were addressed to specific groups within the Gemeine and could thus focus on certain needs common to a particular group. For instance, the hymns for the single sisters and brothers lay heavier stress on sexual abstinence than do those of other choirs. Here again, though, the theme is that the heart united to Christ has no other desires.

The choir hymns in particular stress the Zinzendorfian idea that humans have been created to sleep in the Creator's arms, with each believer being the bride of Christ. This notion is particularly evident in the women's hymns and hymns for married persons, but is virtually absent in the men's hymns, despite Zinzendorf's assertion that men are brides of Christ, too. The most sexually explicit statement of the mystical marriage is the "Lied für dem Braut-Kämmer," where the man is depicted as the proxy for Christ enacting the union of the soul to its Bridegroom.[20] In Bethlehem such hymns were most often sung in the Married People's Choir. For example: "Otherwise everything proceeded quite nicely and happily in the Gemeine, and our Husband blessed all events,

17. *Bethlehem Diary* (Moravian Archives), Oct. 30, 1758.

18. For example, "In the early lesson the material about Jesus Christ as our creator was considered . . . and it was celebrated in song in the evening lesson with a creaturelike attachment of our souls to our God and Lord, who died for us lost humans." *Bethlehem Diary* (Moravian Archives), June 9, 1752.

19. Hamilton, *Bethlehem Diary* 1:48–49.

20. Hymn 2155, 1753 *Gesangbuch*.

especially the Married People's evening quarter-hour service, that Br. Johann Nitschmann held with several stanzas from the hymn, 'O you, in whose arms we sleep,' with a tender feeling for the conjugal love of our husband for his wedded church."[21]

In summary, we can safely conclude from this analysis of major hymnals that the hymns used in Bethlehem were thoroughly Zinzendorfian. If music is the language of the heart, the heart of Bethlehem was attached to the wounds of the Bridegroom, Jesus, and to the Mother Spirit.

LITANIES

The terms "litany" and "liturgy" were used almost interchangeably by Zinzendorf and his followers, but there is an imprecise distinction. A litany is a standardized church prayer, while liturgy may refer to an entire worship service or a long hymn on a single theme. The hymn "O Haupt voll Blut und Wunden" (O head full of blood and wounds) is a liturgy, while the *Te Abba* (O Father) is a litany. I will use litany to refer to the corporate prayers of the Gemeine and liturgy to refer to their worship in general; however, the original sources are not so precise.

Both litanies and liturgies could be shortened or lengthened by the liturgist. Commonly, other elements of worship, such as baptisms and weddings, would occur within a litany. For example, one Sunday in 1748 the *Church Litany (Gemein Litaney)* included a baptism, the reception of twenty-six new acolytes, the blessing of Benigna Antes, the ordination of five deacons, and the consecration of Henry Antes as *senior civilei*.[22]

The basic litany for the Moravians was called the *Gemein Litaney* (Church Litany), but almost as popular was the *Wunden Litaney* (Litany of the Wounds) which will be discussed in detail in a later chapter. In 1744 Zinzendorf wrote several more litanies dedicated to the three persons of the Trinity, using the ancient *Te Deum* hymn as a model. The *Te Patrem* or *Te Abba* is addressed to the Father; the *Te Logos, Te Jehova,* and *Te Agnum* are addressed to Christ; and the *Te Matrem* is addressed to the Holy Spirit.[23]

In addition to these, Zinzendorf (with some help from associates) wrote *Church Prayers* addressed to each person of the Trinity: *to the Father of her Lord, to her Head and Lord,* and *to the Holy Spirit,* as well as a litany to the whole Trinity, *The Trisagion.* Finally, there were two "bridal chamber" litanies, the *Brides' Song* and the *Epithalamium.*[24] While each litany was short enough

---

21. *Bethlehem Diary* (Moravian Archives), Jan. 30 (Feb. 10, n.s.), 1750, (¶ 4).

22. Ibid., Oct. 16 (Oct. 27, n.s.), 1748 (¶ 5).

23. *Herrnhuter Gesangbuch,* no. 1895–1898. Zimmerling, *Gott in Gemeinschaft,* 193–203.

24. English translations of these litanies are found in Appendix 3. See also "Theology in Song: Daily Litanies in the Eighteenth-Century Moravian Church," in Atwood and Vogt, *Distinctiveness of Moravian Culture.*

for daily devotions, together they set forth the main tenets of Zinzendorf's theology in song. Most of the litanies first appeared in *Appendix XII*, but there was a minor revision of these litanies following the so-called Sifting. Some of the litanies were renamed, but their essential ideas remained intact. The revised litanies were published in a separate volume in 1755, but the changes were largely cosmetic.[25]

The litanies used in Bethlehem were the same as those used by the Brüdergemeine in Europe. Because of the delays caused by sea travel, Bethlehem was always behind Europe in adopting changes in the litanies but made an effort to do so as soon as instructions or new liturgy books arrived from Europe. Tables 4 and 5 give the record of usage for the litanies.

Weekend worship ran from Friday evening to Sunday evening, modeling the *tridium* of the Passion-Resurrection cycle of the early church but on a weekly rather than a yearly cycle. Friday evening was devoted to the Passion of Christ. The Sabbath and Sunday schedule implemented by Spangenberg in 1752 was as follows:

Sabbath

6:00 A.M.	the Morning Blessing without a sermon
11:00 A.M.	the Sabbath lovefeast of the children
12:00 A.M.	the Sabbath lovefeast of the entire Gemeine
2:00 P.M.	The liturgy of the Widowers, Widows, and Children
8:00 P.M.	*Congregational service,* with sermon on Daily Text
9:00 P.M.	*Te Pleuram* and then the Evening Blessing

Sundays

6:00 A.M.	*Church Litany*
10:00 A.M.	English preaching service
11:00 A.M.	German preaching service
1:00 P.M.	suckling children's service
1:30 P.M.	the children's hour, and then a sermon
After 2:00 P.M.	reading of the *Gemein Nachrichten.*
7:00 P.M.	*Gemeinstunde* with a sermon or a simple *Singstunde*
8:00 P.M.	*Litany of the Life and Sufferings of Jesus* or the *Hymns of the Wounds of Jesus,* and then the evening blessing.[26]

25. The *Gemein Nachrichten* of 1752 (week 5) gives several paragraphs of changes to the litanies. Some of these were incorporated in the new litany book. None of them affect the theology of the litanies themselves, but deal mainly with meter and rhyme.

26. *Bethlehem Diary* (Moravian Archives), June 30, 1752; cf. Jan. 9, 1752 Conferenz Protocoll (Dec. 11, 1751–Aug. 6, 1752), Moravian Archives.

TABLE 4: MAJOR LITANIES

Year	Gemein Litany	Wunden Litany	Te Jehovah	Te Patrem	Te Matrem	Te Agnum	O Haupt	Te Deum
1742	5	–	–	–	–	–	–	–
1743	9	–	–	–	–	1	–	7
1744	22	3	–	1	–	2	–	2
1745	34	5	2	–	–	–	–	–
1746	24	15	–	–	–	–	–	–
1747	52	39	6	6	14	4	–	1
1748	32	36	1	4	11	2	–	–
1749	8	10	4	8	6	1	–	–
1750	11	36	1	1	–	–	–	–
1751	1	25	1	1	–	1	–	–
1752	36	18	5	2	5	3	–	–
1753	37	11	3	4	2	1	3	–
1754	43	18	4	3	1	7	11	6
1755	52	18	3	4	4	4	17	4
1756	52	25	10	6	2	4	16	–
1757	52	17	20	1	6	5	52	1
1758	48	17	26	0	7	18	48	2
1759	21	11	12	8	3	27	41	3
1760	31	5	9	9	5	21	15	–
1761	36	11	6	6	4	27	16	–

Worship was not confined to the Sabbath and Sunday, however. Because every day was dedicated to the Lord, each day had moments for communal worship. Many of these regularly scheduled worship events included one of the litanies of the Brüdergemeine, although the schedule was subject to changes over the years. The *Bethlehem Diary* records that in April 1747 it was decided to follow the schedule:

Sun.	A.M.	*Te Matrem* [O Mother]
	P.M.	*Te Agnum* [O Lamb]
	Mon.	*Church's Prayer to the Father*
	Tues.	*Church's Prayer to the Mother*
	Wed.	*Church's Prayer to the Husband*
	Thurs.	*Te Jehovah* [Christ]
	Fri.	*Litany of the Wounds of the Husband*
	Sat.	*Singstunde* with *Church Litany* and then *Te Patrem*[27]

Thus the community focused on different persons of the Trinity at different services while devoting special attention to the central blood-and-wounds theology.

27. *Bethlehem Diary* (Moravian Archives), April 5 (April 16, n.s.), 1747 (¶ 3).

TABLE 5: MINOR LITANIES

Year	Mutter Gebet	Vater Gebet	Epitha-lamium	Te Jesum	Te Pleura	Tri-sagion	Braut	Zum Manne	Te Logon
1742	–	–	–	–	–	–	–	–	–
1743	–	–	–	1	–	–	–	–	–
1744	–	–	–	13	–	–	1	–	–
1745	–	–	–	3	–	–	1	–	–
1746	–	–	–	2	–	–	–	–	–
1747	3	2	–	–	–	–	–	2	–
1748	6	2	–	–	–	–	–	4	–
1749	1	–	–	–	18	–	20	2	–
1750	–	–	–	–	8	–	3	2	–
1751	–	–	–	–	18	–	5	0	–
1752	3	2	–	–	9	–	–	1	–
1753	2	1	–	–	5	–	4	3	–
1754	6	3	1	1	6	2	16	2	5
1755	4	2	5	5	8	6	7	2	2
1756	11	7	13	13	12	9	6	7	2
1757	10	5	6	6	4	22	2	16	5
1758	26	13	3	3	1	29	1	23	10
1759	13	13	3	3	4	32	5	11	5
1760	7	3	5	5	6	19	9	9	4
1761	4	8	7	7	1	23	5	6	–

The daily litanies were also connected to the various choirs, which were specially recognized on different days. In 1752, following the return of Spangenberg, it was decided that the daily litanies would be held just before the noon meal, apparently so as not to disrupt work patterns.[28] The new daily schedule was:

5:00 A.M.	Morning Blessing
Midday at 11:30 or 11:45 A.M.	LITURGY CORRESPONDING TO THE CHOIR DAYS:
Mon.	Trisagion
Tues.	*Prayer of the Church to her Mother*
Wed.	*Prayer of the Church to her Husband*
Thurs.	*Prayer of the Church to her Father*
Fri.	A Passion Hymn (such as *O sacred head*)

The Choir Days in 1752 were:

Tues.	Single Sisters
Wed.	Single Brothers
Thur.	Married Brothers and Sisters
Sat.	Widowers, Widows, and Children.[29]

28. Jan. 9, 1752, Conferenz Protocoll (Dec. 11, 1751–Aug. 6, 1752) Moravian Archives.
29. *Bethlehem Diary* (Moravian Archives), June 30, 1752.

The last major change in the scheduling of the litanies came in 1759, when it was agreed to follow Zinzendorf's instructions in the *Jüngerhaus Diarium* (June 4, 1758) concerning the monthly cycle of worship. On the Sunday before Holy Communion they were to sing the first part of the *Wunden Litaney* and then the *Pleurodie* just before communion. The *Te Matrem* was to be used on the Sunday after the *Gemeintag* (a day for reading reports from the mission stations and other communities). On the third Sunday, the *Te Jehovah* was sung.[30]

Throughout the period of the General Economy, then, Zinzendorf's litanies were a part of daily life in Bethlehem. While the frequency of use of individual litanies varied from year to year, it is evident that there was no retreat from blood-and-wounds theology, the motherhood of the Spirit, or the mystical marriage to Christ after 1750. In fact, the increased use of the *Pleurodie* (O side wound) shows an increase in adoration of the side wound after Spangenberg's return to Bethlehem in 1752.[31]

CREATOR AND BRIDEGROOM

There is not space here to give a detailed analysis of each of the litanies, but some general points are important to consider. The litanies addressed to Christ (*Litany of the Wounds, Te Logos, Te Agnum,* and *The Church's Prayer to Her Head and Lord*) were frequently used in Bethlehem, especially during Spangenberg's second term of office, and they stress certain common themes. Each strongly asserts that the Son is the Creator and God of the world. The *Te Logos,* for instance, says "You are the *Ens entium* [being of beings], the *Numen gentium* [God of the nations], the *Causa causarium* [cause of causes]," connecting Christ with common philosophical and mystical names for the deity. Although these are largely philosophical terms, the intention was not to engage in a philosophical discourse but to contemplate the mystical truth behind these words. Thus it was not uncommon for worshippers to lie prostrate at the words "Numen gentium."[32]

Christ is also proclaimed to be the God of the Old Testament who has the ineffable name and before whom the angels veil their faces. "No Angel is so bold and rash, But trembles before your *Shemhamphorash.*" It is interesting that the litany specifically joins this proclamation of the deity of Christ with the Athanasian rejection of Arianism. "Hence does the Church say to this

---

30. Ibid., May 25, 1759. It was noted in this schedule that the members should be able to sing the *Wunden Litaney* by heart.

31. Atwood, "Understanding Zinzendorf's Blood and Wounds Theology," *Transactions of the Moravian Historical Society* (forthcoming).

32. *Bethlehem Diary* (Moravian Archives), Jan. 30, 1752.

Phrase: *Non erat ubi non eras* [There was no time when you were not]. Amen!"
This time Latin is used to emphasize the orthodox nature of this proclamation
of Christ's role as the Creator.

The Zinzendorfian concept of the mystical marriage between Christ and his
church is expressed clearly in *The Church's Prayer to her Head and Lord,* which
was originally known as the *Church's Prayer to her Husband.* None of the original marriage imagery was altered when the name was changed. In fact, the
eroticism actually increased in places. For instance, the phrase "Put the Infants
to the breast" was changed to the more erotic "In your arms and at your breast,
Celebrate the sacrament." In this litany the mystical marriage is not a matter
of ecstasy, nor is it eschatological. Rather, it is related to the intimacy between
God and his redeemed creatures, who are now able to respond directly to his
will.

Two lesser litanies were also often used in the 1750s to express this erotic
devotion to Christ. They are the *Braut-Gesang* (Bride's Song), formally the *Te
Sponsam* (O spouse), and the *Epithalamium* (Bridal chamber song), both of
which were very popular during Spangenberg's second tenure. In the Bride's
Song, the church expresses her joy in her Husband in anticipation of the eschaton: "Wait for us in bliss Until time itself is reborn! For when this has happened, Then you shall be perfected." The union between the soul and the
Savior is even more intimate than marriage. Just as Eve was formed from the
side of Adam in order to be his wife, the *Braut-Gesang* proclaims the Zinzendorfian notion that the church was born out of the side of Jesus (v. 14).

These two litanies were used in a variety of ways in Bethlehem. One or the
other could be part of a special service devoted to the theme of being a bride
of Christ, such as when "in the Gemeinstunde [there] was the discourse about
the blessed connection of the Bride with the Bridegroom, and through him
with the whole Holy Trinity, after which several stanzas from the Epithalamium created a quite pleasing conclusion."[33] They could also be joined with
Holy Communion, as Böhler joined them when he preached on the bride-like
condition of the believers before Christ.[34]

Throughout the 1750s the Bethlehem Gemeine repeatedly reaffirmed its
commitment to the mystical marriage. Spangenberg often preached about the
Bridegroom, and it was reported that in 1757 "the Choirs prostrated themselves
before their Bridegroom and Husband with tender tears."[35] It is recorded that
September 10, 1758, "was a very blessed day, on which much was said, thought,
sung, and played concerning the Bridegroom and his Bride, but the most lovely

33. Ibid., June 19, 1756.
34. Ibid., Nov. 19, 1759.
35. Ibid., Sept. 15, 1757; June 12, 1757.

thing was the way it was experienced. In the Morning Blessing, Br. Petrus [Böhler] sang the festival text: 'The Kingdom of Heaven is like virgins who go to meet the Bridegroom.'"[36]

The *Braut-Gesang* and the Epithalamium were also used as a way to remember the dead in prayer, such as when Spangenberg had the Epithalamium sung on the anniversary of the death of Erdmuth von Zinzendorf.[37] Consistently in Bethlehem's worship life, Zinzendorf's full Christology was celebrated. Christ is the Creator of the universe and the only Redeemer of the world, who unites with each soul in an intimate marriage of the soul. Further implications of this doctrine are discussed in the chapter on the choir system.

THE MOTHER SPIRIT

There is no doubt that Christ was the center of Moravian devotion, but one of the best-kept secrets in the historiography of the Moravian Church was the highly developed worship of the Holy Spirit as the mother.[38] The mother name of the Holy Spirit should not be dismissed as a brief fad. Throughout our period of study, every diarist refers to the Spirit as the mother. Moreover, there is no evidence that Spangenberg, Böhler, Seidel, or the other ministers in Bethlehem were at this time opposed to using the mother imagery.[39]

Two major litanies to the Holy Spirit were used regularly in Bethlehem: the *Te Matrem* and *The Church's Prayer to the Holy Spirit* (or to *Her Mother*). The *Te Matrem* was one of the regularly scheduled weekly litanies in Bethlehem and was particularly associated with the Single Sisters.

In the *Te Matrem,* the Spirit is connected to the work of Christ, as one might expect, based on the earlier discussion of Christocentrism. The Spirit inspired the prophets and the martyrs to praise Christ, and she is the one who brings people to Christ. The Spirit is a mother in this litany in two senses: she is the "Mother of God's children" through her work in regeneration, and she is also the mother of Christ (v. 2). Although the Spirit is proclaimed the "wisdom archetypal," the creative role of the Spirit (Prov. 8:22–23) has already been assigned to Christ in the *Te Logos;* therefore this biblical aspect of the Spirit plays little role in the *Te Matrem.*

---

36. Ibid., Sept. 10, 1758.

37. Ibid., June 19, 1758.

38. Zimmerling, *Gott in Gemeinschaft,* 185–208, integrates his discussion of the Zinzendorf's doctrine of the Holy Spirit with the actual worship life of the community, but even he understates the extent of this devotion.

39. Spangenberg gave liturgies and *Singstunden* to the Mother on Dec. 19, 1755, June 29, 1757, Jan. 10, March 29 and April 12, 1758, as well as on other occasions. On Dec. 19, 1758, Spangenberg instructed the children about the Mother "in a childlike way." Böhler is listed as having "celebrated in song the Mother office of the Holy Spirit, with a blessed feeling" on July 28, 1757, and June 7, 1758, *Bethlehem Diary* (Moravian Archives).

It is interesting that so little attention is given to the role of Spirit as comforter in the *Te Matrem*. She is nowhere identified as the comforter as such, nor is the notion of comfort directly connected with the concept of mother. In contrast, one of the major roles played by the Spirit, according to this litany, is to serve as the agent of communication between God and his people (v. 4). The mother also plays a role in keeping the priesthood of believers holy before God.

The Church's Prayer to the Holy Spirit makes similar claims about the role of the Spirit in the world and in the church. She conceived the Son by the Virgin (v. 1) and is the church's mother. It is interesting that this is the *Church's Prayer* and not the *Gemeine Gebet,* which may indicate that the Moravians believed that the doctrine of the mother office applied to the entire Christian church. She is not simply the special mother of the Brüdergemeine but the mother of all Christians everywhere. This litany is distinct from the *Te Matrem,* however, in the emphasis placed on the daily role of the Spirit in the Gemeine: she is the real consecrator at baptism and the Eucharist and is also an agent of forgiveness.

At the same time, the mother is the one who chastises those who stray. At least some members of the Gemeine accepted this view of the Holy Spirit as a mother who could become displeased and even chastening. It was reported with obvious pleasure that in the little girls' school there was "a special work of the dear Mother on their hearts. A child said to her choir sister, 'the dear Mother is not pleased that I was not allowed to be at the *Anbeten,* but I have prayed to the Savior with many tears.' "[40]

The second half of the 1750s saw an intentional effort to promote the worship of the mother in Bethlehem. She was the focus of two major festivals: Pentecost and the Mother Festival of the Holy Spirit. On December 19, 1756, the first celebration of the Mother Festival was held. Preparations began the night before.[41] The festival itself was considered a special blessing to the Gemeine:

It was announced early with the trombones, and the Brothers and Sisters were also awakened in their respective dormitories with the festival day chorales. In the Morning Blessing, the Gemeine expressed its desire for the visitation of the dear Church-Mother with the old hymn, "Come Holy Spirit, Lord God." Toward 9 A.M. there was a gathering of the whole community. . . . And then Br. Joseph explained the contents: "We were happy that the

40. Ibid., Oct. 17, 1761 (Mädgen Anstalt Diary), 303.

41. "The children had their sabbath lovefeast and the Gemeine its liturgy with the Prayer of the Church to the Holy Spirit, and together they were notified of tomorrow's Mother Festival of the Holy Spirit with the ardent wish that the Holy Spirit would declare and enthrone herself as Mother in every heart." Ibid., Dec. 18, 1756.

long-awaited time had come, when the Holy Spirit chose to let herself be solemnly declared as the Mother of our church.[42]

The Mother Festival the following year was more emotional. The Gemeine gathered at 9:00 A.M. and sang "Come Holy Spirit, Lord God" "with a blessed scenting of the Spirit." After Böhler gave a discourse, they sang, "Welcome in the second year, and that with a thousand joys, you Mother of the suffering band!" There followed many tears, and then the kiss of peace.[43] This celebration made a particular impact on the Single Sisters. "The *Mutter Fest* was an inexpressibly blessed day on which we prayed for every heart to our dear Mother for absolution for everything whereby we had troubled her; we thanked her for her faithful care; and promised her to be completely obedient children from anew; and gave ourselves over to her in her true care."[44] After Zinzendorf's death, the Mother Festival was moved to Pentecost and eventually was abolished. The last recorded celebration of the *Mutter Fest* in the Moravian Church took place in 1774.

THE FATHER

As noted earlier, the Father had no distinct role in his theology despite Zinzendorf's protestations that the Brüdergemeine was the only group to worship the Father properly. This same situation is evident in Bethlehem. Despite the fact that liturgies and litanies were sung to the Father, there are very few references to these having any great impact or meaning in the Gemeine. The litanies themselves are unremarkable.

Two major litanies addressed to the Father were sung on a regular basis. The *Te Patrem* is the older one. Its name was changed in the revised litany book of 1755 from *Te Patrem* to *Te Abba*. I suspect that this was to emphasize Zinzendorf's theology that part of Christ's mission was to reveal the identity of his Father and to give the church the right to call him "Abba."[45] Even so, most of the litany recalls the victory of Christ over sin and death and merely praises the Father for being the Father of the Savior. This fight is on behalf of the Son rather than being the work of the Father. Verses 8 and 9 pray that the

---

42. Ibid., Dec. 19, 1756.

43. The daughters fell down before their divine Mother and sang "Command from us all together the holy honor of the Mother." Br. Petrus made a heartfelt confession, wept, and asked for forgiveness and a new blessing to be obedient and the whole Gemeine with him. But who can express in words the scent of the Holy Spirit and the motherly comfort that expressed itself thereby?" Ibid., Dec. 19, 1757.

44. Dec. 19, 1758, *Single Sisters' Diary*, Moravian Archives. There is a similar record for the Pentecost celebration the following year. Ibid., June 3, 1759.

45. There are other minor revisions and additions to this litany. One of the more interesting is that "Holy Spirit" was changed to "Mother."

Father will help Christ's people in their struggles, and that his angels will protect them from harm, but even here the Spirit plays as great a role as the Father.

The other litany, *The Church's Prayer to the Father of her LORD,* is really a recasting of the Lord's Prayer in verse. In this recasting, however, the litany emphasizes Zinzendorf's belief that the Lord's Prayer is to be understood only through Christ. Six of the eight verses refer directly to Christ, and one of the main works of the Father for which the believer prays is the everlasting bread "from bleeding Side."

This litany does indicate some change in the beliefs of the Brüdergemeine since the founding of Bethlehem, however. In the earliest days the Lord's Prayer was addressed to Christ, not to the Father. The Lord's Prayer "is to be prayed each Monday, a chorale being appended to each phrase. We retain the opening formula as an act of condescension on our part; but we denote thereby the eternal Father, the person of Jesus Christ, through Whom honor is given to the Father."[46] The *Te Abba* is clearly addressed to the Father, but even so, the petitions remain tied to Christ.

Moravian litanies continually reinforced Zinzendorf's theology in Bethlehem throughout the period of the General Economy. According to the records, the residents of Bethlehem were profoundly moved by many of these litanies and there is no indication of disagreement over the content. It is also clear that Spangenberg, Böhler, and the other leaders of Bethlehem used the litanies and preached on their meaning regularly. We can therefore safely conclude that Spangenberg and his co-workers embraced Zinzendorf's understanding of the Trinity, including mystical marriage and adoration of the Spirit as mother. All of the major sources for determining the belief structure of Bethlehem are in agreement with the main features of Zinzendorf's theology. In short, the theology of Bethlehem was that of Zinzendorf.

SYMBOLIC ACTIONS

Nearly every aspect of life in Bethlehem was incorporated into communal rituals in order to bring the secular into the sacred sphere by connecting daily life to the life and death of Jesus. Rituals thereby helped to preserve the community and keep it directed toward its mission. Gillian Gollin expresses the role of ritual in Bethlehem quite well when she says, "The religious rituals associated with such activities represented an attempt to capture the sacred character of all human endeavor in a socially standardized form. Such rituals served not only to keep alive the individual's awareness of the sacred but also to provide a strong basis for the social cohesion and integration of the group."[47]

46. Hamilton, *Bethlehem Diary* 1:80.
47. Gollin, *Moravians in Two Worlds,* 20–21.

Moravian rituals were intended to foster the Christocentric heart religion of Zinzendorf; thus there were changes from time to time so that they would continue to "speak to the heart." This was true to Zinzendorf's assertion that "in a congregation [Gemeine] of Jesus nothing should be done apathetically and by half measures but everything should go on with constant uniformity and conscientiousness."[48] Even with changes in practice, however, the rituals in Bethlehem had a core set of symbols that remained constant.

RITUALS OF INCLUSION

During the General Economy the closed nature of Bethlehem was rigorously enforced, because residents had to be prepared to devote themselves economically and socially to the Gemeine. Moreover, the subdivision of the Gemeine into choirs meant that there were concentric circles of intimacy within Bethlehem that included one's choir, co-workers, and gender group, the Bethlehem Gemeine, the American Gemeine, and finally the worldwide Brüdergemeine. In such an intimate society the entry of new persons could be very dangerous to the harmony of the organization; therefore the means of inclusion was carefully ritualized.

According to Smaby, 22 percent of the immigrants to Bethlehem in its second decade (1754–63) were converts, compared to 78 percent who had come from other settlements of the Brüdergemeine.[49] This averages to about ten converts per year, but it is not certain how many of the one-hundred-plus converts in Bethlehem in the 1750s were also converts to Christianity. Another major source of new Moravians were children of members. One thing common to children and converts was that they had to be brought into the religious and linguistic world of Bethlehem. As the Moravians would have put it, they had to be blessed by the blood of Christ. The two ways to do this were baptism and reception.

Baptisms were very important in Bethlehem. Newborns were baptized as soon as possible in some type of corporate worship. "In the evening, in the eighth hour, the Sister Oesterlein, the wife of our smith in Gnadenhutten, gave birth to a little son, who soon thereafter, at 9:00 P.M., during the liturgy, which was held with the *Te Pleuram*, was baptized in the death of Jesus after the words 'Look up and see the crevice in the rock [i.e., the side wound]—dug out and

---

48. Hamilton, *Bethlehem Diary* 1:105. Zinzendorf reminded the residents of Bethlehem of the difference between a Gemeine and a church when it comes to rituals: "In our sacred rites, such as baptism and Communion, we as a congregation [*Gemeine*] of Jesus are not able to follow an accepted and established and permanent usage and form as the state churches do; alterations within the congregation and its sacred functions can always be anticipated." Hamilton, *Bethlehem Diary* 1:127.

49. Smaby, *Transformation of Moravian Bethlehem*, 64–65.

hewn,' and was named Matthäus.''[50] Sometimes a separate meeting of the Gemeine was held just for a baptism, such as when Elizabeth Utley and Johann Pyrlaeus, "two blood-worms sent to us by the Lamb today," were baptized.[51]

The ritual could produce religious ecstasy, such as was reported early in Bethlehem's history. When one person was baptized into the wounds of Jesus, "The lights flashing from the blood of the Lamb circulated through the *Saal*, and many of the brethren and sisters dissolved in tears."[52] After her baptism, Lea Robins's youngest daughter "was conducted half-dazed from the *Saal* to rest while the Gemeine sang 'Thus more you Blood ignite' after her with warm hearts."[53]

Although water was used in the ceremony, blood was invoked liturgically. Pyrlaeus and other ministers baptized children with the blood of Christ and "buried [them] in the hollow of His wound."[54] The baptism ritual was subject to variations, but it maintained this connection to the blood and wounds of Christ throughout the period of the General Economy. A hymn typically sung at baptism reads: "The Eye sees Water, nothing more, / How it is poured out by Men; / But Faith alone conceives the Pow'r / Of Jesu's Blood to make us clean: / Faith sees it as a purple Flood, / Colour'd with Jesu's Blood and Grace / Which heals each Sore, and makes all good, / What Adam brought on us his Race, / And all what we ourselves have done."[55]

The cardinal points of Zinzendorf's heart religion were communicated through the baptism ritual. Children were buried in death with Christ, so that from that point their lives might be lived with Christ. The minister said to the infant, "Now live, yet not you but Christ live in you." There followed a brief exorcism and a blessing.[56]

The baptism of adults was similar, but it also included reception into a choir. The ceremony typically included a sermon about baptism and the theology of the Brüdergemeine, and then the person's application for baptism would be read. This document put forth the person's religious experience and reasons why she or he felt called by God to be part of the Bethlehem community. Adults would have to be absolved through a hymn such as "The bloody Sweat which with such Heat did from Thee flow," which stresses Christ's penitence

---

50. *Bethlehem Diary* (Moravian Archives), March 11, 1752.

51. Ibid., April 2 (April 13, n.s.), 1748 (¶ 6).

52. Hamilton, *Bethlehem Diary* 1:181.

53. *Bethlehem Diary* (Moravian Archives), April 17, 1748.

54. Hamilton, *Bethlehem Diary* 1:204, 214.

55. 1759 *Litany-book*, 171–72; cf. 1757 *Litaneyen-büchlein*, 190.

56. 1759 *Litany-book*, 172; cf. 1757 *Litaneyen-büchlein*, 190–93. The literal translation of the hymn verse is: "When one points out to him the dear Lamb and his entire works, so flees the evil spirit." The exorcism was much stronger in persons converted from tribal religions. According to the *Zeremonienbüchlein*, this was to impress converts with the seriousness of their break from their former lives in the wild. ZE 6:36–37.

for his people. Members of the choir joined in the blessing by imposing their hands on the baptized person's head. The person was then welcomed into the choir with a kiss.[57] In the case of native peoples and Africans, a new name was generally given at baptism in order to stress their break with tribal religion.

A member of the Brüdergemeine could be received into the Bethlehem congregation after a period of examination and with the approval of the leaders and the lot. If everything was duly approved, he or she was received during a liturgical service, usually the Sunday singing of the Litany during the stanza, "Pale lips, kiss him/her/them on the Heart(s)" or "Open arms, receive them."[58] A long account is given of the reception of Maria Berothin:

Then the *Wunden Litaney* was sung. At the beginning the Gemeine fell down and then stood again at the words, "Your painful first birth." After the words, "Bring the scattered children of God into the ark of the holy Christendom," Br. Joseph (Spangenberg) said, "The heart of the Savior is well-disposed toward all people, and it wills that all be made blessed. On that account let him call to everyone, whoever comes to him is welcome. . . . It [the reception ceremony] is no mere ceremony but we believe that what the Gemeine does, the Savior says "Amen" to, and he does not let such grace to be poured out in vain. Unless a person rips himself away [from the Savior], he has the grace to cleave to him and to carry the yoke of the Savior through the world." Then sister Anna Maria Berothin was received with kiss of love into the Gemeine during the words "O for a poor sinner" and "Pale Lips." Thereupon [the service] was concluded and closed with the *Litany of the Wounds.*[59]

Another form of inclusion ritual was that of reconciliation with the Gemeine. One of the harshest punishments the Gemeine inflicted on a member was expulsion; however, this was not necessarily a permanent action. There are several instances where persons repented and were allowed back into the Gemeine. Generally this readmission was done liturgically. For instance, Br. Nicodemus was received back and forgiven during the singing of "Take them into the wounds."[60]

Likewise, Br. Mack, the head of the native community of Nain, gave absolution to Br. Samuel, who had asked for forgiveness. In the presence of several brothers and sisters he was reconciled to the Gemeine with the stanza "Your sweat in penitential struggle make him wet in body and soul."[61] The ritual of

---

57. Hamilton, *Bethlehem Diary* 1:130.

58. For instance, "in the Litany of the Wounds, at the words, *Offne Arme! nehmet uns* (Open arms, receive us!), the two single brothers Michael Ruch and Friedrich Antes were received into the congregation." *Bethlehem Diary* (Moravian Archives), March 16 (March 27, n.s.), 1746; cf. ibid., Jan. 9, 1752.

59. Aug. 1752, Beylage A, "Gemein-Tag in Bethlehem den 6. Aug. 1752," *Bethlehem Diary* (Moravian Archives).

60. Ibid., May 21, 1757, 278.

61. *Bethlehem Diary* (Moravian Archives), March 2, 1760, Nain Diary, 281–83.

readmission, like those of baptism and reception, connected the persons involved directly to Christ and his struggles for them. It was *his* sweat that did
penance for them and allowed them to return to their place in his wounds.

RITUALS OF *GEMEINSCHAFT*

In a sense, all of the rituals of the community were rituals of Gemeinschaft;
however, there were a number of religious ceremonies whose primary purpose
was to strengthen the ties among members of the community. Included in
these were the lovefeast *(agape)*, the kiss of peace *(pacem)*, and the footwashing
(pedalavium). These rituals were extremely flexible in terms of scheduling and
the conduct of the ritual itself. Sometimes they were used as part of a larger
observance. At other times they were used independently. Although their frequency of use varied, all were used often throughout the period of the General
Economy.

The lovefeast was simply a meal shared in common, but it differed from a
regular meal in that it was a liturgical action. *Dieneren* (from the word for
serving) served the worshippers in the lovefeast. While the *Dieneren* distributed
beverages and some type of bun, the participants sang or listened to specially
prepared music. Frequently the participants had the opportunity to talk during
the lovefeast, but "worldly" talk was not permitted. Worshippers were expected
to discuss their personal religious experience or other religious themes and
concepts. New hymns were introduced and significant events were discussed.

Throughout the ritual the theme of communion with Christ and the Gemeine was stressed. We see this in the account of a lovefeast from 1742, when
residents of the new Gemeine, obviously homesick, "had a blessed Sabbath day
lovefeast." "We thought of our brethren and sisters in Europe who at this very
time of day are letting the Lamb feed and refresh them with the sacrament of
His body and blood, and joined with them in our hunger and thirst for them,
and desired for them and ourselves well-being in every respect within the cleft
of Jesus' wounds."[62]

In Bethlehem there was a regular Sabbath lovefeast on Saturdays that focused on Christ's rest in the grave and the biblical day of rest. Major church
and choir festivals were also celebrated by lovefeasts, sometimes by the Gemeine, sometimes by a particular choir. These simple liturgical meals could be
very emotional. It is recorded that in 1752 "We observed Great Sabbath with a
blessed and contented Sabbath's rest, half-intoxicated from yesterday's lovefeast, from which a pleasant echo was perceived at our lovefeast during the

---

62. Hamilton, *Bethlehem Diary* 1:90.

singing of a hymn that Br. Hermann had written about the body of Jesus resting in the grave."[63]

Lovefeasts gave an opportunity to celebrate specific aspects of the Gemeine's life while reaffirming the fundamental beliefs of the Gemeine. This is seen in the lovefeast for the Children's Festival in 1758. It was held in place of the noontime meal, and the thirty-three children celebrating for the first time "were greeted by the others with a welcome and the verses, 'Enclose them in the Wounds,' 'Let your sweat and blood rain over them,' and 'Preserve them enclosed.'"[64] Lovefeasts were often held in connection with Holy Communion and heightened the emotion of that ritual. In one communion lovefeast, the Gemeine was "so extraordinarily in a mind to sing that we could do nothing but sing 'Glory to the Side' and begin all over again."[65]

Art and other visual effects were used at lovefeasts and other festivals to foster the religious imagination. Paintings of Christ bleeding on the cross, suffering under the crown of thorns, being placed in the tomb, and similar themes were displayed in the chapel. The *Saal* could be decorated elaborately for the choir festivals, with greenery, paintings, and so forth. For one Single Sisters festival:

The *Saal* was quite prettily decorated with green leaves. On the side across from the choir was to be seen a writing with decoratively painted letters which said, 'We who here find ourselves together shake hands in order to bind ourselves to his suffering,' 'Eternal thanks be to you.' The ceiling and both sides were decorated very prettily with white and green works, across the room was the verse 'The Bridegroom Comes,' and on the other, 'Make your lamps ready and fill them with oil,' both of which were prettily decorated with flowers and choir bands. On the third side of the *Saal* were to be seen the portraits of our most beloved Mama and Anna Johanna (Nitschmann), and on the fourth side was the Savior as a corpse. In the four corners of the Saal were green trees. It looked right lovely and pretty.[66]

One of the more elaborate decorations was for the children's lovefeast during a synod in 1748. In the middle of the new *Saal* in the Single Brothers' House a green tree had been erected, like a Christmas tree. Apples and "Side-hole verses" were hung on the tree for the children to take with them. Above the tree "the Side-hole was to be seen painted quite blood red inside of a beautiful heart."[67] Such decorations served to enhance the special nature of certain lovefeasts while communicating the essentials of heart religion and Christocentrism.

63. *Bethlehem Diary* (Moravian Archives), April 24, 1748, and April 1, 1752.

64. Ibid., Aug. 17, 1758.

65. Ibid., July 23 (Aug. 3, n.s.), 1748.

66. Ibid., May 4, 1758, "Der led. Schwester Relation von ihrem Chor-Fest," 370–71.

67. Oct. 15, 1748, Relation von dem vom 12–16 (Oct. 23–27, n.s.), Oct. Synod; Moravian Archives, Bethlehem.

Smaller lovefeasts could also be held among particular subgroups of the Gemeine for special occasions or to honor particular persons. "Our dear Father Demuth, whose 65th [sic] birthday was today, was invited to a children's lovefeast and congratulated by the children with quite nice stanzas, which wrung tears from him and us. After the lovefeast the children all came to him and with feeling kissed his mouth and hands. Their dear old Father completely broke down and praised the little Lamb for his election by grace, and celebrated Jesus' wounds in song."[68]

Married couples might give a lovefeast for their own anniversary or the anniversary of other couples. Since so many people were married in group ceremonies, it was possible for them to share a joint anniversary celebration.[69]

The kiss of peace was another way in which the Gemeine helped to build a sense of community. The kiss could be fitted into almost any liturgical service, such as baptisms, receptions, and Holy Communion. At times it was shared only between certain persons, such as between the baptized person and the sponsors. More often there was a general kiss within a choir or the Gemeine as a whole; however, there was a strict separation of the genders. Men kissed only men, and women only women.[70]

One hymn for use at the kiss of peace in the 1757 litany book has twenty stanzas.[71] Presumably certain stanzas were used for particular occasions or according to how many people were in worship. Here again we see the twin themes of union with God and the Brüdergemeine. The kisses each member gave and received came from the Savior with "the bleeding face," but in the act of kissing, all of the Gemeine was joined, including the saints who have died.

The third major Gemeinschaft ritual was the *pedalavium,* or footwashing. Like the kiss of peace, footwashing was performed only in same-sex groups, and here also there were warnings about sensuality. It appears that there was more than one way to do the footwashing. Either each washed each other's feet, or the minister, eldress, or choir leader did all of the washing.

Footwashing is of course a biblical practice that, according to the Gospel of John (13:14) was commanded by Jesus for his disciples. Thus it is not surprising

---

68. *Bethlehem Diary* (Moravian Archives), Nov. 9, 1752.

69. E.g., the Russmyers held a breakfast lovefeast for several couples on July 15, 1755.

70. Even this precaution could not exclude all sensuality in the kiss of peace, however. Atwood, "Zinzendorf's 1749 Reprimand."

71. 1757 *Litaneyen-büchlein,* 150–51. The Gemeine sang "wir wollen Sünder bleiben" during the kiss of peace on Sept. 20, 1758 (*Bethlehem Diary,* Moravian Archives.) This hymn must have been known in Bethlehem even before the publication of the new litany book. Jacob Roger's mss. litany book (c. 1749), 40, contains an independent English translation of this hymn. His verse to the Holy Spirit reads, "And from the Holy Ghost, To whom the Sinner's heart Gives the Dear Mother's Title O! Spirit, who settest forth The Lamb in all the Bible, In the Heart's Recess, and Makes all Confess Show his wounds and bless." Moravian Archives.

that many biblically oriented sects, including the Brüdergemeine, should institute this practice. The hymn for *pedalavium* in the 1757 litany book basically
relates in verse the Johannine account of Jesus washing his disciples' feet. It is
interesting that the hymn emphasizes that Jesus washed Judas's feet, too.

According to the hymn, disciples follow Jesus' example of washing his disciples' feet, but the footwashing itself was more than a mere imitation of Jesus'
action. It was also an invisible grace, akin to a sacrament, in which the "Watch-
ers" (the angels) participated (v. 11).

Footwashing originated in Herrnhut in the 1720s and was instituted in Bethlehem from the beginning. According to a hymn used in one of the first foot-
washings in Bethlehem, the purpose was to wash away sins, invoking the water
that flowed from the spear wound in Jesus' side.[72] Thus footwashing was directly tied to the death of Jesus and was seen as an absolution. Because of this
connection with absolution, footwashing was frequently used in preparation
for Holy Communion.[73]

Footwashing could be used as a ritual of inclusion as well as of absolution.
One of the more tender instances of this took place in 1744, when the Second
Sea Congregation arrived in Bethlehem. "Following the lovefeast we welcomed
our new brothers and sisters with the kiss of love and washed their weary and
wounded pilgrim feet."[74] The intimacy of this ritual also lent itself to expressions of the mystical marriage. The liturgy "Conversation of the Bridegroom
and the Bride" was sung in Bethlehem for the first time during the Festival of
the Husband following the footwashing.[75]

The lovefeast, the kiss of peace, and footwashing were three of the ways in
which Bethlehem preserved its communal life. They were moments of intimate
contact with members of one's subgroup (choir, co-workers, etc.) and with the
whole Gemeine. They provided a visible means for absolution, inclusion, and
reconciliation, as well as a dramatic way to communicate the essence of Zinzendorf's religion of the heart. Emotion, intellect, and will were brought together in these moments of ritual drama. Moreover, they helped keep the
Gemeine focused on its primary goal. The context and content of the ritual
stressed the primary relationship to the Savior that was the only allowable basis
for community life.

HOLY COMMUNION

The rituals discussed above were important for keeping the community together by strengthening the ties of intimacy, but the ritual of Holy Communion

---

72. Hamilton, *Bethlehem Diary* 1:59.

73. E.g., *Bethlehem Diary* (Moravian Archives), July 5, 1743; Sept. 19 (Sept. 30, n.s.), 1747.

74. Hamilton, *Bethlehem Diary* 1:171.

75. *Bethlehem Diary* (Moravian Archives), Nov. 23 (Dec. 4, n.s.), 1750.

was the center of religious life. In communion the Moravians were physically able to enjoy the body and blood of Jesus that they enjoyed mentally every day in their liturgies. In the eighteenth century, the Moravians consistently promoted the Lutheran doctrine of the real presence, which they described as a "sacramental presence." The wine and the bread were infused with the body and the blood of Jesus, so that the diarist could say that "the eternal Husband spread his cold body sacramentally over his married persons and gave them his blood to drink during an incomparable liturgy of Br. Joseph."[76]

This sacramental partaking of Christ was nourishment and refreshment for the communicants. In the early days of Bethlehem they "arose again before daylight and assembled in the *Saal* to eat and drink the flesh and blood of the Lamb. His holy, tormented body laid hold of us and His precious shed blood refreshed our hearts."[77] Some fifteen years later, the diary records in similar tones that "the congregation satisfied its hunger and thirst for the husband, Jesus Christ, in the most worthy sacrament of his flesh and blood."[78] In this and many other references, Holy Communion is understood as a consummation of the mystical marriage, when the Bridegroom became present to the soul.[79]

Holy Communion was generally celebrated once a month and included several steps. The process began on the Sunday before communion with the singing of the *Litany of the Wounds.* During the week, each communicant had to "speak" with his choir leader. This was the functional equivalent of confession, but it was a face-to-face encounter with an individual intimately aware of the details of one's life. If the communicant's heart was not well disposed for communion, then he or she was not supposed to take part in the ritual. This decision might come from the communicant or from the choir leader.[80] The Gemeine leaders could also ban individuals from communion as a form of discipline. Through this process, the Gemeine could be reasonably assured that all persons joining in Holy Communion were in agreement with the Gemeine, its mission, and its worship.

Generally there was a lovefeast before the communion ritual along with one of the Christ litanies, such as the *Litany of the Wounds,* the *Pleurodie,* or the *Bride's Song.* Communion itself began with a long process of absolution. The congregation lay prostrate before the communion table, which often had a painting of Christ hanging on the wall behind it, and prayed silently while the liturgist offered a corporate prayer of confession. Things deemed destructive to

76. Ibid., Sept. 8, 1757.

77. Hamilton, *Bethlehem Diary* 1:153.

78. "Und denn stillete die Gemeine ihrer Hunger und Durst am Mann Jesu Christ in hochwurdigen Sacrament seines Fleisches und Blutes." *Bethlehem Diary* (Moravian Archives), Oct. 28, 1758.

79. "The Gemeine held its liturgy to its lover concerning his sacramental embrace." Ibid., Oct. 29, 1758.

80. Smaby, *Transformation of Moravian Bethlehem,* 18.

the souls of the brothers and sisters and of the communal mission were symbolically transferred to Christ, who acted as the scapegoat for their sin.

Confession could be very emotional, but the emotions were generally a blend of shame and sorrow for having displeased the Savior and joy over having been forgiven. During confession and absolution during one communion, the Gemeine "fell to the floor and shed innumerable tears during Br. Petrus' [Böhler's] confession in the name of the Gemeine, and the longer one lay there, the sweeter and more pleasing became the little tears, through the absolving merit of his upraised, pierced hands, which one incidentally could not only see but so gently and inwardly feel that no one can pretend to describe it."[81]

The Brüdergemeine published a separate "Absolution and Communion Book" in the 1750s, portions of which were included in the 1757 *Litaneyen Büchlein*. This set out a complete communion service entirely in song.[82] Unfortunately, it is too long to include here, but some excerpts may help give a sense of the communion experience. The communicants were invited to the ritual with verses such as "In a moment stands before us / The Prince with his open Side, / And one feels He's most desirous / Our poor Souls therein to hide."[83]

The call to confession recalls the reproachful look of Jesus to Peter on the night of his betrayal, and evokes a similar sense of shame among the worshippers. The congregation made confession through such prayers as, "O bespittled Cheeks, that the Father may not spit on us! Bloody Gore from thy Body, wash our Feet! Besweated Hair, wipe them!" from the *Litany of the Wounds*.[84] Following absolution and reconciliation through the kiss of peace, the bread and wine were consecrated through the singing of Jesus' words at the Last Supper. This could produce a type of religious ecstasy, as when Böhler liturgized and was "transported" in a communion service in 1758.[85]

The congregation usually sang throughout the time of communion, sometimes antiphonally between choirs, or between the liturgist and the congregation. The communion songs listed in the *Bethelehem Diary* revolve around the same core group of images: the mystical marriage, the Atonement for sins, the presence of Christ, the wounds and corpse of Jesus, and the life flowing through the blood. Throughout the communion ritual the congregation was

---

81. *Bethlehem Diary* (Moravian Archives), Nov. 13, 1758. There is a similar description from a communion service on Nov. 13, 1759: "Br. Petrus reminded the Gemeine of today's great memorial day on which eighteen years ago in Europe and eleven years ago in America our dear Lord made himself known to us as our Elder. . . . We confessed to him with tears more than with words. We gave ourselves to him anew, and sealed everything at the end with the verse 'We say Amen, and that remains eternally true' . . . during a kiss of peace that was moist (with tears) but blessed by his absolution."

82. 1757 *Litaneyen-büchlein*, 246–72.

83. 1759 *Litany-book*, 218.

84. Ibid., 225.

85. *Bethlehem Diary* (Moravian Archives), Nov. 25, 1758.

directed to Christ on the cross and to his wounds from the circumcision, the crown of thorns, the nails, and the spear. The Atonement and the mystical marriage were joined in many verses, such as "Draw us to thee, and we will come / Into thy Wounds' deep Places, / Where hidden is the Honey-comb / Of thy sweet Love's Embraces."[86]

At the point of partaking of the bread, the communicants sang a variety of hymns to the corpse of Jesus, including the often-used verses from the *Litany of the Wounds:* "Pale lips, kiss us on the Heart! Open arms, take us!" Of particular emphasis was the image of the dead Christ acting like Elisha the prophet, who revived a child by lying on his body.[87] After the eating of the body of Christ, there was a time for reflection known as the "Echo after the Holy Corpse," which was also in song.

The blessing of the cup was preceded with verses about the blood and the side wound, such as "On Heart and Mouth, / O Lamb, do Thou bleed, / We smiling look to thy holy side: / To thy Heart now put us, / On thy Wounds press us, / In these blest Sacrament-Hours so precious, / Lamb, Lamb, O Lamb!"[88] Then the cup was consecrated and distributed. Similar hymns were repeated during the drinking of the wine and also in the moments after the sacrament.

Holy Communion served several functions in Bethlehem. It was a dramatic monthly means of impressing upon the hearts of the members the core of Zinzendorf's theology, namely, the Atonement. It was a ritual of spiritual renewal by which the religious experience of the brothers and sisters was reaffirmed through the experience of communing with their Husband, and it was also a ritual of community renewal. Every month difficulties within the community were addressed through the process of speaking and then resolved through absolution and communion.

THE EASTER CYCLE

The Brüdergemeine believed in the sanctification of time. Every New Year's Eve was spent in a watch-night service during which worshippers recalled the blessings of the Lord in the previous year and prayed for an even closer relationship to him in the coming year. The church calendar included observances for particular doctrines, such as the Chief Eldership of Christ and the mother office of the Holy Spirit.

They also commemorated the unique history of the Brüdergemeine with festivals in honor of the founding of Herrnhut, the anniversary of Bethlehem,

---

86. 1759 *Litany-book,* 232; 1757 *Litaneyen-büchlein,* 256.
87. 1759 *Litany-book*; 1757 *Litaneyen-büchlein,* 258–59.
88. 1759 *Litany-book,* 240; 1757 *Litaneyen-büchlein,* 263.

the beginning of the missionary enterprise, and so forth. Conspicuously missing in this calendar were festivals in memory of the Unitas Fratrum, such as
the founding of that church. The martyrdom of Jan Hus was not celebrated
until 1761 in Bethlehem, yet in 1755 they observed Yom Kippur as a biblical
festival.[89]

The key festivals, though, were those connected to the Son of God. The
stages of Jesus' life blessed the yearly cycle; thus the Bethlehem year was largely
a recollection of the life of Jesus with festivals for the conception, birth, and
circumcision of Jesus. Most sacred was the week-long celebration of Jesus' last
week, especially his death and Resurrection. Throughout the week, they read
the gospel accounts of Jesus' last week on earth with a particular emphasis on
his sufferings. His anguish in the garden of Gethsemane was given special attention in the readings and in songs about the "bloody sweat" shed in the
garden. "Today was the material of his death struggle in the garden, which so
affected the children that they could not read and sing enough over it. . . . They
are so eager for their beautiful hour [worship] that they can hardly wait, and
then they spend almost the entire day reading and singing about it."[90]

On the Thursday before Easter, Maundy Thursday, the Moravians celebrated communion with "many juicy blood stanzas." The day of Jesus' Crucifixion was one of the holiest and most emotional for the residents of
Bethlehem:

All the suffering scenes of our Lord, from hour to hour, were read aloud from the descriptions of the evangelists and were sung about in a most devout manner with the most
exquisite passion verses, for the most part from our blessed Christel's [Christian Renatus's]
liturgies. And when at the fourth hour in the afternoon came the story of how our Lord
died, the Gemeine fell quite softly on the knees as one person, and in the Spirit, completely
overcome by holy awe and inner affection for her most loved and beautiful corpse, cried,
greeted, and kissed it with the pouring of countless tears for the heart and eyes, certainly
no fewer than Joseph and Nicodemus (John 19:38f.) might have shed.[91]

The account of Jesus being stabbed by the centurion's spear received special
attention on Good Friday since that event marked the beginning of the church
and the giving of the Holy Spirit.[92]

89. Smaby, *Transformation of Moravian Bethlehem*, 19, is in error on her listing of festival days. Her list
reflects a later stage in the development of the Moravian church calendar. It appears that Bethlehem observed
all of the Brüdergemeine festivals listed in the *Losungen* for each year. For the martyrdom of Jan Hus, see
Bethlehem Diary (Moravian Archives), July 6, 1761. That entry includes a brief history of the Unitas Fratrum,
with a lot of attention given to Comenius. On Yom Kippur, see Gemein Conferenz, Sept. 15, 1755, Moravian
Archives, Bethlehem.
    90. *Bethlehem Diary* (Moravian Archives), March 16, 1761, Kinder Anstalt, 202–3.
    91. *Bethlehem Diary* (Moravian Archives), March 20, 1761.
    92. Ibid., April 13, 1759, 243.

The day after Good Friday was also a holy day for the Gemeine since it marked the time that Jesus spent among the dead. They called the day Great Sabbath, thus relating Jesus' rest in the grave on Saturday with the Old Testament sabbath. It was observed with two separate lovefeasts, one for children and one for adults. Liturgies about the corpse of Jesus, especially those written by Christian Renatus von Zinzendorf, were "the spice" for the lovefeast.[93]

Easter was the denouement of this yearly drama. Two things marked the Easter celebration: the visiting of the graves of dead brothers and sisters and an affirmation of faith. The visitation of the *Gottes Acker,* the cemetery, was in conscious imitation of the visiting of Jesus' tomb by the women disciples and then the men. Before sunrise the sisters gathered and heard the story of the women sung from the *Harmony of the Gospels;* and then the men gathered for the same thing, except that they would hear about the male disciples.[94]

Just before sunrise the Gemeine proceeded by choir to the God's Acre and held the Easter service in the midst of their dead companions. Included in the litany was a prayer to be kept in union with those who had died in Bethlehem and elsewhere in the Gemeine, naming them individually. "I believe that our Brethren {name} and our Sisters {name} are gone to the church above, and entered into the joy of the Lord; the Body was buried here."[95]

Most of the Easter Litany was taken from Luther's Small Catechism, but it had a distinctly Zinzendorfian cast. For instance, it was Trinitarian in form, but the only thing related to the Father was the Lord's Prayer. Most of the litany concerned the life and work of the Son, particularly the affirmation that he "redeemed me a lost and undone human Creature, purchased and gained me from all Sin, from Death, and from the Power of the Devil, Not with Gold or Silver but with his holy precious Blood."[96] It also contained a lengthy section on the believer's desire to die and be with Christ rather than live separated from him in this life. It ended with a glorification of the resurrected Lord.

On Easter morning in Bethlehem they did not sing Resurrection hymns but hymns to the wounds of Christ. Spangenberg opened the 1757 Easter service with the traditional words of the Easter Litany: "The Lord is risen." To this the Gemeine answered: "He is risen indeed." Then they sang, "He has shown his disciples his hands and side." The sun "arose just as we were singing 'Bright wounds of Jesus, Sun-Wounds of Jesus.' And after we had hailed all his holy wounds in communion with the heavenly choir, we parted God's Acre."[97]

93. Ibid., March 25 1758; April 14, 1759; March 21, 1761.

94. Ibid., April 6, 1760.

95. Easter Litany, 1759 *Litany-book,* 216; 1757 *Litaneyen-büchlein,* 244. Cf. *Bethlehem Diary* (Moravian Archives), March 26, 1758.

96. *Litany-book,* 214; 1757 *Litaneyen-büchlein,* 242.

97. *Bethlehem Diary* (Moravian Archives), Easter 1757. At 9 A.M. Spangenberg also led Zinzendorf's liturgy "Ave Agnus Dei" in "Silentia et Pleura."

The Good Friday–Great Sabbath–Easter cycle was an intense form of the weekly cycle of worship. Every Friday was Good Friday, every Saturday was the Sabbath, and every Sunday was Easter, but even more deeply, every day was lived in this awareness. All of the rituals of the Gemeine connected the members to their mystical Husband and Head by celebrating his life, sufferings, and death. The rituals and observances we have examined were to greater and lesser degrees tied to Zinzendorf's Christocentric heart religion with its focus on the Atonement.

Yearly, monthly, weekly, and even daily, the Gemeine reaffirmed its connection to its bloody Savior, and, in doing so, to Zinzendorf's theology. However, these rituals not only served the purpose of keeping the Gemeine focused on its religious life and mission, they also joined the Gemeine together. Whether it was the sharing of a meal, the kiss of peace, or prayers for the dead on Easter, these ritual actions helped preserve the community by continually redirecting the residents to their reason for existence.

FIGURE 6. Marriage of twelve couples in Marienborn, 1743. Unity Archives, Herrnhut.

CHAPTER 6

UNION WITH CHRIST

Analysis of religious symbols and theological concepts is necessary but not sufficient for understanding a society. It is important to show how these elements are related to social life. In Bethlehem, worship and social structure were inextricably joined to create a unique Christian community that valued each individual's development while forming a cohesive society. The idea that God became a real flesh-and-blood human being was the basis of the Moravian social order and it allowed the residents of Bethlehem to make sense of their life together.[1]

Life in the Gemeine was maintained not simply by the unique social structure and practices but by the continual recollection of the physical reality of the life of Jesus. The weekly recollection of Jesus' physical life, including his illnesses, through the *Gemein Litany* reminded the worshippers that the Incarnation blessed normal human existence in all of its weakness while transforming it. Their vivid worship of Christ helped the members live the lives they idealized, but liturgy alone did not accomplish that task.

THE CHOIR SYSTEM

As noted earlier, the most distinctive aspect of Moravian social life in a Gemeine was the choir system. The choirs were not singing groups but bands based on age, gender, and marital status. These were an expansion of Spener's theory of the *ecclesiolae in ecclesia*. Just as the Brüdergemeine was an *ecclesiola* within the Lutheran church, the choirs were *ecclesiolae* within the Brüdergemeine. Even during his school days, Zinzendorf developed various types of Spenerian bands; thus it was natural that during the formative period of Herrnhut in the 1720s he encouraged people to form voluntary associations for spiritual growth.[2]

Gradually these groups became homogeneous in terms of gender, age, and marital status. It was the single men who in 1728 first joined themselves together in an exclusive society. In 1730 the eldress Anna Nitschmann gathered a group

1. Faull, *Moravian Women*, xxiii–xxiv; Smaby, *Transformation of Moravian Bethlehem*, 10–13; cf. Zimmerling, *Nachfolge zu lernen*.
2. Uttendörfer, *Alt Herrnhut*.

of single women in a similar covenant. The Single Brothers set up separate housing and common industry on May 7, 1739, and the Single Sisters likewise in 1740. By the mid-1740s the entire population of Herrnhut had been divided into choirs, although not every choir had its own house.[3]

In an Ortsgemeine, such as Herrnhut, there were *Anstalten* (institutions) for the children, such as boarding schools, orphanages, and nurseries. Children generally left home between the ages of six and twelve (at the point of clear sexual differentiation) and went to live in an Anstalt. Although this was modified in Herrnhut in the 1760s so that parents would take more responsibility for their children, many preferred the older approach.[4]

Even in communities where parents raised their children, though, the church supervised childrearing and could force parents to place their children in an Anstalt if it were deemed better for the children. Moreover, at the onset of puberty most children moved into their choir house. They still had regular contact with their families, sometimes daily, but the focus of their lives was in the choir. In the Ortsgemeinen of the eighteenth century, therefore, we can hardly speak of traditional family structures.[5]

In addition to regular community worship throughout the week, each choir held numerous services separately. Choirs sang their own hymns and litanies appropriate for their status in life.[6] Moreover, each choir had "Helpers" whose function was to provide spiritual direction and supervise the morality and piety of the members. Since Zinzendorf's heart religion was based on experience, hypocrisy was a great fear for him and his fellow workers. They were afraid that persons in the Gemeine, particularly children growing up in the choirs, would learn to speak the language of Christian experience without having the experience itself; therefore religious conversation and examination were intended to prevent hypocrisy by uncovering the true nature of someone's feelings.

Heart-searching conversation was as important for the choir workers as for the members. "The Single Brothers' Choir workers had their regular night watch on this Sabbath night. . . . They discussed thoroughly and at length with one another their own and their Choir's present state."[7] This examination was institutionalized in the practice of *Sprechen* (speaking). Members had to

---

3. Sommer, *Serving Two Masters*, 30. It should not be assumed that separate dwellings were necessary for a choir, although that was considered the ideal. According to Gollin, *Moravians in Two Worlds*, 72, about one third of the 120 Single Sisters in Herrnhut were living with their families as late as 1742.

4. Sommer, *Serving Two Masters*, 66–69.

5. Ibid., 29–31.

6. See Nelson, "Herrnhut: Friedrich Schleiermacher's Spiritual Homeland," chaps. 5–9, for a full discussion of the devotional life of Herrnhut; however, it should be noted that most of Nelson's sources represent a later period than we are studying. Smaby, *Transformation of Moravian Bethlehem*, 14–23, gives a concise and helpful summary of Nelson's work.

7. Hamilton, *Bethlehem Diary* 1:100.

"speak" with one of the elders in order to uncover the true state of their souls before going to the Lord's Table.[8] Slackening of piety or a lack of discipline could be quickly dealt with and the wayward member restored to grace. If no change in behavior or attitude was evident, the person could be excluded from communion or even from the community.[9]

The primary purpose of such religious conversation, however, was to assist people in coming to a personal experience of Christ and maintaining a vital relationship with him. The choir helpers and pastor frequently reminded the choirs of this goal. For example,

In the evening after the Singstunde, Br. Gottlieb gave an unctuous, blessed, and impressive talk to the entire Choir. [It concerned] the faithful and watchful eye of our Lord and how his all-seeing eye gives everything such exact attention and sees into the bottom of the heart of all things existing; therefore no hypocrite . . . could slip through. Whoever has a poor sinner's heart, however, and honestly and uprightly lives to please the Savior alone is always welcomed by him.[10]

Religious conversation was seen as a way to assist the Lord's "all-seeing eye," and was thus a centerpiece of Zinzendorf's heart religion and the backbone of the choir system.

Bethlehem showed a more extreme expression of communal life than any other Moravian community. Spangenberg, with the encouragement of Zinzendorf, made Bethlehem a Pilgergemeine in which every member of the community was to be a servant of the Lord ready to do whatever was needed for the work of the Lord (and the Gemeine). The economic potential of both men and women was maximized, and the members were to be ready to answer the call to mission work. There had to be a supply of women leaders to minister to women both within Bethlehem and in the mission field. It was strongly preferred to send married couples into the various mission areas (including the Caribbean islands and South America). Since missionaries were not expected to take their children with them, their children were raised by the community.[11]

---

8. The requirement of *Sprechen* echoes the discipline of the Unitas Fratrum, where priests heard private confessions of their entire flock on a regular basis. Fousek, "Spiritual Direction and Discipline," 211–13.

9. Punishment could be swift and severe, particularly in Herrnhut. For instance, in 1734 two youths were given twelve blows; in 1735 an apprentice was imprisoned; in 1736 three members were whipped for insubordination; and in 1744 four Sisters were caught in an illicit relationship with a stranger. One received 300 blows, another 170, another 160, and the last was expelled. Sommer, *Serving Two Masters*, 184, n. 60. Such punishments became less frequent after 1745, which may indicate that the choir system became more effective in preventing abuses. According to Gollin, *Moravians in Two Worlds*, 88, Bethlehem did not need to resort to this degree of harsh punishment, and she concludes that Bethlehem was more successful than Herrnhut in controlling its residents.

10. May 25, 1756, *Single Brothers' Diary*, Moravian Archives.

11. The practice of sending children of missionaries to one of the Moravian communities to be raised (usually after age seven) continued into the early twentieth century. One of the major purposes of Moravian boarding schools was to provide a home for missionary children.

In Bethlehem this practice of raising children communally was extended to every family, since each person in Bethlehem was a potential missionary. Throughout the period of the General Economy (1742–62) there were no families in Bethlehem, at least by conventional definitions. As Erbe puts it, "Every trace of family life was abolished in this organism."[12] Children were raised by the Single Sisters in the nursery from the time they were weaned. The nursery was opened in Bethlehem in 1746, and in 1749 it was transferred to Nazareth, which meant that parents and children did not even live in the same village. At that time, the nursery contained twenty-nine boys and twenty-six girls. At times it had as many as seventy residents under the age of five.

Most studies of Bethlehem have examined this elaborate choir system primarily in terms of the economy and social control. Therefore attention has been directed mainly to the Single Brothers' and Single Sisters' Choirs, the major loci of both economic activity and disciplinary action in Bethlehem. Smaby has taken the discussion further by addressing the communal values and norms expressed through the choir system, but there has been little discussion of how the entire choir system grew out of Zinzendorf's heart theology.

The choir system was more than an effective way to organize the economy of the Gemeine; it was a practical expression of Zinzendorf's theory that the earthly existence of the Son of God has sanctified all aspects of human life. According to Zinzendorf, as persons progress through the various choirs, their piety should change to reflect their changing life situations as they meditate upon and celebrate different aspects of the Incarnation.[13] For instance, the Single Brothers were reminded in one of their hymns that "So was Abiad, El Gibbor; So went his pulse, his breath, So he experienced changes; So his brow sweated; So he stood up, So lay down upon a wretched bed; So he was tired, So he was hungry, So spoke when he spoke. That everything he did on earth in human fashion is an immeasurably praise-worthy blessing to us."[14]

Even the most mundane aspects of human life, such as eating and sleeping, were blessed by the Incarnation. The youths of Bethlehem were reminded of this in their daily worship so that they would avoid the common temptation to divide life into sacred and secular realms or to disparage their own earthly

---

12. Erbe, *Bethlehem, Pa.*, 38.

13. Zinzendorf, *Kinder Reden* ZE 6:47:260.

14. "So was Abiad, Elgibbor, So ging sein puls, sein odem, So ging verändrung bey Ihm vor, So dünstete sein Brodem, So stund Er auf, so legt' Er sich Auf schlechte lager-stätte, So ward Er müde, hungerig, So redt Er, wenn er redte; . . . Das Er auf menschen-weise So macht; ist uns ein meritum Von unschätzbarem preise." 1757 *Litaneyen-büchlein*, 207–8. The translation in the 1759 English litany book is interesting: "So was the everlasting God, So He felt Alteration, So He drew Breath, so mov'd his Blood, So was his Perspiration, So He lay down on a poor Bed, So He did rise each Morning, So He felt Hunger, so eat Bread, So spoke, and so was turning. . . . In short, by ev'ry Thing He did on Earth in human Manner He hath great blessings merited And brought our State to Honour."

needs. In 1758 Br. Lemke reminded the community "that everything that we do can be done in the name of Jesus, small or large, and thus in this way the most insignificant act becomes for us a liturgy."[15] Each choir used a different aspect of the life of Jesus as a model for their own lives. In this way all of life became a liturgy. Every task could be an act of worship and identification with the Savior.

In Bethlehem the blessing of human existence began in the womb and continued into death. This connection between the doctrine of the Incarnation and the choir system was made explicit in 1761 when the All Choirs Festival was joined to the Festival of the Conception of Our Lord in Mary. Among the songs highlighted in that festival was "Creator of all Creatures, take on yourself our nature."[16] The unusually detailed description of the All Choirs Festival of 1752 demonstrates how elaborate this system was.

From early until the night, the twenty-fifth was an uncommonly blessed day, when the whole human existence of our Creator was so present and near in all the events, as if he stood there, and his wounds were sparkling very much. The festival was announced to the Choirs in the morning at arising with singing and music at their respective dormitories. After that was the general Morning Blessing. At 8:00 A.M. in a private service in the Sisters' House eleven girls who had been transferred from the Children's Choir into the Older Girls' Choir were given the red band instead of the green ones they had worn up until then. At 9:00 A.M. the whole Gemeine assembled in the *Saal*, where today's festival material was sung with the Text-words of the Festival Gospel, and the Gemeine sang chorales in between. Then Br. Hermann gave a discourse on the Incarnation of our Creator and of the blessing and sanctifying of all ages, classes, genders, and offices of our human life that flows from the Incarnation.

Then the children from the Girls Choir assembled in the little Gemeine Saal. . . . After the general children's lovefeast, there was a little lovefeast in the conference room for the sucklings, fifteen in number, at which they were amused with singing, music, and affection, and in such a manner they also received their congratulations for the Incarnation of their Creator.

At noon, in the Saal, there was a general lovefeast for the Sisters from all the Choirs. During the lovefeast, a part of hymn No. 1407 "A choir of sinners and sinneresses," was sung from the choir loft. After the lovefeast some of their Festival materials for today were read and then at the end a sermon that our dear Ordinary [Zinzendorf] had given for the Sisters in Herrnhut the year before was read. After this there was a lovefeast of a similar sort for all the Brothers. During the lovefeast the stanzas about the humanness of the Savior were sung solo from the hymn "When I can eat him." . . . During this lovefeast, the Sisters in the confinement room [room for new mothers] with their children were visited by some Sisters, and some stanzas were sung to them for today's festival. . . . Finally,

15. *Bethlehem Diary* (Moravian Archives), Dec. 7, 1758.
16. Ibid., March 25, 1761.

out of an inner thankfulness that the Spirit had overshadowed a virgin who bore our little Jesus, [the festival] was concluded with a general liturgy using the *Te Matrem.*[17]

In this way every member of the community was directly involved in the worship of the Gemeine and blessed by the Incarnation of Christ. Suckling babies, new mothers, single men and women, and married adults celebrated their physical and spiritual connection to the Creator who became a human being.

CHILDHOOD

The choirs were the major means by which members of the Brüdergemeine, particularly the children, learned how to be faithful members of the community. Through instruction, ritual, and the example of their choir workers, children learned communal norms and were enabled to experience a relationship with their Savior. Choirs also assisted in the often painful process of conversion, during which a person's ego was reshaped to conform to the will of Christ manifested through the communal ethos as each individual appropriated the Moravians' mission.[18]

The religious life of children was of such concern to the Gemeine that Spangenberg himself sometimes led their devotions. For example, in 1761 he led devotions in the *Mädgen* Anstalt (young girls' school) on the theme of "the love-fire toward the Savior, which the dear Mother kindles in your heart." The children joined in a liturgy that included the verses "My heart burns so that I feel," "His Cross, the shame," and "That is the fire."[19] Here we see not only how doctrines such as the mother office of the Spirit were taught through liturgy and ritual but also how the Gemeine attempted to communicate the emotional zeal of heart religion to a new generation.

As was shown earlier, Zinzendorf's heart religion is not a matter of maturity or intellect; therefore he could assert that infants and even embryos have religious faith. A typical child in Bethlehem became a member of a choir even before birth, and the process of religious instruction and socialization began *in utero.* When a woman's pregnancy became advanced, she moved into a special dormitory for the pregnant sisters and became part of the pregnant sisters' choir. Wisely, the pregnant sisters' choir met at the same time as the embryo choir for the unborn children. Their devotions focused on the Virgin Mary's pregnancy.

17. Ibid., March 25, 1752.
18. Smaby, *Transformation of Moravian Bethlehem,* 151–52, describes this process. Many of the *Lebensläufe* found in Faull, *Moravian Women,* focus on their "awakening" during adolescence or young adulthood. This is true of both those who converted and those raised in the community.
19. *Bethlehem Diary* (Moravian Archives), Oct. 7, 1761, 302–3 (Mädgen Anstalt).

In the afternoon, on account of today's festival of Mary's visitation, those Sisters, whom the Lamb before now deigned to carry side hole creatures for Him under their hearts, had a very nice lovefeast. There were eleven of them in all, whom our dear Husband had provided with this church-marriage blessing, who were placed according to the time sequence of their expected delivery and they formed a quite nice circle. . . . At the conclusion of the lovefeast they greeted and kissed each other formally during the intonation of the words from the *Te Patrem,* "That your child lay naked and bare on your lap."[20]

Older studies of Bethlehem and Zinzendorf have ridiculed the embryo choir as Sifting Time nonsense, but in light of modern psychology and sociology one can only marvel at the foresight of this community in establishing a means of caring for the emotional, intellectual, physical, and spiritual needs of pregnant women. Industrialized society has only recently begun to establish such intentional "support groups" for women. However, we should not equate the pregnant sisters' choirs with such modern organizations, as the primary purpose of the choirs was religious, not psychological. Nonetheless, in addressing religious needs, the choirs met psychological ones as well.

After delivery and baptism, a child, along with its mother, would become part of the *Säugling Chor* (suckling choir). Once a year, on July 2, there was a special festival for the pregnant women, new mothers, and the sucklings all together. "The lovefeast was begun with the beloved 'Ave my dear Husband, Ave for your Plan!' . . . During the lovefeast the little sucklings made much cross-air-bird joy for us, and each one sang and cried 'Ave' according to his manner."[21] The pregnant women and sucklings festival in 1752 was celebrated "in remembrance of the childlike joy of little John in the womb over the presence of his Lord," recalling Zinzendorf's frequent allusions to the story of John the Baptist in the womb as a paradigm for the Christian life. The babbling of the children was considered part of the liturgy.[22]

Once it had been weaned, a child would be moved into the nursery as part of the *Kinder Chor.* The *viertelstunde* (quarter-hour) liturgies for the infants started as soon as there were infants in Bethlehem, and the Diary records happily that the infants "were as attentive as though they understood it."[23] The "as though" is interesting. One must remember Zinzendorf's idea that some things, especially religious things, can be experienced even if people do not fully understand them. Thus the children may have been experiencing the lit-

20. Ibid., June 21 (July 2, n.s.), 1749 (¶ 2).
21. Ibid., July 2 (July 23, n.s.), 1748.
22. Ibid., July 2, 1752. The sucklings' liturgies continued at least until 1760 (ibid., May 5, 1760), and the Spangenbergs were very much involved (see entry for July 1, 1755, where the Sisters Lawatsch, Spangenberg, and Graft are said to have journeyed to Nazareth for the pregnant women's festival, bearing a special liturgy for the occasion).
23. Hamilton, *Bethlehem Diary* 1:168.

urgy even though they could not understand it. These services continued in 1751 under the choir leaders Br. and Sr. Graff, who were called the children's parents.[24]

From their earliest days children were taught Zinzendorf's doctrines and learned the internal discourse of the Brüdergemeine. They learned to speak fondly of the blood and wounds of Christ and to long for a heart's union with him. Maria Spangenberg testified to this Christocentric goal when she wrote to Zinzendorf about the nursery children: "The dear little lambs astonish the whole land. They know nothing except the wounded Lamb, and they don't want to know anything else. They think and talk and sing and play and dream of him."[25] Years after the so-called Sifting Time, the Memorabilia of 1757 notes that the nursery children have "the Man of Sorrows as their sole object, they sing and play to Him quite lovely and have amazing love for everyone who is around them."[26] The love the children showed each other was seen as the natural consequence of their exclusive devotion to the suffering Christ.

The Gemeine believed that the particular need of the children's choir was to develop moral purity and obedience to God and the Gemeine. Their choir hymns, particularly after 1750, reveal this concern. Most of the references to obedience in the 1753 hymnal are in the children's hymns, but they do not simply demand that children obey. The idea of salvation by grace is preserved. It is by drawing the children to his own heart that Christ leads them away from sinful desires.

The Bethlehem Diary records how children learned the doctrines of the community and could even manipulate community norms to their advantage when dealing with their elders. When Sophia, a native child, heard her parents talking about the coming of the Savior, she said that she was waiting for him to come. When her mother replied that she was often a disobedient child, Sophia responded, "It is true, dear Mother, I am a poor child, but I hold the Savior dear, and when he comes, I shall sing to him the verse: I have been baptized with his blood."[27] Sophia understood surprisingly well the Zinzendorfian paradox of being a justified sinner. Notice also how easily she used the blood language of the Gemeine in a familial conversation.[28]

A similar story from the same period regards the girls' institution. A girl was

24. *Bethlehem Diary* (Moravian Archives), Nov. 21, 1751. The diary states that the services were "resumed" by the Grafs, who had recently come from Europe. This may indicate that these services had been discontinued by Nitschmann.

25. Maria Spangenberg to Zinzendorf, April 21, 1746 (R. 14, A 18, 5 Herrnhut Archives), quoted in Erbe, *Bethlehem, Pa.,* 44.

26. Memorabilia, 1757, 904, Moravian Archives, Bethlehem.

27. *Bethlehem Diary* (Moravian Archives), Feb. 14, 1761, 128–29 (Nain Diary).

28. It should be noted that even though children were not raised in families, they still had contact with their parents.

crying, and when she was asked why, she said, "I have been considering how often in the past year I have troubled the Savior, and have not been a proper joy to him." She continued to cry silently, but after a while she said, "I feel that the Savior has forgiven me." She then sang "I am a poor little child" and three other songs with her playmates.[29]

Notice that this interchange is actually between the child and Christ. She was not crying because she had offended anyone around her, but because she felt she had displeased Christ. Moreover, the choir workers did not try to convince her otherwise. They left her crying in the night until she had experienced forgiveness, not from her elders but from the Savior. This is a good illustration of the religious purpose of the choirs: to help individuals, even children, come to an intimate and exclusive relationship with Christ, and to let that relationship inform their behavior. Some may question whether the experience of this child and others in Bethlehem was "real" in the sense that they comprehended the word "Christ" as an adult would. For our purposes, the question is irrelevant. The child and the community believed that she was having direct contact with Christ and acted accordingly.

Such predilection for religious experience was not merely the provenance of the girls. It was noted that in the boys' Anstalt in Nazareth some of the older boys formed a band after hearing the day's sermon. They wrote some of their thoughts in verse on a writing slate. "They complained to the Savior that their hearts were still not burning enough toward his wounds. Afterwards they sang their verse with one another, and a blessed peace of God ruled over them."[30]

The children's choirs held their own liturgies, which included the basic doctrines of the Brüdergemeine. In the Kinder Conferenz of 1756: "The question of whether the children should have more liturgies was discussed. It was observed that they had as many liturgies as the other choirs, especially their weekly Choir Liturgy. In our little children's book is a complete theology of the Father, the Mother, the Husband, the church, the Jerusalem above, the Angels. Is that not sufficient to excite the liturgical feeling of the youth?"[31] The children also learned to sing many of the same hymns and litanies as the adults. At their lovefeasts they often sang "Pale lips, kiss him on the heart" and "You Man of Sorrows so beautiful."[32] At least as late as 1758 the children were joining in the *Litany of the Life, Sufferings, and Death of Jesus* (the first part of the *Litany of the Wounds*).[33]

29. *Bethlehem Diary* (Moravian Archives), Nov. 18, 1761, (Mädgen Anstalt), 432–33.

30. Ibid., Sept. 1761 (entry after Sept. 30), 199.

31. May 27, 1756, Kinder Conf. Moravian Archives, Bethlehem.

32. *Bethlehem Diary* (Moravian Archives), Sept. 29, 1756, 661–64, Beilage 7.

33. Ibid., Jan. 1, 1758. In 1752 it was decided that the *Kinder Chor* liturgy would be on Saturday and that they would alternate between the *Te Agnum* and the *Litany des Lebens und Leiden*. *Bethlehem Diary* (Moravian Archives), Beilage B, 1227–31.

Christmas was a special time each year to remind the entire Gemeine, especially children, that Christ had been a human child; that "Eternity's great Father Had a little Boy's weak Nature."[34] A Christmas liturgy written in 1747 "praised God the child that lay in the crib." This liturgy makes little mention of shepherds, angels, and magi. Instead, the focus is on the Christ child and how he grew and was obedient. It even asserts that Jesus learned his Hebrew alphabet just the way the Gemeine children must learn to write in their own language.[35]

The connection between the Gemeine children and the God-Child was reinforced every Christmas through liturgy, song, drama, and even sculpture. A nativity scene was erected yearly in the *Saal* (a variation on an old German custom that modern Moravians call the *Putz*), with the words "Come, Creator, into my heart!" inscribed below. The children held a separate service during which they worshipped before the Christ image.

Toward evening, first the children assembled at the little Jesus in the stable and in the manger and held their vigil, partly with repeating of the Christmas story, and partly and particularly with singing the same [story] in old and also new Christ child verses. Some among them performed a beautiful cantata during their lovefeast, and during it some small presents were distributed among them, for example beautifully written verses. They themselves suggested all sorts of psalms of joy, until their little candles were lit. Then Br. Petrus sang "Christ, you who are the bright day," "Jesus sends such little flames hither," "How beautiful shines the wound-star," and "The fire which ignites us" with an uncommonly lovely and joyful feeling.[36]

Spangenberg began the Boys Choir Festival of 1761 with petitions from the *Litany of the Life, Sufferings, and Death of Jesus.* "Your painful first birth—your holy boyhood time, sanctify our dear boys." Through the litany and hymns, such as "by your holy boyhood anoint these boys," the Gemeine reminded the boys that Jesus had also been a boy.[37] During the festival a painting of Jesus as a twelve-year-old was prominently displayed in the *Saal* in order to visualize this point.

Spangenberg also took the opportunity to tell the children about Christian Renatus's work among the boys choir in Herrnhaag more than ten years earlier. Then the congregation sang some of Renatus's hymns written for the Boys Festival. Among them was "When we want to enliven ourselves, we go to the little rose-red garden." Older boys were then received into the *Jünglinge Chor*

---

34. 1759 *Litany-book*, 180.
35. Manuscript liturgies, Box 3, Moravian Archives, Bethlehem.
36. *Bethlehem Diary* (Moravian Archives), Dec. 24, 1758.
37. Ibid., Feb. 28, 1761.

(young men's choir) with the words, "Your sweat in penitential struggle." Thus in a single worship service we see that the life of the boys was joined to that of Jesus Christ through the litany, the hymns, a painting, and the recollection of his Passion.

For the Brüdergemeine, the suffering of Jesus was the focal point of the Incarnation. Every drop of blood or sweat was seen as a special blessing. Thus the Gemeine as a whole could sing, "All of our Choir regulation, all Choir instruction and practice, all sinner's holiness, comes to us out of the side of Jesus. Hail, complete human existence, in which we read divinity! Hail, medicine for the original fall! Hail, glimmering wick of the primal light! From your own side-hole came the wife's body and soul; therefore our boys can have their own Elisha."[38] All of the children were directed to enjoy the blood and wounds of Christ, especially the side wound. As late as 1772 the little girls in Bethlehem were singing: "His true blood, the highest good, in heaven and also on earth, sprinkle you every day to make you ever more lovely. May his suffering image, painted in pain, day and night be your spirit's pasture, to your eternal joy. . . . And that his pain cure your sinful heart, unhealthily suffering compunction, and whatever is sick in body and soul, cure forever. Thus would your path on life's way be always a true blessing, if you only hope and wish and believe for the sake of his wounds."[39]

LABOR

The primary purpose of the choirs was to increase individual devotion to the Savior and commitment to his mission; however, as we have seen, the theology of the Brüdergemeine eschewed a strict separation of sacred and secular activities within a Gemeine. One of the cardinal tenets of Zinzendorfian Christocentrism is that when a person is converted, his or her entire life becomes a liturgy to Christ. The difference between the sacred and the secular is a difference between being converted and being dead in sin, not between different spheres of an individual's life.

Therefore economics had to be brought into the religious realm. Much of the economic activity of the Moravian settlements was conducted in and through the choirs. This was where young men were apprenticed into trades in which they showed skill or which the Gemeine needed, rather than simply following their father's trade.[40] Women also practiced trades considered appro-

---

38. 1759 *Litany-book*, 175; cf. 1757 *Litaneyen-büchlein*, 195.

39. Mädgen Fest Liturgy, 1772, Manuscript Liturgies, Box 3, Moravian Archives, Bethlehem. Consider also this verse for the Girls' Choir from the 1759 *Litany-book*, App., 10: "The rosy Tint and ruddy Streak, The bloody Balsam it doth make, Which with their Mouth of Faith, our Bees Suck from the holy Side's Recess."

40. For a history of the economic activity of the Brüdergemeine in the mission fields, see William J. Danker, *Profit for the Lord: Economic Activities in Moravian Missions and the Basel Mission Trading Company* (Grand Rapids: William B. Eerdmans, 1971).

priate to their gender, such as spinning and sewing. These tasks also played a major role in the communal economy. Work was a major feature of Bethlehem life. As Erbe points out, the Single Brothers built their enormous choir house by moonlight so as not to neglect the day's labor.[41]

This blessing of labor was expressed in the many lovefeasts held for the workers in the various occupations: spinners, harvesters, and so forth. For instance, when a barn was completed in Nazareth in 1747, there was a special celebration that related this effort directly to Jesus, "the dear carpenter in Nazareth."[42] The liturgy for that festival drew a mental image of Jesus in his father's shop surrounded by tools familiar to eighteenth-century German woodworkers. The Savior, like his followers, experienced a stiff back and *Arbeits Schweiß* (sweat of labor).

The liturgy elegantly presented the paradox that lies at the heart of Zinzendorf's theology, that the Creator became a creature, by connecting the divine activity of the Son of God with the manual labor of Jesus. "You who merely spoke when the world was made now must bring your strength together day by day." The workers celebrated the notion that Christ "gives a thousand joys to our work" and that "no job is too small to be blessed."

In a similar vein, Spangenberg wrote to Zinzendorf that the brothers and sisters "mix the Savior and his blood in their rail-splitting, land-clearing, fence-making, plowing, harrowing, sowing, mowing, washing, spinning, in short, in everything."[43] Special liturgies were sung for important communal workdays, such as the harvest. "Immediately after breakfast there was a mowers lovefeast, at which a hymn prepared by the late Br. Cammerhof for a similar occasion was sung. Thereafter the sickles were distributed and the whole house, the Brethren and Sisters separately, went with music into the field and began to harvest with joy."[44]

Marriages, too, were part of the economic and missionary activity of Bethlehem. All marriages in Bethlehem had to be approved by the Gemeine, and most were arranged by the leaders according to the economic and religious needs of both the individuals and the Gemeine. This was in accordance with Zinzendorf's concept of the *Streiter Ehe,* such as he had contracted with Erdmuth, in which the emotional aspect of marriage is superseded by the communal/religious purpose of the Brüdergemeine.[45]

Moreover, many of the vocations, especially mission stations, were restricted

41. Erbe, *Bethlehem, Pa.,* 90, estimates that the brothers and sisters worked sixteen hours per day.
42. Manuscript Liturgies, Box 3, Moravian Archives, Bethlehem.
43. April 26, 1746. Herrnhut Archives, R.14, A18, 31, quoted in Erbe, *Bethlehem, Pa.,* 92.
44. *Bethlehem Diary* (Moravian Archives), July 10, 1752.
45. Smaby, *Transformation of Moravian Bethlehem,* 159–65, and Gollin, *Moravians in Two Worlds,* 110–27.

to married persons. But even the marriages of common artisans and tradesmen were arranged, since their activities were part of the overall mission of Bethlehem. The leadership wanted to ensure that a married couple could contribute economically and spiritually. There were times when the married persons in the Hausgemeine worked communally on their various tasks. On such occasions, we are told, "It went quite cheerful and lively: one worked on shoes, another made clothes, a third made powders for the apothecary, a fourth copied, some peeled turnips, some knitted, others spun, sewed, etc. and with it all love was discussed quite heartily and freely and in the midst of everything beautiful blood verses were sung."[46]

Labor and rest were both part of the daily liturgy and a way of worshipping Christ as well as serving him.[47] The Incarnation of the Son of God demonstrated that economic activities were no less important and sanctified than "religious" ones. The Moravians in Bethlehem took Luther's idea of vocation far beyond what the reformer had envisioned and turned secularization theory on its head. Instead of the idea of vocation leading to increased secularization, in Bethlehem it led to a sacralization of daily life. Nothing was to be separated from the sacred realm, because God in Christ had experienced full humanity.

SEXUALITY

One of the more controversial and important aspects of Zinzendorf's theology is his understanding of human sexuality.[48] It might be expected that this aspect of his thought would not have been fully received by his followers, but the evidence demonstrates that Bethlehem followed the logic of Zinzendorf's ideas about sexuality very closely. There was, though, a fundamental ambivalence toward sexuality in the theology and practice of the Brüdergemeine, and it originated with Zinzendorf.

On the one hand, human sexuality was valued highly. The appreciation of the full humanity of the God-man included sexuality. Zinzendorf saw this idea as one of the marks of the true religion proclaimed by the Brüdergemeine. According to Zinzendorf, whoever does not find a blessing in the conception, birth, and circumcision of Jesus belongs to the devil's religion because the devil always tries to turn the Incarnation into mere mythology.[49] Furthermore, the sexual act was viewed as the highest expression of spirituality and worship of God. It was a sacramental expression of the mystical marriage. Sex re-creates God's love for his people, and thus there is no sin in the sex act itself.

---

46. *Bethlehem Diary* (Moravian Archives), Oct. 12, 1745, quoted in Erbe, *Bethlehem, Pa.*, 92.

47. On the Moravian understanding of the Sabbath, see Peter Vogt, "Zinzendorf's Theology of the Sabbath," in Atwood and Vogt, *Distinctiveness of Moravian Culture.*

48. I have explored this topic more deeply in my article "Sleeping in the Arms of Christ."

49. Zinzendorf, *Gemeinreden* 1:31.

On the other hand, the threat of uncontrolled sexuality was so great that the genders were strictly separated in all Gemeinen from about the age of five, even within the family home. Zinzendorf was afraid that the emotionality of the Moravians' worship would quickly spill over into sexual expression unless that outlet was closed to the brothers and sisters.[50]

In the taverns, for instance, women served only women, and men served only men. In worship, men sat on one side and women on the other.[51] Such separation extended even into death. The corpses of men and women were prepared in separate chambers and buried in separate sections of the cemetery.[52] Any illicit conversation between persons of the opposite sex could be punished severely. Natural brothers and sisters could not even be trusted together. Some of the perceived danger during the Sifting Time stemmed from the fact that this barrier between men and women was crumbling.[53]

The separation of genders was most extreme in Bethlehem. Even married persons lived in single-sex choir houses. Spangenberg wrote in 1755 that "our married folk still live as if they were on a journey: the husbands by themselves and the wives by themselves and the children by themselves."[54] This separation of husbands and wives was the most distinctive feature of Spangenberg's General Economy and appears to have been Spangenberg's idea. Before joining the Moravians, Spangenberg had adopted celibacy.[55] It has sometimes been asserted that the separation of husbands and wives was primarily related to economic concerns, but no one has yet put forward compelling evidence to that effect. Bethlehem's approach to married life was unique not only in colonial America but within the Brüdergemeine itself. Had it simply been a response to life in the wilderness, one would expect to see similar arrangements among other immigrant groups. When the decision came from the leadership in Germany in 1758 that Bethlehem should move to single-family dwellings, it was a long and difficult transition. In November 1758 twelve couples received their own rooms in the former Men's House.[56] It was not until 1771 that all couples in Bethlehem had their own residences.

---

50. Gollin, *Moravians in Two Worlds,* 69, attributes this to a fear of scandal, while Smaby, *Transformation of Moravian Bethlehem,* 10–11, emphasizes the conscious sublimation of sexual energy to religious purposes. Both are correct.

51. See the plates in ZE 6, *Zeremonienbüchlein,* which are reproduced in Sessler as well. Particularly noteworthy for our discussion are plates 8 and 9, which clearly depict a deaconess in clerical-style garb (white alb) serving communion to the women. She thus has a position equal to that of the male deacon. See Nelson, "Ordination of Women."

52. Graf Heinrich Casimir Gottlieb von Lynar, *Nachricht von dem Ursprung und Fortgange, und hauptsächlich von der gegenwärtigen Verfassung der Brüder-Unität* (Halle: Johann Jacob Curt, 1781), 124–26.

53. Atwood, "Zinzendorf's 1749 Reprimand."

54. Spangenberg to Corn. v. Laer, (R. 14, A 18, Herrnhut Archives), quoted in Erbe, *Bethlehem, Pa.,* 39, n. 173.

55. Reichel, *Spangenberg,* 126–28.

56. *Bethlehem Diary* (Moravian Archives), Nov. 17, 1758.

Before that time, husbands and wives lived in communal male and female dormitories. The records do not make clear just how conjugal relations between husbands and wives were handled during this period, but, consistent with the Moravians love of order, time together appears to have been arranged carefully. "It has been worked out for each pair of our dear married folk to have their own day and place for their holy joining; however, the warriors [missionaries and ministers] have the Sabbath for that."[57] Records show that were two double beds in the Married Sisters' dormitory, possibly for that purpose.

Smaby notes that the birth rate shows that there must have been frequent contact between couples. In fact, according to Smaby, the birth rate was actually higher when couples lived separately.[58] The reaffirmation of the communal system by the residents of Bethlehem in 1754 indicates that there was general satisfaction with the marital arrangements.

Part of the reason for the Moravian ambivalence toward sexuality, other than its being a legacy of the New Testament itself,[59] is that the demand of absolute devotion to Christ was also a demand for devotion to the Brüdergemeine of which Christ was Chief Elder. Sexual desire not only leads to sin, it creates a force destructive of community. Sexual desire, marital devotion, and even parental love compete with communal devotion; therefore every successful communal society must struggle with the issue of sex and marriage.

The Brüdergemeine rejected the traditional Christian solution of celibacy for all members.[60] The other obvious solution, communal marriage, such as was practiced in the next century at Oneida, was also unthinkable.[61] Instead, Zinzendorf and Spangenberg created a unique system in Bethlehem that allowed marriage but made the choir the primary social group.[62]

Virginity was absolutely required before marriage, but even after marriage sex was communally regulated. Moreover, in both the single and the married state, it was Christ who was the only focus of desire. Married persons were to remain virgins spiritually by not giving in to their lust.[63] The longing for union

57. This system was established even while Zinzendorf was in Bethlehem. Erbe, *Bethlehem, Pa.*, 39, n. 173.

58. Smaby, *Transformation of Moravian Bethlehem*, 103.

59. 1 Cor. 7:9, Eph. 5:31–32; Matt. 9:15, 25:1–12; Luke 5:34; John 3:29; Rev. 18:23. Vogt, "Ehereligion," 39.

60. This was the source of the conflict between the Moravians and Conrad Beisel and his Ephrata cloister. Vogt, "Ehereligion."

61. Ira Mandler, *Religion, Society, and Utopia in Nineteenth-Century America* (Amherst: University of Massachusetts Press, 1984).

62. I am in complete agreement with Gollin, *Moravians in Two Worlds*, 67, that one of the main purposes of the choir system was to break up traditional loyalties for the sake of the community. Smaby, *Transformation of Moravian Bethlehem*, 10–13, also highlights this aspect of the choirs. Erbe, *Bethlehem, Pa.*, 40, calls the choir an ersatz family.

63. Spangenberg, *Apologetische Schluß-Schrift*, 603–5, 650–54, and 367–68.

with Christ helped members live by the communal standards of sexual behavior.

As Smaby indicates, adolescence was a critical time for the residents of Bethlehem, primarily because of the emergence of sexual needs and desires.[64] Here, too, the Incarnation of Christ helped young people, particularly men, deal with their emerging drives. Earlier we saw that Zinzendorf asserted that the circumcision of Jesus sanctified the male genitals. The male choirs in Bethlehem fully accepted and promoted this view. Their liturgical life included the veneration of the circumcision of Jesus that sanctified their own maleness. Even the women in the Gemeine were told to have special respect for the boys, because Jesus also had a penis.[65]

The circumcision cut was the most important wound of Christ for the boys' and single men's choirs. Their choir hymns and liturgies stress the theory that in submitting to having his penis cut, the God-man would also preserve the boys from sexual sins. Consistent with Zinzendorf's view of ethics, young men struggling with sexual awakening did not need to hide in secret or use penitential acts to try to control natural urges. Instead, they could look to the sinless Jesus, a sexual being who lived without sin. He would preserve them.

I see the priest standing there, who, under the Spirit's breezes, circumcised (according to the Covenant status and religious duty) the boy without sin who was made sin for us. O holy Covenant slit, O holy wound, govern the true maleness of the sinful creature, whom you have sanctified as an honor-pot [or marriage vessel] with the circumcision blood. The boys veil and hide themselves from all secret prohibited [acts] because of this covenant. The young men protect themselves before nature with seals, which only the Creator can open.[66]

At the Single Brothers' Festival of 1761, "the virgin men were blessed by Brothers Gottlieb and Dencke. . . . Then they sang, 'Pale lips, kiss them on the heart! Open arms, receive them! Your chaste virginity transform them into maidens [from the *Wunden Litaney*].' 'That the mind may be like that of the

64. Smaby, *Transformation of Moravian Bethlehem*, 152.

65. 1759 *Litany-book*, 174; cf. "Wird eine gnaden-Esther, Und nach dem leibe schwester, Ein knäbelein gewahr; So beugt es herz und sinne Der kinder-wäreterinne, Daß GOttes Sohn ein knabe war" (1757 *Litaneyen-büchlein*, 194). The language is toned down somewhat from the time of the Sifting, but the imagery is the same.

66. 1759 *Litany-book*, 174, cf. 1757 *Litaneyen-büchlein*, 193–94. The theme that Jesus' circumcision preserves the boys' purity is echoed in various liturgies preserved in the Moravian Archives for this period. Manuscript liturgies, Boxes 1–3, Moravian Archives, Bethlehem.

Lamb and the body like his corpse.'"[67] In their choir liturgies they sang: "If only all the boys would think each Minute, 'Open Pleura, your are mine,' and heart and body were brought in, then they would sleep away the pangs, but the poor childhood still in their usual blindness are excited in the flesh, they become immoral through a wild, natural intoxication."[68]

This and other hymns for the boys and single men make frank admission of sexual excitement and temptation, but they always direct the brothers to turn to the wounds of Jesus for protection and release. The hymn just quoted goes on to say that there is a great difference between youths raised in the choir system and those who come from outside. Moravian boys have already experienced the Lord's Passion and death and have the support of their choir in their temptations. The latter must experience a conversion to the Lord and try to control their urges on their own.[69] Therefore the Moravians acknowledged that it was useless to try to impose the morality and religious methods of the Brüdergemeine on those who were not called by the Savior.

One of the weaknesses, already noted, in Zinzendorf's theory of the Incarnation and sexuality is that the blessing of the Incarnation falls most directly on those who share Christ's gender. Although the women in Bethlehem were directed toward adoration of the earthly life of Jesus as a blessing for their own lives, the Virgin Mary plays an equally vital role for them. "Where, without our Toil, He blesses; / Then's this Train of Sinneresses / Led up joyful, though ashamed, / By the Virgin, Mary named."[70] Girls and single women were reminded frequently of the blessedness of the single life, using Mary as their model. "Rest, dear bodily members. They were like yours, when the Word came down to earth, when he was born: Shall the lust of the flesh profane your breast, and Mary's breasts gave drink to little Jesus?"[71]

The single life had a special holiness, not superior to marriage but still holy in its own right. Many women in the Brüdergemeine never married, and that was perfectly acceptable.[72] The chastity of the virgins had a message even for those who were married: that they should remain virginal in their own hearts.

---

67. "Jünglinge von den Brr. Gottlieb und Dencke zu led. Brr. gesegnet wurden. . . . Es wurde dabey gesungen: Blasse Lippen, küsst ihnen aufs Herz! Ofne Arme, nehmet sie! Dein keuscher Jünglings-Standwandle sie zu Jungfrauen. Dass der Sinn des Lamms Sein gleiche und die Hütte seiner Leiche." *Bethlehem Diary* (Moravian Archives), Nov. 1, 1761 (¶ 9). This reference to men being made into "maidens" (Jungfräuen) came a decade after the so-called Sifting. It is also clear in context that this was not referring to some type of gender change.

68. 1759 *Litany-book,* 181; cf. 1757 *Litaneyen-büchlein,* 202.

69. 1759 *Litany-book,* 182 (vv. 6–7); cf. 1757 *Litaneyen-büchlein,* 203.

70. 1759 *Litany-book,* 179; cf. "Wo es huld gibt ohne mühe: Da kömts jungfräulein Marie, Mit dem ganzen Mädgen-hafsen, Froh und sünderhaft gelaufen," *Litaneyen-büchlein,* 199.

71. 1759 *Litany-book,* 190; cf. 1757 *Litaneyen-büchlein,* 212.

72. Smaby, "Female Piety Among Eighteenth-Century Moravians," *Pennsylvania History* 64 (1997); Faull, *Moravian Women,* xxvii–xl, 4.

"In old Times was Virginity Preserved but indiff'rently; / For one did scarce a Virgin see, / But she was Bride immediately. . . . When I a Virgin-Choir behold, / And think of their Grace manifold: / I wish, each Heart disposed be / Like Mary's in her Pregnancy."[73]

It is interesting that, although women could not look directly to Jesus as the model for stages of their life (e.g., the onset of puberty), they ritualized their stages more than the men. As they progressed from choir to choir, women had a liturgical ceremony in which they received colored ribbons to indicate their new status. The ribbon colors were red for young girls, green for older ones, pink for single women, blue for married ones, and white for widows.[74] The women always wore these ribbons in public, but there was no similar uniform for the men. This ribbon-giving ceremony took place during the All Choirs Festival, which "was an uncommonly blessed day, when the whole human existence of our Creator was so present and near in all the events, as if he stood there, and his wounds [were] the flame in the events."[75] A lovefeast was then held for each of the choirs.

As important as Mary was, as both virgin and mother, the Moravians believed that single women could preserve their virginity best by viewing themselves as brides of Christ. Their liturgies and choir hymns are filled with references to being married to Christ and to him alone. This theme was continually reinforced in their choir devotions, such as when the new dormitory for the Single Sisters was completed in 1752. "After the Singstunde, the entire choir went up to the sleeping room and our most dear choir mother Anna Rosel [Anders] held our Evening Blessing and at the same time dedicated this sleeping area with a penetrating feeling and nearness of our bleeding husband."[76]

MARRIAGE

In Zinzendorf's religion of the heart, sin is a matter of intention, not action, and thus in order to keep marriage holy, it had to be preserved from the corruption of sinful lust. Marriage could not be simply a legitimation of sinful

---

73. 1759 *Litany-book*, 280–81; cf. 1757 *Litaneyen-büchlein*, 306–7.

74. "Br. Matthäus explained to them that the Choir ribbons were a beautiful regulation of the *Gemeine*. Formerly the Single Sisters would have had a green Choir ribbon, they saw however that for a long time they had already worn the red ribbon, that now according to the regulation of the Gemeine it was the children who should receive the green Choir ribbon, as a sign of the good hope that we had about our children, as plants in Jesus' garden and little trees in his tree school, just as they now were going to see that the trees would sprout and receive green branches and leaves, as a sign that summer is near. Then the red ribbons were removed and the green put on these 67 children, by the Sisters, during which stanzas and also a hymn were sung by heart and accompanied." *Bethlehem Diary* (Moravian Archives), March 25, 1752. The use of green ribbons for the girls is not well known. For another description of the ribbon-changing ceremony, see ibid., May 4, 1758, Der led. Schwestern Relation von ihrer Chor-Fest, 371.

75. Ibid., March 25, 1752.

76. May 15, 1752, *Single Sisters' Diary*, Moravian Archives.

desire. On the contrary, Zinzendorf asserted that married persons could have sex and remain virgins, at least in their souls.[77] In order to sanctify the married state, sexuality had to be divorced from lust and sensuality; therefore the Married Choir's devotions included prayers to "Bless the Breasts, which for to such our Babes look, / And thus doubly are connected / With the Bodies so respected / Of the Sisters who bore them." Husbands and wives, "chaste and praying, either give or receive; and in closest Love cemented, As He it himself invented, Raise a Church-Seed in his Name."[78] Children conceived in such chaste intercourse would indeed be innocent.[79] In this way the Brüdergemeine sought to overcome the old Augustinian connection between procreation and original sin without losing the Augustinian view of sin as a corrupted will or heart.

The Married Choir and its theology was based on Zinzendorf's idea of the "procurator marriage" or the "proxy marriage," which was frequently celebrated in worship. A proxy marriage means that earthly marriage does not interfere with the mystical marriage with Christ. We have already seen how often the language of marriage was used to describe the church and Christ in the hymnals of the Brüdergemeine and in the litanies in Bethlehem, but the imagery of the mystical marriage had special application within the Married Choir.

Sexual union was a sacramental action of the mystical marriage with an invisible grace. The man served as Christ for the woman, who represented the church. Wives and virgins both were married to Christ and only to Christ. This was reinforced in many verses from the liturgies for the Married Choir, such as: "The Virgins have devoted / Body and Soul unspotted / A thousand Times to Him, / Who with the Bride's Attire / Decks them, and does desire, / Soon as they're ripe, to marry them. / . . . O God, O chaste Lamb, Jesus! / Blow up thy clean Flame in us; / Our Marriage stands in / Need of thy Blood's Overspreading, / The Int'rim Proxy-Wedding / Was done in Jesu's Name indeed."[80]

The marriage rite itself gave expression to this understanding of the proxy

---

77. Beyreuther, "Sexualtheorien im Pietismus," 32–34. Zinzendorf followed Luther in distinguishing between the "feeling necessary" for sexual intercourse and the "sinful lust" that often accompanies it. Ibid., 34–35, 50; cf. *Apologetische Schluß-schrift*, ZE 3:605, 650–54. Zinzendorf went so far as to criticize Paul's understanding of marriage in 1 Corinthians 7:1–9 as an outlet for those who can't exercise self-control. Zinzendorf called this a "canine principle," and accused husbands of turning their wives into prostitutes when they viewed them only as objects of sexual satisfaction. *Apologetische Schluß-schrift*, 270; *Büdingische Sammlungen*, ZE 7:4:514.

78. 1759 *Litany-book*, 195; cf. 1757 *Litaneyen-büchlein*, 218–19.

79. "The modification of conception makes [children] not sinful, but they remain pure. 'Otherwise your children would be impure'" (1 Cor. 7:14). *Apologetische Schluß-schrift*, ZE 3:607.

80. 1759 *Litany-book*, 192; cf. 1757 *Litaneyen-büchlein*, 215.

marriage. The Bethlehem Diary contains the following description of a marriage on August 25, 1755:

"At 8 P.M. the communicants assembled in the *Saal* for the wedding of the six couples betrothed on Aug. 10. First, Br. Joseph sang some stanzas from the hymn, 'O Head full of Blood and Wounds.' During the stanza 'God, you chaste little Lamb' the procurator-wedding took place in the name of Jesus Christ, the hands of these six couples were joined, their conjugal ties validated, and they were blessed by the congregation with a cordial song."[81] A wedding of four couples near the end of the General Economy is similarly described:

First was sung, "O Creator of my soul, etc." "You are indeed to our souls their husband and Lord alone, etc." . . . [Böhler spoke.] Then the Wedding-Liturgy was sung by the choir: "Lord our God, you who have yourself established and blessed the holy marriage, you wanted them to be bound together through the band of holy marriage, in order to do your work together. Sprinkle their union with your blood and spread out on them all of your thoughts of peace." And after was sung, "O God, you chaste little Lamb, blow on your Marriage flames" "The Procurator Wedding is sent in the name of Jesus Christ," then the following four pairs . . . were bound in holy marriage under the blessing of the liturgists: "in the name of Jesus Christ, our Head, Bridegroom, and Elder; in the name of our dear Father in heaven; in the name of our dear Church Mother; and in the name of the Gemeine above and that which is still here below, we bring you honorably together."[82]

On the wedding day of fourteen couples in 1757, Peter Böhler reminded the Gemeine of its special relationship to the Bridegroom, and the day was concluded with a "Singstunde about our destination, to sleep in his arms."[83] At least until the 1760s the annual Married Choir's Festival celebrated this mystical union of the soul with Christ through earthly marriage. The "Creator of our souls" was the "Male principal." With tears in their eyes they sang hymns asking for Christ's blessing on their marriage, proclaiming that they were "predestined to sleep in his arms," after which the kiss of peace was shared with members of the same sex.[84]

Every week in the *Church Litany*, the congregation was reminded about gender relations as the congregation prayed that Christ would bless the preg-

---

81. *Bethlehem Diary* (Moravian Archives), Aug 25, 1755. Group weddings were the norm during the General Economy. Paul Peucker notes that married couples in the second "Sea Congregation" bound for Bethlehem received implicit pre-marriage counseling, and one brother had to be cautioned on being too "fleshly" in his intercourse with his wife after the ceremony. Peucker, "Heerendijk—Link in the Moravian Network: Moravian Colonists Destined for Pennsylvania," *Transactions of the Moravian Historical Society* 30 (1998): 13–14.

82. *Bethlehem Diary* (Moravian Archives), Nov. 29, 1761, 412–13.

83. "Br. Petrus beschloß auch bald darauf diesen remarquablen Tag mit einem lieblichem Singstunde von unsrer Destination, in Seinem Arm zu schlafen." Ibid., April 20, 1757.

84. Ibid., Sept. 7, 1760, 193–94.

nant and nursing sisters. They also reaffirmed their understanding that faith in Christ will help both men and women to bridle their lusts:

> Be the Sanctification of all the Choirs, thro' the maternal Care of the Holy Ghost;
> Let our Marriage be honourable among all Men,
> And our Bed undefiled;
> Make the Wife subject unto the Man, as unto the Lord,
> And teach the Husband to be benevolent to the Wife, as unto the Church;
> But let no Warrior entangle himself with Affairs of this life,
> Nor the Creature take Place to the Prejudice of the Creator, or divide with Christ;
> Regulate and keep in Order the festival Seasons of Matrimony (Especially of the newly married Pair N.N.) *(Deut. xx. 8. ch. xxiv. 5. I Cor. vii. 5.),*
> Let our pregnant Sisters reap the Blessing of thy having lain under a human Heart,
> And let those who give Suck, enjoy the Blessing of thy having sucked the Breasts of a Mother;
> Sanctify all bodily Fathers to the spiritual Father,
> And all who bear Children, to the Mother of us all;
> Bless thy Gift, the Children;
> Visit them even in their Mother's Womb!
> If they have but Thee, they lose nothing though they should never see this World, for they all live unto Thee;
> But if they must feel the Troubles of this Tabernacle, then bury them with Thee in Baptism unto Death!
> Through the Merit of thy Covenant -Wound circumcise the Hearts of our Boys;
> And thy becoming Man in a Virgin's Body, make the Girls chaste;
> Thy holy Celibacy till Death, transform thy Choir-Companions into Virgins; *(Rev. xiv. 4)*
> Let the Bands of Virgins go in the Odour of thy Bridegroom'-Name;
> May Faith in the Marriage of the Lamb be the Girdle of the Reins of the espoused Sisters,
> Call their Chamberlains thy espoused ones, and this will be a Girdle to their Loins;
> Be thyself the Reward of those Brethren, who have discharged their matrimonial Ministry with Faithfulness,
> And be Thou the blessed Hope of those Sisters, who are lonely and Widows indeed;
> Pour out thy Holy Spirit on all thy Servants and handmaids!
> Purify their Souls in obeying the Truth thro' the Spirit, unto unfeigned Love of the Brethren! *(I Pet. i. 22.)*
> *Hear us, O dear Lord and God!*[85]

These petitions recall the points already examined. Every week in worship the congregation proclaimed that pregnancy, birth, nursing, circumcision, virginity, and marriage were all blessed by the Incarnation of Christ.

---

85. The translation is from the 1759 English Litany book, which is an accurate translation of the 1757 German litany book, *Litaney-büchlein.*

Despite the fact that Zinzendorf taught that men are equally the brides of Christ, it is evident that this was not emphasized in Bethlehem. There are just a few references in the diary to the Brothers' celebrating their "conjugal connection" with Christ.[86] It is interesting in this light that although the choir liturgy books contain several hymns for the widows expressing their marriage to Christ, there are only a few verses for widowers. None of them mentions the mystical marriage. After their earthly marriage is over, widowers no longer have a role in the mystical marriage. They still can suck like babies at the side of Christ, but they no longer serve as his representatives in the mystical marriage.[87]

DEATH

Just as the Incarnation of Christ blessed all stages of life, it also sanctified death. Death was not meaningless but was considered one of the holiest moments of a life lived with Jesus. Clifford Geertz's general statement about the usefulness of religious symbolism to bring meaning to suffering applies in the Moravian context as well: "As a religious problem, the problem of suffering is, paradoxically, not how to avoid suffering but how to suffer, how to make of physical pain, personal loss, worldly defeat, or the helpless contemplation of others' agony something bearable, supportable—something, as we say, sufferable."[88]

For the Moravians in Bethlehem, suffering and death were meaningful and "sufferable" because the Savior had also suffered and died. Christ himself was the agent of death who plucked flowers from the gardens of each choir.[89] He was the Bridegroom who gave the kiss of death that was the final consummation of his love. "Around 9:00 in the morning the Single Sister, Maria Elisabeth Engfer, received the long-expected final kiss from her beloved Bridegroom, and her soul flew home to its mother city. It was immediately announced to the Gemeine with the trumpet sound. We sang some other verses and could scarcely stop singing for affectionate congratulation and gazing longingly into our eternal homeland."[90]

Death in Bethlehem, for men and women, was not a loss or a tragedy but the passage into wedded union with the Husband of their souls. As such, death was not to be feared but to be longed for. According to Böhler, death was the

---

86. E.g., *Bethlehem Diary* (Moravian Archives), April 22 (May 3, n.s.), 1749 (¶ 5).

87. 1759 *Litany-book*, 197.

88. Geertz, *Interpretation of Cultures*, 104.

89. "Our girls' institution also had a beautiful lovefeast in the afternoon in thankfulness that the Savior had wished to pluck a little flower from their [flower] bed, and afterwards they held a delightful Home-Going Liturgy." *Bethlehem Diary* (Moravian Archives), Oct. 4, 1758. Such language was not reserved for children, however. It was also used to describe the death of thirty-eight-year-old Friedrich Weber (ibid., Aug. 11, 1760).

90. Ibid., Nov. 28, 1752.

greatest festival to expect on earth.[91] In 1759, when a Single Sister received the long-awaited final kiss, all of her choir sisters longed to be the next to die.[92]

This consummation of the marriage with Christ was often described as an entering into the body of Christ through the spear wound in his side. This was an image of complete union with the Savior through the atoning wounds that had made salvation possible. The side wound acted as a magnet drawing souls home. It was the mother city of the Christian and the location of final happiness. "During the English sermon during the eleventh hour, the noble soul of our faithful deacon and dear Brother, Brownfield, abandoned its wearied body and flew with a look of longing toward the magnet of the wounds of Jesus, into its mother city. He passed away during the words of benediction, 'At the End of all Need' and 'Now you Side hole, you have carried him home.'"[93] Among the verses that the Single Sister Catharina Leibertin sang with her sisters as she died was "In my Husband's Death and Pain, there is my element." She died during the words "Deep into the dear Side!"[94]

Generally the choir leader or spouse would take charge of such a death scene by leading the singing and giving the final blessing of the dying sister or brother. The dying persons also sang hymns and liturgies to Christ as long as they were able. Frequently they chose their favorite hymns but almost invariably these focused on the suffering and death of Jesus. This was natural since people's minds were on death, but these hymns were also the center of the community's worship life. In every worship act the members of the Gemeine were reminded of the details of Jesus' death and the salvific effect of it, but they were also frequently reminded of their own mortality. All of life was in many respects a preparation for death.

When it became evident that the death of a brother or sister was near, those gathered at the bedside joined in a standard litany that appears to have been made up of portions of the *Church Litany, O Sacred Head now Wounded,* and the *Litany of the Life and Sufferings of Jesus* (the first part of the old *Litany of the Wounds*). The verses sung at the time of death were familiar to the Gemeine through its worship. They included such stanzas as the following from "O Haupt voll Blut" (O head full of blood): "When my mouth grows pale in his arms and lap, so shall the myrrh of the corpse, which flowed out of the side, give the final anointing to the dying body; that I will journey to the Gemeine.

91. Ibid., Sept. 25, 1760.

92. Aug. 13–14, 1759, *Single Sisters' Diary,* Moravian Archives.

93. *Bethlehem Diary* (Moravian Archives), April 23, 1752. During his first synod upon his return to Bethlehem in 1751, Spangenberg had read the funeral ode Zinzendorf wrote for Julianna Nitschmann, "Side Wound open yourself." Ibid., Dec. 11 (Dec. 22, n.s.), 1751.

94. Ibid., May 22, 1760, 529–31.

My flesh will live again."[95] It was considered especially good if a person died during the words "Open arms, Receive him/her!" or "Pale lips, Kiss him/her on the heart."

Even a seven-year-old like Anna Schaub could participate in her dying liturgy. "In the afternoon the children began to sing, and indeed a proper Going-Home liturgy. When she [Anna Schaub] heard them, she joined her voice with them and gave some verses of her own. When she became so weak that she could no longer sing, she still moved her lips. . . . When her eyes were broken, she called out, 'Ave, my dear Husband!'"[96]

The process of dying itself was blessed by the Incarnation. The details of Jesus' slow dying and agony were a comfort to the suffering. His corpse was a blessed object of devotion in hymns and liturgies used throughout the year during the period of the General Economy. Dying persons often requested the "corpse hymns" of Christian Renatus to be sung so that the memory of Jesus' own dying, death, and burial would encourage them as they faced the same process.[97]

As Sarah Reinke died in 1758, "the late Christel's 'corpse liturgies,' which were sung for her, were her sweets through the night, in which she joined many a time. . . . She gently went to sleep into Jesus' arm and lap."[98] Joseph Healy was blessed with the verses "Your sweat in penitential struggle," "Open arms, Receive him," "Pale lips, Kiss him on the heart"; and then Healy "received the last little kiss and his soul went over into the wounds."[99]

At times the dying person would have a vision or give words of comfort to those left behind. This frequently involved the idea of union with Christ and continued communion with members of one's own choir. The death delirium of Jonathan Becks (1742–59) was more vivid than most, but it was not considered unusual.

Toward evening the fever took the upper hand and he fantasized very pleasantly. . . . He said, "Oh look there, there I see the dear Savior sitting. He looks amazingly beautiful and friendly. Christel [Christian Renatus] is sitting next to him, and he waves to me and says,

---

95. "Wenn mein mund wird erbleichen In seinem Arm und schooß, So soll die Myrrh der Leichen, Die aus der Seite floß, Dem sterbenden gebeine Die letzte ölung geb'n; Dann fahr ich zur Gemeine Mein fleisch wird wieder leb'n." 1757 *Litaneyen-büchlein*, 20. This differs slightly from the translation in the English *Litany-book* of 1759, which reads, "And when my Mouth grows pallid In Jesu's Lap and Arms, The Corpse's Myrrh so valid, Which in his Heart's Blood swarms, Embalm my Body dying; No other Salve at all! Myself to Salem flying, Shall once that Flesh recall" (18).

96. *Bethlehem Diary* (Moravian Archives), Jan. 20, 1761.

97. The hymns of Christian Renatus have often been consigned to the so-called Sifting Time; however, they were frequently used in Bethlehem after the Sifting. For instance, "After those who are sick had also received their portion of the body, Br. Nathanael [Seidel] sang the corpse-bees completely to sleep with the late Christel's corpse liturgies for a blessed rest in His grave!" Ibid., Nov. 27, 1756.

98. Ibid., Aug 31, 1758, 142. Such references could be multiplied greatly.

99. March 18, 1753, *Single Brothers' Diary*, Moravian Archives.

I shall continue like that, I'll be there soon. I see also Sven Roseen, who is beautiful. My old master is already there. Oh how tenderly Kapp is as he kisses the feet of the dear Savior. Now I will be there in an instant."[100]

Craig Koslofsky indicates that the Reformation marked a change in Western attitudes toward the dead. Whereas "medieval Christians dwelt in a community of the living and the dead," the Reformation moved the dead from the community by placing cemeteries outside the city walls and abolishing prayers for the dead.[101] If Koslofsky is correct, then the Moravians represent a return to an earlier practice and point of view. Death was a normal part of life in Bethlehem and the dead remained a part of the community in many ways. Members gathered on the cemetery at least once a year to commemorate the dead and to celebrate the resurrection. Deaths were announced immediately through the playing of trombones so that the whole Gemeine could pray for the departed and also contemplate their own end.

Br. Petrus read then the text for today which was very appropriate for these events, and then he explained the homegoing liturgy, customary in the Gemeine, which is played upon the trombones, namely: the first melody, of "O Head full of Blood and Wounds" signifies that the Bridegroom has kissed home someone from our midst. With that one should think, "Someone has just died." The second melody indicates from which choir. And the third, which is also the melody "O Head," brings each person to himself, and reminds him of the blessed moment when he will also have the great grace, and therefore one may sing in his soul 'When *my* mouth grows pale.' "[102]

Even the anniversary of the massacre of the Moravian mission station at Gnadenhütten could be an occasion for celebrating death. "Our children had an afternoon lovefeast to celebrate this remarkable day." They sang "You man of sorrows so beautiful" and "Pale lips! Kiss them on the heart." They remembered the massacre with the "pleasing homegoing sound upon the trombones."[103]

Many of the litanies used regularly in worship, in particular the *Church Litany,* included petitions for the dead and a prayer to be kept in fellowship with them. "Keep us in everlasting fellowship with the whole church triumphant, And let us rest together in thy Wounds from all our Labour."[104] If some-

100. *Bethlehem Diary* (Moravian Archives), June 27, 1759.

101. Craig M. Koslofsky, *The Reformation of the Dead: Death and Ritual in Early Modern Germany, 1450–1700* (New York: St. Martin's Press, 2000), 2.

102. *Bethlehem Diary* (Moravian Archives), Feb. 7, 1758. Choirs would also take other occasions to remember their dead, such as the general gathering on the anniversary of Christian Renatus's death to remember him and several members of the Bethlehem Gemeine who had recently died. Ibid., May 28, 1760.

103. Ibid., Nov. 24, 1756.

104. 1759 *Litany-book,* 55, cf. 1757 *Litaneyen-büchlein,* 61.

one had died recently, the liturgist would add the following phrase to the litany: "His Eyes, his Mouth, his Side, His Body crucify'd, / Whereon we lean unshaken, / {Name of person} to see is taken; / [Cong.]: Where he/she now thankful kisses / The hands and feet of Jesus."[105]

The final act in life's drama was the funeral. The ceremony itself was held in the worship hall and was quite simple. There would be a litany, usually portions of the *Litany of the Wounds*, and the reading of the *Lebenslauf* (memoir) of the departed. In contrast to Lutheran practice in Germany, there was a public ceremony with an address for every member of the community, regardless of status.[106] The Lebenslauf indicated that the life and death of every member of the community was valued. It was a validation of the individual and of the community at the same time.

Following the litany and the Lebenslauf, the Gemeine would proceed by choir with the body to the cemetery, which was called *Gottes Acker* (God's Acre) because bodies were planted there as seeds for the resurrection.[107] The precise order of procession varied, but men and women were always kept separate (according to German Lutheran tradition). In some funerals women even served as the pall bearers for members of their own choir. Men and women were also buried separately, and in general by choir.[108]

According to the *Zeremonienbüchlein*, during the procession the community played and sang "lively and frisky music" *(mit Musik lieblich und munter)*.[109] After a brief burial liturgy, the body was interred with the words: "Keep us with the entire perfected congregation (Church Triumphant), especially with our brother {or sister} N.N. in eternal fellowship, and let us rest in the same manner with them in your wounds!"[110]

Virtually these same words were used each year at Easter in the eighteenth century. Each Easter the congregation gathered to visit the graves of their

105. 1759 *Litany-book*, 55; cf. 1757 *Litaneyen-büchlein*, 61. The German version emphasizes the nail wounds in the hands and feet. This entire passage was dropped from the litany in the 1790s.

106. Koslofsky, *Reformation of the Dead*, 107–14; 144–47.

107. The first Single Sister to be buried in Bethlehem was Elizabeth Brazier: "She was the first seed from the maiden's choir in the God's Acre in America." April 3, 1750, *Single Sisters' Diary*, Moravian Archives.

108. Burial by choir was not followed precisely in the time of Bishop Nitschmann, as the burial of his wife, Johanna, demonstrates. Another example is the stillborn son of Sister Cammerhof, who was buried beside his father. *Bethlehem Diary* (Moravian Archives), July 20 (July 31, n.s.), 1751. An examination of the cemetery reveals the surprising fact that there is no stone marking the grave of the son. It seems likely that the son was buried in the grave of his father.

109. Anonymous, *Zeremonienbüchlein*, 57. This should not be confused with a New Orleans "jazz funeral." The music of German chorales was known for the use of minor keys.

110. "Und nach den Worten: Bewahre uns mit der ganzen vollendeten Gemeine, insonderheit mit unserm Bruder (oder Schwester) N.N. in ewiger Gemeinschaft, und lass uns dermaleins mit ihr ausruhen bey deinen Wunden!" This is essentially the ritual prescribed in the revised liturgy book of 1778. *Gesangbuch zum Gebrauch der evangelischen Brüdergemeinen* (Barby: Spellenberg, 1778), 220. "Wounds" was changed in 1789 to "presence" as Moravian devotion moved away from its Zinzendorfian roots.

brothers and sisters.[111] There they confessed their faith in the eschatological Resurrection and read the names of members of the congregation who had died in the previous year, using words taken from the funeral liturgy.

I believe, that our brethren N.N. [name] and our sisters N.N. are gone to the church above, and entered into the joy of their Lord; the body was buried here.
We poor sinners pray Thee to hear us, O dear Lord and God;
And keep us in everlasting fellowship with the church triumphant; especially also with those servants and handmaids of the whole church, whom Thou hast called home within this year, as N.N. and to let us once rest with them at Thy wounds.[112]

Each person who had died in the community was named at Easter, and the community reaffirmed that death does not separate the Gemeine. This reading of the names of the dead and praying for ongoing communion with them was a form of the ancient church practice of reading the diptychs on which names of the dead were recorded. Zinzendorf acknowledged this connection, saying, "the Diptychs belong to the ritual of a congregation of God, [because] therein lies a connection with the invisible [World]."[113] In this way, the Moravians were assured that they would not be forgotten in death.

Interestingly, they also believed that the individuals they knew and loved were acting as their intercessors in heaven. The prayers of the dead were considered just as valid as those of the living. This marks an interesting departure from normal Protestant practice, but in Bethlehem they believed that "The more who depart out of a choir to go to our Savior, so much the better it is for that choir, the more blessed it is, so many more helpers that choir gets, so many reminders who charm the Savior, and remind him of a day, or of a person, such as the Single Brothers' festival, that he may well be very near then with his sweet presence."[114]

Easter, then, was a yearly affirmation, not only of the unique Resurrection of Christ and a general resurrection of the church but also of the eternal life of specific members of the community.[115] This sense of community extending beyond the grave changed dramatically as the Moravians moved out of intimate communities and into the impersonal world of nineteenth-century America.[116]

111. Anonymous, *Zeremonienbüchlein*, ZE 6:58.

112. *A Collection of Hymns chiefly extracted from the Larger Hymn-Book of the Brethren's Congregations* (London: Brethren's Chapel, 1769), 306–7.

113. Zinzendorf, *Einundzwanzig Diskurse*, 325.

114. Ibid., 327.

115. April 18, 1756, *Single Sisters' Diary*, Moravian Archives.

116. Atwood, "The Joyfulness of Death in Eighteenth-Century Moravian Communities," *Communal Societies* 17 (1997): 39–58.

From conception to burial, heart religion and the Christocentric theology
of Zinzendorf shaped life in Bethlehem. Throughout their lives, the brothers
and sisters lived in the knowledge that the incarnate God blessed every stage of
their lives, and that his death was their salvation. This concept was not simply
communicated in hymns and sermons, it was embodied in the most basic element of Bethlehem's social structure, the choir. The Zinzendorfian understanding of the Incarnation and the unique social structure of Bethlehem were
united through the ritual and worship of the community. Their vivid, even
shocking, Christocentric worship allowed the Moravians to live the lives they
idealized. From womb to tomb, the men and women of Bethlehem lived in an
intimate and caring community devoted to Christ alone.

FIGURE 7. Moravian brothers and sisters adoring the crucified Christ. Unity Archives, Herrnhut.

CHAPTER 7

LIVING IN THE SIDE
WOUND OF CHRIST

M any aspects of the piety, theology, and society of Bethlehem during the period of the General Economy have been discussed so far, but there is one key aspect of their life that unified their beliefs and practices. Bethlehem was a community dedicated to the blood and wounds of Christ. To understand Bethlehem and its success, it is necessary to understand the nature of the wounds symbolism and its social function during the communal period.

THE LITANY OF THE WOUNDS

When Br. Joseph (Spangenberg) assumed his duties as Chief Elder of the Moravian Church in the fall of 1744, he introduced the newly written *Litany of the Wounds* and taught the residents of Bethlehem how to chant it.[1] During the period of the General Economy this would be one of the most important and frequently used litanies. It was sung in German and English and was quickly translated into more than one tribal dialect. It had such a powerful effect when it was first sung to the natives at Bethlehem's mission outpost of Gnadenhütten that "they forgot all about going to sleep."[2]

According to the Moravians, this litany was a centerpiece of their theology. They asserted that it would be better for those who had questions about their beliefs to read this litany than any theology book they might write.[3] Moreover, the litany was used by those who were already Moravian to renew their love to their Savior and devotion to the Gemeine.

The success of this practice is attested to by notations such as the following: "A new working of grace has been noted in Digeon and his wife. He recently has been taken hold of by the *Litany of the Wounds*."[4] In short, the *Litany of the Wounds* is a prime example of Zinzendorf's heart religion and wounds

---

1. Hamilton, *Bethlehem Diary* 1:210, 214.

2. *Bethlehem Diary* (Moravian Archives), June 14 (June 25, n.s.), 1746. Manuscripts of the translated litany are preserved in the Moravian Archives, Bethlehem. On the use of the *Litany of the Wounds* in Moravian missions to the Northern tribes, see Jane T. Merritt, "Dreaming of the Savior's Blood: Moravians and the Indian Great Awakening in Pennsylvania," *William and Mary Quarterly* 54, 3rd ser. (Oct. 1997): 723–46.

3. Nov. 8 (Nov. 19, n.s.), 1748, Helpers Conference Minutes, Moravian Archives, Bethlehem.

4. March 11 (March 22, n.s.), 1747, Engere Conf. Minutes, Moravian Archives, Bethlehem.

theology, which have already been discussed. As such, it merits a serious discussion. But even though this litany captures the essence of the theology and piety of Zinzendorf and his disciples in America, it has been virtually ignored by scholars until recently.[5]

The litany divides naturally into two parts: the sufferings and death of Jesus and the hymns to the wounds. The first section recalls the form of petition used in the *Church Litany*. It begins with a *Kyrie* to Christ that includes a special *Gloria* specifically to the side wound. Then the community prays that God the Father will look on the five wounds of Christ and remember that these are the atoning ransom for the sins of the world. The worshippers are reminded that the wounds are their consolation because they are the proof of forgiveness of sins.

The Second Person of the Trinity is addressed next, but the words are actually directed to the congregation. They are reminded that the side wound of Christ is "the doorway to heaven." Then the Holy Spirit is addressed, her primary mission being to preach "daily the wounds of the Lamb to his congregations of the Cross which have found him."

Thus the opening lines of the litany give the skeleton of Zinzendorf's Trinitarian doctrine. Both the Father and the Spirit are connected to the Son and his atoning death. The Father looks on the wounds of Christ and has mercy on humankind, while the Spirit preaches the doctrine of the wounds in the church. The Christocentric focus of the Trinity is summed up in the line "Holy Trinity, blessed be you for the sake of the Lamb."

The short series of petitions are clear expressions of Zinzendorf's heart religion in relationship to the blood and wounds theology.

> From all self-righteousness;
> From all lack of discipline;[6]
> From all unbloodied grace;
> From hearts that have not been bled upon;
> From indifference to your wounds;
> From estrangement from your cross;
> From being weaned from your side;
> From unanointed gossip about the blood;
> From eternal mortal sin;
>
> *Preserve us, dear Lord God!*

5. Atwood, "Zinzendorf's Litany of the Wounds"; Faull, "Faith and Imagination."
6. The translation of Jacob Rogers reads, "From all Dryness of Chastisement" (Moravian Archives), and that in the English *Litany-book*, "From the dryness of discipline." The German version was changed to read *zucht-trokkenheit* after 1753. These are actually better expressions of Zinzendorf's theology than the original German version.

The Moravians were in effect praying that they never stray from Zinzendorf's theology. These lines express a fear of turning away from the suffering Christ and accepting some type of grace other than that of the Atonement.

At the same time, however, there is a prayer to be preserved from "unanointed gossip" or "prating" about the blood. The Brüdergemeine understood that familiarity breeds, if not contempt, a taking for granted or even a sense of frivolity about holy matters, particularly among those growing up in the Gemeine.[7] Therefore, whenever this litany was used, the Gemeine prayed to be preserved from being indifferent to the wounds or treating them lightly. We see here that the attitude of the worshipper is crucial to the experience of being in the Gemeine. Wounds theology had a powerful effect, but not on those who were indifferent or "unanointed."

The next series of petitions were sung antiphonally, generally between choirs. They recall the petitions in the *Church Litany* that relate the life of Jesus to the daily life of Moravians in the choirs. Not only does the circumcision of Jesus help to "circumcise our hearts" but even his exile as a child in Egypt (Luke 2) plays a role in redemption. The flight to Egypt is not used here as a symbol of the exodus of the chosen people from slavery, but is a statement that members of the Brüdergemeine should also be ready to go into exile themselves. Just as Jesus was not bound to his home, so too the residents of Bethlehem should not be tied to their homes. They must "be at home everywhere." By being citizens of heaven and sojourners on earth, the Moravians were in fact "citizens of the world." No area was considered beyond the reach of their missionaries.[8]

The litany also asserts that Jesus had studied as a child. This is inferred from his encounter with the scribes in the Temple (Luke 2) and his knowledge of Scripture, but stands in marked contrast with a long tradition of Christian thought that asserted that Jesus was uneducated. This rejection of the tradition is surprising because it appears to conflict with a later line that states, "May your astonishing simplicity make reason hateful to us." This apparent contradiction serves to highlight a point made earlier. Heart religion is not opposed to practical reason or education, only to groundless speculation. Members of the Brüdergemeine were encouraged to study, particularly the Bible and languages, but they were steered away from philosophy and free inquiry.

Jesus, then, is used as the model of the scholar who is obedient first of all to

---

7. This was the problem during the Sifting Time at Herrnhaag and relates to Zinzendorf's admonitions in his Reprimand of 1749 against speaking lightly of the side wound. Craig D. Atwood, "Zinzendorf's 1749 Reprimand."

8. Heinz Motel, in his article "Nikolaus Ludwig von Zinzendorf," in *Concise Dictionary of the Christian World Mission,* ed. Stephen Neill, Gerald H. Anderson and John Goodwin (Nashville: Abingdon Press, 1971), 680, reports that by 1760 more than three hundred members of the community had gone out as missionaries.

God. The simplicity of Jesus means not stupidity but single-heartedness. He spoke what he knew without ratiocination. Moreover, in becoming incarnate, the Son of God laid aside his omniscience, taking on human finitude and ignorance. This is the "meritorious ignorance" referred to in a later line.[9] Here Jesus stands as the model of the person who is content with what can be known, in contrast to those who presume to know the essence of everything. In this way, the *Litany of the Wounds* blesses human finitude.

This sanctification of finitude continues in the following stanzas. The physical weakness of Christ is praised as a blessing of human weakness. Human weakness is a blessed state because it removes the threat of self-righteousness and autonomy. The Son of God himself submitted to the Father in the garden of Gethsemane: "May your reliance on your heavenly Father to suffer and not to suffer / Be our decree of your divinity." The voluntary submission of Jesus demonstrates the importance of relying on God alone in this life. Weakness removes the temptation to rely on human efforts.

The humanness and weakness of Jesus were best revealed in his Passion. For the Moravians, the Passion began with the mental anguish in the garden when the reality of his "fear of suffering and death" was clearly revealed. The Brüdergemeine exulted in Jesus' struggle with his own fears and emotions, even though he appeared more afraid of death than many Christian martyrs. According to the *Litany of the Wounds,* the courage of the martyrs is "put to shame" by Christ's own struggle over his death. This is one way the Brüdergemeine tried to temper the martyr zeal of its members. One might be called to suffer with Christ in the mission fields, but suffering should not be sought out for its own sake. Christ himself feared death and tried to avoid it.

Several lines of the litany concern the physical details of Christ's suffering and death. This graphic recalling of Jesus' ordeal strengthens the connection between the joy of being a Christian and the cost of the victory over Satan. It is also intended to move the heart into devotion of the one who suffered. The blood of Christ sets the earth on fire, presumably with the love for God.

The "pale lips" kiss believers on the heart, drawing them into the community of his death. Believers come into such an intimate relationship with Jesus that the Savior's "dead eyes, look out through our eyes." Christ acts like the woman who anointed his feet and dried them with her hair, but he anoints the believer with "bloody foam" and dries them with "sweat-soaked hair."

Not only blessing but rebirth comes from the wounds. Just as Elisha laid his living body on a dead child to bring him back to life (2 Kings 4:34); so Christ

---

9. The translation of Rogers is helpful, mss. litany book, Moravian Archives. He translates "Fence in our understanding" as "Bridle our penetrations," thus emphasizing the speculative aspect of reason rather than "understanding." This line was dropped after the so-called Sifting Time.

lays his dead body on the believer in order to bring him or her into new life. The wounds also have an eschatological significance. The wounded hands show where names are written in the book of life at the last judgment. The wounded feet will be seen on the Mount of Olives. The glorious Son of God coming in the clouds will bear the marks of his Passion as proof of his identity.[10]

The second part of the litany consists of the hymns to the wounds of Jesus. It is this section, which was separated from the earlier portion in the 1750s, that has attracted the most censure over the years, but there is no indication that anyone in Bethlehem objected to these hymns, at least during Spangenberg's tenure. This section is unusual in that it is neither Christ nor the other members of the Trinity who are addressed but the wounds themselves. They have become a symbol for Christ, the Atonement, and all of the fruits of the Atonement: eternal life, security, and so forth.

They are the "worthy wounds" that merit honor from the believer because they are the source of salvation. They are "dearest" and "wondrous" because they "make sinners holy and thieves saints." That line is intentionally provocative, shocking the worshipper out of complacency or self-righteousness. The paradoxical nature of the joyful worship of the wounds of Christ is united with the paradox of being a graced sinner. It is only the sinner, such as Mary Magdalene, who is saved. Saints must acknowledge their sinfulness in order to be saved through the power of the wounds.

The ability of wounds adoration to affect the heart of the believer is acknowledged directly in the petition "Powerful wounds of Jesus, So moist, so gory, bleed on my heart so that I may remain brave and like the wounds." The litany praises those who have preached the wounds, because it is the wounds of Christ that produce the self-knowledge that comes with the rebirth. Therefore the wounds themselves are a source of truth. They reveal the sinful state of humankind far better than any litany of human depravity, but at the same time they display the glorious mercy of God. They are "clear" and "glistening." They light a torch in the heart that is brighter than lightning beams.

This summary does not exhaust the meaning of the wounds symbolism for the Gemeine. The wounds are a source of security and comfort. They are "juicy" and "succulent" because they nourish the soul. The worshipper is strengthened by sucking at the side of Christ; she "licks it, tastes it." The wounds provide a warm and soft bed in which to lie. They protect the children from the cold, so that the worshipper says, "I like lying calm, gentle, and quiet and warm. What shall I do? I crawl to you." The believer longs to return to

---

10. Zinzendorf, *Pennsylvania Sermons,* 126. There is an unusual version of "First Fruits" by Valentine Haidt that shows Zinzendorf preaching to the nations and pointing to the sky, where one sees the side wound emitting shafts of light. See Meyer and Peucker, *Graf Ohne Grenzen,* 21.

the womb, to crawl inside the "deep wounds of Jesus" and lie there safe and protected.

This vision of the wounds is focused on the individual, but not exclusively. There is an interplay between "My wounds" and "Our wounds." The heat from the wounds, the saving power of Christ's Atonement, will cover the world, and all classes of people will come to salvation; "slaves, beggars and kings, farmers and counts" will become pilgrims who worship at the corpse of Jesus.

This is a good description of the Brüdergemeine and its worldwide perspective. African slaves in St. Thomas, natives in Pennsylvania dispossessed of their ancestral homes, Moravian peasants, and more than one count came together before the image of the wounded God. The brothers and sisters of Bethlehem joined the "many thousand kinds of sinners" who sat in the "treasure hoard" of the "cavernous wounds of Jesus."

From the *Litany of the Wounds* we can see that the wounds were a multivalent symbol in Bethlehem. An entire Christian theology was focused intensely on a single compelling symbol. The doctrine of the Atonement, which could easily become a philosophical abstraction, was transformed into a contemplation of the historical account of the wounding of Jesus.

The doctrine of the soul's eventual union with God, which could easily dissolve into some type of mystical annihilation or pantheism, was portrayed in terms of a physical/spiritual entry into the very being of Christ through his wounds. The individual remains an individual but is completely absorbed into the divine being, along with all those who believe in the Atonement.

The doctrine of providence is anthropomorphized into an image of eternal protection in the womb of the side of Christ. The doctrine of justification by grace through faith, which had become a sterile academic debate, is recast in terms of the ever-present paradox of the beautiful and horrible wounds of Christ.

The paradox of Christianity is not simply the cross, with its opposing bars, but the body of Jesus, whose wounds are repulsive and gory to the world and simultaneously beautiful, glistening, and succulent to the believer. It is in the light of this primal paradox that the paradox of being a justified sinner was to be understood and experienced. The theology of the cross itself, which is forever at odds with a theology of glory, is painted again and again in the *Litany of the Wounds*. The bride of Christ is beautiful only insofar as she embraces the bleeding and battered Bridegroom.

THE *PLEURODY*

This paradoxical worship of the wounds was not confined to the *Litany of the Wounds*. It was expressed in the many hymns to the corpse of Christ and especially in the *Pleurody* that gradually gained in popularity during Spangenberg's second tenure in the 1750s. The *Pleurody* focuses exclusively on the side wound of Christ, even asserting that the victory of Christ came in the piercing of his side. This was a sacred event: "All angels and the heavenly host / Who gaze at that with love, / But soon must veil their faces / Before the ruby light." The wounding of God is thus compared to the theophanies of the Bible where the seraphim must cover their eyes before the glory of God (e.g., Isaiah 6:2–3); however, in this case human creatures are more blessed than the angels.

The church, the bride of Christ, "which was Dug out" of the side, is at home in the side wound and can adore it without shame or fear. The side wound acts as a magnet drawing the bride to Christ and keeping her there for eternity. All true believers belong in the side of Christ, even the Old Testament prophet Isaiah. John the Evangelist, we are told, fainted when he prepared his account of the wounding. Thomas had the special pleasure of placing his hand physically in the side. Through the *Pleurody* the worshipper becomes contemporary with Thomas and looks within the side as in a dream (or trance) and does not wish to awaken.

This litany assures the worshipper that all of the wounds—in fact, the whole corpse of Jesus—are honorable and important, but the wound over Jesus' heart is particularly valued. "Although we honor all the wounds alike And feed upon the entire corpse; Still we concentrate on the breast our Thanks: shame, pain, joy, love, and desire."

This was the place where the bride of Christ was born, just as Eve was born from the side of the first Adam. Thus the church, as the bride of Christ, is doubly flesh of his flesh. Not only did he become human, she was born from his side. This womb symbolism is made explicit in the *Pleurody*:

> In order flesh of his flesh and bone And spirit of his spirit to be;
> That each to the womb Gives his special devotion.
> And at the end of all distress One says to his beloved God:
> What right my body has to the earth, Is because it was formed in this womb;

Because the church was born from the Spirit that flowed with Christ's blood, it shares "God's nature." This mysterious joining through the side of Jesus is not only "the Point of our Religion" but also "the inexpressible things that Paul saw." The litany closes with a pledge that the Brüdergemeine will remain true to the bloody side.

The adoration of the wounds of Christ was far more important during the General Economy than has been indicated in the literature on Bethlehem. Previous scholars have dismissed this cult as being confined to the years of Cammerhof's influence, but it was actually a vital element of life in Bethlehem at least until 1762. Very early in Bethlehem's history the diarist described communion as a time "when we maggots shall attach ourselves individually and eternally to His gaping wounds." In the 1760s, the diarist recorded, "At last the corpse-bees approached the sacramental meal of his corpse and blood."[11] These two entries are nearly twenty years, an entire generation, apart.

WOUNDS DEVOTION IN BETHLEHEM

In 1748 one of the native children, Herzel, presented his personal theology to the Bethlehem Gemeine. It consisted of "Lamb, God's Lamb, Wounds, Blood, Blood of the Lamb, Side-hole, Nail-wounds, Spear gash, God's wounds, etc."[12] Others, such as Spangenberg, explicated the meaning of these symbols more fully. He often blessed "the Gemeine with many nice and bloody stanzas about the side hole" and preached on this theme.[13] From the earliest days the members of the Bethlehem Gemeine learned about the "deity and salvation for sinners which can be learned from the pierced hands and feet and from the gouged-out side."[14]

A dozen years later Spangenberg was still preaching "about the transfiguration of Jesus' wounds in the light of the Holy Spirit, and afterwards [he] celebrated this subject in song during the Singstunde in an uncommonly lovely way."[15] It is clear from the records that the Spangenbergs were no less enamored of the wounds than the rest of the Brüdergemeine. One sign of this is that blood-and-wounds hymns were selected to honor Mary Spangenberg for her fifty-third birthday, "which was quite Good Friday-like."[16]

The adoration of the wounds during Holy Communion was a high point of life in Bethlehem. The residents were like the apostles, especially Thomas, who could see and touch their Lord. "In the Singstunde we felt our Lamb's closeness to his poor little flock of doves in the cross' atmosphere and, like the Apostles, could touch his side hole with their hands, and fly in and out of it."[17] Such experiences were repeated frequently: "Again it was a great and indescribably

---

11. Hamilton, *Bethlehem Diary* 1:176: "Zuletzt naheten sich die Leichnams-Bienen zu dem Sacramentlichen Mahle seines Leichnams und Blutes." *Bethlehem Diary* (Moravian Archives), Jan. 19, 1760; cf. ibid., Dec. 22, 1759, Sept. 26, 1761. Anna Rosel's birthday celebration in 1761 began with the verse, "How good it is to the little worm with the feeling for the wounds from early into the night." Ibid., Aug. 10, 1761.

12. *Bethlehem Diary* (Moravian Archives), March 19 (March 30, n.s.), 1748.

13. Ibid., June 14 (June 25, n.s.), 1748.

14. Hamilton, *Bethlehem Diary* 1:172.

15. "Von der Verklärung der Wunden Jesu in dem licht des h. Geistes, und besung darauf in der Singstunde diese Materir ungemein lieblich." *Bethlehem Diary* (Moravian Archives), Aug. 8, 1757.

16. Ibid., Feb. 26 (March 8, n.s.), 1748 (¶ 6). A few years later her husband wrote a special lovefeast liturgy that was nineteen verses long and had the choral refrain, "Bless him from your holy wounds." "Segne ihn aus deinen heilgen Wunden, mit den Tröpflein aus den Nägel-Schründen, dein balsamiren mach, daß Er sich stets mit Segen rühre." Ibid., May 1, 1756, Beilage 1, 371–74.

17. Ibid., Aug. 14 (Aug. 25, n.s.), 1747 (¶ 7).

blessed day with nothing but corpse ideas and feelings. The communion services received their beginning with the hymn 'O Head full of Blood and
Wounds' up to stanza five. [Spangenberg preached] and in faith we knelt before
him during the stanza 'Recognize me my protector, my shepherd take me in.'
. . . [Spangenberg led communion and was] especially inspired at the liturgy of
the cup."[18] The day concluded with the *Hymns to the Wounds.*

Such adoration could lead to religious ecstasy, such as that recorded on May
11, 1748: "in the Singstunde a lovely and pleasant air of the cross breezed
through and our hearts felt quite blessed in the most beloved side hole. We
crawled completely inside! Hallelujah!"[19]

Residents of Bethlehem frequently adored the wounds of Christ just before
going to sleep at night, especially on the Sabbath. One of the most frequent
images associated with the wounds in Bethlehem was that of resting with
Christ. This was often connected to various images for the mystical marriage
or being a child sleeping in a bed.

The *Bethlehem Diary* is full of references to being "rocked into our Sabbath's
rest with our juicy litany of the wounds."[20] The side wound serves as the cradle
in which the Christian can have a Sabbath rest safe from Satan and the world.
"We were quite happy all day in the side hole, and in the Singstunde and
Gemein-Litaney we felt as if embedded eternally in the side hole."[21]

As part of the All Choirs' Festival of 1756, the communicants had a liturgy
using the hymn "So as one would have a pleasant rest in the bed." During the
lovefeast afterward "the whole Gemeine was inspired by the singing of the late
Christel's death and corpse ideas. And the conclusion of this indescribably
blessed festival took place with the *Litany der Menschheit Jesu [Litany of the
Wounds]*, which hastened each one to rest in the soft bed of his side."[22] This
view of the side wound as a bed is expressed in songs such as "In the soft bed
of your side, my dearest little Jesus," which Spangenberg used in an evening
blessing in 1761.[23]

Every subgroup in Bethlehem worshipped the wounds. There are numerous
references in the *Bethlehem Diary* to the adoration given by children, married
persons, widows, and even infants. The devotion of the Single Brothers is striking, though not unusual. "And then this lovefeast that had lasted five hours
was finally ended. . . . Then the brothers went two by two from the Gemein
Saal with music, and they played and sang throughout the streets of Bethlehem,

18. Ibid., Dec. 28, 1755.
19. Ibid., May 11 (May 22, n.s.), 1748.
20. Ibid., July 24 (Aug. 4, n.s.), 1747.
21. Ibid., Oct. 8 (Oct. 19, n.s.), 1748.
22. Ibid., March 25, 1756.
23. Ibid., Feb. 11, 1761.

and after that they formed a circle and closed by singing together to honor the Pleura of our Husband the tender little verse 'Little Side Hole, Little Side Hole.' "[24]

When the Single Brothers built their capacious choir house in 1748 they inscribed the core of their doctrine on the lintels front and rear. On the south side of the building was a sundial with the superscription *"Gloria Pleurae"* (Glory to the Side), with a star beneath and the year in Roman numerals. An inscription in the wall on the north side said "Father, Mother, and dear Husband, honor the adolescents' plan."[25] Their house was thus suitably dedicated to the divine family and to the side wound of Christ.

Bethlehem celebrated the wounds of Jesus in a number of hymns, in addition to the litanies examined above. One of the most popular was "Little side hole, little side hole, you are mine" (*Seitenhölgen, Seitenhölgen, du bist mein!*), which was popular among the children. The great missionary to the native tribes, Pyrlaeus, translated this into Mahican soon after beginning work among that tribe.[26] The fascination of the *Seitenhölgen* hymn was not confined to the 1740s. In 1752, when Spangenberg was leader of Bethlehem, the anniversary of this hymn was observed, "which was very joyful to us."[27] Six years later the children held a lovefeast that impressed upon them "the account of the opening of the pleura and the Spirit born from it," while the adults declared their own "devotion to the holy side, as the Mother-place of *our* spirit."[28] At the end of the day, the congregation sang the familiar hymn "Side-hole, Side-hole, you are mine."

This idea of the soul's longing for the side wound was a common theme. In 1749 von Watteville led worship on the Daily Text "in which the material about the creation of the Lamb's souls from his side, and their constant tendency to return therein, was nicely treated, blessedly experienced."[29] It is important to note that von Watteville did not merely preach on this topic but that it was "blessedly experienced" by the congregation in its worship. The soul's longing for the womb of Christ was perceived as a reality in Bethlehem.[30]

A similar service in 1760 was particularly impressive to the diarist. It in-

---

24. April 24 (May 5, n.s.), 1748 *Single Brothers' Diary,* Moravian Archives.

25. "Heute wurden in unser ledigen Brüder hause an der South Seite die Sonnen Uhr mit der Uberschrifft Gloria Pleurae und in . . . darunter stehen den gegestern schöne Stern und der Jahr [illegible] MDCCXVIII, und an der North Seite der marmor Stein mit den Uberschrifft Vater, und Mutter und Lieber Mann Habt Ehr vom Jünglings Plan." Ibid., June 13 (June 24, n.s.), 1748 (¶ 3); cf. Levering, *A History of Bethlehem,* 199, which mistranslates *Mann* as "supreme man" rather than "husband."

26. *Bethlehem Diary* (Moravian Archives), Aug. 31, 1748; June 24, 1748.

27. Ibid., March 10, 1752.

28. Ibid., March 24, 1758.

29. Ibid., Aug. 5 (Aug. 16, n.s.), 1749.

30. "And as the Gemeine again assembled at 3:00, in order to testify to its devotion to the holy side, thus the womb of our spirits." Ibid., March 24 (Good Friday), 1758.

cluded hymns that portrayed the wounds as the healing pool of Bethsaida, and "the conclusion of the day took place in the evening with the *Pleurody,* in the deepest devotion to the Mother City."[31]

Spangenberg shared in this adoration of the side wound as the homeland of the soul. In 1757 he sang "Lick on Jesus Christ" and "spoke about the bloody side as our home."[32] This theme of the side wound being the womb of Christ, the birthplace of the soul, and the eternal home of the Christian sums up many levels of meaning of the side wound as the sum of the Christian life.

As we can see from the numerous quotations and descriptions given above, the Gemeine of Bethlehem completely and thoroughly endorsed Zinzendorf's blood-and-wounds theology. They lived, worshipped, worked, and loved within the side wound of Christ. It is no wonder that one diarist could relate, "We all felt homesick for the side."[33]

It should be impossible to deny that throughout the 1740s and 1750s the Gemeine of Bethlehem was thoroughly imbued with the blood-and wounds-theology of Zinzendorf. The litanies, liturgies, and hymns were filled with this imagery, and it was the major mode of discourse within the Gemeine. Children were raised singing praises to the side wound, and the dead were laid to rest in the open side.

It should also be clear that the traditional understanding of the Sifting Time does not explain the piety of Bethlehem. The adoration of the wounds, marriage mysticism, and the motherhood of the Holy Spirit were persistent and consistent facets of life in Bethlehem throughout the period of the General Economy. Spangenberg, Böhler, and the other leaders in Bethlehem were active participants in this piety.

Yet the question remains, why would Bethlehem embrace such a form of devotion and discourse, which was and remains offensive to many people? What was the magnetic attraction of the wounds of Christ? Despite the usefulness of a theological explanation for the meaning of the wounds cult, it does not completely answer this vexing question of why it was embraced so wholeheartedly, without reservation, by the community. Part of the answer to the attraction of the wounds cult lies in its social usefulness within a communal society.

INTERPRETING THE WOUNDS CULT

Many modern observers view Zinzendorf's blood-and-wounds theology as an expression of some type of psychological pathology. The psychologist and pas-

---

31. "Der Schluss des Tages geschahe Abends mit der Pleurodie, in der innigsten Andach zur Mutterstadt." Ibid., Jan. 20, 1760; cf. June 2, 1759.

32. Ibid., Oct. 20, 1757. Earlier in the year Böhler (March 14) had also preached on this theme.

33. Ibid., Sept. 3 (Sept. 14, n.s.), 1748.

tor Oskar Pfister subjected the hymns of the Brüdergemeine in the 1740s to a thorough Freudian analysis and concluded that they revealed a deeply troubled psyche struggling to cope with childhood repression. Pfister's diagnosis was that Zinzendorf had transferred his severely repressed sexual drive to Jesus, making the side wound a vaginal symbol. Zinzendorf found sexual release in fantasizing about sucking and licking this ersatz vagina.[34]

Pfister also raised questions about possible homosexuality as well as sado-masochism in Zinzendorf. He based this diagnosis on Zinzendorf's promotion of the mystical marriage with Christ for both men and women and the connection of that mystical marriage with the graphic details of the torture and murder of Jesus.

Reichel, Bettermann, Beyreuther, and other scholars of the modern Brüdergemeine in Germany understandably rejected the conclusions of Pfister. Bettermann offered the most sophisticated refutation of Pfister by demonstrating the deep theological concerns addressed in Zinzendorf's metaphors. In various ways, though, they followed the lead of Zinzendorf's first great apologist, Spangenberg, who argued that Zinzendorf adapted his language for the benefit of his listeners and experimented with strange expressions in order to better communicate the truth of the gospel.[35]

The eighteenth-century translator of Zinzendorf's discourses on the Augsburg Confession, Francis Okeley, defended Zinzendorf in a similar manner. "Some Sentiments and Expressions of his may possibly seem new and strange at first sight; but Experience has shewn, that they will gradually approve themselves, and discover their solid Truth and Propriety, in proportion as Men are willing to hear the holy Spirit's preliminary Lessons to their Heart, and with Simplicity to enter deep into the practical divine Science of the Cross and Wounds of Jesus, their only Creator and Redeemer."[36] Zinzendorf himself defended the hymns of the infamous *Appendix XII,* as thoroughly scriptural. "Our phrases cannot be attacked without reproaching the Holy Scriptures, especially the New Testament."[37]

Linguistic and theological explanation does not solve every problem associated with blood-and-wounds theology, however, because it does not adequately explain why Zinzendorf fixated so much on the side wound of Christ. Why did this image become the dominant symbol in his theology? We have to acknowledge some soundness in Pfister's insight that psychology as well as theology is

---

34. Pfister, *Die Frömmigkeit des Grafen Ludwig von Zinzendorf,* 5, 57–64.

35. E.g., Erich Beyreuther, "Einführung in die Öffentlichen Gemein-Reden", ZH 4, vii.

36. Zinzendorf, *Twenty-one Discourses or Dissertations upon the Augsburg-Confession which is also the Brethren's Confession of Faith,* trans. Francis Okeley (London: W. Bowyer, 1753), iii.

37. Zinzendorf, *Einundzwanzig Diskurse* 7:148.

at work here. It is undeniable that the death of Jesus was eroticized in the wounds cult. It does not take Freud to recognize that the side wound is a vaginal symbol, especially when Zinzendorf and the Moravians repeatedly identified it as a womb or birth canal, as we have seen.

There are, however, two major problems with the Pfister thesis. One is that such symbolism is not *ipso facto* pathological. It is possible that Zinzendorf's fantasy life was very healthy for him and his community. One must beware of equating the unusual or even abnormal with the pathological. Zinzendorf was an amazingly effective person who earned the admiration and devotion of thousands of people from dozens of countries. He had a prodigious capacity for work and fathered several children. It is not to be denied that he was an extremely eccentric person and prone to arouse hatred as much as love, but it is hard to see him as pathological if one ignores his religious language.

Pfister takes the only symptom of a supposed pathology as the proof of that pathology without corroborating evidence. There is little or nothing in Zinzendorf's life to suggest a deep-seated psychosis other than his adoration of the wounds. Second, Pfister largely ignores the Brüdergemeine. Zinzendorf was the author of many blood-and-wounds hymns, and he was certainly the architect of that theology, but the hymns were read and sung and cherished by thousands of people, many of whom wrote their own hymns and poems in this style.[38] Therefore, even if Pfister adequately explains Zinzendorf's psyche and his use of wounds language, his theory fails to account for the enduring popularity of the wounds cult in Bethlehem.

A variation on Pfister's theme would be some type of group pathology. This theory lies behind some of the scholarship on the Sifting Time that presents the 1740s as a time of religious fanaticism infecting the Brüdergemeine. The theory of group pathology has drawbacks as well, however. One of them has been noted frequently in this study: the language and concepts of the 1740s were the same as those of the 1750s and even the early 1760s in the Brüdergemeine and were used by individuals who all scholars agree were rational and healthy persons.

A second problem is that, as with the question of Zinzendorf's supposed pathology, one seeks in vain for evidence of pathology in the Brüdergemeine apart from the religious language. In an age in which witch hunts were still a fresh memory and messianic pretenders appeared in many places, the Brüdergemeine seems rather conventional.[39] Observers were more impressed with the Bethlehem Moravians' industry and harmony than with any deviant behavior.

38. See, for example, Pfeifer-Quaile, "Self-Expression of Moravians in North Carolina."
39. David S. Lovejoy, *Religious Enthusiasm in the New World* (Cambridge: Harvard University Press, 1985).

Some of us might be tempted to say that Bethlehem, with its discipline, love, and order among persons of many different races was healthier than the rest of colonial American society, which was routinely murdering native peoples, enslaving Africans, and abusing women and children. Could it be that the cult of the wounds was a major factor in the remarkable success of Bethlehem?

THE FUNCTION OF THE WOUNDS CULT

Theories of pathology fail to account for the phenomenon, but we should not minimize blood-and-wounds theology. It is no accident that this theology thrived during the period of the General Economy in Bethlehem. In fact, the preservation of that communal system depended in part on the emotional, graphic, and disturbing language of the cult of the wounds. Pfister's insights into the unconscious psychological nature of the wounds language are valid, but that language should be examined on an anthropological, not an individual, level.

As long as Bethlehem remained a carefully regulated communal society, wounds theology was useful, indeed vital. Wounds language represented the unique dialect of the Brüdergemeine, setting its members apart from the rest of the world. Outsiders are often most offended by what is most meaningful to insiders.

As Zinzendorf put it, the brides of Christ had their own "jargon," which the unconverted do not understand and should not attempt to speak. It was a language for intimate moments with the Bridegroom, an erotic language based on the Song of Solomon and the cross of Jesus, which identified its speakers as brides of Christ.[40] Likewise, according to Zinzendorf, the language of the motherly care of the Holy Spirit is for the Gemeine alone, not the world. Only those who have experienced the motherhood of the Spirit can speak this language authentically.[41]

Such an internal discourse serves at least three related purposes: (1) It provides a strong sense of personal identity with the community and its mission by providing a common language. (2) It marks the boundary with the outside world so that members know who does not belong. In this respect, the attack of Whitefield on the language of *Appendices XI* and *XII* marked his final break with the Moravians. "From New York we hear that Mr. Whitefield has declared himself more clearly in opposition to us—that he is not only against us, but rather also against the things of the Savior. He ridicules our litany of the wounds and speaks ill about our 2nd Part of Hymns [Engl. 1746]. It is to be

---

40. Zinzendorf, *Gemeinreden* ZH 4:41:208.
41. Ibid., 46:248, cf. 255–56; ibid., 36:134.

feared that he himself no longer knows what he believes."[42] (3) The wounds cult also helps keep people within the society by marking them as "strange" to the outside world. For instance, a Brüdergemeine minister named "Hagen, in Chekomeco, went to visit Rhinebeck and encountered a minister who had recently come from Germany who was so disturbed over the *Litany of the Wounds* that he came close to striking Hagen."[43]

All of this increased the tendency of Bethlehem to isolate itself from the world and to keep the heart of its worship a secret.[44] As early as 1747 the Gemeine was urged to keep some things, such as "cross-air bird" language, secret from the world. "Such books, letters, and hymns should be handled carefully and not communicated so freely because it is unbearable for the wounds of Jesus and similar things to be prostituted to the ridicule of the world."[45]

This remained a concern long after the so-called Sifting Time. What has sometimes been interpreted as a pulling back from wounds language after 1750 was simply a new caution about putting such language into print. In 1760 the members were informed that "Everyone who has a liturgy book should take care that it does not fall into strange hands. The word of the Lord applies here, 'You shall not throw holy things in front of dogs nor pearls before swine.' The deep, divine truths that are in the *Büchlein* must never become material for controversy, and therefore no one should get hold of it, other than who will use it with an inner feeling."[46] Even today the boundary between insiders and outsiders has been preserved; but the outsiders now include modern Moravians. Only those who lived in the Gemeine and shared the religious experience and mission of the Gemeine could speak the language of the wounds.

Mary Douglas argues that the social body and the physical human body are closely related. "The social body constrains the way the physical body is perceived. The physical experience of the body, always modified by the social categories through which it is known, sustains a particular view of society."[47] In Douglas's terms, rituals are a restricted code or a condensed set of symbols, and the body is a key component of that code. The Moravians, as we have seen, certainly controlled their physical bodies, even to the point of regulating sexual relations among married persons.

42. July 15, 1747, Helper's Conference Minutes, Moravian Archives, Bethlehem.

43. *Bethlehem Diary* (Moravian Archives), June 30 (July 11, n.s.), 1746.

44. Fogleman, "Jesus Is Female," argues that this was a major source of conflict between the Brethren and their neighbors.

45. Feb. 24 (March 7, n.s.), 1747 (¶ 7), Engere Conferenz Minutes, Moravian Archives, Bethlehem. This was motivated by the fact that "some of the Brüdergemeine works, including the 'Salt for the Sheep and Lambs' and the *Litany of the Wounds,* are coming into the hands of the public and being misused."

46. *Bethlehem Diary* (Moravian Archives), June 28, 1760, Verlass des von 26ten bis 29ten June 1760 in Lititz gehaltenen Brüder-Synodi (¶ 7), 605.

47. Douglas, *Natural Symbols,* 69.

Following Douglas's anthropological ideas, we would expect that the strict ordering of Bethlehem society would be connected to symbols of bodily separation from pollution and violation.[48] However, the central symbol of Bethlehem was an open wound in the body of Christ. This does not seem to fit Douglas's theory. How could a society with such strict boundaries and rules of behavior worship a bleeding orifice?

The body of Christ did indeed represent Bethlehem's social structure, as Douglas's theory predicts, but in ways unique to Bethlehem's paradoxical nature as a missionary settlement that valued both personal experience and communal structure. The wounds cult was an essential feature of the ritual and social system that strengthened community boundaries by providing an internal discourse while allowing a point of entry for new members.

As we have seen, persons entered the community through the side wound of Christ. This was more than just a graphic expression of the traditional Christian doctrine that all are saved by the death of Jesus. It was also an expression of the community's own clear boundaries from the outside world. Residence within the community was rigidly controlled and visitors were isolated as much as possible.[49]

Entrance into the community, whether by birth or conversion, was literally an act of violence to the social structure. Rather than simply stagnate, though, the Moravians actively sought new members through conversion and procreation; therefore there had to be a way to bring them into the Gemeine ritually. The entry through the side wound of Christ helped serve this purpose. The violence experienced by the Gemeine when new members joined was ritualized as violence on the body of Christ. The metaphorical body was forced to yield a new and unique orifice through which persons could enter. The boundary was provided in the form of a bloody hole that allowed the flow of people in and out that was necessary for survival.

WOUNDS AS SUBLIMATION

Life in a communal society such as Bethlehem had many personal benefits in terms of security and intimacy, but it also involved a tremendous personal cost. Personal needs had to be sacrificed for the mission and harmony of the community. Individuals were required to give up much of their privacy and autonomy. The adoration of the wounds and corpse of Jesus served to sublimate a variety of personal needs and fears that would have otherwise destroyed the community.

48. In Douglas's terminology, the Moravians had both high "grid" and high "group," meaning that there was a focus on socially determined roles (*Natural Symbols,* 55–60).

49. Daniel Thorp's theory that the Moravian community of Bethabara had permeable boundaries applies equally well to Bethlehem. Thorp, *Moravian Community in Colonial North Carolina,* 178–98.

In Victor Turner's terminology, the graphic, even taboo, quality of wounds worship provided the "anti-structure" that allowed the residents of Bethlehem to experience *communitas* on a regular basis without destroying the structure itself.[50] In short, the wounds of Christ acted in more than one way to create the sense of the sacred that allowed the Bethlehem community to thrive.

One of the ways communal tension was dealt with in Bethlehem was through the eroticization of the wounds. Here is where Pfister's insight into the sexual nature of the blood-and-wounds theology is most helpful, but one must transpose his personal psychological theory about Zinzendorf to a social key. Residents of Bethlehem repressed their own erotic drives in favor of the community through the choir system, but such needs can be repressed only so far. The wounds cult provided an outlet for sexual energy that was community-enhancing rather than community-destroying.

As we have seen, even traditional marriage was dangerous and prone to destroy the Gemeine. Husbands and wives as well as single women and men were directed to focus sexuality on Christ rather than each other. This was accomplished through the mystical marriage combined with the wounds worship. Release came in worship when "the whole Gemeine fell before its bloody husband and his *pleura,* and lay there trembling in the presence of the side hole."[51] The adoration of the side wound of Jesus, with its compact symbolism (womb, vagina, breast, bed, etc.), could incite and satisfy the erotic desires of the whole Gemeine. "Our Morning Blessing was especially bloody and juicy. The Married People sang from its place in the pleura, its 'Ave,' and the youthful flock trembled behind in the side hole, whose new manifestation they observed today with a blessed sensation of shaking from love's fever."[52]

It was important to the Gemeine to keep the erotic tied to the wounds of Christ because a too-overt sexualizing of religion in Bethlehem would have brought the Gemeine under legal censure and would also have made it difficult to keep the members from acting physically on their mental imagery. Thus the erotic was combined with the repulsive. The side wound could be a sexual image only so long as it remained a wound. If it were to become too clearly a vagina, the ability of this symbolism to sublimate sexuality would be lost.[53]

Another psychological toll paid in a communal society is the repression of aggression, particularly against fellow members of the society. This was com-

50. Turner, *The Ritual Process,* 96–96, 131–40.

51. *Bethlehem Diary* (Moravian Archives), Dec. 31, 1748.

52. Ibid., April 29 (May 10, n.s.), 1748.

53. I strongly suspect that this is what happened during the so-called Sifting Time. Since some of the pertinent documents have been destroyed, we many never know for sure. I suspect that the way some single men referred to the side wound, which upset Zinzendorf so, came too close to making this identification of wounds theology and sexuality. Cf. Peucker, "Blut' auf unsre grünen Bändchen," 55–77.

pounded in the case of Bethlehem because the Moravians were functionally pacifist and theologically called to love their enemies.[54] Through the choir system and the intricate structure of pastoral supervision, the Gemeine worked hard to keep members from harboring ill feelings toward one another.

Community rituals supported this structure of conflict resolution. Shortly after Spangenberg began his second term, he restored order in Bethlehem, in part through personal leadership and in part through the rituals of the Gemeine. He brought erring brothers to repentance and absolved them through community ritual that focused on wounds imagery.

The ritualized torture and murder of Jesus served to transfer violent emotions out of the Gemeine and into the mythical realm. Night after night they witnessed the dying of Jesus, often in gory detail. There are numerous descriptions of the cathartic release that residents experienced as a result. Violence was imaginatively expressed and at the same time forgiven. The worshipper participated in the act of violence while at the same time receiving absolution for his sins from the one being wounded.

Thus Jesus served as the ultimate scapegoat for the Gemeine, both theologically and in daily practice. The community imaginatively acted out destructive and self-destructive impulses in a safe environment. As René Girard has argued, the violence of Christian liturgy can help overcome society's tendency toward actual violence.[55] This was evidently the case in Bethlehem.

The wounds cult helps us understand the ability of the Brüdergemeine to repress the natural fear of death, as well. For centuries Christian doctrine has taught that death is not to be feared by those who have faith in Christ, but rarely are people, even the devoutly faithful, able to repress this fear successfully. The Brüdergemeine did a remarkable job in replacing the fear of death with a sense of joy in dying. During the communal period in Bethlehem, there was an overwhelming sense of joy and celebration, even a longing for death. This is the result, in part, of the breakup of traditional emotional ties through the choir system, but it is also related to the wounds cult. The dying were comforted by the contemplation of the wounds.

It was not surprising that Caspar Boekcel enjoyed hymns such as "My wounds of Jesus, Yes mine!" as he was dying, or that "he faded away nicely and happily with the words, 'At the end of all need.'"[56] Br. Steifel was similarly

---

54. For instance, during the violence of the French and Indian War the Moravians were often in danger, but the fear and desire for revenge could be channeled through the wounds cult, as when Spangenberg applied the Hymns to the Wounds to the situation of Seidel, who had barely escaped hostile natives. *Bethlehem Diary* (Moravian Archives), Oct. 31, 1756.

55. René Girard, *I See Satan Fall Like Lightning,* trans. James G. Williams (Maryknoll, N.Y.: Orbis, 2001); René Girard, *Violence and the Sacred,* trans. Patrick Gregory (Baltimore: Johns Hopkins University Press, 1972).

56. *Bethlehem Diary* (Moravian Archives), Aug. 9, 1758, Beilage, 131–32.

comforted by verses about the side hole that were sung by the Single Brothers as he died. "They formed a circle around him and sang him many beautiful side hole stanzas with music for going home; and then his spirit was revived and he came back to himself because his soul lives so entirely in the material of the side hole, so that he babbled much along with them, as well as he could, and raised up his hands in joy, which, for such an old Separatist, was a quite nice sight."[57] He died while Nathanael Seidel sang "wounds hymns" to him.

This contemplation of the wounds of Jesus at the time of death was in part an expression of the desire for union with God and a sense of the assurance of salvation through the Atonement, but it was also related to the scapegoating of Christ. The horrors of dying were not denied in Bethlehem, but they were transferred from the dying individual to his or her Savior-God.[58]

By enduring all of these things and rising to new life, Christ removed their horror. This overcoming, at least partially, of the fear of death helped the Gemeine survive and thrive. Its members could give themselves entirely to the Gemeine without being distracted by their own mortality. Moreover, they were prepared to face death in the mission fields whenever the Gemeine determined that it was time to go.

In summary, the vivid imaginative life of the Brüdergemeine was not pathological. In fact, it was a key factor in the success of Bethlehem's communal society. It provided a mythology and ritual that allowed the members of the society to sublimate a variety of personal drives and fears to the mystical realm for the good of the Gemeine and its mission.

The sense of ecstasy and joy experienced in the worship of the wounds, so often reported in the Bethlehem Diary, was real. It was a religious experience inextricably connected to a deep psychological experience of catharsis. The brothers and sisters of Bethlehem did indeed sleep in the arms of their Creator and were drawn into his side wound. There they found both ecstasy and security.

57. Ibid., Oct. 2 (Oct. 13, n.s.), 1748, (¶ 4).

58. Atwood, "The Joyfulness of Death"; Philippe Ariès, *The Hour of Our Death,* trans. Helen Weaver (New York: Knopf, 1981), 110–23.

CONCLUSION

Nikolaus Ludwig Graf von Zinzendorf was certainly one of the most creative and controversial figures within the Pietist movement, and his Brüdergemeine was the most successful of the radical Pietist groups in the eighteenth century. Although Zinzendorf and his movement remained in the orbit of the Lutheran Church, his theology combined elements of radical, mystical Pietism with Luther's theology of the cross in provocative and compelling ways.

The theology of Zinzendorf was an organic rather than a mechanistic system. On the surface it might appear inconsistent and even at times contradictory. Certainly it lacked the scope and completeness of a systematic theology or a *summa,* but it had an internal coherence. Once one enters into the thought and accepts the fundamental principles of Zinzendorf's heart religion, the rest of his theology makes sense. His sermons, litanies, and hymns focus on a few multifaceted and evocative images that can be summed up in two related phrases: "Your Creator is your Savior" and "Your Creator is your Husband." His teaching on sexuality, Christian community, ethics, salvation, and mission all revolve around these two points.

For those who entered into Zinzendorf's imagery, it proved to be extremely creative and powerful, providing a belief system with which they could confront the challenges of modernity. The form of Christianity that Zinzendorf developed served as a bulwark against the forces of anomie in a changing world and unleashed the power of the human spirit to create community.

Life in Bethlehem was a clear reflection of Zinzendorf's basic principles and doctrines. The Gemeine read his sermons, prayed his litanies, sang his hymns, and wrote in his style. He provided the language with which they interpreted their world and the framework on which they built their society. From conception to burial, the life of the residents in Bethlehem was shaped by the theology of Zinzendorf; or, as he would put it, all aspects of life in Bethlehem were born out of the side wound of the Savior. Spangenberg was the craftsman who created the General Economy and organized the life of Bethlehem, but Zinzendorf provided the soul and motivating spirit of the endeavor. It was his theology that gave birth to Bethlehem and underlay every facet of its social life.

This theology met the intellectual and religious needs of the Moravians, but it also met various social and psychological needs that otherwise could easily have destroyed a religious commune. The embodiment of Zinzendorf's theology in the choir system and in the community's ritual life helped to erase the line between the sacred and the secular so that all activities, even marital intimacy, could become part of the work and worship of the Gemeine. Likewise, a wide range of human desires and emotions were brought into the religious realm and safely resolved without threat to the communal welfare.

Zinzendorf's paradoxical theology allowed the Moravians to create a community that resolved many of the contradictions of human life. Conflicting human needs and drives, even those of Eros and Thanatos, could be transcended by the exclusive devotion to the wounded and bleeding Husband whose own body revealed the violent forces of human life. Theology, piety, and society were united to create an effective and stable communal society in colonial Pennsylvania.

THE END OF THE GENERAL ECONOMY

Zinzendorf died in 1760, and the Brüdergemeine lost its creative genius. Through the years he had been able to introduce new devotions and festivals, such as the Chief Eldership of Christ and the Enthronement of the Holy Spirit as Mother, as needed, but his successors could only blow upon the dying embers of his creativity. Johannes von Watteville and Spangenberg failed to institutionalize his charisma, and the Brüdergemeine became more orthodox and less vigorous.[1]

More important for the Bethlehem story, soon after Zinzendorf died, the leadership in Europe, in particular the financial director Koeber, decided to dissolve Bethlehem's communal structure. Spangenberg resisted this action, but in April 1761 he was ordered to proceed with the dissolution of the system he had carefully constructed.[2] He did so reluctantly, but he believed that once the process had begun, only a full transformation of the economy could preserve the spiritual well-being of the membership. The news of the proposed change affected morale in the community, immediately lessening the missionary and communal spirit. The transition itself proved to be very painful and took nearly ten years to complete.

Unfortunately for the Brüdergemeine in Europe, the dissolution of the General Economy did not achieve the desired results. In fact, it created a social

---

1. Nelson, "Herrnhut: Friedrich Schleiermacher's Spiritual Homeland," chap. 13, discusses the Spangenberg era.
2. Erbe, *Bethlehem, Pa.*, 127–36, gives the story of the negotiations between Spangenberg and the financial director, Koeber.

and economic crisis that nearly destroyed Bethlehem. The effect of the forced dissolution of the General Economy was more damaging and lasting than the deleterious effects of the so-called Sifting Time. The mission of Bethlehem was curtailed, schools were reduced in size, people renounced the Brüdergemeine, and once-profitable industries began to lose money.[3]

One clear indication of the harm caused by the dissolution was that the population of Bethlehem began to decline after 1761. By 1766 there were almost a hundred fewer people in the village than in 1761. This decrease continued until 1818.[4] In her detailed examination of the demographic picture of Bethlehem over its first hundred years, Smaby shows that the dissolution affected every aspect of social life, including birth rates, marriage age, and migration. "There is considerable demographic evidence that the fifty-year period between the end of the Communal Economy and the General Synod of 1818 was socially stressful. The long slow decrease in the population, the increasing rates of withdrawal, the negative figures for natural increase, the drop in marriage rates, the even steeper drop in birth rates, and the astoundingly high average age at first marriage all point to extreme stress."[5]

Bethlehem persisted as a closed society (only members of the Brüdergemeine could live there) until 1844, but the last fifty years of its existence witnessed a steady decline of social, economic, and religious vitality. The American Revolution hastened its demise by introducing ideas of freedom and independence. Gradually the younger generation abandoned the unique practices and social structures of the original settlers. It grew increasingly difficult to enforce choir discipline and the segregation of the genders.

Young men and women stopped obeying the lot or even the advice of the elders in deciding their marriages. Violations of the authority of the elders grew more common after 1800, and residents chafed under the economic restrictions imposed by the church. At the General Synod of 1818, the American Moravians asked for permission to dispense with some of the more unique practices, such as *Sprechen*, arranged marriages, the use of the lot (in most matters), and having pastors in charge of financial affairs.[6] It was during this period that the Brüdergemeine in America became the Moravian Church and more or less consciously rejected its Zinzendorfian heritage.

The decline of Bethlehem is related to a rejection of Zinzendorf's theology in favor of a moderate form of American evangelicalism during this same period. Since the communal structure of Bethlehem and the theology of Zinzen-

3. Ibid., 145–46; Smaby, *Transformation of Moravian Bethlehem*, 35.
4. Smaby, *Transformation of Moravian Bethlehem*, 51.
5. Ibid., 83.
6. Hamilton and Hamilton, *History*, 233–34.

dorf had a symbiotic relationship, it is to be expected that as Bethlehem declined as a religious community so would its appreciation of Zinzendorf's theology. This issue merits further research, but for now we can see some illuminating signs of this retreat from Zinzendorf's theology.

First, the sermons distributed through the *Gemein Nachrichten* include virtually none of Zinzendorf's sermons after 1775. A Zinzendorf revival in 1774 did not last long. Second, hymnals after 1780, especially the English-language ones, contain more typically Anglo-American Protestant hymns. Hymns about blood, wounds, sex, and death were slowly replaced by hymns about providence, conversion, and consecration. As the Brethren began to sing like other people, they began to live like them.

Third, there is the surprising history of the translation of Zinzendorf's works into English.[7] During Zinzendorf's life, there was a vigorous attempt to communicate his ideas to the non-German world. The Brüdergemeine translated portions of many of his works, and in some cases long discourses. These are honest translations that do not draw back from Zinzendorf's less traditional expressions of religious faith. The Gemeine clearly felt the need to communicate its beliefs to the literate public. Soon after Zinzendorf's death, however, translation ceased entirely. For nearly two hundred years no one was translating Zinzendorf in America, not even as the American Moravians switched from German to English in work and worship.

Fourth, there is the bookstore record in Bethlehem. In the 1750s the shelves were filled with thousands of volumes of Zinzendorf's published works, to be distributed throughout the colonies. Yet by the 1790s virtually none of his works were available. Even the preachers and teachers of Bethlehem had turned away from Zinzendorf. Ideas and images that had been compelling to their parents and grandparents seemed embarrassing or anachronistic to a generation that had lived through a revolution. This is seen in John Ettwein, the leader of Bethlehem at the end of the eighteenth century. He attached an interesting note at the beginning of the Bethlehem Diary for the year 1747: "For memory: I pray that whoever reads this diary in future times will overlook the overwrought expressions, of the side hole, brown hearts, black hearts, the marriage, and etc. If someone were to have the time and desire to copy [this diary] and leave out such words and phrases, he would do a good service to future generations."[8]

---

7. Atwood, "Introduction."
8. "Pro memoria: Wer in kunftigen Zeiten diese Diaria lesen will wird gebeten: die übertrieben Redens-Arten, vom Seiten-hölgen, Braunen Herzten, schwarzen Herzten, der Ehe, zu übersehen. Wer Zeit und Lust dazu hätte, sie zu copiren und solche Worte und Phrases weg zu lassen, thäte der Nachwelt einen Guten dienst damit."

Thankfully, no one took this advice. Still, we can safely conclude that as Bethlehem's communal society declined, so did the use of Zinzendorf's theology and piety. The Moravians became virtually indistinguishable from their neighbors in how they worshipped and worked, prayed and loved, lived and died. As a new generation turned away from the graphic imagery of Zinzendorf, they lost the intense relationship with Christ that their parents had considered their reason for being. Correspondingly, they lost the ability to live in an intimate communal setting and aggressively serve Christ.

Zinzendorf's creative genius gave birth to a city in the wilderness and infused it with strength to endure through many crises, but later generations successfully exorcised from their doctrine and worship what they considered a dangerous demon. The Moravians of the 1780s and 1790s gradually purged their liturgy of its devotion to the mother, the side wound of Jesus, the heavenly community, and other "unseemly" practices, without realizing that they were cutting off their Gemeine from its source of life.

The nineteenth century witnessed the gradual transformation of the Brüdergemeine, a vigorous and distinctive international community, into the Moravian Church in America, a small American evangelical denomination. The provocative and creative theology of Zinzendorf could have no place in such a conventional church. The nineteenth-century Moravians did what the Saxon government and Halle fathers could not; they silenced Zinzendorf.

APPENDIX 1

Membership Statistics of the Brüdergemeine in 1743

In the *Gemeinorten:*[1]
 Herrnhut, 750
 Heerendyk (Holland), 30
 Montmirail, 10
 Marienborn, 150
 Herrnhaag, 400
 The Ronneburg (also in Wetteravia), 100
 Official church workers, 700

Members of the Brüdergemeine scattered in various areas:
 Upper Lusatia, 1,700
 Saxony, 100
 Bohemia, 300
 Silesia, 2,000
 Wetteravia, 200
 Holland, 300
 Sweden, 100
 Württemberg, 200
 Augsburg, 30
 Franconia, 300
 Thuringia, 500
 Iceland, 1
 Vogtland, 200
 Berlin, 100
 Magdeburg and Pommerania, 300
 Holstein and Jutland, 500
 St. Petersburg, 2
 Denmark, 500
 Sweden [*sic*], 520
 Livonia, 7,000

1. Hamilton and Hamilton, *History*, 657, n. 32.

London, 300
Lamb's Inn (Fulneck), 100
Yorkshire, 1,200
Scotland, 4
Isle of Man, 1
Pennsylvania, 300
Georgia, 12
New York, 53
Hungary and Transylvania, 57

Converts in the mission fields:
Greenland, 20
Cape of Good Hope, 30
Ceylon, 5
Berbice and Surinam, 27
St. Thomas, 300
St. Croix and St. John, 3
North America (natives), 45

APPENDIX 2

Bethlehem Bookstore Catalog, March 10, 1755

Zinzendorf's Works Available in Bethlehem

170	Homiliae über die Wunden-Litaney
182	Zeyster Synod Reden von 1746
282	Augsburg Confession Discourses
175	Gemein Reden von 1747 in 2 Theilen
5	" " Erster Theil, separ.
189	Oeffentliche Gemein Reden
6	" " Eingebunden
11	Der 32 Homilien von 1744, 45, und 46
150	" " 8 Homil. fehlen
24	Einer Predigt, vom Zeugniß der grosser Religions Wahrheiten in 1754 in London gehalten
69	Sixteen Discourses from Berlin, 2d ed.
12	Maximes (London 1754)
89	Discourse of the Augs. Confession
34	Plain Case
2	Pensylv. 7 Synodos von 1741
43	Periteauta
7	Der Jüngers naturelle Reflexiones
91	Sieben letzte Reden von 1741
96	Wacte [sic] des Treuen und Wahrl. Zeugen auf 1754
32	Collectio 2nd Flohculi Theol. Patrist.
220	Der Jüngers Predigten in Lond. seit 1751
297	Texte von [seine] lieben Nähe
50	Enchirid. Biblic. Genes
50	Texte auf Genese und Exodo
200	Stück der neuem Reden des Ord. seit 1751
200	Kinder Reden ungebunden
300	Berliner Reden
300	Bertholdsdorfer [sic] Reden
50	Harmonien

[This represents nearly 3,500 volumes of Zinzendorf's writings, not including his daily watchwords *(Losungen)* and liturgical pieces.]

Other Items:

67	M. A. G. Spangenbergs Declaration
16	" " Darlegung
10	" " Einigebunde
39	" " *Schluß-Schrift*
4	" " Erste separat.
400	Wilcoks honig Tropfen
1,500	A.B.C. büchlein English von New York
28	Wärtlichen Extract auß dem Pro memoria in sachen Herr-nhaags
5	Le Synodie de Berne del' An. 1532 (London 1752)
6	Büdingsche Sammlungen 2nd Theil (1 defective)
5	Representation of the Engl. Cong. with the Morav.
199	Buchstabia-buchlein
600	" " Phil. Edit.
1	Krasse Bauler Bibel mit grobe. druck

APPENDIX 3
Moravian Litanies Used in Bethlehem

THE LITANY OF THE WOUNDS OF THE HUSBAND[2]

First Choir	Second Choir
Hail!	Lamb of God.
Christ,	Have mercy!
Glory	to the side wound!

Lord God Father in Heaven!

Remember the bitter death of your son. Look at his five holy, red wounds which are indeed the payment and ransom for the whole world. May we console ourselves with this at all times, and hope for mercy.

Lord God, Son, Savior of the World!

We would all be ruined by our crimes, except that you have gained for us the doorway to heaven. Glory and memory to the side wound.

Lord God, Holy Spirit!

Preach daily the wounds of the Lamb to his Communities of the Cross which have found him. It is your office.

You Holy Trinity, blessed be you for the sake of the Lamb.

Lamb of God, holy Lord and God, receive the prayer of our need. Have mercy on us all!

---

2. The German originals may be found in ZE 2. The *Litany of the Wounds of the Husband* is taken from Zinzendorf, *Wundenlitanei Homilien,* ZH 3, pages not numbered. Translated with the assistance of Ricarda Fröhlich.

From all self-righteousness;
From all lack of discipline;
From all unbloodied grace;
From hearts that have not been bled upon;
From all beauty without streaks of blood;
From indifference to your wounds;
From estrangement from your cross;
From being weaned from your side;
From unanointed gossip about the blood;
From eternal mortal sin;

Preserve us, dear Lord God!

May your painful first birth	*Make us love our humanness!*
May your holy first wound[3]	*Help us circumcise our hearts!*
May your childlikeness	*Help us to have childlike joy!*
May your first exile	*Teach us to be at home everywhere!*
May your first maturity	*Make our adolescence holy!*
May your diligence with your study	*Make us learned for the Kingdom of God!*
May your youth	*Bless the unmarried choirs!*
May your faithful sweat of labor	*Make all labor easy for us!*
May your faithfulness to your craft	*Make us true on our part!*
May your astonishing simplicity	*Make reason hateful to us!*
May your proper Bible foundation	*Make us all know our Bible!*
May your meritorious ignorance	*Fence in our understanding!*
May your exemplary temple devotion	*Make us faithful people of religion!*
May your powerlessness and weakness	*Make our weakness welcome to us!*
May your theology of the cross	*Remain our confession of faith!*
May your righteousness to the last will	*Make us faithful to your will!*
May your will, validated by your death	*Remain the rule of your heirs!*
May the fulfillment of your will	*Bring the scattered children of God into the ark of holy Christianity!*
May your fear of suffering and death	*Put to shame the courage of the martyrs!*

---

3. I.e., circumcision.

May your reliance on your heavenly Father to suffer and not to suffer

Be our decree on your own divinity!

May your willing passion

Teach us tolerance!

May your holy baptism of blood

Ignite all of God's earth!

May your sweat in penitential struggle

Pour over us in body and soul!

Your scratches from the crown of thorns,

Mark us on our foreheads!

Pale lips,

Kiss us on the heart!

Mouth dripping spittle,

That you would not have to spit out anyone!

Cheeks spat upon,

That the Father may not spit upon us!

Dead eyes,

Look out through our eyes!

Bloody foam from your back,

Wash our feet!

Sweat-soaked hair,

Dry them!

Open arms,

Receive us!

O your holy five wounds

Do like Elisha! We want to be the child!

Pierced hands,

Show us where we are written!

Nail-bored feet,

When you stand again on the Mount of Olives!

You sign of the Son of Man,

Appear to Israel according to the flesh, before you come in the clouds!

You large side hole,

Take in the entire world!

But also side chasm,

To you I pray especially, oh, keep your people, and me!

May your pierced heart

Beat and leap over us!

May you unnamed and unknown wounds,

Be greeted, all of you!

Worthy wounds of Jesus,

Who will keep us from honoring you here and there forever? You have earned it.

Covenant wounds of Jesus,

One must praise God, who has preserved us up to your time, where one has something.

Dearest wounds of Jesus,

Whoever does not love you, and does not give his whole heart to you, holds nothing dear.

Wondrous wounds of Jesus,

Holy fissures, you make sinners holy, and thieves from saints. How amazing!

Powerful wounds of Jesus,

So moist, so gory, bleed on my heart so

	that I may remain brave and like the wounds.
Closing wounds of Jesus,	*If I could rest and feed my soul between you, close again.*
Mysterious wounds of Jesus,	*I thank the pastors, who made me known with the bruises and gashes of my Lamb.*
Wound-Shadow[4] of Jesus	*By your Light, may I still paint many an image of your tortured visage in the heart.*
Clear wounds of Jesus,	*With whom it is true, the way is white, when it is clear in heaven and the word looks at it.[5]*
Glistening wounds of Jesus,	*You make my heart a dazzling candle of grace before the rays and lightning.*
Cavernous wounds of Jesus,	*In your treasure hoard, roomily sit many thousands kinds of sinners.*
Purple wounds of Jesus,	*You are so succulent, whatever comes near becomes like wounds and flowing with blood.*
Juicy wounds of Jesus,	*Whoever sharpens the pen and with it pierces you just a little, and licks, tastes it.*
Near wounds of Jesus,	*I do not want to be even a hair's-width from your hole.*
Painful wounds of Jesus,	*Sensitive to the Lamb, and for that reason, so grounded to the cure and so proven.*
Warm wounds of Jesus,	*In no pillow can a little child feel itself so secure before cold air.*
Dainty wounds of Jesus,	*So tender, so delicate, you are to such children proportional to little beds.*
Soft wounds of Jesus,	*I like lying calm, gently, and quiet and warm. What should I do? I crawl to you.*
Hot wounds of Jesus,	*Go on heating, until you are able to*

4. I.e., silhouette.

5. This rather confusing petition is replaced in later versions by *We want to paint still more crucifixion scenes under your streams, only bring more in the hearts!* and the previous petition is omitted.

	cover the entire world with your warmth.
Treasure wounds of Jesus,	*To them, the slaves, beggars and kings, farmers and counts make a pilgrimage.*
Eternal wounds of Jesus,	*[You are] my house to dwell in. In a million eons you will still be new.*
Our wounds of Jesus,	*Which are traveled upon by every band, young and old, great and small.*
My wounds of Jesus,	*Mine, yes mine! To me it is then, as though you were there entirely for my heart alone.*
At the end of all trouble,	*Anoint us, you red wounds.*[6]

In the meantime, I believe the death-streaked eyes, the spit-dripped mouth, the fire-baptized corpse, the thorn-scratched head, the furrows on the back:

Until I, at the proper hour, can see in my flesh the body wounded for me, on which we build so firmly, and greet close by, the works in his hands and feet.

Hail!	*Lamb of God.*
Christ,	*Have mercy!*
Glory	*To the side wound!*

The Trisagion[7]

(Choir) [1.] Congregation, come near!
(Lit.)   Before the One in Three,
          Who in these days
          Is your Father and Mother and Bridegroom!
L.   2. To the Father,
Gem.   [Come] as dust,
          Nevertheless to the believer
          [He] gives a holy and chaste
          Right to marry Jehovah in the flesh.
L.   3. To the Spirit,
Gem.   [Come] as a child
          With running eyes and heart,

6. This is probably an allusion to extreme unction.
7. Zinzendorf, *Litaney Büchlein,* 64–65.

	To hear the Mother

To hear the Mother
Declare the Lamb's wounds and boils.

Ch.   4. To Christ,

G.   [Come] as his body,
And his sinful spouse,
Redeemed and reconciled,
And attended by his holy angels.

Ch.   5. You martyr-seed,

Gem.   By the grace of God,

Lit.   The representative of his economy,

Ch.   And for the time the female disciple whom Jesus loves.

L.   6. What is He to you, then?

Gem.   My eternal Husband!
My only pain!
My only joy, my love, my heart!

Te Abba[8]

LORD GOD, we praise you.
    Your Spirit calls out, "Abba."
The only God of the Church,
    Loves to be honored by his dear children.
All angels and the host of heaven
    And those who serve to honor the Creator,
Also Cherubim and Seraphim,
    Always sing with a clear voice:
Holy FATHER God,
Of the God of Sabaoth,
Who is the God of the whole World,
And God of his Christian flock.
The Holy Twelve messengers
    Knew and named you first of all:
The faithful martyrs at all times
Faced death trusting in your gracious election (John 17:6).
    The four who rest neither Night nor Day,
    Are having to do with You
    As much as with the One who is standing on the mountain
And is moving in the sevenfold flame.
    The twenty-four Elders are

---

8. Originally, *Das Te Patrem*. Ibid., 66–68.

Twenty four who are crying "Abba!"
Your divine Glory and your Power
    Are shining out from the Son far and wide. Amen!
[1.] Indeed, you loved the world so much
    That your heart surrendered itself
    To give your Son, your joy and life,
Over to suffering and death.

    2. So that everyone who believes in him
Might be included in your household.
    But you did not leave him all alone,
You aided him at all times;
    3. Until he, having won the victory
Rose into highest heaven,
Attended by those legions
    That did not join him in his fight (Matthew 26:53).
    [4.] And when he approached the throne
You took command of the battle, (1 Cor. 15:25)
And you drew the sword and will not sheath it
Until the devils are made into footstools;
5. Until the day Hell consumes no more,
    Until death is also at an end,
Flesh, world, and sin are no more,
    And love has won its place.
    [6.] Since that time he now appears
In the sanctuary through his blood
    And sits on the seat of honor
    And rests now from his labors,
7. But you are putting on your power
That works wonders above all wonder:
Help us, your champions,
    Who are consecrated by his blood.
    [8.] Give us part in your One's salvation,
And in all of his victory.
    Help your faithful Christ's people
    And bless what he says: it is.
    9. Yes, send your dear angels to those
    Who are in the service of your dear Souls:
    Care for and nurse them for all time

And give them a powerful guidance.

[The Married Choir Sings:] *What your Christ represents*

   Daily honors you, O Father.

10. Daily, O FATHER, you are praised

   By those who claim Christ Jesus for themselves,

   Because you gave your child bare and naked

Into the womb of a maiden.

   11. Because you have favored us to be the Bride

At the marriage feast of the Son;

And because we here on this earth,

   Are becoming one in spirit with him.

   12. Because you have sent the MOTHER

   Who has already concerned herself so much with us;

Because you will be the Consecrator

When the creature weds the Creator.

   THE CHURCH'S PRAYER TO THE FATHER OF HER LORD[9]

[1.] You who are in heaven,

   Since your Son, the only one,

   God the Lord, is their brother,

  [You are] **Father of the congregation**

 2. What a name; sanctify it!

   Speak to his praise,

All ye creatures on your knees:

   JESUS,

have mercy!

  3. Father, come with your kingdom,

   That to the guiltless Lamb,

Who took on himself our punishment,

   His humanity may pay homage.

  4. As things are accustomed to go in heaven,

So also on earth:

   Your holy will shall happen

Through the flock of your Lamb.

  5. Give to us our dear bread.

   Give it to us also today:

The Righteousness before God

   From the bloody Side.

---

9. Ibid., 69–70.

6. And forgive us our sins,

As we also forgive!

For we recognize the patience

Of the Lord as our life.

7. Lead us not into temptation,

But help everyone

To be free from the evil one

And into the peace of God.

8. God, in whom the Church believes,

Jesus to please (John 17:26)

Become the Father everywhere

When he is all in all.

THE CHURCH'S PRAYER TO HER HEAD AND LORD[10]

[1.] O *Yahweh Elohim,* (Gen. 2:4)

Word of the joyous sound

From all of God's Cherubim, (Heb. 1:6, Ps. 97:7)

You are God above all! (Rom. 9:5)

2. When your name bedews us, (Song of Sol. 1.3)

It wafts through all the choirs!

And what would the Bride be

If there were no Bridegroom?

3. Sit in your kingdom

Until your champion is at hand;

For ever more be like the man

Who was exiled for us.

4. If your Body, filled with God

Holds a church festival

(L.) Father, just say, "it is my will"

(Ch.) So the saying is done *[dictum factum]*

5. Let your little flock, known by you

In the closeness of the corpse,

In your arms and at your breast

Celebrate the sacrament.

6. If to the Father something is harmed,

You can quickly arbitrate;

If the Mother is not obeyed,

10. Ibid., 80–81.

Your eye must judge it.

      7. From the false angel's light

      May you protect us!

You know how the Evil One

Had once tempted you.

      8. **Kyrie Eleison!**

The Blood of the Lamb is the master,

Before whom Satan's throne

      And all his spirits tremble.

      9. You who are all in all,

Father of all Beings!

Let us read in your eyes

      Who your Father is.

10. **Amen!**

      Our Joshua!

      Be present with this story (2 Cor. 4:6)

Of the Father's glory

      That shines in your face!

TE LOGOS[11]

Praised be the prophet (Deut. 18:15, Heb. 1:2, John 1:1)

      Who speaks from the bosom. (John 1:18)

You, maker of all creatures,

      Are naturally God to all the world.

      Thus we give to you the honor due to God.

All angels and the host of heaven,

Also the Cherubim and Seraphim,

And we sing with clear voice:

      You are the source of being *[Ens entium]*,

      The God of the nations *[Numen gentium]*,

      The Cause of Causes *[Causa causarum]*,

      Thus the God above all that is!

OR   O Father of Nature

      The Intercessor of the Creatures

      Yahweh Sabaoth

      The Living One who was dead!

No Angel is so bold and rash,

11. Ibid., 75–78.

But trembles before your *Shemhamphorash!*[12]

> The Morning Stars gazed at you,
> They saw and veiled their eyes.

There, beyond place and time,

> You were named, God the Son.

Therefore in the church it is said,

There was no time when you were not.

[Non erat ubi non eras]

> **Amen.**[13]

[1.] Your divine power and majesty

> Is recognized by the heathen in creation,

But your twelve apostles

> Saw it through your wounds.

2. The Martyrs, now resting in you,

> Who awaited them, but you? (Acts 7:55)

The entire worthy Christendom

> Praises you, Father of eternity. (Isa. 9:9)

3. The twenty-four Elohim[14] (Rev. 4:5)

> Know what is proper for their Head,

Who sits on the throne of all the world

> Still wearing the form of the slaughtered Lamb.

4. The seven flames before the throne

> Illuminate this vision.

The harmony of the four beasts

> intones day and night:

We are atoned.

5. Through your creative power

You have made the heavens and the earth;

> Humankind you have formed,
> According to your image to be your Bride.
> 6. And when humanity lost all that
> You stepped forward in a new form,

And departed from eternity

> Into this limited time.

7. The Spirit illumined a young virgin

> That bore you as little Jesus,

---

12. This is the word for the seventy-two names of God in Jewish Kabbala.

13. Given in Latin: *Non erat ubi non eras.* This was a succinct anti-Arian phrase indicating the eternity of the Son.

14. This refers to the heavenly court, uniting Genesis 1:26 with Revelation 4:5.

And lay in the manger:

    Abi-ad, El-gibbor, Shiloh.[15]

8. Terror accompanied your cradle,

    Terror defended your teaching!

Terror overcame all nature

    When your spirit fled your body!

9. O you, named the God of all the world,

    Are recognized both by the world and your people,

By the world in the lightning marks;

By your people in your nail marks.

      11. What you are doing with your people

    While you sit enthroned and rest,

That we want, more than ever, to behold

In the villages of Christians.

12. But when the convolution of the world

    Proclaims the approach of judgment;

When you command the angels,

    "Gather my people to me."

13. When your sign appears in the clouds,

    And the world cries for clefts in the rocks,

    When the mountains shall no longer be

We doves will fly in through the window (Isaiah 60:8).

      14. And we will gaze fully on the Godhead

That so blinded us here;

Before that glorious lightning we had

    To take flight deep within the wounds (Song of Sol. 2:14).

      15. Now, Abba, remain until then

In Jesus' Name, God of the community,

Until the bride has become one with Christ,

    Clinging with heart and mind to her flesh and bone,

16. For GOD, who is named the God of all the world,

Became flesh, and she

One spirit with him.

    And his arrival in the flesh

    Will keep our bodies and souls chaste.

TE AGNUM[16]

Unblemished LAMB of God

    Holy Bridegroom

---

15. These are names for God found in Isaiah 6:9 and Genesis 49:10 and later were used as names for the Messiah.

16. *Litaney Büchlein,* 79–80.

Who came from the Throne
And assumed humanity.
[1.] The four who do not rest day or night,
 Always converse with you.
The twenty-four throne lords
 Gladly give you your honor;
2. The Father on the Father's throne,
His true and only Son,
The Holy Spirit and Comforter joyful:
 And worship you in the person of the Lamb.
 3. You slaughtered Lamb! We praise you,
And trembling, we honor your office,
 That you receive the book from the Father (Rev. 5:7)
And break its seven seals.
 4. You are no longer in this world;
You have placed us within it:
So seal us from sin
 And all the sorrow of the earth!
5. Daily, O Heart, we love you,
 For your name and for yourself:
The name that no one else knows,
 Is pronounced over your people.
 6. Keep our robes bright and pure
 Through your blood and your blood alone
Until the day when you will become forever
 The church's Lamb and Light and Temple.

TE MATREM[17]

LORD GOD, now be praised,
 You worthy HOLY SPIRIT!
You, the mother of Christendom
 The church honors in unity.
All angels and the host of heaven
 And whoever serves the honor of the Son;
Also the cherubim and seraphim:
 They all sing with a clear voice:
Divine majesty,
 Who proceeds from the Father,

17. Ibid., 70–72.

Praising the Son as the creator (Heb. 1:8–10).
And pointing to his suffering!
Your divine power and teaching craft
    Have carried millions over.
The holy twelve apostles through you
    Became everything they were.
You spoke in the highest degree through the martyrs,
When death sat on their tongues.
    That the Four do not rest day and night,
    Does not happen without your activity.
The four and twenty kings,
    Who were faithful in little,
And now are set over much,
You help them to cry the Holy, Holy!
    Amen.
[1.] O Mother of all God's people,
    O wisdom archetypal!
You are the informer of all hearts
    And the purifier of body and soul!
2. The Virgin's womb was not rejected
    For the holy temple site,
    Which was delivered of the Child
Who is the Father of all beings.
    3. You led him to the arena
Where he warded off the accuser,
    And then, since it went hard with him,
He became the judge of both parties.
[4.] The holy Trinity
    Speaks with Christendom through you
    To the Bride and her Christ
    You are the friend and private counselor.
5. You come to us, spelling out 'Abba,'
    And take our word back home,
Bring our prayers into heaven
    And also bring back the Amen.
[6.] Now help us, your servants,
    (Who are consecrated by you yourself)
Make us ashamed of self-righteousness
    And hinder all self-help.
7. Help your folk, God the Holy Spirit!
    Direct them often to the Lamb of God;

Keep and nurse his own people for all time
    With the bloody righteousness.
[8.] Daily, O MOTHER! You are praised
    By whoever knows the Savior and you
Because you guide the Gospel
    Over all the world around;
9. Because you teach the princes of the people
    To walk before the cloud of witnesses;
Because you ordain prophets and
    Adorn with wonders and gifts;
10. Because you sanctify priests for the Lamb,
And strew incense in their censors.
    The married people and the virgins
You sanctify as your temples.
    [11.] That when he comes, the friend,
[And when] the signature of the Son of Man appears
And fills all the world with fear,
    You will comfort our eyes with that sign.

THE CHURCH'S PRAYER TO THE HOLY SPIRIT[18]

[1.] You, who from the Father joyful
    Were sent here to us,
Spirit, of whom the Virgin received
The Son at the proper time;
    2. Since the Lamb of God, so red,
    Is the Brother of his own people,
And their Father is God of Christ (John 20:17),
    [You are] **Mother of the Congregation!**
        (Gal. 4:26; Song of Sol. 6:8)
    3. Your name, our dear God,
    Be always near us.
So that the word of Jesus' death
Shines clearly among our souls
4. Whoever the Savior calls from the grave
To return into life,
    Those bring into your Ark,
And teach them to pray, Abba!
5. As in your holy heights (Ps. 102:20),
    Thus also on earth,

18. Ibid., 73–74.

Your holy will shall be done
By the flocks of Jesus.
6. The righteousness before God,
   Through the blood atonement,
Our dear daily food,
Comes through your serving.
    7. MOTHER! Our Father's grace
    Is the life of the church,
Our dear Lord's patience,
    And your manifold forgiveness.
8. We would not want to be tempted,
   Do not wish it to any member;
But if you lead one into trial,
   The discipline leads to peacefulness.
9. And until the one who is called evil
Lies at the feet of God (Ps. 110:1, Heb. 2:8),
The church remains in the Holy Spirit
   Consecrated before him.
10. Amen,
Breath of Elohim! (Gen. 1:2)
   Come in Jesus' name,
And rule the Sanhedrin
   Of your children.
     Amen.

THE BRIDE'S SONG[19]

  The Daughters bow
Quite reverently
Before the residents of that City
   Which has the Bridegroom within.
The Angels all, the escort of honor
   of the holy Trinity,
The throne-princes and the lords
   Delight to see you in your beauty.
Blessed Kyria (2 John 1)
   Jerusalem (Gal. 4, 26),
You daughter of God,
   (And sister as well),

---

19. Originally *Das Te Sponsam*. Ibid., 102–5.

Women of the man Joshua,[20]
>Out of his side
—Hallelujah!—
By Christ in his death labors,
>Born to be the immortal "She"!
Amen.

[1.] The twelve apostles' number
And the dear prophets all,
The ever faithful martyrs
>Help complete your number.
2. The people who are concerned about Jesus' suffering
>Bye and bye will be included.
>Those who do not sleep day or night[21]
Drive your chariot through the world.
>3. The anointed locks of your hair
Are the liturgists of the altar;
>They lie before Joshua,
To wipe away his sweat.
[4.] GOD, the Father of eternity,
>Henceforth known as the Son of Man,
Became in the womb of a young virgin
>one with mortal flesh.
5. The eternal light was his raiment;
>[But] God prepared for him a body,
>And so the virgin received the Son
In person from the Holy Spirit.
[6.] And why, dear Bride of Christ,
Did God appear in the flesh?
>To his honor, and to your shame be it said:
>You had placed your bed away from him:[22]
>7. You were in his enemy's arms.
>He held you tightly
—May God help us!—
Until GOD, the powerful, came himself
>And took the virgin from the strong man.
[8.] GOD, the independent Wisdom,

20. The Hebrew version of the name Jesus.
21. I.e., seraphim.
22. A reference to the book of Hosea in the Old Testament.

Who helped prepare,
> As the Creator's master builder,
> The created eternity according to his mind,
9. That sovereign majesty
> Who proceeds from God the Father,[23]
Whom the Bridegroom, in his stead,
> Has left to his Bride as a comfort,
> 10. She celebrates her own festival with you
And with your wedding adornment;
> She transforms the embarrassment
Into divine consideration.
> [11.] Now then, sit at home in his joy
> And be ashamed for all eternity,
And the higher your Husband exalts you,
> Rejoice in him as long as he lives.
> 12. Wait for us in bliss
Until time itself is reborn!
> For when this has happened,
Then you shall be perfected.
13. When your husband draws near to judgment
And heaven and earth are fleeing before him;
> For we are waiting, as he commanded,
> For a new heaven and earth.
14. Then march after him in triumph
> And place yourself around his side's cote
From whence you were dug out
> When your Savior departed [this life].
> [15.] Meanwhile, remember the church
That must remain imperfect,
> Which indeed lies in the Blood of the Lamb
And is victorious in all her wars.
14. [sic] Because the dove sits in the rock-cleft
And the Lion guards the dove:
> Which, however, because of faults and defects,
> Always cries for the soul of Christ.
[17] Daily, O Church, makes us
> Mindful of our Mother.

---

23. The Moravians since the time of Zinzendorf have not used the *filioque* clause when speaking of the Holy Spirit.

The spiritual race of Shem
        May never be forgotten by Jerusalem.
        18. When the church prays in her mind,
Then it turns itself toward the capital city,
Where the One with the five red wounds
        Is the temple; her light and her God;
There, there is no death.
[19.] The sick at the healing pool
        All enter the realm of health,
        One part is awaiting in its nest,
You, wife of the lamb, your entry feast.[24]

EPITHALAMIUM[25]

[1.] Happiness to the faithful bride of the Lamb,
To the holy wife of the Bridegroom,
The Church, who amuses her Husband,
        Whom his Father himself dearly treasures,
2. The Mother dressed in her best attire,
Gives her princes as attendants
So that also heaven and her hosts
Rejoice and wonder about her honor;
        3. That a wretched creature
        Partakes in God's nature;
And on the command of their Lord
They delight to honor the Bride.
4. Cherubim and Seraphim stand there
Astonished before their Jehovah,
        Observe what the Godhead
        Had intended from deep counsel,
5. The counsel of the Trinity,
Which so greatly delights the sinner;
        What was before a deep mystery
And was first made clear at the appointed hour,
6. When the Son forsook the throne
        And lowered himself to be among people,
And after bitter death pain,
        Entered again into rest.

---

24. The 1759 English text reads "consummation" rather than "entry feast." In either case, the reference is to the "marriage supper of the Lamb."
25. *Litaney Büchlein*, 106–8.

7. The faithful patriarchs all the time,
And the dear prophets all,
      Who waited for it in the old covenant,
He carried away with him when he arose.
      8. The twelve apostles of the Church
      Took up their chairs around the dear Lamb;
And then there are still in this array,
Twelve other thrones, whosesoever they are.
[9.] When Stephan and the martyrs
Sometimes looked around, there He stood,
      Waiting for their readiness,
In order to leave with the spirit.

10. And Christendom follows them
      With joy out of this temporal sphere,
To see the Husband and his Bride,
      And to be among their flock.

11. The twenty-four kings are
      Certainly members of the Church:
And when the Church surrounds them,
      So the choir worships with them and sings:
[12.] Bride! Your bridal grandeur
      Has its sources from the Side
Of Jehovah, your Christ,
Which for your sake, was split apart.
      13. Your Husband was made a curse for you
And atoned for your adultery:
You may now cover up your brokenness and sinful edges
with his bloody vestment.
15. [sic] So you can stand before Jehovah,
      And gaze at him with your eyes,
While the brilliant Seraphim
      Bow their countenance before him;
16. Because heaven is not pure enough for Him
      Nor the angels holy enough,
And for this reason as well, in awe
      Are hiding themselves in their wings.
[17.] Now, God's Church above!
      Bless us, your comrades,

Who in spirit see the seats,
>   That stand prepared for them.
18. But remember, yet before the wedding takes place,
>   And before the Husband leads his wife home,
>   We too must be perfected:
For there is only One Church.
>   19. Administer your office among us,
In private, as well as openly!
So that, when the Lamb reveals himself to You,
>   We may also experience something of it.
20. That will help us poor sinners
>   Until we are all under one roof!
The eye and the watcher of Israel,
Preserve spirit and body and soul!

THE PLEURODY (FORMERLY TE PLEURA)[26]

Praise the election by grace
In the holy mark in the side!
O dear Lamb, be blessed
For the opening of your side!
All angels and the heavenly host
Who gaze at that with love,
But soon must veil their faces
Before the ruby light.
The church alone, Jesus' bride,
Because from there it was dug out and built,
Looks directly into the sunlight
With uncovered face.

Pax tibi, Gloria,
Cultus, memoria,
Tu pallor faucium!
Ave, Cor saucium!

That is:
Peace to you and glory,
Worship and remembrance,

---

26. Ibid., 91–94; my translation.

You, face so pale!
Hail, broken heart!

1. Go deep within, my heart, the riven side,
Deep, deep, I say, deep within!
In its proper time, Jesus' faithfulness brings
What is earthly to the Spirit's house.

2. The one who in a dream looks in,
Does not want to awaken again.
In short, the magnet of the holy side
Attracts far beyond heaven and earth.

3. When the Lamb of God appears visibly,
And the world cries for caves in the cliffs;
Then will place of the spear-piercing
Be the medal that honors him.

The living blood from the side
Cries out,
Cries out,
Mercy!

4. Prince Isaiah saw the wound
Through the viewpoint of the old covenant:
Behold, and see the cleft in the rock
And in that cleft, the tomb's fountain,
Through which you chosen people
Are dug out and hewn.

5. John, Jesus' close comrade,
Saw how he was opened.
(When he was pacing in his room
And beginning his Gospel;
It thundered, said Seribent (his secretary):
But as he came to the writing
About the holy pierced side;
What must it have been to him then?)

6. Jesus Christ showed the rest
Who he was through this wound,
And Thomas, whom the Lord commanded,
Felt in the side and the nail marks.

7. Which moved him so much
That he paid the first homage.
Now the feeling congregation calls out:
Honor to the holy pierced side!
Amen.

8. Although we honor all the wounds alike
And feed upon the entire corpse;
Still we concentrate on the breast our
Thanks, shame, pain, joy, love, and desire.

9. When the new work of God originated,
So that the wife embraces her husband
(Jer. 31:22, Rev. 1:13);
The God's suffering sheep gave birth
To his beloved She in sleep.

10. We are poor little children,
Who have nothing in ourselves but sin,
But whom Jesus wound-bloom
Has broken through to holiness.

11. In order flesh of his flesh and bone
And spirit of his spirit to be;
That each to the womb
Gives his special devotion.

12. And at the end of all distress
One says to his beloved God:
What right my body has to the earth,
Is because it was formed in this womb;

13. That I have a poor soul, indeed,
More naturally to the side hole,

Out of which my Creator bore me anew,
When Jesus was crucified.

14. Daily, sings your Christendom,
Lamb! and wishes itself to be in the side.
The Vine and the branches
Belong in one another in there.

15. That the church shares in God's nature,
Is ascribed only from there.
The point of religion
Remains, at least, in that aeon.

16. The one whom creatures never see,
To him one holds the liturgy there.
The inexpressible things that Paul saw,
One finds there all together.

17. To where God the worthy Holy Spirit
Points so diligently,
There the assembly of Christians
Account it for their own proper place.

18. What wonder, that at this time
The evening red shines of bright?
The Brethren's church at this time
Is a brother to the holy side,
The bloody side.

BIBLIOGRAPHY

PRIMARY SOURCES

Reproductions

Zinzendorf, Nikolaus Ludwig. *Hauptschriften in sechs Bänden.* Ed. Erich Beyreuther and Gerhard Meyer. Hildesheim: Georg Olms, 1962–65 (abbreviated ZH).

———. *Nikolaus Ludwig von Zinzendorf: Ergänzungsbände zu den Hauptschriften.* Ed. Erich Beyreuther and Gerhard Meyer. Hildesheim: Georg Olms, 1965–71 (abbreviated ZE).

———. *Nikolaus Ludwig von Zinzendorf: Materialien und Dokumente,* series 1–4. Ed. Erich Beyreuther et al. Hildesheim: Georg Olms, 1971– (abbreviated ZM).

Printed Materials

A Collection of Hymns chiefly extracted from the Larger Hymn-Book of the Brethren's Congregations. London: Brethren's Chapel, 1769.

A Collection of Hymns, for the Use of the Protestant Church of the United Brethren. London: Brethren's Chapel, 1789.

A Collection of Hymns. Part 3. London, 1749.

Acta Fratrum Unitatis in Anglia. London, 1749.

XII. Anhang und Zugaben I-IV zum Herrnhuter Gesangbuch. N.p., 1743–48. (ZE 2.)

Arndt, Johannes. *True Christianity.* Trans. and ed. Peter Erb. New York: Paulist Press, 1979.

Bayle, Pierre. *The Dictionary Historical and Critical of Mr. Peter Bayle.* 2d ed. London, 1735.

Bengel, Johann Albrecht. *Abriß der so genannten Brüdergemeine* N.p., 1751. (ZM 2:10.)

Chelčický, Peter. "On the Triple Division of Society." Trans. and ed. Howard Kaminsky. In *Studies in Medieval and Renaissance History.* Vol. 1. Ed. William M. Bowsky, 137–73. Lincoln: University of Nebraska Press, 1964.

Cranz, David. *Alte und Neue Brüder-Historie oder kurz gefaßte Geschichte der Evangelischen Brüder-Unität.* Barby, 1772. (ZM 2:11.)

———. *Ancient and Modern History of the Brethren.* Trans. Benjamin LaTrobe. London, 1780.

Das Litaneyen-Büchlein nach der bey den Brüdern dermalen hauptsächlich gewöhnlichen Singe-Weise von neuem revidirt, und in dieser bequemen Form ausgegeben von dem Cantore Fratrum Ordinario. 4th ed. Barby, 1757.

Die Täglichen Losungen der Brüder-Gemeine. Years 1756 through 1774. Barby, 1755–73.

Gesangbuch zum Gebrauch der evangelischen Brüdergemeinen. Barby: Spellenberg, 1778.

Hahn, Hans-Christoph, and Hellmut Reichel. *Zinzendorf und die Herrnhuter Brüder: Quellen zur Geschichte der Brüder-Unität von 1722 bis 1760.* Hamburg: F. Wittig, 1977.

Hamilton, Kenneth G., trans. and ed. *The Bethlehem Diary.* Vol. 1, 1742–44. Bethlehem, Pa.: Moravian Archives, 1971.

Hamilton, Kenneth G., and Lothar Madeheim, trans. *The Bethlehem Diary.* Vol. 2, 1744–1745. Ed. Vernon Nelson, Otto Dreydoppel Jr., and Doris Rohland Yob. Bethlehem, Pa.: Moravian Archives, 2001.

Herrnhuter Gesangbuch: Christliches Gesang-Buch der Evangelischen Brüder-Gemeinen von 1735 zum drittenmal aufgelegt und durchaus revidirt, Part 2, Anhänge I-XII. (ZM 4:3.)

Kurze, zuverlässige Nachricht von der, unter dem Namen der Böhmisch-Mährischen Brüder bekanten, Kirche Unitas Fratrum 1757. (Zeremonienbüchlein.) (ZE 6.)

Liturgic Hymns of United Brethren. Rev. and enl. ed. London, 1793.

Lynar, Graf Heinrich Casimir Gottlieb von. *Nachricht von dem Ursprung und Fortgange, und hauptsächlich von der gegenwärtigen Verfassung der Brüder-Unität.* Halle: Johann Jacob Curt, 1781.

Rimius, Henry. *A Candid Narrative of the Rise and Progress of the Herrnhuters, Commonly call'd Moravians or Unitas Fratrum, with a short Account of their Doctrines, drawn from their own Writings.* London, 1753.

Schrautenbach, Ludwig Carl. *Der Graf von Zinzendorf und die Brüdergemeine seiner Zeit.* Ed. Friedrich Wilhelm Kölbing. Gnadau and Leipzig, 1851. (ZM 2:9.)

Spangenberg, August Gottlieb. *Antworten.* N.p., 1751. (ZE 5.)

———. *Apologetische Schluß-Schrift, worinn über tausend Beschuldigungen gegen die Brüder-Gemeinen und ihren zeitherigen Ordinarium nach der Wahrheit beantwortet werden.* N.p., 1752. (ZE 3.)

———. *Idea Fidei Fratrum or An Exposition of Christian Doctrine as taught in the Protestant Church of the United Brethren or Unitas Fratrum.* Trans. Benjamin LaTrobe. 1778; London: Hazard, 1790. Republished with foreword by J. Kenneth Pfohl and Edmund Schwarze. Winston-Salem, N.C.: Board of Christian Education of the Southern Province of the Moravian Church, 1959.

———. *Declaration über die Zeither gegen uns ausgegangene Beschuldigungen, Sonderlich die Person unsers ORDINARII.* Leipzig, 1751. (ZE 5.)

———. *Darlegung richtiger Antworten auf mehr als dreyhundert Beschuldigungen.* (ZE 5.)

———. *Apologetische Erklärung über einige Beschuldigungen gegen den Ordinarium Fratrum.* Barby, 1750. (ZE 5.)

———. *Leben des Herrn Nikolaus Ludwig, Grafen von Zinzendorf und Pottendorf.* Barby: Brüdergemeine, 1773–75. (ZM 2:1–8.)

———. *The life of Nicholas Lewis, Count Zinzendorf, Bishop and Ordinary of the Church of the United (or Moravian) Brethren.* Trans. and ed. Samuel Jackson. London: S. Holdsworth, 1838.

Spener, Philipp Jakob. *Pia Desideria.* Trans. Theodore G. Tappert. Philadelphia: Fortress Press, 1964.

The Litany-book, According to the Manner of Singing At present mostly in Use among the BRETHREN, Again revised, and in this convenient Form set forth by the Brethren's CHANTOR. Trans. from the 4th German edition. London, 1759.

Vogt, Peter, ed. *An Authentic Relation of the Occasion, Continuance, and Conclusion of the First Assembly of some Labourers out of most of the Christian Religions and other private religious People in Pensilvania kept in German Town 1st and 2nd January 1741–42.* Vol. 30 of *Nikolaus Ludwig von Zinzendorf: Materialien und Dokumente,* series 11. Hildesheim: Georg Olms, 1998.

Zinzendorf, Nikolaus Ludwig. *Büdingische Sämmlung,* vols. 1–3. (ZE 7–10.)

———. *Der Teutsche Sokrates.* 1732. (ZH 1.)

———. *Inhalt dererjenigen Reden, welche zu Berlin vom 1ten Januario 1738. bis 27ten Aprilis in denen Abend-Stunden sonderlich für die Manns-Personen gehalten worden.* Berlin, 1738. (*Berliner Reden,* ZE 14.)

———. *Pennsylvanische Nachrichten von dem Reiche Christi Anno 1742.* (ZH 2.)

———. *Des Herrn Grafen Ludwig von Zinzendorf Sieben letzte Reden, so er in der Gemeine vor seiner am 7. August erfolgten abaermaligen Abreise nach Amerika gehalten, 1742.* (ZH 2.)

———. *Eine Sammlung öffentlicher Reden von dem Herrn, der unsere Seligkeit ist und über di Materie von seiner Marter. In dem Jahr 1742 mehrenteils in dem nordlichen Teil von Amerika.* (ZH 2.)

———. *Neun Offentliche Reden über wichtige in die Religion einschlagende Materien, Gehalten zu London Anno 1746.* (ZH 6.)

———. *Die an den Synodum der Brüder in Zeist vom 11. May bis den 21. Junii 1746 gehaltene Reden.* 1746–47. (*Zeister Reden,* ZH 3.)

———. *Der Öffentlichen Gemein-Reden im Jahr 1747.* (*Gemeinreden,* ZH 4.)

———. *Vier und Dreßig Homiliae über die Wunden-Litaney der Brüder.* 1747. (*Wundenlitanei Reden,* ZH 3.)

———. *Einundzwanzig Diskurse über die Augspurgische Konfession.* 1748. (*Einundzwanzig Diskurse,* ZH 6.)

———. *Naturelle Reflexionem.* 1746–48. (ZE 5.)

———. *Twenty-one Discourses or Dissertations upon the Augsburg-Confession which is also the Brethren's Confession of Faith.* Trans. Francis Okeley. London: W. Bowyer, 1753.

———. *Londoner Gesangbuch: Vorwort und Elenchus zu Teil 1 und 2.* 1753–54. (ZH 5.)

———. *An Exposition, or True State, Of the Matters objected in England to the People known by the Name of Unitas Fratrum.* London: J. Robinson, 1755.

———. *Der Predigten, die der Ordinarius Fratrum von Anno 1751 bis 1755 zu London gehalten hat.* (ZH 5.)

———. *Des Ordinarii Fratrum Berlinische Reden, 2. revidierte Ausgabe von 1758.* (ZH 1.)

———. *Zuverlässige Nachricht.* 1760. (ZH 6.)

———. *Samlung einiger von dem seligen Ordinario Fratrum während seines aufenthalts in den Teutschen Gemeinen von Anno 1755 bis 1757 gehaltenen Reden an die Kinder.* Barby, 1761. (*Kinder Reden,* ZE 6.)

———. "Christian David: Servant of the Lord, A Translation of the Memoir of Christian David as written by Count Nicholas L. von Zinzendorf." Trans. Carl John Fliegel and ed. Vernon Nelson. Bethlehem, Pa.: Moravian Archives Publications, 1962.

———. *Nine Public Lectures on Important Subjects in Religion Preached in Fetter Lane Chapel in London in the Year 1746.* 1746. Trans. and ed. George W. Forell. Iowa City: University of Iowa Press, 1973.

———. *A Collection of Sermons from Zinzendorf's Pennsylvania Journey.* 1742. Trans. Julie Weber and ed. Craig D. Atwood. Bethlehem, Pa.: Moravian Publication Office, 2001.

Archival Material
Bethlehem Diary. Moravian Archives, Bethlehem, Pa.
Catalog of the Bookstore. Moravian Archives, Bethlehem, Pa.

Engere Conferenz Minutes. 1747. Moravian Archives, Bethlehem, Pa.

Gemein Conferenz Minutes. Sept. 15, 1755. Moravian Archives, Bethlehem, Pa.

Gemein Nachrichten. Moravian Archives, Bethlehem, Pa.

General und Special Sachen, 1744. Moravian Archives, Bethlehem, Pa.

Conferenz Protocoll. Moravian Archives, Bethlehem, Pa.

Helpers Conference Minutes. Moravian Archives, Bethlehem, Pa.

Journal of the Diaconat. Moravian Archives, Bethlehem, Pa.

Kinder Conferenz Minutes. 1756. Moravian Archives, Bethlehem, Pa.

Manuscript liturgies. Boxes 1–3. Moravian Archives, Bethlehem, Pa.

Musicological card index to the Bethlehem Diary. Moravian Archives, Bethlehem, Pa.

Nelson, Vernon. "Index to the Gemein Nachrichten." Moravian Archives, Bethlehem, Pa.

Relation von dem vom 12/23–16/27, 1748 Oct. Synod. Moravian Archives, Bethlehem, Pa.

Relation von dem in Salisburg in May 1756 gehalten Brüder-Synode. Moravian Archives, Bethlehem, Pa.

Single Brothers' Diary. Moravian Archives, Bethlehem, Pa.

Single Sisters' Diary. Moravian Archives, Bethlehem, Pa.

Spangenberg, A. G. "General-Plan mit welchem ich an. 1744. von Europa nach America abgereißt." Folder 1, 1-a. Moravian Archives, Bethlehem, Pa.

Zinzendorf, N. L. "Strafbrief, Feb. 1749," R3A.8.L3a (original and copy). Archiv der Brüder-Unität, Herrnhut; copy, Zinzendorf Box A, NZ VI.3. Moravian Archives, Bethlehem, Pa.

SECONDARY SOURCES

Aalen, Leiv. *Die Theologie des jungen Zinzendorf.* Berlin: Lutherisches Verlagshaus, 1966.

———. "Zinzendorf als Kommentator der Confessio Augustana." *Unitas Fratrum* 17 (1985): 57–67.

Adeney, Walter F. "Waldenses." In *Encyclopaedia of Religion and Ethics,* ed. James Hastings. Edinburgh: T. & T. Clark, 1980.

Ahlstrom, Sidney. *A Religious History of the American People.* 2 vols. Garden City, N.Y.: Image Books, 1975.

Alderfer, E. G. *The Ephrata Commune: An Early American Counterculture.* Pittsburgh: University of Pittsburgh Press, 1985.

Ariès, Philippe. *The Hour of Our Death.* Trans. Helen Weaver. New York: Knopf, 1981.

Atwood, Craig D. "Zinzendorf's 1749 Reprimand to the Brüdergemeine." *Transactions of the Moravian Historical Society* 29 (1996): 59–84.

————. "Sleeping in the Arms of Christ: Sanctifying Sexuality in the Eighteenth-Century Moravian Church." *Journal of the History of Sexuality* 8 (1997): 25–51.

————. "The Joyfulness of Death in Eighteenth-Century Moravian Communities." *Communal Societies* 17 (1997): 39–58.

————. "Zinzendorf's Litany of the Wounds of the Husband." *Lutheran Quarterly* 11 (1997): 189–214.

————. "The Mother of God's People: The Adoration of the Holy Spirit as Mother in the Eighteenth-Century Brüdergemeine." *Church History* 68 (1999): 886–910.

————. "Theology in Song: Daily Litanies in the Eighteenth-Century Moravian Church." In *The Distinctiveness of Moravian Culture: Essays and Documents in Honor of Vernon Nelson on his 70th Birthday,* ed. Craig D. Atwood and Peter Vogt. Nazareth, Pa.: Moravian Historical Society, 2003.

————. "The Persistence of Zinzendorfian Piety in Colonial America." In *German Moravians in the Transatlantic World,* ed. Michele Gillespie and Robert Benchy. Forthcoming.

Atwood, Craig D., and Peter Vogt, ed. *The Distinctiveness of Moravian Culture: Essays and Documents in Honor of Vernon Nelson on his 70th Birthday.* Nazareth, Pa.: Moravian Historical Society, 2003.

Jane Augustine, "The Mystery: H. D.'s Unpublished Moravian Novel, Edited and Annotated Towards a Study in the Sources in a Poet's Religious Thinking." Ph.D. diss., City University of New York, 1988.

Bartos, F. M. *The Hussite Revolution, 1424–1437.* Trans. J. Weir and ed. John Klassen. East European Monographs ser., no. 203. New York: Columbia University Press, 1986.

Beck, Hartmut. *Brüder in vielen Völkern: 250 Jahre Mission der Brüdergemeine.* Erlangen, 1981.

Becker, Bernhard. *Zinzendorf und sein Christentum im Verhaltnis zum kirchlichen und religiosen Leben seiner Zeit.* 2d ed. Leipzig: F. Jansa, 1900.

Beckwith, Sarah. *Christ's Body: Identity, Culture, and Society in Late Medieval Writings.* London: Routledge, 1993.

Bell, Catherine. *Ritual: Perspectives and Dimensions.* New York: Oxford University Press, 1997.

Benad, Matthias. *Toleranz als Gebot christlicher Obrigkeit: das Büdinger Patent von 1712.* Hildesheim, 1983.

Bettermann, Wilhelm. *Theologie und Sprache bei Zinzendorf.* Gotha: Leopold Klotz, 1935.

Beyreuther, Erich. *Der junge Zinzendorf.* Vol. 1. of *Die große Zinzendorf Trilogie.*

Marburg an der Lahn: Verlag der Francke-Buchhandlung, 1957; reprint 1988.

———. *Zinzendorf und die sich allhier beisammen finden.* Vol. 2 of *Die große Zinzendorf Trilogie.* Marburg an der Lahn: Verlag der Francke-Buchhandlung, 1959; reprint 1988.

———. *Zinzendorf und die Christenheit.* Vol. 3 of *Die große Zinzendorf Trilogie.* Marburg an der Lahn: Verlag der Francke-Buchhandlung, 1961; reprint 1988.

———. *August Hermann Francke: Zeuge des lebendigen Gottes.* Marburg, 1961.

———. *Studien zur Theologie Zinzendorfs.* Neukirchen-Vluyn: Kreis Moers, 1962.

———. "Einführing in die Öffentlichen Gemein-Reden." (ZH 4.)

———. *Geschichte des Pietismus.* Stuttgart: J. K. Steinkopf, 1978.

———. "Einleitung" to Spener's *Sendschreiben.* In Philipp Jacob Spener, *Schriften,* vol. 1, ed. Erich Beyreuther and Dietrich Blaufluß. Olms: Hildesheim, 1979.

Beyreuther, Gottfried. "Sexualtheorien im Pietismus." Ph.D. diss., Ludwig-Maximillians-Universität, Munich, 1963. (Reproduced in ZM 2:13, 509–96.)

Bintz, Helmut. "Die Begründung der christliche Ethik in der Inkarnationslehre bei Zinzendorf." In *Pietismus-Herrnhutertum-Erweckungsbewegung: Festschrift für Erich Beyreuther,* ed. Dietrich Meyer, 177–302. Cologne: Rheinland-Verlag, 1982.

Bloch, Maurice, and Jonathan Parry, eds. *Death and the Regeneration of Life.* Cambridge: Cambridge University Press, 1982.

Bloesch, Donald. G. *The Evangelical Renaissance.* Grand Rapids: Wm. B. Eerdmans, 1973.

Bonomi, Patricia U. *Under the Cope of Heaven: Religion, Society, and Politics in Colonial America.* New York: Oxford University Press, 1986.

Bradley, Ritamary. "Patristic Background of the Motherhood Similitude in Julian of Norwich." *Christian Scholar's Review* 8 (1978): 101–13.

Brecht, Martin. "Pietismus." In *Theologische Realenzyklopädie,* 26:606–13. Berlin: Walter de Gruyter, 1996.

———, ed. *Geschichte des Pietismus.* Vol. 1, *Der Pietismus vom siebzehnten bis zum frühen achtzehnten Jahrhundert.* Vol. 2, *Der Pietismus im achtzehnten Jahrhundert.* Göttingen: Vanderhoeck & Ruprecht, 1993, 1995.

Brock, Peter. *The Political and Social Doctrines of the Unity of the Czech Brethren in the Fifteenth and Early Sixteenth Centuries.* Vol. 11 of *Slavistic Printings and Reprintings.* Ed. Cornelis H. van Schooneveld. The Hague: Mouton & Co., 1957.

Brown, Dale. *Understanding Pietism.* Grand Rapids: Wm. B. Eerdmans, 1978.

Brown, Peter. *Body and Society: Men, Women, and Sexual Renunciation in Early Christianity.* New York: Columbia University Press, 1988.

Bultmann, Rudolf. *Theology of the New Testament.* Trans. Kendrick Grobel. 2 vols. New York: Charles Scribner's Sons, 1954.

Burke, Barbara Ellen. "Parallels Between Moravianism and Selected Works by H. D." Master's thesis, University of Louisville, 1991.

Bushman, Richard L. *The Great Awakening: Documents on the Revival of Religion, 1740–1745.* New York: Atheneum Publishers, 1970.

Butler, Jon. *Awash in a Sea of Faith: Christianizing the American People.* Cambridge: Harvard University Press, 1990.

Butler, Jon, and Harry Stout. *Religion in American History: A Reader.* 3rd ed. New York: Oxford University Press, 1998.

Bynum, Caroline Walker. *Jesus as Mother: Studies in the Spirituality of the High Middle Ages.* Berkeley and Los Angeles: University of California Press, 1982.

———. "The Blood of Christ in the Later Middle Ages." *Church History* 71 (2002): 685–714.

———. "Violent Imagery in Late Medieval Piety." *Bulletin of the German Historical Institute* 30 (2002): 3–36.

Caldwell, Alice May. "Music of the Moravian 'Liturgische Gesange' (1791–1823): From Oral to Written Tradition." Ph.D. diss., New York University, 1987.

Campbell, Ted. *Religion of the Heart: A Study of European Religious Life in the Seventeenth and Eighteenth Centuries.* Columbia: University of South Carolina Press, 1991.

Camporesi, Piero. *Juice of Life: The Symbolic and Magic Significance of Blood.* Trans. Robert R. Barr. New York: Continuum, 1995.

Coalter, Milton J., Jr. "The Radical Pietism of Count Nicholas Zinzendorf as a Conservative Influence on the Awakener, Gilbert Tennent." *Church History* 49 (1980): 35–46.

———. *Gilbert Tennent, Son of Thunder: A Case Study of Continental Pietism's Impact on the First Great Awakening in the Middle Colonies.* New York: Greenwood Press, 1986.

Cohn, Norman. *The Pursuit of the Millennium: Revolutionary Millenarians and Mystical Anarchists of the Middle Ages.* 2d ed. New York: Oxford University Press, 1970.

Corbett, Julia Mitchell. *Religion in America.* 3rd ed. Upper Saddle River, N.J.: Prentice-Hall, 1997.

Cragg, Gerald. *The Church in the Age of Reason, 1648–1789.* Vol. 4 of *Pelican History of the Church.* New York: Viking Penguin Books, 1970.

Crews, C. Daniel. *Zinzendorf: The Theology of Song.* Winston-Salem, N.C.: Moravian Archives, 1999.

———. "Die Stellung der Musik im gottesdienstlichen Leben der Brüdergemeine." *Unitas Fratrum* 47 (2000): 12–28.

Crews, C. Daniel, and Richard Starbuck. *With Courage for the Future: The Story of the Moravian Church, Southern Province.* Winston-Salem, N.C.: Moravian Archives, 2002.

Crist, Robert, ed. *Penn's Example to the Nations: 300 Years of the Holy Experiment.* Harrisburg: Pennsylvania Council of Churches, 1987.

Dalton, Hermann. *Daniel Ernst Jablonski.* Berlin: Warneck, 1903.

Danker, William J. *Profit for the Lord: Economic Activities in Moravian Missions and the Basel Mission Trading Company.* Grand Rapids: Wm. B. Eerdmans, 1971.

Darnton, Robert. *The Great Cat Massacre and Other Episodes in French Cultural History.* New York: Vintage Books, 1985.

Dentan, R. C. "Heart." In *The Interpreter's Dictionary of the Bible,* ed. George Buttrick, 2:549–50. Nashville: Abingdon Press, 1962.

Deppermann, Klaus. *Der hallesche Pietismus und der preussiche Staat unter Friedrich III.* Göttingen, 1961.

———. "Pennylvanien als Asyl des frühren deutschen Pietismus." *Pietismus und Neuzeit* 10 (1984): 190–212.

Deppermann, Klaus, et al. *Pietismus und Neuzeit: Ein Jahrbuch zur Geschichte des neueren Protestantismus.* Göttingen: Vandenhoeck & Ruprecht, 1974–.

De Schweinitz, Edmund. "Some of the Fathers of the American Moravian Church: John Christian Frederick Cammerhoff." *Transactions of the Moravian Historical Society* 2: 175–83.

Dithmar, Christiane. *Zinzendorfs nonkonformistische Haltung zum Judentum.* Heidelberg: Universitätsverlag, 2000.

Douglas, Mary. *Natural Symbols: Explorations in Cosmology.* New York: Vintage Books, 1973.

———. *Purity and Danger: An Analysis of the Concepts of Pollution and Taboo.* 1966; New York: Ark Paperbacks, 1989.

Durkheim, Émile. *Elementary Forms of the Religious Life.* Trans. J. W. Swaim. 1915; New York: Free Press, 1965.

Durnbaugh, Donald F. "Radical Pietist Involvement in Early German Emigration to Pennsylvania." *Yearbook of German-American Studies* 29 (1994): 29–48.

———. "Communitarian Societies in Colonial America." In *America's Communal Utopias*, ed. Donald E. Pitzer. Chapel Hill: University of North Carolina Press, 1997.

Engel, Katherine Carté. "Br. Joseph's Sermon on the *Oeconomie*, February 11, 1758." In *The Distinctiveness of Moravian Culture: Essays and Documents in Honor of Vernon Nelson on his 70th Birthday*, ed. Craig D. Atwood and Peter Vogt. Nazareth, Pa.: Moravian Historical Society, 2003.

Erb, Peter. *Pietists: Selected Writings*. Mahwah, N.J.: Paulist Press, 1983.

Erbe, Hans-Walter. *Zinzendorf und der fromme hohe Adel siner Zeit*. Leipzig, 1928. (ZM 2:12.)

———. *Herrnhaag: Eine religiose Kommunität im 18. Jahrhundert*. Hamburg: F. Wittig, 1988.

———. "Herrnhaag—Tiefpunkt oder Höhepunkt der Brüdergeschichte?" *Unitas Fratrum* 26 (1989): 37–51.

Erbe, Helmut. *Bethlehem, Pa.: Eine Herrnhuter-Kolonie des 18. Jahrhunderts*. Herrnhut: Gustav Winter, 1929.

Evans, R.J.W. *The Making of the Habsburg Monarchy*. New York: Oxford University Press, 1979.

Faull, Katherine M. "The American *Lebenslauf*: Women's Autobiography in Eighteenth-Century Moravian Bethlehem." *Yearbook of German-American Studies* 27 (1992): 23–48.

———. "Faith and Imagination: Nikolaus Ludwig von Zinzendorf's Anti-Enlightenment Philosophy of Self." In *Anthropology and the German Enlightenment: Perspectives on Humanity*, ed. Katherine M. Faull, 23–56. Lewisburg: Bucknell University Press, 1995.

———, trans. and ed. *Moravian Women: Their Related Lives*. Lewisburg: Bucknell University Press, 1997.

Fogleman, Aaron S. *Hopeful Journeys: German Immigration, Settlement, and Political Culture in Colonial America, 1717–1775*. Philadelphia: University of Pennsylvania Press, 1996.

———. "The Decline and Fall of the Moravian Community in Colonial Georgia: Revising the Traditional View." *Unitas Fratrum* 48 (2001): 1–22.

———. " 'Jesus ist weiblich': Die hernhutische Herausforderung in den deutschen Gemeinden Nordamerikas im 18. Jahrhundert." *Historische Anthropologie: Kultur, Gesellschaft, Alltag* 9 (2001): 167–94.

———. "Jesus Is Female: The Moravian Challenge in the German Communities of British North America." *William and Mary Quarterly* 60, 3rd ser. (2003): 295–332.

Fousek, Marianka Sasha. "Spiritual Direction and Discipline: A Key to the

Flowering and Decay of the Sixteenth-Century Unitas Fratrum." *Archive for Reformation History* 62 (1971): 207–24.

Freeman, Arthur J. "The Hermeneutics of Count Nicolaus Ludwig von Zinzendorf." Ph.D. diss., Princeton Theological Seminary, 1962.

———. *An Ecumenical Theology of the Heart: The Theology of Count Nicholas Ludwig von Zinzendorf.* Bethlehem, Pa.: Moravian Publication Office, 1998.

Fries, Adelaide. *The Moravians in Georgia.* Raleigh, N.C.: Edwards and Broughton, 1905.

Fudge, Thomas A. *The Magnificent Ride: The First Reformation in Hussite Bohemia.* Aldershot, Eng.: Ashgate, 1998.

Gaustad, Edwin Scott. *The Great Awakening in New England.* New York: Harper and Brothers, 1957.

Gawthrop, Richard L. *Pietism and the Making of Eighteenth-Century Prussia.* Cambridge: Cambridge University Press, 1993.

Gay, Peter. *The Enlightenment: An Interpretation.* 2 vols. New York: Norton, 1969.

Geertz, Clifford. *The Interpretation of Cultures.* New York: Basic Books, 1973.

Geiger, Erika. *Countess Erdmuth Dorothea von Zinzendorf: 300th Anniversary of her Birth.* Trans. Irene Geiger. Niesky: Gudrun Schiewe, 2000.

———. *Erdmuth Dorothea Gräfin von Zinzendorf. Die 'Hausmutter' der Herrnhuter Brüdergemeine.* Holzgerling: Hännsler, 2000.

Gembicki, Dieter. "From *Kairos* to *Chronos*: Time Perception in Colonial Bethlehem." *Transactions of the Moravian Historical Society* 28 (1994): 31–57.

Gill, Theodor. "Zinzendorf und die Mähren." In *Graf Ohne Grenzen: Leben und Werk von Nikolaus Ludwig Graf von Zinzendorf,* ed. Dietrich Meyer and Paul Peucker, 37–42. Herrnhut: Unitätsarchiv im Verlag der Comeniusbuchhandlung, 2000.

Girard, René. *Violence and the Sacred.* Trans. Patrick Gregory. Baltimore: Johns Hopkins University Press, 1972.

———. *I See Satan Fall Like Lightning.* Trans. James G. Williams. Maryknoll, N.Y.: Orbis, 2001.

Godfroid, Michel. "Le Piétisme allemande a-t-il existé? Histoire d'un concept fait pour la polémique." *Études Germaniques* 101 (1971): 32–45.

Goen, C. C. *Revivalism and Separatism in New England, 1740–1800.* New Haven: Yale University Press, 1962.

Gollin, Gillian Lindt. *Moravians in Two Worlds: A Study of Changing Communities.* New York: Columbia University Press, 1967.

Hamilton, J. Taylor. *A History of the Church Known as the Moravian Church, or the Unitas Fratrum, or the Unity of the Brethren, During the Eighteenth and Nineteenth Centuries. Transactions of the Moravian Historical Society* 6. Nazareth, Pa.: Moravian Historical Society, 1900.

———. *The Recognition of the Unitas Fratrum as an Old Protestant Episcopal Church by the Parliament of Great Britain in 1749.* Nazareth, Pa.: Moravian Historical Society, 1925.

Hamilton, J. Taylor, and Kenneth G. Hamilton. *History of the Moravian Church: The Renewed Unitas Fratrum 1722–1957.* Bethlehem, Pa.: Interprovincial Board of Christian Education of the Moravian Church in America, 1967.

Havens, Mary B. "Zinzendorf and the Augsburg Confession: An Ecumenical Vision?" Ph.D. diss., Princeton Theological Seminary, 1990.

Hazard, Paul. *European Thought in the Eighteenth Century: From Montesquieu to Lessing.* Trans. J. Lewis May. London: Hollis & Carter, 1954.

———. *The European Mind: 1680–1715.* Trans. J. Lewis May. Cleveland: Meridian Books, 1963.

Heimert, Alan. *Religion and the American Mind: From the Great Awakening to the Revolution.* Cambridge: Harvard University Press, 1966.

Hök, Gösta. *Zinzendorfs Begriff der Religion.* Uppsala: Lundequistska Bokhandeln, 1948.

Holloway, Mark. *Utopian Communities in America, 1680–1880.* 2d ed. Mineola, N.Y.: Dover, 1966.

Hutton, J. E. *A History of the Moravian Church.* 2d ed. London: Moravian Publication Office, 1909.

———. *A History of Moravian Missions.* London: Moravian Publication Office, 1922.

Kaminsky, Howard. *A History of the Hussite Revolution.* Berkeley and Los Angeles: University of California Press, 1967.

Kinkel, Gary Steven. *Our Dear Mother the Spirit: An Investigation of Count Zinzendorf's Theology and Praxis.* Lanham, Md.: University Press of America, 1990.

Kortz, Edwin W. "The Liturgical Development of the American Moravian Church." *Transactions of the Moravian Historical Society* 18: 267–302.

Koslofsky, Craig M. *The Reformation of the Dead: Death and Ritual in Early Modern Germany, 1450–1700.* New York: St. Martin's Press, 2000.

Leach, Edmund. *Culture and Communication: The Logic by Which Symbols Are Connected.* Cambridge: Cambridge University Press, 1976.

Lehmann, Hartmut. *Pietism und Weltliche Ordnung in Württemburg vom 17. bis zum 20. Jahrhundert.* Stuttgart: Kohlhammer, 1969.

———. "Zur Definition des 'Pietismus.'" In *Zur neueren Pietismusforschung,* ed. Martin Greschat, 82–90. Darmstadt: Wissenschaftliche Buchgesell-schaft, 1977.

———. "'Absonderung' und 'Gemeinschaft' im frühen Pietismus. Allgemein-historishe und sozialpsychologische Überlegungen zur Entstehung und Entwicklung des Pietismus." *Pietismus und Neuzeit* 4 (1977–78): 54–82.

Levering, Joseph Mortimer. *A History of Bethlehem, Pennsylvania, 1741–1892, with Some Accounts of its Founders and the Early Activity in America.* Bethlehem, Pa.: Times Publishing Co., 1903.

Lewis, Arthur James. *Zinzendorf, the Ecumenical Pioneer: A Study in the Mora-vian Contribution to Christian Mission and Unity.* Philadelphia: West-minster Press, 1962.

Lindberg, Carter. *The Third Reformation?* Macon: Mercer University Press, 1983.

Longenecker, Stephen L. *Piety and Tolerance: Pennsylvania German Religion, 1700–1850.* Metuchen, N.J.: Scarecrow Press, 1994.

Lovejoy, David S. *Religious Enthusiasm in the New World.* Cambridge: Harvard University Press, 1985.

Macek, Josef. *The Hussite Movement in Bohemia.* London: Lawrence & Wishart, 1965.

Mandler, Ira. *Religion, Society, and Utopia in Nineteenth-Century America.* Am-herst: University of Massachusetts Press, 1984.

Matthias, Markus. "Collegium pietatis und ecclesiola." *Pietismus und Neuzeit* 19 (1993): 47–59.

May, Henry F. *The Enlightenment in America.* New York: Oxford University Press, 1976.

McLoughlin, William. *Revivals, Awakenings, and Reform: An Essay on Religion and Social Change in America, 1607–1977.* Chicago: University of Chi-cago Press, 1977.

Merritt, Jane T. "Dreaming of the Savior's Blood: Moravians and the Indian Great Awakening in Pennsylvania." *William and Mary Quarterly* 54, 3rd ser. (Oct. 1997): 723–46.

Meyer, Dietrich. *Der Christozentrismus des späten Zinzendorf.* Bern: Herbert Lang, 1973.

———. *Bibliographisches Handbuch zur Zinzendorf-Forschung.* Düsseldorf: C. Blech, 1987.

———. *Zinzendorf und die Herrnhuter Brüdergemeine, 1700–2000.* Göttingen: Vandenhoeck & Ruprecht, 2000.

———. "The Moravian Church as a Theocracy: The Resolution of the Synod of 1764." In *The Distinctiveness of Moravian Culture: Essays and Docu-ments in Honor of Vernon Nelson on his 70th Birthday,* ed. Craig D.

Atwood and Peter Vogt. Nazareth, Pa.: Moravian Historical Society, 2003.

Meyer, Dietrich, and Paul Peucker, eds. *Graf Ohne Grenzen: Leben und Werk von Nikolaus Ludwig Graf von Zinzendorf.* Herrnhut: Unitätsarchiv im Verlag der Comeniusbuchhandlung, 2000.

Mezezers, Valdis. *The Herrnhuterian Pietism in the Baltic.* North Quincy: Christopher Publishing, 1975.

Miller, Katherine. "A Short History of the Life of Benigna, Baroness von Watteville, nee Countess von Zinzendorf." *Transactions of the Moravian Historical Society* 27 (1992): 53–61.

Molnár, Amedeo. "The Synod of the Unity of the Brethren at Lhotka near Rychnov, 1467–1967." Unpublished lecture. Bethlehem, Pa.: Moravian Theological Seminary, 1973.

———. "The Theology of the Brethren." In Rudolf Ríčan, *The History of the Unity of Brethren: A Protestant Hussite Church in Bohemia and Moravia.* Trans. C. Daniel Crews. Bethlehem, Pa.: Moravian Publication Office, 1992.

Molnár, Enrico. "The Pious Fraud of Count Zinzendorf." *Iliff Review* 11 (1954): 29–38.

Motel, Heinz. "Nikolaus Ludwig von Zinzendorf." In *Concise Dictionary of the Christian World Mission,* ed. Stephen Neill, Gerald H. Anderson, and John Goodwin. Nashville: Abingdon Press, 1971.

Müller, J. T. *Zinzendorf als Erneuerer der alten Brüderkirche.* Leipzig: Friedrich Jansa, 1900.

Müller, Karl. *Das erste Missionsjahrhundert.* Vol. 1 of *200 Jahre Brüdermission.* Herrnhut: Verlag der Missionsbuchhandlung, 1931.

Murphy, G. Ronald, trans. *The Heliand: The Saxon Gospel.* New York: Oxford University Press, 1992.

Murray, Edward Gene. "Fruit That Should Remain: An Analysis of Christian Spiritual Formation as Experienced in the Renewed Moravian Brethren Colony at Bethlehem, Pennsylvania, from 1742–1762." Ph.D. diss., Kansas State University, 1995.

Nelson, James David. "Herrnhut: Friedrich Schleiermacher's Spiritual Homeland." Ph.D. diss., University of Chicago, 1963.

Nelson, Vernon. *The Bethlehem Gemeinhaus: A National Historic Landmark.* Bethlehem, Pa.: Moravian Congregation of Bethlehem, 1990.

———. "John Valentine Haidt's Life and Work." Bethlehem, Pa.: Moravian Archives, 1996.

———. "Ordination of Women in the Moravian Church in America in the

Eighteenth Century." *TMDK: Transatlantic Moravian Dialogue Correspondence* 17 (1999): 14–23.

———. "The *Geistliche Gedicht* of Zinzendorf and the Brüder-Unität 1745–1748." In *"Alles ist euer, ihr aber seid Christi": Festschrift für Dietrich Meyer*. Ed. Rudolf Mohr, 827–38. Cologne: Rheinland-Verlag, 2000.

———. "Johann Valentin Haidt und Zinzendorf." In *Graf Ohne Grenzen: Leben und Werk von Nikolaus Ludwig Graf von Zinzendorf*, ed. Dietrich Meyer and Paul Peucker. Herrnhut: Unitätsarchiv im Verlag der Comeniusbuchhandlung, 2000.

———, trans. and ed. "Peter Boehler's Reminiscences of the Beginnings of Nazareth and Bethlehem." *Transactions of the Moravian Historical Society* 27 (1992).

———. "Index to the German Nachrichten." Manuscript. Bethlehem, Pa.: Moravian Archives, n.d.

O'Brien, Susan. "A Transatlantic Community of Saints: The Great Awakening and the First Evangelical Network, 1735–1755." *American Historical Review* 91 (1986): 811–32.

Oestreich, Gerhard. *Neostoicism and the Early Modern State*. Trans. David McLintock and ed. Brigitta Oestreich and H. G. Koenigsberger. New York: Cambridge University Press, 1982.

O'Malley, J. Steven. *Early German-American Evangelicalism: Pietist Sources on Discipleship and Sanctification*. Metuchen, N.J.: Metuchen Press, 1995.

Pagels, Elaine. "Whatever Happened to God the Mother? Conflicting Images of God in Early Christianity." *Signs: Journal of Women in Culture and Society* 2 (1976): 193–303.

———. *Adam, Eve, and the Serpent*. New York: Random House, 1988.

Patzelt, Herbert. *Der Pietismus im Teschener Schlesien, 1709–1730*. Göttingen, 1969.

Pelikan, Jaroslav. *The Spirit of Eastern Christendom* and *Christian Doctrine and Modern Culture Since 1700*. Vols. 2 and 5 of *The Christian Tradition*. Chicago: University of Chicago Press, 1989.

Petig, William E. *Literary Antipietism in Germany During the First Half of the Eighteenth Century*. New York: Peter Lang, 1984.

Peucker, Paul. "Heerendijk—Link in the Moravian Network: Moravian Colonists Destined for Pennsylvania." *Transactions of the Moravian Historical Society* 30 (1998).

———. "Gegen ein Regiment von Schwestern: Die Stellung der Frau in der Brüdergemeine nach Zinzendorfs Tod." *Unitas Fratrum* 45–46 (1999): 61–72.

———. "'In Staub und Asche': Bewertung und Kassation im Unitätsarchiv

1760–1810." In *"Alles ist euer, ihr aber seid Christi": Festschrift für Dietrich Meyer.* Ed. Rudolf Mohr. Cologne: Rheinland-Verlag, 2000.

———. "Blut' auf unsre grünen Bändchen: Die Sichtungszeit in der Herrnhute Brüdergemeine." *Unitas Fratrum* 49–50 (2002).

———. "A Painter of Christ's Wounds: Johann Langguth's Birthday Poem for Johann Jakob Müller, 1744." In *The Distinctiveness of Moravian Culture: Essays and Documents in Honor of Vernon Nelson on his 70th Birthday,* ed. Craig D. Atwood and Peter Vogt. Nazareth, Pa.: Moravian Historical Society, 2003.

Pfeifer-Quaile, Wendy. "The Self-Expression of Moravians in North Carolina." Ph.D. diss., Rutgers University, 2001.

Pfister, Oskar. *Die Frömmigkeit des Grafen Ludwig von Zinzendorf: Ein psychoanalytischer Beitrag zur Kenntnis der religiösen Sublimierungsprozesse und zur Erklärung des Pietismus.* Leipzig: F. Deuticke, 1910.

Pitzer, Donald, ed. *America's Communal Utopias.* Chapel Hill: University of North Carolina Press, 1997.

Plitt, Hermann. *Die Brüdergemeine und die Lutherische Kirche in Livland.* Gotha, 1861.

———. *Zinzendorfs Theologie.* Vol. 1, *Die ursprüngliche gesunde Lehre Zinzendorfs* (1723–42); vol. 2, *Die Zeit krankhafter Verbildungen in Zinzendorfs Lehrweise* (1743–50); vol. 3, *Die wiederhergestellte und abschließende Lehrweise Zinzendorfs* (1750–60). Gotha: F. A. Perthes, 1869–74.

Podmore, Colin. *The Moravian Church in England, 1728–1760.* Oxford: Clarendon Press, 1998.

Porteous, N. W. "Soul." In *The Interpreter's Dictionary of the Bible,* ed. George Buttrick, 4:428–29. Nashville: Abingdon Press, 1962.

Reichel, Gerhard. *August Gottlieb Spangenberg.* Tübingen, 1906.

———. *Zinzendorfs Frömmigkeit im Licht der Psychoanalyse.* Tübingen: J.C.B. Mohr, 1911.

Reichel, Helmut. "Das Ende des Brüdergemeine Herrnhaag, 1750." *Unitas Fratrum* 26 (1989): 52–72.

Řican, Rudolf. *The History of the Unity of Brethren: A Protestant Hussite Church in Bohemia and Moravia.* Trans. C. Daniel Crews. Bethlehem, Pa.: Moravian Church in America, 1992.

Risler, Jeremias. *Leben August Gottlieb Spangenbergs, Bischofs der evangelischen Brüderkirche.* Barby: Brüdergemeine, 1794.

Ritschl, Albrecht. *Geschichte des Pietismus in der lutherischen Kirche des 17. und 18. Jahrhunderts.* 3 vols. Bonn: Adolph Marcus, 1882–86.

———. *Three Essays.* Trans. Philip Hefner. Philadelphia: Fortress Press, 1972.

Roeber, Gregg. *Palatines, Liberty, and Property: German Lutherans in Colonial America.* Baltimore: Johns Hopkins University Press, 1993.

———. "Der Pietismus in Nordamerika im 18. Jahrhundert." In *Geschichte des Pietismus,* ed. Martin Brecht, vol. 2. Göttingen: Vandenhoeck & Ruprecht, 1995.

Sames, Arno. *Anton Wilhelm Böhme (1673–1722): Studien zum ökumenische Denken und Handeln eines Halleschen Pietisten.* Göttingen, 1989.

Sawyer, Edwin Albert. "The Religious Experience of the Colonial American Moravians." *Transactions of the Moravian Historical Society* 18:1–227.

Schattschneider, David A. "Souls for the Lamb: A Theology for the Christian Mission According to Count Nikolaus Ludwig von Zinzendorf and Bishop August Gottlieb Spangenberg." Ph.D. diss., University of Chicago, 1975.

Schmidt, H., H. Bintz, and W. Günther, eds. "Protokoll des Gesprächs zwischen Professor Karl Barth und Vertretern der Brüdergemeine am 12. Oktober 1960 in Basel." *Civitas Prasens,* no. 13, special issue (1961).

Schmidt, Martin. *Pietismus als theologische Erscheinung.* Göttingen, 1984.

Schneider, Hans. "Der radikale Pietismus im 17. Jahrhundert." In *Geschichte des Pietismus,* ed. Martin Brecht, 1:391–437. Göttingen: Vandenhoeck & Ruprecht, 1993.

———. "Der radikale Pietismus im 18. Jahrhundert." In *Geschichte des Pietismus,* ed. Martin Brecht, 2:107–97. Göttingen: Vandenhoeck & Ruprecht, 1995.

———. "Geheimer Brief-Wechsel des Herrn Grafens von Zinzendorf mit denen Inspirten." *Unitas Fratrum* 49–50 (2002): 213–18.

Schutt, Amy. "Forging Identities: Native Americans and Moravian Missionaries in Pennsylvania and Ohio, 1765–1782." Ph.D. diss., Indiana University, 1995.

Schwartz, Hillel. *The French Prophets.* Berkeley and Los Angeles: University of California Press, 1980.

Sensbach, Jon. *A Separate Canaan: The Making of an Afro-Moravian World in North Carolina, 1763–1840.* Chapel Hill: University of North Carolina Press, 1998.

Sessler, Jacob John. *Communal Pietism Among Early American Moravians.* New York: Henry Holt, 1933.

Smaby, Beverly Prior. *The Transformation of Moravian Bethlehem from Communal Mission to Family Economy.* Philadelphia: University of Pennsylvania Press, 1989.

———. "Female Piety Among Eighteenth-Century Moravians." *Pennsylvania History* 64 (1997).

———. "Forming the Single Sisters' Choir in Bethlehem." *Transactions of the Moravian Historical Society* 28 (1994): 1–14.

Sommer, Elisabeth Watkins. "A Different Kind of Freedom? Order and Discipline Among the Moravian Brethren in Germany and Salem, North Carolina, 1771–1801." *Church History* 63 (1994): 221–34.

———. *Serving Two Masters: Moravian Brethren in Germany and North Carolina, 1727–1801.* Lexington: University Press of Kentucky, 2000.

Spinka, Mathew. *John Amos Comenius: That Incomparable Moravian.* New York: Russell & Russell, 1943.

———. *John Hus at the Council of Constance.* New York: Columbia University Press, 1965.

———. *John Hus: A Biography.* Princeton: Princeton University Press, 1968.

Steinberg, Leo. *The Sexuality of Christ in Renaissance Art and in Modern Oblivion.* 2d ed. Chicago: University of Chicago Press, 1996.

Sterik, Edita. "Mährische Brüder, böhmische Brüder, und die Brüdergemeine." *Unitas Fratrum* 48 (2001): 106–14.

Stockwell, Foster, ed. *Encyclopedia of American Communes, 1663–1963.* Jefferson, N.C.: MacFarland, 1998.

Stoeffler, F. Ernest. *The Rise of Evangelical Pietism.* Vol. 9 of *Studies in the History of Religions.* Leiden: E. J. Brill, 1965.

———. *German Pietism During the Eighteenth Century.* Vol. 24 of *Studies in the History of Religions.* Leiden: E. J. Brill, 1973.

———, ed. *Continental Pietism and Early American Christianity.* Grand Rapids: Wm. B. Eerdmans, 1976.

Strauss, Gerald. *Luther's House of Learning: Indoctrination of the Young in the German Reformation.* Baltimore: Johns Hopkins University Press, 1979.

Strom, Jonathan. "Problems and Promises of Pietism Research." *Church History* 71 (2002): 536–54.

———. "Early Conventicles in Lübeck." *Pietismus und Neuzeit* 27 (2003).

Strupl, Milos. "Confessional Theology of the Unitas Fratrum." *Church History* 33 (1964): 279–93.

Surratt, Jerry Lee. *Gottlieb Schober of Salem: Discipleship and Ecumenical Vision in an Early Moravian Town.* Macon: Mercer University Press, 1983.

Sykes, Norman. *Daniel Ernst Jablonski and the Church of England.* London: SPCK, 1950.

Tappert, Theodore G. "The Influence of Pietism in Colonial American Lutheranism." In *Continental Pietism and Early American Christianity,* ed. F. Ernest Stoeffer. Grand Rapids: Wm. B. Eerdmans, 1976.

Thierry, William of St. *On Contemplating God; Prayer; Meditation.* Vol. 1 of *The*

Works of William of St. Thierry, trans. Sister Penelope. Spencer, Mass.: Cistercian Pub., 1971.

Thorp, Daniel B. *The Moravian Community in Colonial North Carolina: Pluralism on the Southern Frontier.* Knoxville: University of Tennessee Press, 1989.

Turner Conrad, Maia. " 'Struck in their Hearts': David Zeisberger's Moravian Mission to the Delaware Indians in Ohio." Ph.D. diss., College of William and Mary, 1998.

Turner, Victor. *The Ritual Process: Structure and Anti-Structure.* Ithaca: Cornell University Press, 1969.

Tweed, Thomas, ed. *Retelling U.S. Religious History.* Berkeley and Los Angeles: University of California Press, 1997.

Uttendörfer, Otto. *Zinzendorf und die Frauen: Kirchliche Frauenrechte vor 200 Jahren.* Herrnhut, 1919.

———. *Alt Herrnhut: wirtschaftsgeschichte und Religionssoziologie Herrnhuts während seiner ersten zwanzig Jahre (1722–1742).* Herrnhut: Missionsbuchhandlung, 1925.

———. *Zinzendorfs religiöse Grundgedanken.* Herrnhut: Missionsbuchhandlung, 1935.

———. *Zinzendorf und die Mystik.* Berlin: Christlichen Zeitschriften-Verlag, 1952.

Vacovsky, Adolf. "History of the 'Hidden Seed.'" In *Unitas Fratrum*, ed. Mari P. van Buijtenen, Cornelius Dekker, and Huib Leeuwenberg, 35–54. Utrecht: Rijksarchief, 1975.

Van Gennep, Arnold. *The Rites of Passage.* Trans. M. B. Vizedom and G. L. Caffee. 1906; Chicago: University of Chicago Press, 1960.

Vogt, Peter. "A Voice for Themselves: Women as Participants in Congregational Discourse in the Eighteenth-Century Moravian Movement." In *Women Preachers and Prophets Through Two Millennia of Christianity,* ed. Beverly Mayne Kienzle and Pamela J. Walker, 227–47. Berkeley and Los Angeles: University of California Press, 1998.

———. "Herrnhuter Schwestern der Zinzendorfzeit als Predigerinnen." *Unitas Fratrum* 45–46 (1999): 28–60.

———. "*Ehereligion:* The Moravian Theory and Practice of Marriage as a Point of Contention in the Conflict Between Ephrata and Bethlehem." *Communal Societies* 21 (2001): 37–48.

Wagner, Murray L. *Peter Chelčický: A Radical Separatist in Hussite Bohemia.* Scottsdale, Pa.: Herald Press, 1983.

Wagner, Walter H. *The Zinzendorf-Muhlenberg Encounter: A Controversy in*

Search of Understanding. Bethlehem, Pa.: Moravian Publication Office, 2002.

Wallace, Paul. *Conrad Weisser (1696–1760): Friend of Colonist and Mohawk.* Philadelphia: University of Pennsylvania Press, 1945.

Wallmann, Johannes. *Philipp Jakob Spener und die Anfänge des Pietismus.* Tübingen, 1970.

———. "Die Anfänge des Pietismus." *Pietismus und Neuzeit* 4 (1977–78).

———. *Der Pietismus.* Göttingen: Vandenhoeck & Ruprecht, 1990.

———. "Was ist Pietismus?" *Pietismus und Neuzeit* 20 (1994).

Ward, W. R. "The Renewed Unity of the Brethren: Ancient Church, New Sect, or Transconfessional Movement." *Bulletin of the John Rylands Library* 70 (1988): lxvii–xcii.

———. *The Protestant Evangelical Awakening.* Cambridge: Cambridge University Press, 1992.

———. "German Pietism, 1670–1750." *Journal of Ecclesiastical History* 44 (1993): 476–505.

Warner, Paul. *History of the First Moravian Church, Philadelphia, Pa.* Nazareth, Pa.: Moravian Historical Society, 1942.

Weigelt, Horst. "Interpretations of Pietism in the Research of Contemporary Church Historians." *Church History* 39 (1970): 236–41.

Weinlick, John R. "Moravianism in the American Colonies." In *Continental Pietism and Early American Christianity,* ed. F. Ernest Stoeffler, 123–63. Grand Rapids: Wm. B. Eerdmans, 1976.

———. *Count Zinzendorf.* New York: Abingdon Press, 1956; reprint, Bethlehem, Pa.: Moravian Church in America, 1989.

Wessel, Carola. "Connecting Congregations: The Net of Communication Among the Moravians as Exemplified by the Interaction Between Pennsylvania, the Upper Ohio Valley, and Germany (1772–1774)." In *The Distinctiveness of Moravian Culture: Essays and Documents in Honor of Vernon Nelson on his 70th Birthday,* ed. Craig D. Atwood and Peter Vogt. Nazareth, Pa.: Moravian Historical Society, 2003.

Wheeler, Rachel. "Living upon Hope: Mahicans and Missionaries, 1730–1760." Ph.D. diss., Yale University, 1998.

Wilson, Bryan. *The Social Dimensions of Sectarianism.* Oxford: Clarendon Press, 1990.

Wokeck, Marianne. *Trade in Strangers: The Beginnings of Mass Migration in North America.* University Park: Pennsylvania State University Press, 1999.

Yeide, Harry. *Studies in Classical Pietism: The Flowering of the Ecclesiola.* New York: Peter Lang, 1997.

Zeiser, Samuel R. "Moravians and Lutherans: Getting Beyond the Zinzendorf-Muhlenberg Impasse." *Transactions of the Moravian Historical Society* 28 (1994): 15–29.

Zimmerling, Peter. *Nachfolge zu lernen: Zinzendorf und das Leben der Brudergemeine.* Moers: Brendow-Verlag, 1990.

———. *Gott in Gemeinschaft: Zinzendorfs Trinitatslehre.* Giessen/Basel: Brunnen Verlag, 1991.

———. "Zinzendorfs Bild der Frau." *Unitas Fratrum* 45–46 (1999): 9–27.

INDEX

Made in the USA
Lexington, KY
09 March 2016